W.G. SEBALD IN CONTEXT

The German academic and writer W.G. Sebald made an astounding ascent into the canon of world literature. In this volume, leading experts from the English- and German-speaking worlds explore his celebrated prose works published in the short span from 1996 to his premature death in 2001. Special attention is paid to Sebald's unpublished texts and books awaiting translation into English. The volume – illustrated with many unpublished archive images – scrutinizes the dual nature of Sebald's life and work, located between Germany and England, academic and literary writing, vilification and idolization. Through nearly forty essays on a broad range of topics, *W.G. Sebald in Context* achieves a revision of our understanding of Sebald, defying many clichés about him. Particular attention is paid to the manifold ways in which Sebald's writings exert a legacy far beyond literature, especially in the areas of art, cinema and popular music.

UWE SCHÜTTE worked as Reader in German in British higher education until Brexit. He has edited over ten volumes and written more than fifteen monographs on contemporary German-language literature and German pop music, with a focus on W.G. Sebald, Heiner Müller and Kraftwerk.

W.G. SEBALD IN CONTEXT

EDITED BY

UWE SCHÜTTE

Georg-August-University, Göttingen

CAMBRIDGE
UNIVERSITY PRESS

Shaftesbury Road, Cambridge CB2 8EA, United Kingdom

One Liberty Plaza, 20th Floor, New York, NY 10006, USA

477 Williamstown Road, Port Melbourne, VIC 3207, Australia

314–321, 3rd Floor, Plot 3, Splendor Forum, Jasola District Centre, New Delhi – 110025, India

103 Penang Road, #05–06/07, Visioncrest Commercial, Singapore 238467

Cambridge University Press is part of Cambridge University Press & Assessment, a department of the University of Cambridge.

We share the University's mission to contribute to society through the pursuit of education, learning and research at the highest international levels of excellence.

www.cambridge.org
Information on this title: www.cambridge.org/9781316511350

DOI: 10.1017/9781009052313

First published 2023

A catalogue record for this publication is available from the British Library.

A Cataloging-in-Publication data record for this book is available from the Library of Congress

ISBN 978-1-316-51135-0 Hardback

When you grow up promises are held up in front of you. Get your O levels done and your A levels and then everything will be fine. And then you do your BA and your PhD, but the more you are lured along this road, the more is taken away from you, the less the scope becomes. Day by day you leave things behind, ultimately your health, and so loss becomes the most common experience we have. I think somehow this has to be accounted for and as there are few other places where it is accounted for it has to be done by writing. It is quite clear to me that many people can identify with this view of life. It is not necessarily a pessimistic one; it is just a matter of fact that somehow this whole process is one in which you get done out of what you thought was your entitlement.

W.G. Sebald, 12 January 2001

Contents

Illustrations

Notes on Contributors

DAVID ANDERSON is Leverhulme Early Career Fellow in the Department of Comparative Literature and Culture at Queen Mary University of London, where he is an associate of the Centre for Anglo-German Cultural Relations. His monograph *Landscape and Subjectivity in the Work of Patrick Keiller, W.G. Sebald and Iain Sinclair* (2020) was published by Oxford University Press.

CATHERINE ANNABEL has completed a PhD with the School of Languages and Cultures at the University of Sheffield, on labyrinths and intertextuality in the work of Michel Butor and W.G. Sebald. She is co-editor of the new edition of the English translation of Butor's *L'Emploi du temps* (*Passing Time*) which was published in June 2021 by Pariah Press. Catherine is retired, after a long career in higher education administration.

LUISA BANKI is Research Assistant in Comparative and German Literature at the University of Wuppertal. Her research interests include modern German and German Jewish literature, post-Shoah literature and the history of gendered reading. Recent publications on Sebald include: *Post-Katastrophische Poetik: Zu W.G. Sebald und Walter Benjamin* (2016) and 'Poetik der Restitution: Zur Theorie und Praxis der Zeugenschaft bei W.G. Sebald', in: A Eusterschulte et al. (eds.), *Videographierte Zeugenschaft: Geisteswissenschaften im Dialog mit dem Zeugen* (Weilerswist-Metternich: Velbrück, 2016), pp. 302–314.

JO CATLING was a senior lecturer at the University of East Anglia (UEA), Norwich, which she joined in 1993 as Lecturer in German Literature and Language. She taught alongside W.G. Sebald until his untimely death in 2001. Jo has published widely on Rilke, translation and W.G. Sebald. Books include the edited volumes *A History of Women's Writing in Germany, Austria and Switzerland* (2001) and, together with Richard

Hibbitt, *Saturn's Moons: W.G. Sebald – A Handbook* (2011). She is also translator of three volumes of Sebald's essays: *A Place in the Country* (2013); his essays on Austrian literature, *Die Beschreibung des Unglücks* and *Unheimliche Heimat*, are forthcoming as *Silent Catastrophes*.

IAN ELLISON is a DAAD PRIME postdoctoral research fellow, dividing his time between the University of Kent in Canterbury, their Paris School of Arts & Culture and the University of Frankfurt. His first book, *Late Europeans and Melancholy Fiction at the Turn of the Millennium* (2022), is the first comparative study of novels by W.G. Sebald, Patrick Modiano and Antonio Muñoz Molina.

MELISSA ETZLER is Senior Lecturer of German and First Year Seminar at Butler University in Indianapolis, which she joined in 2014. Her PhD thesis, *Writing from the Periphery: W.G. Sebald and Outsider Art*, explores intersections of pathology, marginalization, creative production and politics. In addition to two book chapters she has published on Sebald, she has written on topics ranging from ecocritical thought and ecofeminism in German Gothic works to German horror films. She has co-edited two volumes, one on rebellion and revolution (2010) and one on German pedagogical strategies (2021).

IAIN GALBRAITH is a poet and translator. His recent publications include a volume of poems, *The True Height of the Ear* (2018), as well as translations of Esther Kinsky's prose work *River* (2018), Esther Dischereit's *Sometimes a Single Leaf: Selected Poems* (2020) and *Flowers for Otello: On the Crimes that Came out of Jena* (2022), Reinhard Jirgl's novel *The Unfinished* (2020) and Ulrike Draesner's *this porous fabric. Selected Poems* (2022). He has received several prizes, including the Stephen Spender Prize (2014), the Popescu Prize for European Poetry Translation (2015) and the Schlegel-Tieck Prize (2016, 2019). He translated and wrote a commentary upon Sebald's *Across the Land and the Water: Selected Poems 1964–2001* (2011).

RÜDIGER GÖRNER is Centenary Professor of German with Comparative Literature and Director of the Centre for Anglo-German Cultural Relations at Queen Mary University of London. His most recent books include *Romantik: Ein europäisches Ereignis* (2021), *Hölderlin and the Consequences: An Essay on the German 'Poet of Poets'* (2021), *Die versprochene Sprache: Über Ilse Aichinger* (2021), *Im Zeichen des Windrads: Literarische Orientierungen* (2019), *Franz Kafkas akustische Welten* (2019) and *Oskar Kokoschka: Jahrhundertkünstler* (2018). On

Sebald he has published several essays with the main focus on his literary and poetic topologies.

JAKOB HESSING is Professor Emeritus of German Literature at the Hebrew University of Jerusalem. He specializes in German Jewish literature and contributes regularly to the *Frankfurter Allgemeine Zeitung*. His numerous publications include a biography of Else Lasker-Schüler (1985) as well as books on Sigmund Freud (1989) and Heinrich Heine (2005). With Verena Lenzen, he co-authored *Sebalds Blick* (2015).

RICHARD HIBBITT is Senior Lecturer in French and Comparative Literature at the University of Leeds, where he co-directs the Centre for World Literatures. His research is on aesthetics, poetics and cultural exchange from the eighteenth century to the present day, with a particular interest in the long nineteenth century. He is a general editor of *Comparative Critical Studies* and on the Executive Committee of the European Society of Comparative Literature. With Jo Catling he co-edited *Saturn's Moons: W.G. Sebald – A Handbook* (2011; paperback reprint 2020). His current projects include a co-edited volume of war poetry from Gallipoli (with Berkan Ulu).

TORSTEN HOFFMANN is Professor of Modern German Literature at the University of Stuttgart and President of the International Rilke Society. His work focuses on literature around 1800, classical modernism and contemporary literature. In recent years, he has worked on intermediality, author interviews and the literary politics of the New Right, among other topics. His recent book publications include *Rainer Maria Rilke* (2021), *Verfilmte Autorschaft: Auftritte von Schriftsteller*innen in Dokumentationen und Biopics* (co-edited, 2020) and *Navid Kermani* (edited, 2018).

MICHAEL HUTCHINS is Associate Professor and Chair of German and International Studies at Indiana University Southeast. His Sebald-related publications include his PhD thesis on Sebald's reception of the Jewish messianic tradition (*Tikkun: W.G. Sebald's Melancholy Messianism*, 2011), 'Intent to Mislead: W.G. Sebald's Notion of Authenticity', in: Antonius Weixler (ed.), *Authentisches Erzählen* (2012) and '"Der Gedanke kommt ihm wie eine Erlösung": Restitution and False Redemption in Dramatic Texts by W.G. Sebald', in: U Schütte (ed.), *Über W.G. Sebald* (2017). In addition to Sebald's work, Hutchins is interested in contemporary German literature and cinema.

BEN HUTCHINSON is Professor of European Literature at the University of Kent and Consultant Editor for German at the *Times Literary Supplement*. His books include *Lateness and Modern European Literature* (2016), *Comparative Literature: A Very Short Introduction* (2018), *The Midlife Mind* (2020) and *On Purpose* (2023). He has published extensively on Sebald, including the books *W.G. Sebald: Die dialektische Imagination* (2009) and *A Literature of Restitution: Essays on W.G. Sebald* (co-edited with Jeannette Baxter and Valerie Henitiuk, 2013).

LEONIDA KOVAČ is curator and Professor at the University of Zagreb, Academy of Fine Arts. The main fields of her interest are contemporary art, feminist theories and critical theories. She has published nine books among which are *Anonimalia: Normative Discourses and Self-Representation of Twentieth Century Women Artists* (2010), *Tübingen's Box: Essays on Visual Culture and Biopolitics* (2013), *In the Mirror of the Cultural Screen: Jagoda Kaloper* (2013) and *Mrdjan Bajić: Disenacting Transversals* (2017).

LISA KUNZE is Research Assistant at the Göttingen University Library, currently working on Günter Grass. She was awarded her doctorate in 2021 with the thesis *Der Schamane mit der Feder: Ökologie und „Mitleidenschaft" in W.G. Sebalds ›Nach der Natur‹* (2022), supervised by Heinrich Detering. Her on-going projects include co-editing the anthology *Günter Grass als Büchermacher: Die Jahre mit Steidl*, the critical edition *Benjamin Franklin / Gottfried Achenwall: Amerika 1766: Anmerkungen über Nordamerika, und über dasige Grosbritannische Colonien* as well as a Marbach booklet on *Hans Christian Andersen in Baden-Baden*. Also forthcoming is an annotated edition of the Romantic poet Friedrich Begemann's lyrical œuvre.

DUNCAN LARGE is Academic Director of the British Centre for Literary Translation at the University of East Anglia in Norwich. He is Professor of European Literature and Translation at UEA, and Chair of the PETRA-E Network of European literary translation training institutions. Duncan has authored and edited six books about Nietzsche and German philosophy; he has also published two Nietzsche translations with Oxford World's Classics (*Twilight of the Idols, Ecce Homo*), and one translation from the French (Sarah Kofman's *Nietzsche and Metaphor*). His most recent book publications are the co-edited volumes

Untranslatability: Interdisciplinary Perspectives (2019) and *Nietzsche's ›Ecce Homo‹* (2021).

FLORIAN LEITNER is Director of the Media Theatre and Head of the Media Dramaturgy in the Department of Media Studies at Humboldt University of Berlin. He studied dramaturgy in Munich and Paris and was a fellow at the doctoral school 'Image/Body/Medium: An Anthropological Perspective' at Karlsruhe University of Arts and Design. At the University of Munich, he was responsible for the film studies section within the Master's programme 'Aisthesis'. He has also worked as a theatre director, dramatic advisor and screenwriter. His recent books include *Medienhorror: Mediale Angst im Film* (2017).

BERNHARD MALKMUS is Professor of German Studies at Newcastle University. His research focuses on theories and narratives of modernity and the environmental humanities. He is currently working on a study of German literature and the Great Acceleration, which includes an in-depth exploration of Sebald's *After Nature, The Rings of Saturn* and the abandoned Corsica Project.

SVEN MEYER is a Project Manager at the Hamburg Patriotic Society of 1765. He studied German and English Literature in Kiel and Göttingen as well as Cultural Management in Hamburg. Sven is the editor of the posthumous Sebald volumes *Campo Santo* and *Über das Land und das Wasser* and has co-edited anthologies on Immanuel Kant and Friedrich Schiller. He has written essays on Sebald, Wilhelm Raabe and Jan Wagner.

HENDRIK OTREMBA is a writer, visual artist and singer with the group Messer. He also works as a lecturer in creative writing and occasionally as a curator, also writing sporadically about music for journalistic outlets. His paintings are regularly exhibited and feature on record covers and in various magazines. Hendrik's novels include *Über uns der Schaum* (2017), *Kachelbad's Erbe* (2019) and *Benito* (2022). With Messer he has released five albums so far, most recently *No Future Dubs* (2021).

TERRY PITTS was until 2013 Executive Director of the Cedar Rapids Museum of Art and the Center for Creative Photography, University of Arizona. His books include *Reframing America: Points of Entry* (1995) and *Edward Weston* (1999). Since 2007, he has written the Sebald-centred blog, *Vertigo* (https://sebald.wordpress.com).

FLORIAN RADVAN is Professor of Fachdidaktik Deutsch at the University of Bonn and Director of the Bonn Centre for Teacher Training (BZL). A PhD student of W.G. Sebald, he has published on twentieth-century German theatre and drama. His research focus is on the use of learning materials in classrooms and he co-edited the *Handbuch Lehr- und Lernmittel für den Deutschunterricht* (2019). For over ten years now, he has cooperated with Cornelsen publishing company as the editor of literary texts for German secondary schools.

RITCHIE ROBERTSON was Taylor (latterly Schwarz-Taylor) Professor of German at Oxford from 2010 to 2021. His books include *Kafka: Judaism, Politics, and Literature* (1985), *The 'Jewish Question' in German Literature, 1749–1939* (1999), *Mock-Epic Poetry from Pope to Heine* (2009), *Enlightenment and Religion in German and Austrian Literature* (2017) and *The Enlightenment: The Pursuit of Happiness, 1680–1790* (2020), besides short introductory studies of Heine, Kafka, Goethe and Nietzsche. On Sebald he has previously published 'W.G. Sebald as a Critic of Austrian Literature', in: *Journal of European Studies* 41 (2011), pp. 305–322.

MARTIN SCHAUSS is a Teaching and Research Fellow of Twentieth-Century Literature in English at the University of Edinburgh. His most recent publications include '"With an Eye to Their Later Existence as Ruins": Language, Materiality and the Ruin in the Work of W.G. Sebald', in: *Critique: Studies in Contemporary Fiction* (2021) and '"The Absolute Impossibility of all Purchase": Property and Translation in Beckett's Post-war Prose', in: *Samuel Beckett and Translation* (2021). His research focuses on twentieth-century and contemporary literature, experimental writing, environmental humanities, ecopoetics, global modernism and cultural translation. He previously held an IRC-funded Postdoctoral Research Fellowship at University College Dublin, following his PhD at the University of Warwick.

UWE SCHÜTTE was Reader in German until Brexit and is Privatdozent at Göttingen University. An MA and PhD student of W.G. Sebald, he has published widely on contemporary German-language literature and pop music, with a focus on Kraftwerk and Sebald. His book publications include *W.G. Sebald: Einführung in Leben & Werk* (2011), *Figurationen: Zum lyrischen Werk von W.G. Sebald* (2014), *Interventionen: Literaturkritik als Widerspruch bei W.G. Sebald* (2014), *Über W.G. Sebald: Beiträge zu einem neuen Bild des Autors* (edited, 2017), *W.G.*

Sebald (Writers and their Work) (2018), *Annäherungen: Sieben Essays über W.G. Sebald* (2019) and *W.G. Sebald: Leben und literarisches Werk* (2020).

CHRISTOPH SINGER is Professor for British and Anglophone Cultural Studies in the Department of British Literary and Cultural Studies at the University of Innsbruck, Austria. He has published anthologies on intersections of middlebrow and modernism, the iconography of Dante and Milton and on spaces of well-being. His PhD thesis explored shorelines as liminal spaces and he has published on the legacies of the Partition of India. His second book discusses the temporality of narratives in times of crisis, particularly the experience of existential waiting. He is one of the editors of the recently established series Narratives and Mental Health (Brill).

CHRISTOPH STEKER is programme director at C.W. Leske publishers and a freelance editor in Cologne. He co-edited *Künstler, Kunden, Vagabunden: Texte, Bilder und Dokumente einer Alternativkultur der zwanziger Jahre* (2020). On Sebald, he published several chapters in edited volumes and *Böhmische Erinnerungsräume in W.G. Sebalds ›Austerlitz‹* (2015). Christoph is currently working on his PhD thesis exploring the role of botany in Sebald's work.

PAUL THOMPSON obtained his PhD at the University of St Andrews. Previously he gained a Master's with distinction from the University of Edinburgh for a dissertation entitled *Time and Relative Dimensions in Sebald: Time, Space, and Distance as Phenomena in W.G. Sebald's Documentary Fiction*, which applied phenomenology as a tool of literary criticism. Though his current field of research is lesbian pulp fiction of the 1950s and 1960s, Paul has retained a keen interest in Sebald since he was an undergraduate. Before becoming a scholar, Paul was a career civil servant.

NICK WARR is Lecturer in Art History at the University of East Anglia, specializing in twentieth-century avant-garde and "outsider" modes of practice with a particular interest in film and photography. He is also Academic Director of the East Anglian Film Archive and Curator of the University of East Anglia's Photographic Collection. Nick has prepared a comprehensive catalogue of all Sebald's photographic materials, *Shadows of Reality* (forthcoming) in collaboration with Clive Scott and Michael Brandon-Jones. In 2019 he curated two exhibitions of Sebald's photography, *Lines of Sight: W.G. Sebald's East Anglia* (Norwich Castle Museum) and *Far Away – But from Where?* (UEA Sainsbury Centre).

ANDREW J WEBBER is Professor of Modern German and Comparative Culture at the University of Cambridge and a Fellow of Churchill College. He has published widely on the textual and visual cultures of Germany and Austria since 1800. His monograph publications include *The Doppelgänger: Double Visions in German Literature* (1996), *The European Avant-Garde. 1900–1940* (2004) and *Twentieth-Century Berlin: A Cultural Topography* (2008). Edited volumes include *A Companion to the Literature of Berlin* (2017) and *Placing Schnitzler* (*Austrian Studies* 27 (2019)), with J Beniston. He is currently co-authoring a book on the films of Christian Petzold.

ADRIAN NATHAN WEST is a literary translator and the author of *The Aesthetics of Degradation* (2016) and *My Father's Diet* (2022). His translations have been shortlisted for the International Booker Prize and the National Book Award, and his criticism appears frequently in such journals as *The Baffler* and *The New York Review of Books*.

PAUL WHITEHEAD is Research Associate in Modern German Literature at Johannes Gutenberg University Mainz. His publications include *Im Abseits: W.G. Sebalds Ästhetik des Marginalen* (2019) and *Heinrich Mann-Handbuch* (2022, co-edited with Andrea Bartl and Ariane Martin). He has published articles on Heinrich Mann, Sebald, Thomas Lehr, Andreas Maier and the cultural history of modernity. He is currently completing a *Habilitation* on the reception of Heinrich Heine's works in Austria and Germany (1871–1906) and a volume comprising the correspondence between Heinrich Mann and René Schickele.

LYNN L WOLFF is Associate Professor of German and Affiliate Faculty in Jewish Studies at Michigan State University. Her research focuses on German-language literature of the twentieth and twenty-first centuries, Holocaust and memory studies, text-image studies and translation. She is the author of *W.G. Sebald's Hybrid Poetics: Literature as Historiography* (2014) and editor of *A Modernist in Exile: The International Reception of H.G. Adler* (2019). With Helen Finch she edited *Witnessing, Memory, Poetics: H.G. Adler and W.G. Sebald* (2014), and with Hans Adler she edited *Aisthesis und Noesis: Zwei Erkenntnisformen vom 18. Jahrhundert bis zur Gegenwart* (2013). Her current work explores modes of abstraction in visual forms of Holocaust testimony.

KAY WOLFINGER is a teaching assistant at the University of Munich and received his doctorate in 2014 for a thesis on Robert Walser and the theory of context. He was a Research Assistant at the Deutsches Literaturarchiv Marbach and is a founding member of the German Sebald Society. His most recent publications include *Das Archiv der Geister oder Was sollen Okkultisten lesen?* (2021). Publications on the literary world in the twentieth century and on contemporary literature include *Eleganz und Eigensinn. Studien zum Werk von Hans Pleschinski* (co-edited with Laura Schütz, 2019) and *Mystisches Schwabing: Die Münchner Kosmiker im Kontext* (edited, 2020). He is currently writing a *Habilitation* on media interpretation of occultism.

Preface

'Ein Schriftsteller sollte zufrieden sein, wenn er in seinem Leben *ein* wirklich gutes Buch geschrieben hat' ('An author should think himself fortunate if he writes *one* really good book during his lifetime'), W.G. Sebald once said to me around 1993. At this point, he had written *Die Ausgewanderten*, which, translated into English as *The Emigrants*, was to bring him international acclaim as an author of prose fiction. Over the next five years, he made a vertiginous ascent into the canon of world literature, the mark of an extraordinary professional progression that was cut short by his premature death in December 2001.

Even over the span of a career curtailed, it is beyond dispute that Sebald wrote *more* than one good book, even that he may have written *only* good books. These quickly attracted academic interest, especially in the anglophone world, supported, no doubt, by his position in British academia and the curiosity he aroused in his colleagues there. After all, he was 'one of us'. (Or at least seemed to be.)

To his *Germanistik* colleagues in German academia, by contrast, Sebald was a rebellious outsider who as a junior academic had already made a questionable name for himself through his savage attacks on sacred cows of German literature and leading representatives of his discipline. Even after he emerged as a literary author in the 1990s, German academia continued to treat Sebald's work with a considerable level of suspicion, if not outright hostility. He was disparaged as an author of 'Germanistenprosa', intellectualized maunderings of a professor struggling to transcend the day job, while his style – a nod to nineteenth-century writers such as Adalbert Stifter – was dismissed as dated or twee by critics who were missing the point of his writing.

In 1993, Sebald's highly polemical essay on Alfred Andersch, previously a sacrosanct idol of the political left, sparked outrage on the German literary scene. His public lectures at the University of Zurich on the failure of German post-war literature to engage with the Allied bombing campaigns and their devastation of cities such as Dresden and Hamburg had a similar effect towards the end of the same decade. Journalists, literary critics and many academics baulked at his wholesale attacks, as did several leading German writers, prominent among them Günter Grass.

Without question, Sebald's reception in Germany differed greatly from that in his adopted country, where he was overwhelmingly held in high esteem. Amongst the small German Studies community in the United Kingdom, Sebald was considered a respected, well-liked colleague, known under his adopted name of Max, and in British literary circles he soon gained the admiration of fellow distinguished writers such as Will Self, Iain Sinclair and Marina Warner.

This conflicting appraisal raises an important consideration that also fundamentally informs the approach of the present volume: there is no single Sebald. The aim of drawing together this collection of essays is to present Sebald's biography, his critical writings and his literary œuvre under different aspects, from different perspectives and in different contexts. More than any homogeneous, monolithic analysis, it is hoped that such a composite, multi-vocal portrayal may be in a position to do justice to the complexity of the academic and author's multi-faceted life and body of work.

There are many books on Sebald. Some might say too many. (I certainly have to accept some blame in this respect.) Though we may be observing a slowdown of the 'Sebald-industrial complex',[1] the 'Sebald-industry'[2] is far from exhausted. On the contrary, even two decades on from Sebald's death, the effect of his writing endures, especially beyond academia, and draws ripples more intricate and extensive than almost any other author's since Kafka.

What we are witnessing in the anglophone world, as his work has entered 'into a process of recycling, reformulation, transformation and adaptation',[3] is nothing short of a Sebald cult. Sebald lives on in the works of other writers, of visual artists across a range of media, but also in pop music, internet blogs and through the audio, film and stage adaptations of his texts. *W. G. Sebald in Context* is, not least, a response to this ripple effect and proposes to take stock of the many shores, old and new, to which the author and his legacy have taken us.

*

To this end, and in keeping with its aspiration to complexity and multi-facetedness, my aim with *W. G. Sebald in Context* is to challenge existing secondary literature in two main ways: first, as even a cursory overview shows, current research, especially in an anglophone context, continues almost without exception to focus on a narrow range of key themes, chief among them trauma, the Holocaust, intermediality, memory and melancholy. As early as 2007, JJ Long was already forced to conclude that Sebald scholarship was generally 'repetitive and predictable'.[4] Extensive omnibus reviews of existing research by Richard Sheppard,[5] a former colleague of Sebald, support this claim. As a consequence of such a restricted focus, these themes, usually investigated through the lens of the novel *Austerlitz*, have long dominated Sebald research at the considerable expense of his other publications.

Over the past decade, there has been some diversification in this regard, as becomes apparent not least from the contributions to the present volume on newer theoretical approaches from the fields of ecocriticism and media theory. At the same time, it is probably fair to say that some recent academic trends (such as digital humanities) may not be able to yield many significant new insights into Sebald's work.

However, there is a great deal of work to be done simply in the area of textual and contextual analysis, and many of Sebald's intertextual references or allusions to the history of ideas, beyond the usual suspects, remain unexplored. Additionally, Sebald's estate in the Deutsches Literaturarchiv (German Literature Archive, DLA) in Marbach promises fruitful new impulses for future research. To give but one example: a thorough investigation into the underlinings and marginalia in his personal library should produce many surprising insights into where his literary as well as critical writings take their material from.

A second notable weakness of much existing research on Sebald is that 'too many essays about [him] are cast in the kind of rebarbative idiom' which Richard Sheppard resoundingly if rightly condemns for its lack of accessibility, 'since the effect of such writing is to veil Sebald's texts from mortal gaze within a mystery accessible only to a priestly elite'.[6] Sheppard has in mind here the sort of jargon-heavy discourse that cares little about Sebald's texts themselves and more about parading a '*prêt-à-porter* theory'[7] around an echo chamber of academic self-adulation. As a literary critic, Sebald himself always rejected this approach to literature, finding 'smug critical cleverness to be a special form of stupidity'.[8]

Unlike offerings by 'the general run of German critics, whose plodding studies [on Kafka] regularly become a travesty of scholarship',[9] *W.G. Sebald in Context* hopes to do justice to its subject by dispensing with 'the frustratingly opaque mode that Sebald has excited in some critics',[10] as

David Anderson put it, and by filling in gaps existing scholarship has insufficiently addressed or has failed to engage with entirely.

For instance, this volume will discuss the formative impact Sebald's grandfather, Josef Egelhofer, had on him as a person and writer, it will highlight the significance of the British Centre for Literary Translation (BCLT) founded by Sebald, it will read his interviews as authorial self-staging and embed them in the context of his literary œuvre, and it will emphasize the importance of the polemical for Sebald's life and work. The transnational and transmedial nature of Sebald's work is reflected in several essays in this collection, but also in its broad range of contributors, comprising leading Sebald scholars, early career researchers and artistic practitioners from both Germany and the anglophone sphere.

The volume is expressly dedicated to the "German Sebald". That is to say, in keeping with the many facets of Sebald, this volume is mindful of the significant difference between the "German Sebald" and the "English Sebald" in analyses of his writing. The sequence in which Sebald wrote his books in German differs markedly from the order in which they were published in translation, resulting in a significantly diverse author profile across German- and English-speaking countries. In German, Sebald made his literary debut in 1988 with *Nach der Natur*, the intricate lyrical prose style of which informs all his future prose writing. In English, this early work only came out posthumously as *After Nature* in 2002, whereas the instant success of his English-language debut *The Emigrants* in 1996 earnt Sebald the misleading label of a 'Holocaust author', which some still assign to him to this day.

Consequently, my editorial decision was to treat the German texts as the original version of Sebald's work. Despite his being heavily involved in the translation process, the English-language editions are alternative versions that do not capture the same range of meaning and nuance as the originals. This is not so much purely a question of subtleties, overtones and allusions being 'lost in translation'.[11] Mark McCulloh rightly refers to Sebald's 'tandem literary œuvres'[12] and emphasizes the shift in literary 'key' or modulation between the two languages, in which, for instance, the English version's preference for 'severity over playfulness' may lose some of the 'graver mood of Sebald's German originals'.[13] As Sebald himself observed, his own active participation in the process notwithstanding: 'Some of the finer grain vanishes in translation, inevitably. I mean you can make small gains in the process of translation also, but, on the whole, I think you tend to lose some of the finer grain, particularly as regards shadings of earlier forms of German.'[14] Conducting research exclusively on the basis of Sebald's works in translation, as is often the case in the area of English studies, is thus evidently problematic.

A related difficulty arises when scholars who do not have German are unable to access the extensive and important body of German-language research or archival materials. Significant texts from Sebald's estate, including, especially, his critical writings, remain unpublished or untranslated, which is regrettable, to say the least, in view of the sustained anglophone interest in his work. Here, too, *W. G. Sebald in Context* is designed to act as a corrective in two regards. For one thing, it aims to reveal crucial cross-connections between Sebald's fiction and his literary criticism. It is impossible to arrive at a differentiated understanding of Sebald as an author without an appreciation of how organic and close the relationship between his literary and his critical work is. One is inconceivable without the other, as his late essays from *Logis in einem Landhaus* (*A Place in the Country*, 1998) show very clearly: in these, the two components of his work merge into a new hybrid form of writing which was precluded from further development only because of his untimely death.

Secondly, *W. G. Sebald in Context* will serve as an introduction to those critical and literary writings still awaiting translation, with the intention of affording those who do not read German insight into the full extent of Sebald's œuvre. In addition to his juvenilia and scripts for unrealized films on Immanuel Kant and Ludwig Wittgenstein, this untranslated archival material comprises his Corsica Project, which far exceeds in scope and comprehensiveness the partial piecemeal excerpts of it published in the *Campo Santo* collection.

This volume also explores what is known about the World War Project Sebald was working on when he died. Slated to appear after *Austerlitz*, the book seems to have had all the potential for literary greatness of the earlier novel and then some. 'I am convinced that the book Max was writing when he died would have been his greatest yet',[15] stated his former colleague, the distinguished historian Richard J. Evans.

*

A central problem with academia's wholescale appropriation of Sebald is the risk this runs of perpetuating a distorted image of him. This is due not least to complex ways alluded to at the outset in which he straddled irreconcilably different contexts, Germany and England, academia and literature, adulation and ostracism.

Cliché-ridden German misconceptions of UK academia as a kind of Oxbridge idyll have a counterpart in the erroneous or ignorant assumptions concerning German peculiarities that we encounter in English-language publications on Sebald.[16] Two different countries, two different perceptions of the same author: from a British perspective, Sebald's contentious standing in Germany, due to his polemics against revered figureheads of German literature, seems astonishing. Meanwhile, his German reception is bemused by his international acclaim and taken aback by his cultural pessimism.

He was indisputably a complex and many-layered individual who resisted any easy pigeonholing. One readily available myth that informed how he was perceived from the outside was the image of him as a pathologically morose melancholic. From my own experience of Sebald, nothing could be further from the truth. He had a bitingly sarcastic sense of humour and we laughed a great deal, even, or especially, in the face of the preposterously outrageous absurdities of the world.

From the outside, Sebald appeared as a man of contradictions. His intellectual biography, as Andrew Sutcliffe argues, 'presents a strange case for the critic. Despite having lived and worked in England for the vast majority of his adult life, ... Sebald appears to have had almost no scholarly interest in Anglophone literature'.[17] Repeatedly, English-speaking interviewers were also puzzled by Sebald's steadfast refusal to switch to English as his writing language.

He had a mind of his own, sometimes obstinately so. When external inspectors were due to conduct the first Teaching Quality Assessment in the mid-1990s, he simply showed them the door, despite the consequences this had for himself and his department. His long-standing friend, the artist Jan Peter Tripp, was similarly surprised when, just a few days before Sebald's death, *For Years Now* was published. A collaboration between Sebald and the graphic artist Tess Jaray, the volume combined Sebald's English-language 'micro-poems' with Jaray's minimalist artwork. For years, Tripp had been planning precisely such a collaboration with Sebald, in which the German versions of the 'micro-poems' were to be juxtaposed with etchings by Tripp, and which finally came out after Sebald's death under the title of *Unerzählt* (*Unrecounted*). But Sebald had never once mentioned his parallel project with Jaray to his close friend. He could be completely unpredictable like that or, as his Swiss colleague, the Germanist Peter von Matt, put it: 'Sebald was someone you thought capable of anything, because you were never quite sure what to expect next.'[18]

And yet, the non-conformist, order-averse, obstinate sides of Sebald's character are often smoothed over in the interest of painting a more palatable public picture of him, just as Sebald scholarship may choose to overlook or exclude any facets of his thinking that do not seem to conform to established interpretative frameworks or conventional academic wisdom, such as his predilection for the superstitious and heretical. It is easier to censor or suppress the discomfiting views of one individual than it is to challenge prevailing institutional presumptions.

This strikes me as particularly regrettable in the current political climate, in the context of which Sebald's indomitable independence of mind takes on an extra-literary relevance. His work has an important ethical dimension which is too often understood in a purely retrospective sense. He is romanticized as the author of a "literature of restitution" (and this is again understood narrowly in terms of the Holocaust, even though he always had in mind all victims of modernity's history of violence).

His ethical focus, however, was always as much on our deplorable present as on the past and, even more so, on our acutely uncertain future, as evidenced, for instance, by the fact that more than thirty years ago he was already expressing vehement concern over the destruction of the environment and climate change, marking him out as an early prognosticator of the devastating impact of the Anthropocene.

The resurgence of deadly conflict across Europe in February 2022 should put us in mind of his admonitions about the ineradicable human drive to destruction. 'Nothing gives us a sense of safety like scorched earth', he writes in the Corsica Project, 'And so we keep on laying waste to the lands of our enemies with fire'.[19]

Likewise, Sebald's impassioned, and sometimes provocative, interventions on behalf of animals or the socially marginalized as paradigmatic representatives of disenfranchised groups should be taken seriously at a time in which society and culture are being radically restructured under the post-democratic primacy of profit maximization. We have yet to discover Sebald as the quiet but insistent critic of capitalism whose work is by no means as apolitical as it may appear at first glance.

Finally, his unwavering non-religious faith in the transcendental and metaphysical is deserving of greater attention in our ruthlessly immanent society in which such categories have long been consigned to the scrapheap. Significantly, Sebald never claimed to be in possession of any absolute truths about the inexplicable. On the contrary, 'I am not seeking an answer', as he once explained to an interviewer, 'I just want to say, This is very odd indeed'.[20]

For all these reasons, it is high time for academia to accept Sebald more fully as 'one of us', not despite, but because of the fact that he has continually criticized the ideological foundations and hidden contradictions of our discipline, and because our privileged position in the rarefied bubble of the academy, where we were – at least during his time – free to read think write, made him feel ashamed.

There are important lessons to be learnt from Sebald about moral courage, the spirit of dissent, solidarity and independence of mind. It is a particular concern of the present volume to offer an introduction to the contradictory, oppositional Sebald, for it should be the responsibility of academic scholarship to counter misinformation and suggest a corrective to misrepresentations propagated by distortive journalistic or simplistic biographical accounts.

As goes without saying, though, *W.G. Sebald in Context* lays no claim to any absolute truth either. To pretend otherwise would be a travesty of the complexities of Sebald's person and work. On the contrary, what we owe him, more than two decades after his death, is a volume compiled under the sign of contradiction and in the spirit of defiance.

Notes

1. N Pages, Crossing Borders: Sebald, Handke, and the Pathological Vision, in: *Modern Austrian Literature* 40:4 (2007), pp. 61–92 (84).
2. M Swales, W.G. Sebald: History – Memory – Trauma [review], in: *Arbitrium* 26:1 (2008), pp. 128–130 (128).
3. S Cooke, Cultural Memory on the Move in Contemporary Travel Writing: W. G. Sebald's ›The Rings of Saturn‹, in: A Erll, A Rigney (eds.), *Mediation, Remediation, and the Dynamics of Cultural Memory* (Berlin/New York: De Gruyter, 2009), pp. 15–30 (27).
4. JJ Long, *W.G. Sebald: Image, Archive, Modernity* (Edinburgh: Edinburgh University Press, 2007), p. 28.
5. R Sheppard, Dexter – Sinister: Some Observations on Decrypting the Mors Code in the Work of W.G. Sebald, in: *Journal of European Studies* 35 (2005), pp. 19–63 and Woods, Trees and the Spaces In-Between, in: *Journal of European Studies* 39:1 (2009), pp. 79–128.
6. Sheppard, Woods, Trees, pp. 80–81.
7. Ibid., p. 84.
8. Sebald, Gerhard Kurz, ›Traum-Schrecken. Kafkas literarische Existenzanalyse‹ [review], in: *Literatur und Kritik* 161/162 (1982), pp. 98–100 (98).
9. Sebald, Kafka Goes to the Movies, in: *Campo Santo* (London: Penguin, 2006), pp. 156–173 (158). Subsequent references to Sebald's writings are provided with abbreviations in the main text.

10. D Anderson, *Landscape and Subjectivity in the Work of Patrick Keiller, W.G. Sebald and Iain Sinclair* (Oxford: Oxford University Press, 2020), p. 110.
11. M Zucchi, Zur Kunstsprache W.G. Sebalds, in: S Martin, I Wintermeyer (eds.), *Verschiebebahnhöfe der Erinnerung: Zum Werk von W.G. Sebald* (Würzburg: Königshausen & Neumann, 2007), pp.163–183.
12. M McCulloh, Two Languages, Two Audiences: The Tandem Literary Œuvres of W.G. Sebald, in: S Denham, M McCulloh (eds.), *W.G. Sebald: History – Memory – Trauma* (Berlin/New York: De Gruyter, 2006), pp. 7–20.
13. Ibid., pp. 11, 10.
14. Qtd. in: J Catling, R Hibbitt (eds.), *Saturn's Moons: W.G. Sebald – A Handbook* (Oxford: Legenda, 2011), p. 359.
15. The quote is from an online obituary that has disappeared but can still be found on the *Vertigo* website, https://sebald.wordpress.com/2007/06/05/the-chronicler-of-damages-caused-more-on-"the-book-that-will-never-be".
16. A paradigmatic case is Robert Macfarlane's opening chapter in J Cook (ed.), *After Sebald: Essays and Illuminations* (Woodbridge: Full Circle, 2014), where, inter alia, Sebald's first name is misspelt, or Freiburg and Fribourg are confused.
17. A Sutcliffe, *Reimagining Melancholia, Melancholy and Psychiatry in the Work of W.G. Sebald and David Foster Wallace* (PhD thesis: King's College London, 2020), p. 71.
18. Qtd. in: T Honickel, *Curriculum Vitae: Die W.G. Sebald-Interviews*, ed. U Schütte, K Wolfinger (Würzburg: Königshausen & Neumann, 2021), p. 200.
19. U Bülow et al. (eds.), *Wandernde Schatten: W.G. Sebalds Unterwelt* (Marbach: Deutsche Schillergesellschaft, 2008), p. 209.
20. A Lubow, Crossing Boundaries [Interview], in: L Schwartz (ed.), *The Emergence of Memory: Conversations with W.G. Sebald* (New York: Seven Story, 2007), pp. 159–172 (165).

Acknowledgements

Sebald scholarship in English began to prosper even before the author's premature death in December 2001 and continues to flourish more than two decades later. Arguably few and far between, however, are publications which provide a framework for a more differentiated understanding of his life and works. This is what this volume hopes to achieve by illuminating the various contexts surrounding his life, work and legacy.

Even though there is only one name on the cover, edited volumes are always collaborative efforts. First and foremost, I must thank Nick Warr, curator of the W.G. Sebald Photographic Archive at the University of East Anglia, for making available a cornucopia of never-before published photographs taken by Sebald. Luke Ingram at the London office of the Wylie Agency helped in securing the permission to quote from Sebald's papers held at the Deutsche Literaturarchiv in Marbach. I am grateful, too, to the photographers who gave permission to include their images in this volume. Finally, Bethany Thomas at Cambridge University Press provided steadfast support during the bumpy road this project took until its completion.

I am indebted, last but not least, to the translators contributing to this volume: the essays by Kay Wolfinger, Florian Radvan, Lisa Kunze, Torsten Hoffmann and Sven Meyer were translated by Suzanne Nater, while Imran Hashmi took care of Hendrik Otremba's essay. Special thanks to Kirstin Gwyer who expertly transformed my German-English hotchpotch into the fine, elegant essays of this volume.

W.G. Sebald in Context developed under difficult circumstances and is my first book after leaving both academia and Brexit Britain behind for good. It is a relief to close chapters and change direction, allowing for a new phase of my life to begin.

Note on Text

All references in this volume are to the widely available paperback editions of Sebald's works in German and English (UK editions). Where a published translation is available, all quotations are referenced first to the English version, followed by the German original. On occasion, translations have been tacitly modified. For works that have not been translated, contributors provided their own translations.

Please note that pagination in the German paperback edition of *Die Ausgewanderten* from 2008 onwards differs from earlier editions due to the omission of several illustrations. Similarly, German paperback editions of *Schwindel. Gefühle.* from 2005 onwards feature a different pagination to those before. References are always to the first paperback edition.

Several sections of the chapters by Sven Meyer, Florian Radvan and Paul Thompson include rewrites and additions by me.

Chronology

1944   18 May (Ascension Day): Born Winfried Georg Sebald in Wertach, Allgäu (Bavaria), to Georg Sebald (1911–99) and his wife Rosa Genoveva, *née* Egelhofer (1914–2003)

1947   January: Georg Sebald returns home from a prisoner-of-war camp in Haut Plateau de Larzac, France

1952   December: Sebald family moves to nearby Sonthofen where Georg Sebald had worked as a clerk for the local police since 1947

1956   March: Georg Sebald becomes a captain in the newly established *Bundeswehr* (German Army)
          14 April: Death of grandfather Josef Egelhofer (born 1872)

1963   October: Matriculates at the University of Freiburg, where he studies German and English literature for four semesters

1965   October: Transfers to the Université de Fribourg (Switzerland) and lives with his older sister Gertrud (born 1941)

1966   July: Receives his Fribourg *licence ès lettres* for a dissertation on playwright Carl Sternheim
          September: Takes up an appointment as a German language teaching assistant (*Lektor*) at the University of Manchester

1967   March: Completes an unpublished, autobiographical novel
          April: Writes to Theodor W. Adorno with a query regarding Sternheim
          September: Marries Ute Sebald *née* Rosenbauer in Sonthofen
          December: Applies to the Goethe-Institut, Munich, to train as a German-language teacher

1968   March: Submits an MA dissertation on Sternheim at the University of Manchester
          Autumn: Takes up a post as a teacher of German and English at an international boarding school in St. Gallen, Switzerland
          December: Applies unsuccessfully for a Junior Research Fellowship at Sidney Sussex College, Cambridge

1969 October: Revised version of Sebald's MA dissertation is published as *Carl Sternheim: Kritiker und Opfer der Wilhelminischen Ära* (*CS: Critic and Victim of the Wilhelmine Era*)
May: Returns to Manchester, where he is re-appointed as *Lektor*

1970 October: Takes up an appointment to an Assistant Lectureship in German Language and Literature at the University of East Anglia (UEA), Norwich, Norfolk
October: The Sebalds rent a flat in a large house in Vicar Street, Wymondham, Norfolk

1971 April: The Sebalds move into a house they purchased in Orchard Way, Wymondham, where he continues work on a PhD thesis on Alfred Döblin
September: Begins writing polemical reviews for the *Journal of European Studies* at UEA

1973 August: Submits PhD thesis, entitled *The Revival of Myth: A Study of Alfred Döblin's Novels*
October: Promotion to Lecturer

1974 July: Receives his PhD despite unorthodox nature of the thesis
July: Presents paper at Kafka conference organized at UEA

1975 Summer: Application to train as a German-language teacher is accepted by Goethe-Institut. The Sebalds subsequently sell their house in Wymondham and move back to Germany with their family labrador, Jodok
October: Signs contract with Goethe-Institut

1976 January to August: Attends a teacher training course in Munich but decides to withdraw and return to UEA for the autumn term
May: Visits Jan Peter Tripp in Stuttgart for the first time since school
June: Purchase of dilapidated Old Rectory in Poringland, Norfolk
November: Participates in 90-minute TV documentary on Carl Sternheim broadcast by RIAS Berlin station

1979 May: Gives paper on Elias Canetti at a symposium in Vienna, with Canetti in attendance

1980 March: Revised German version of PhD thesis published *as Der Mythus der Zerstörung im Werk Döblins* (*The Myth of Destruction in Döblin's Work*)
October: Sebald visits the Haus der Künstler (Artists' House) on the grounds of the Lower Austrian Psychiatric Institution in Gugging and befriends the schizophrenic poet Ernst Herbeck

1981 Spring: Starts work on a screenplay entitled *Jetzund kömpt die Nacht herbey: Ansichten aus dem Leben und Sterben des Immanuel Kant (Night Now Draweth Nigh: Scenes from the Life and Death of Immanuel Kant)*
September: Interviews Solly Zuckerman on the Allies' World War Two aerial bombing campaign
December: Travels to New York to give a paper at an academic conference on Döblin and later visits relatives in New Jersey

1982 Autumn: Publishes an essay on the literary representation of the aerial bombing campaign against Germany in the academic journal *Orbis Litterarum*

1983 Spring: Starts work on a prose poem on the botanist and explorer Georg Wilhelm Steller, which is later included in his first literary publication *Nach der Natur (After Nature, 1988)*

1984 January: Rosa Sebald informs him of the suicide of his former primary school teacher Armin Müller, which ultimately leads to the story 'Paul Bereyter'
September: A first essay collection on Austrian literature, *Die Beschreibung des Unglücks (Describing Disaster)*, is published
Winter: Submits *Beschreibung des Unglücks* to University of Hamburg to gain his *Habilitation* (second doctorate)
October: Promotion to Senior Lecturer

1986 April: Receives his *Habilitation*, intended as a failsafe if job situation worsens in the UK

1987 February: Unsuccessfully applies to the Deutsche Literaturfonds (German Literature Fund) for a grant to develop his 'Prosaprojekt' (Prose Project), which would later develop into *Schwindel. Gefühle. (Vertigo)* and parts of *Die Ausgewanderten (The Emigrants)*
March: Sebald chairs a conference on Contemporary German Drama at UEA, presents paper on Herbert Achternbusch
July–August: Sebald goes to Vienna prior to travelling through northern Italy (Venice, Lake Garda, Milan – where a new passport is issued by the German Consulate – and Verona) to Munich
October: Promotion to Reader

1988 Late summer: *After Nature*, Sebald's first literary book, is published
October: Promotion to Professor of European Literature

1989   Spring: Founds the British Centre for Literary Translation (BCLT) at UEA, assumes position as Director until April 1994

1990   March: *Schwindel. Gefühle.* (*Vertigo*) is published

June: Takes part in the televised Ingeborg Bachmann Prize competition in Klagenfurt, Austria, where he reads excerpts from the story 'Paul Bereyter', later published in *The Emigrants*, but the work is not recognized by the jury

1991   February: Sebald's essay on the Holocaust survivor Jurek Becker is rejected by the editor of a volume on Becker who commissioned it

March: Second essay collection on Austrian literature *Unheimliche Heimat* (*Strange Homeland*) is published

December: Receives his first literary prize, the Fedor Malchow Prize, for *After Nature*, in Hamburg

1992   September: *Die Ausgewanderten* (*The Emigrants*) is published

December: On behalf of the BCLT, Sebald organizes the European Writers' Forum at UEA featuring original language readings by eight leading European writers and their respective translators

1993   January: *The Emigrants* is discussed on the prestigious German television programme *Das Literarische Quartett* (*The Literary Quartet*), where it is snubbed by leading German critic Marcel Reich-Ranicki

Spring: Sebald publishes a polemical essay on Alfred Andersch, leading to protests and scandal in Germany

Throughout the year, Sebald takes individual walks through various parts of East Anglia that are later fictionalized in *The Rings of Saturn*

August: Admitted to Norfolk and Norwich Hospital for a back operation

1994   February: Sebald receives the Berlin Literature Prize along with several other writers

June: Awarded the Johannes Bobrowski Medal but, considering it ugly and unwieldy, throws it into the waters of the Lesser Wannsee near the grave of writer Heinrich von Kleist

Deaths of colleagues Michael Parkinson (April) and Janine Dakyns (August) leave Sebald distraught

November: He is awarded the LiteraTour Nord Prize for *The Emigrants*

1995   September: Travels to Corsica in connection with research for a prose book on the natural history and anthropology of the island

October: *Die Ringe des Saturn* (*The Rings of Saturn*) is published

1996   April: *The Emigrants*, translated by Michael Hulse, is published by Harvill to huge acclaim amongst anglophone literary critics
September: Undertakes second research trip to Corsica but later in the year abandons that book project, parts of which posthumously appear in the collection *Campo Santo* and in *Wandernde Schatten* (*Wandering Shadows*), the catalogue to the 2008–09 Sebald exhibition at the Deutsche Literaturarchiv (German Literature Archive) in Marbach
October: Elected member of the prestigious Deutsche Akademie für Sprache und Dichtung (German Academy of Language and Literature)

1997   October to December: Delivers three controversial lectures on the air war and German literature in Zurich
Receives the *Jewish Quarterly*/Wingate Prize for Literature (for *The Emigrants*) in London (March), the Mörike Prize in Fellbach (April) and the Heinrich Böll Prize in Cologne (November)

1998   June: *The Rings of Saturn*, translated by Michael Hulse, is published by Harvill
September: *Logis in einem Landhaus* (*A Place in the Country*), an essay collection on Swiss and Alemannic authors, is published

1999   March: Zurich lectures are published under the title *Luftkrieg und Literatur* (*The Natural History of Destruction*)
April: Visits Prague, Terezín and Nuremberg to undertake research for his next prose book
June: Georg Sebald dies
August: German programmes are discontinued at UEA; Sebald is transferred from the School of Modern Languages and European Studies to the School of English and American Studies
December: *Vertigo*, translated by Michael Hulse, is published by Harvill

2000   April: Awarded a NESTA (National Endowment for Science, Technology and the Arts) Fellowship, which would have allowed Sebald to take leave during four consecutive spring semesters in order to concentrate on literary writing
Spring: Teaches creative writing to MA students at UEA
Receives two prestigious literary awards in Germany, the Joseph Breitbach Prize in Mainz (July) and the Heinrich Heine Prize in Düsseldorf (December)

2001 February: *Austerlitz* is published by Hanser in Germany and, translated into English by Anthea Bell, in Britain (October) by Hamish Hamilton

More than in previous years, requests for interviews, invitations to attend official functions, participations in conferences, commissions to deliver opening addresses, informal small group and national broadcast readings and extensive reading tours to promote *Austerlitz* in Germany, Austria, Switzerland and the United States are evidence of his international success, causing him great strain and exhaustion

11 December: Receives his copy of *For Years Now*, a collection of short poems in English in collaboration with the visual artist Tess Jaray (born 1937)

14 December: Dies of heart aneurysm while driving near his home

2002 3 January: Buried near his home in St Andrew's churchyard, Framingham Earl, Norfolk

2002 August: *After Nature*, translated by Michael Hamburger, is published by Hamish Hamilton

Bremen Literary Prize (January), National Book Critic's Circle Award (March) and Wingate Literary Prize are awarded posthumously for *Austerlitz*

2003 March: *Unerzählt* (*Unrecounted*), a collaboration with visual artist Jan Peter Tripp, is published

September: *Campo Santo*, a collection of short texts from the abandoned Corsica Project, along with journalistic pieces and essays on German literature, is published

2004 *Unrecounted*, translated by Michael Hamburger, is published by Hamish Hamilton

2008 September: *Über das Land und das Wasser: Ausgewählte Gedichte 1964–2001* (*Across the Land and the Water: Selected Poems, 1964–2001*), a collection of mostly unpublished poetry, edited by Sven Meyer, is published

Winter: Exhibition *Wandernde Schatten: W.G. Sebalds Unterwelt* opens at Literaturmuseum der Moderne (Museum of Literary Modernism), Marbach, accompanied by an exhibition catalogue (runs until February 2009)

2011 November: *Across the Land and the Water. Selected Poems, 1964–2001*, translated and edited by Iain Galbraith, is published by Hamish Hamilton

2014 February: *A Place in the Country*, translated by Jo Catling, is published by Hamish Hamilton

Abbreviations

Literary Writings

Ae   *Austerlitz*, transl. A Bell (London: Penguin, 2002)
Ag   *Austerlitz* (Frankfurt: Fischer, 2003)
AN   *After Nature*, transl. M Hamburger (London: Penguin, 2003)
AW   *Die Ausgewanderten. Vier lange Erzählungen* (Frankfurt: Fischer, 2008)
E   *The Emigrants*, transl. M Hulse (London: Vintage, 2002)
FYN   *For Years Now: Poems by W.G. Sebald. Images by Tess Jaray* (London: Short Books, 2001)
LWe   *Across the Land and the Water: Selected Poems, 1964–2001*, ed. & transl. I Galbraith (London: Penguin, 2012)
LWg   *Über das Land und das Wasser. Ausgewählte Gedichte 1964–2001*, ed. S Meyer (Frankfurt: Fischer, 2012)
NN   *Nach der Natur. Ein Elementargedicht* (Frankfurt: Fischer, 1995)
RSe   *The Rings of Saturn*, transl. MHulse (London: Vintage, 2002)
RSg   *Die Ringe des Saturn. Eine englische Wallfahrt* (Frankfurt: Fischer, 1997)
SG   *Schwindel. Gefühle.* (Frankfurt: Fischer, 1994)
Ue   *Unrecounted*, transl. M Hamburger (London: Penguin, 2005)
Ug   *Unerzählt. 33 Texte und 33 Radierungen* (Munich: Hanser, 2003)
V   *Vertigo*, transl. M Hulse (London: Vintage, 2002)
KP   *Wandernde Schatten. W.G. Sebalds Unterwelt*, ed. U Bülow et al. (Marbach: Deutsche Schillergesellschaft, 2008)

Critical Writings

BU   *Die Beschreibung des Unglücks: Zur österreichischen Literatur von Stifter bis Handke* (Frankfurt: Fischer, 1994)
CSe   *Campo Santo*, ed. S Meyer, transl. A Bell (London: Penguin, 2006)
CSg   *Campo Santo*, ed. S Meyer (Frankfurt: Fischer, 2003)
LH   *Logis in einem Landhaus* (Frankfurt: Fischer, 2000)

LL   *Luftkrieg und Literatur* (Frankfurt: Fischer, 2001)
MZ   *Der Mythus der Zerstörung im Werk Döblins* (Stuttgart: Klett, 1980)
NHD *On the Natural History of Destruction*, transl. A Bell (London: Penguin, 2003)
PC   *A Place in the Country*, transl. J Catling (London: Penguin, 2014)
RM   *The Revival of Myth: A Study of Alfred Döblin's Novels* (PhD thesis: UEA 1973)
SH   *Carl Sternheim: Kritiker und Opfer der Wilhelminischen Ära* (Stuttgart: Kohlhammer, 1969)
UH   *Unheimliche Heimat: Essays zur österreichischen Literatur* (Frankfurt: Fischer, 1995)

Other Sources

DLA Archive W.G. Sebald (Deutsches Literaturarchiv, Marbach)
EM   *The Emergence of Memory:Conversations with W.G. Sebald*, ed. LS Schwartz (New York: Seven Stories, 2007)
G   *Auf ungeheuer dünnem Eis:Gespräche 1971 bis 2001*, ed. T Hoffmann (Frankfurt: Fischer, 2011)
SM   *Saturn's Moons:W.G. Sebald – A Handbook*, ed. J Catling, R Hibbitt (Oxford: Legenda, 2011)

Works by W.G. Sebald

German		English	
1969	Carl Sternheim: Kritiker und Opfer der Wilhelminischen Ära (Kohlhammer) revised MA dissertation	1973	Revival of Myth: A Study of Döblin's Novels PhD thesis, UEA Norwich
1980	Der Mythus der Zerstörung im Werk Döblins (Klett) German version of PhD thesis	1996	The Emigrants, transl. M Hulse (Vintage/New Directions)
1985	Die Beschreibung des Un-glück: Zur österreichischen Literatur von Stifter bis Handke (Residenz/ Fischer)	1998	The Rings of Saturn, transl. M Hulse (Vintage/New Directions)
1988	Nach der Natur: Ein Ele-mentargedicht (Greno/ Fischer)	1999	Vertigo, transl. M Hulse (Vintage/New Directions)
1990	Schwindel. Gefühle. (Andere Bibliothek/ Fischer)	2001	Austerlitz, transl. A Bell (Penguin/Modern Library)
1991	Unheimliche Heimat: Essays zur österreichischen Lite-ratur (Residenz/Fischer)	2001	For Years Now: Poems by W.G. Sebald. Images by Tess Jaray (Short Books)
1992	Die Ausgewanderten: Vier lange Erzählungen (Andere Bibliothek/ Fischer)	2002	After Nature, transl. M Hamburger (Penguin/ Modern Library)
		2003	On the Natural History of Destruction. With Essays on Alfred Andersch, Jean Améry and Peter Weiss, transl. A Bell (Penguin/ Modern Library)

1995 *Die Ringe des Saturn: Eine englische Wallfahrt* (Andere Bibliothek/ Fischer)

1998 *Logis in einem Landhaus: Über Gottfried Keller, Johann Peter Hebel, Robert Walser und andere* (Hanser/Fischer)

1999 *Luftkrieg und Literatur. Mit einem Essay zu Alfred Andersch* (Hanser/Fischer)

2001 *Austerlitz* (Hanser/Fischer)

2003 with Jan Peter Tripp: *Unerzählt: 33 Texte und 33 Radierungen* (Hanser/ Fischer)

2003 *Campo Santo: Prosa, Essays*, ed. S Meyer (Hanser/ Fischer)

2008 *Über das Land und das Wasser: Ausgewählte Ge-dich-te 1964–2001*, ed. S Meyer (Hanser/Fischer)

2004 with Jan Peter Tripp: *Unrecounted: 33 Poems*, transl. M Hamburger (Penguin/New Directions)

2005 *Campo Santo*, ed. S Meyer, transl. A Bell (Penguin/ Modern Library)

2011 *Across the Land and the Water: Selected Poems, 1964–2001*, ed. & transl. I Galbraith (Penguin/ Modern Library)

2013 *A Place in the Country*, transl. J Catling (Penguin/Modern Library)

This synopsis compares the sequence of book publications by Sebald in German and English during his lifetime and posthumously. The information in brackets indicates the publishers of the German hardcover and paperback editions and the publishers of the British and American paper back editions, respectively.

The pagination of corresponding editions is mostly, though not necessarily, identical. Canadian editions were omitted.

A detailed bibliography, compiled by Richard Sheppard, can be found in J Catling, R Hibbitt (eds.), *Saturn's Moons: W.G. Sebald – A Handbook* (Oxford: Legenda, 2011), pp. 446–496.

PART I

Biographical Aspects

CHAPTER I

Allgäu

Kay Wolfinger

W.G. Sebald came from the Allgäu, an alpine region of south-western Germany. The local people here speak a Swabian-Alemannic dialect that bears a greater resemblance to Swiss dialects than the Bavarian variant of German normally spoken in the south of Germany. The rural village of Wertach, where Sebald was born in May 1944, is nowadays a tourist and winter sports destination.

When Sebald was eight years old, his family moved about eleven miles to the market town of Sonthofen, which was officially granted its town status in 1963. During the years 1952 to 1954, Sebald attended the local primary school, which now accommodates the municipal library and music school. From 1954, Sebald made the daily six-mile train journey to Immenstadt, where he attended the Catholic Maria Stern grammar school. Two years later, he moved to the secondary school in Oberstdorf and graduated with his *Abitur* school-leaving certificate in 1963. Sebald left Sonthofen later that year to begin his student life in Freiburg. He then transferred to Fribourg, Switzerland, and afterwards to England where he worked as a *Lektor* (language assistant). After his emigration to England, Sebald only returned to the Allgäu region for occasional visits.

To what extent can the Allgäu be described as his *Heimat*, if we define this specific German concept as the native town, the locations and youthful reminiscences that intrinsically shape our personal identity? Mark Anderson summarized the extent to which the Allgäu homeland influenced Sebald's character as well as his literary work: 'Many of Sebald's passions later in life – for long walks, gardening, maps and country almanacs, for the natural world in general – can be traced back to these early lessons with his grandfather' (SM 32). His special attachment to his grandfather, who was a firm connection for Sebald with his childhood upbringing in the Allgäu, was an important element of his positive appreciation of his home region (see chapter 2 in this volume).

However, the title for Sebald's 1990 essay collection on Austrian literature established his ambivalence towards *Heimat*. In his volume
Unheimliche Heimat (Strange, or: Uncanny Homeland) – the word
'unheimlich' alludes to Sigmund Freud's essay *Das Unheimliche* (*The
Uncanny*, 1919) – Sebald sought to emphasize how the familiar homeland
can simultaneously be an alien, inhospitable and possibly even fear-laden
place. In Austrian literature in particular, Sebald sees an especially problematic relationship with *Heimat*, yet this also applies for Sebald's work
and his self-enactment as a writer. In Sebald's literary phantasmagoria
Heimat is tellingly always presented as a strange, inhospitable homeland.
This portrayal influences his work as a whole, as well as characterizing the
first-person narrator's *Heimat* descriptions and those of the uprooted
protagonists of his narrative texts.

In interviews, Sebald's assertions about his idea or experience of *Heimat*
almost entirely re-enact that ambivalent perception of his homeland that
he develops in his work. In conversation with Doris Stoisser, Sebald offered
the following explanation: '*Heimat*, or what one defines by this term, is
only visible from afar. Hence, it was only since the nineteenth century that
this concept began to have the precise relevance that we associate with it
today. *Heimat* is then a kind of mirage that one sees from a great distance'
(G 225).

Heimat and Images of Destruction

The mirage of Sebald's Allgäu *Heimat* emerges as central theme of his
literary texts. He outlines experiencing *Heimat* as getting to know oneself –
and the 'otherness' in oneself – in the supposedly authentic and autobiographical style of the lectures he delivered in Zurich in 1997 on the theme
of air war and literature. His main argument that German post-war
literature had failed, because of its lack of narratives about the aerial
bombing campaign against German cities, is illustrated through his personal experience of his *Heimat*. Sebald writes here that the 'scandalous
deficiency' (NHD 70/LL 76) of keeping quiet about past events overshadowed his life:

> At the end of the war I was just one year old, so I can hardly have any
> impressions of that period of destruction based on personal experience. Yet
> to this day, when I see photographs or documentary films dating from the
> war I feel as if I were its child, so to speak, as if those horrors I did not
> experience cast a shadow over me, and one from which I shall never entirely
> emerge. (NHD 70–71/LL 76–78)

Sebald juxtaposes his childhood upbringing in the idyllic Allgäu country-side with the 'images of destruction' (NHD 71/LL 78) with which he was not confronted as a child and adolescent growing up in Wertach and Sonthofen. Tellingly, it is the images of destruction, which 'make me feel rather as if I were coming home', and certainly not the 'now entirely unreal idylls of my early childhood' (NHD 71/LL 78) that in fact ought to have been intermingled with the concept of *Heimat*. This example already shows how Sebald re-enacts the real *Heimat* as sinister or surreal and insinuates a feeling of intimacy with the destruction as a substitution for *Heimat*.

In *Luftkrieg und Literatur* (*On the Natural History of Destruction*), the book-length version of his Zurich lectures, Sebald also mentions the bombing raid on Sonthofen, the site of one of the *Ordensburg* training institutions for elite Nazis. Sebald had reportedly asked the chaplain during the religion class at the grammar school in Oberstdorf, 'how we could reconcile our ideas of divine providence with the fact that neither the barracks nor the Ordensburg had been destroyed during this air raid, only, and as if in place of them, the parish church and the church of the hospital foundation' (NHD 74–75/LL 80). Interestingly, Sebald at that point made no mention of the event that became known as the 'Miracle of Sonthofen'. Undoubtedly, he ought to have known about Sonthofen parish church being the target of an air raid during the middle of a church service. However, since the parish priest instructed the congregation to stand in the aisles alongside the walls, there were no fatalities when the nave collapsed.

It was his schoolmates who shed light on what, for Sebald, is described as a traumatic experience during his youth. In an interview with the film-maker Thomas Honickel, Sebald's school friend, Jürgen Kaeser, remem-bered that the teachers 'showed . . . us the film of Bergen-Belsen after the liberation presumably by the Americans'.[1] The shocking documentation of the crimes committed during the Holocaust was profoundly distressing for Sebald precisely because of society's overwhelming silence (EM 105, G 82, G 226–227).

Birth and War

In his self-representation as a melancholic and an observer of the 'natural history of destruction', Sebald writes the horrors of war into his fiction-alized biography, when he makes his literary debut with his book *Nach der Natur* (*After Nature*). In this poetry volume, the mother of the narrator – who is not yet aware that she is pregnant – is described watching the devastation of the bombing raids in Franconia in August 1943: 'During the night of the 28th / 582 aircraft flew in / to attack Nürnberg. Mother, / who on the next day planned / to return to her parents' / home in the Alps, / got no further than / Fürth. From there she / saw Nürnberg in flames' (AN 84/NN 73).

This inferno already marks the narrator's life, even before his birth, and continues in the Allgäu idyll when the narrator is born here: 'At the moment on Ascension Day / of the year 'forty-four when I was born, / the procession for the blessing of the fields / was just passing our house to the sounds / of the fire brigade / band, on its way out / to the flowering May meadows' (AN 86/NN 76). What appears initially to be interpreted as a positive anticipation of life is interrupted in the following verses of the poem and has a tragic outcome because 'the cold planet Saturn ruled this hour's / constellation' (AN 86/NN 76), and an approaching storm kills one of the canopy bearers in the procession.

The alignment of the planets and the town's tragic history suggested that the birth in the real and figurative sense was under the rule of Saturn. Sebald continues further: 'I grew up, / despite the dreadful course / of events elsewhere, on the northern / edge of the Alps, so it seems / to me now, without any / idea of destruction' (AN 86–87/NN 76). The destruction only loomed in the distance, and yet it stayed in the subconscious; moreover, it would be later reconstructed in Sebald's work and become the actual *Heimat* transcending the 'strange homeland'.

Wertach as Fictionalized Location

To mark the publication in 1990 of his first collection of prose texts, *Schwindel. Gefühle.* (*Vertigo*), in discussion with the critic Andreas Isenschmid, Sebald refers to the region of his native Allgäu, which appears as a fictionalized place, and bears the hallmarks of an unwelcoming, strange homeland:

> I never went back to spend any real time there since the old days, until I made a spontaneous trip to rediscover, or to see first-hand, whether I could still find the place as I imagined it to be. I had the feeling of reaching a state that I could genuinely compare with that of the Hunter Gracchus, namely, caught in a no-man's land, neither here nor there, neither completely alive nor completely dead, because many of the characters I remembered from my childhood had meanwhile passed away. (G 59–60)

Sebald refers here to the narrative 'Il ritorno in patria', in which the first-person narrator, who shares many similarities with the real writer, W.G. Sebald, hikes down into the village W. after decades of absence.[2] The locality of W. bears unmistakeable and verifiable characteristics of his birthplace, Wertach, but Sebald just uses the first initial (as he does later with S. for Sonthofen). Consequently, Sebald tells the story of a fictionalized and distinctive literary 'Wertach' and not any realistic topography; he engages in a skilful narrative game of hide-and-seek, superimposing onto real facts another layer of reminiscences and references to literary and cultural history.

When the book was first published many local residents saw Sebald as denigrating his birthplace (a so-called *Nestbeschmutzer*), because his literary portrait of the village showed it in a partly unfavourable light and was not entirely respecting of the facts. The first part of 'Il ritorno in patria' later became the inspiration for the 'Sebald Walk' (Sebaldweg), a tourist attraction shadowing the narrator's path along the walk from Oberjoch to his native village, featuring quoted extracts from the story.

The treatment of his birthplace gives a perfect example of Sebald's poetological strategy: leitmotifs are repeated throughout the stories, memory is conveyed through quoted media, the narrator's research reconstructs the blurred traces, hidden connections are exposed and even the remotest

Illustration 1 – Wertach in the 1940s

points of cultural history turn out to be interlinked and mutually reference each other. Nevertheless, reconstruction and pursuit of hidden traces are potentially misleading: 'The more images I gathered from the past, . . . the more unlikely it seemed to me that the past had actually happened in this or that way, for nothing about it could be called normal: most of it was absurd, and if not absurd, then appalling' (V 212/SG 241).

Sonthofen and the Literary Primary School Teacher

The literary figure of Paul Bereyter, who is based on the real person and teacher Armin Müller, is paradigmatic for the core theme of *Die Ausgewanderten* (*The Emigrants*). Sebald's prose book addresses what it means to be somebody who voluntarily or forcibly leaves his *Heimat*, and who no longer frees himself abroad from the influences of his place of origin. The story again begins with the reflection of Sebald's first-person narrator who finds out about his former teacher's suicide on 30 December 1983 when he reads an obituary in the local paper: 'Almost by way of an aside, the obituary added, with no further explanation, that during the Third Reich Paul Bereyter had been prevented from practising his chosen profession' (E 27/AW 42).

This note first elicits the characteristic tendency towards research and reconstruction that is typical of Sebald's narrator. He discovers that Paul Bereyter was a so-called 'quarter Jew' (*Vierteljude*) who was no longer allowed to pursue his career during the Third Reich and suffered painful losses because of it.

While the narrator explores the background to his teacher's suicide, he gradually understands how, in his old age, Bereyter increasingly perceived his *Heimat* as sinister. This was a direct contrast to previous decades when he still worked as a teacher. The narrator recalls how Bereyter and his pupils got to know the places in Sonthofen like 'the electric power station with the transformer plant, the smelting furnaces and the steam-powered forge at the iron foundry, the basketware workshops, and the cheese dairy' (E 38/AW 57–58). Together with his pupils, he also visited 'Fluhenstein Castle, explored the Starzlach Gorge, went to the conduit house above Hofen and the powder magazine where the Veterans' Association kept their ceremonial cannon, on the hill where the stations of the cross led up to the Calvary Chapel' (E 39/AW 58).

This appreciation for his former hometown could almost be interpreted as an implicit tribute, if it were not for Lucy Landau, who gives the first-person narrator an insight into Bereyter's later life. In her analysis, the onset of age made him bitter and he rails against the 'miserable place S. . . . which in fact he loathed and, deep within himself, of that I am quite sure, said Mme Landau, would have been pleased to see destroyed and obliterated, together with the townspeople, whom he found so utterly repugnant' (E 57/AW 84).

The Horrors of Childhood?

In recent years there has been a steady progression in acknowledging the importance of Sebald in the Allgäu, his former *Heimat*, thanks to cultural events, readings, guided hiking tours on the 'Sebald Walk' and the Sebald Society (Deutsche Sebald Gesellschaft) in Kempten. Yet there are also some lingering reservations. Many local people are resentful of Sebald because of passages like the following excerpt from his book *Austerlitz* in which Sebald's first-person narrator describes a visit to Fort Breendonk, a former place of Nazi torture:

> As I stared at the smooth, grey floor of this pit, which seemed to me to be sinking further and further, the grating over the drain in the middle of it and the metal pail standing beside the drain, a picture of our laundry room at home in W. rose from the abyss and with it, suggested perhaps by the iron hook hanging on a cord from the ceiling, the image of the butcher's shop I always had to pass on my way to school, where at noon Benedikt was often to be seen in a rubber apron washing down the tiles with a thick hose. (Ae 32–33/Ag 41)

Real memories of his birthplace, Wertach, are localized here in the fictional place W., and they are merged with the brutal crimes of the National Socialist period that Sebald's first-person narrator encounters at a much later point elsewhere. Sebald links the quoted passage with this conclusion: 'No one can explain exactly what happens within us when the doors behind which our childhood terrors lurk are flung open' (Ae 33/Ag 41).

This oppressive example is representative of Sebald's memories of his birth town of Wertach in the context of a history of genocide. Certainly, Sebald must have experienced some good moments during childhood in his *Heimat*. For example, he was a member of a youth group, which transformed into a circle of friends with a keen interest in literature, for whom Sebald often organized readings of the major titles of world literature to initiate further discussion.[3] This is also a facet of what was once possible in the 'strange homeland' and that later probably led to *Heimat* becoming the fictionalized theme of W.G. Sebald's literary work.

Notes

1. T Honickel, *Curriculum Vitae. Die W.G. Sebald-Interviews*, ed. U Schütte, K Wolfinger (Würzburg: Königshausen & Neumann, 2021), pp. 27–38 (36).
2. R Tabbert, Früher Schulweg im Allgäu: Zwei Kindheitserinnerungen des Schriftstellers W.G. Sebald, in: *Literatur in Bayern* 97 (2009), pp. 28–30.
3. K Wolfinger, Freundschaft mit Sebald: Ein Gespräch mit Jürgen Kaeser, in: K Wolfinger (ed.), *Die literarische Provinz: Das Allgäu und die Literatur* (Berlin: Lang, 2021), pp. 133–137.

CHAPTER 2

Grandfather

Christoph Steker

Josef Egelhofer, Sebald's maternal grandfather, was born in 1872 in the Swabian town of Binnroth in south-west Germany, where he grew up on a small farm. A blacksmith by trade, he later secured a position as a village police constable in the Allgäu market town of Wertach and moved there in 1912, with his wife Theresia, whom he had married in 1905.[1] Egelhofer was widely respected not just by virtue of the office he held, but also because of his tall stature and smartly dressed appearance (SM 26–27).[2]

Not least because of his social status, the long-retired constable made a profound impression on the young Sebald. Egelhofer formed a close bond with his grandson and became far more of a father figure to him than Sebald's actual father Georg, who was mostly absent during the formative early years of his son's life, kept away by his stints in the military and as a prisoner of war and later by his commute for work to the town of Sonthofen, some eleven miles away.

These circumstances meant that young Winfried spent the first years of his life largely in the loving care of his grandfather. And they explain why Sebald never got over Egelhofer's death in April 1956: 'As a boy I felt protected. His death when I was 12 wasn't something I ever quite got over. It brought an early awareness of mortality and that the other side of life is something horrendously empty',[3] he explained in an interview. The traumatic sight of the laid-out corpse returns in a poem from *For Years Now*, Sebald's last book publication: 'The smell / of my writing paper / puts me in mind / of the woodshavings / in my grandfather's / coffin' (FYN 42).

The grandfather is not just a key figure in Sebald's life; he also looms large in his work as a literary figure. It is this literary manifestation, not the real Josef Egelhofer, that will be the primary concern of this essay. Yet, as will be shown, an adequate appreciation of Sebald's literary work is only possible against the background of Sebald's very close relationship with his grandfather. 'My interest in the departed, which has been fairly constant, comes from the moment of losing someone you couldn't really afford to

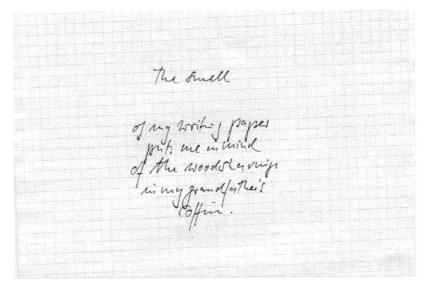

Illustration 2 – Autograph of 'The smell'

lose' (EM 171), he once acknowledged. And it is in this sense that Sebald, according to Uwe Schütte, 'can be described as a "ghost writer", haunted by the memory of his grandfather'.[4]

Hiking Companion, Teacher, Natural Philosopher

Sebald spent a sheltered childhood in the secluded setting of the Allgäu in south-west Germany. Remote and untouched by the destruction of war, the village of Wertach existed in a kind of time warp. While elsewhere modernisation had long since begun, everyday life in the mountain village resembled nineteenth-century conditions: 'Life moved at a slower, more elemental pace, in rhythm with the seasons, the sun, and the moon. Without a rail link to the outside world, few travellers came here, and few of its residents had reason to leave' (SM 25).

Accordingly, Sebald's childhood years spent with his grandfather were dominated by joint hikes through the alpine landscape. Even after his retirement, Josef Egelhofer kept up his regular, extended walks, on which he liked to take his grandchildren – young Winfried and his older sister Gertrud. On these rambles through a rich natural landscape, he never tired of teaching the children the names of plants and animals and of sharing his knowledge of the natural world with them, communicating insights into its diversity and its mysteries that were to have a lifelong effect on Sebald.

Sebald was educated early on about the effects of herbs and their use for healing purposes. Together with Egelhofer, he collected plants that were kept dried in labelled jars in the kitchen and brought out when needed to prepare suitable remedies in case of illness on the basis of recipes that Egelhofer had jotted down in a notebook reserved specifically for this purpose. This detail found its way into Sebald's fragmentary early novel from 1967, in which a student named Josef always carries a recipe book with him as a memento of his deceased grandfather (see chapter 8 in this volume).[5]

Like the folkloristic art of predicting the weather and interpreting it with the aid of a farmer's almanac, such orally transmitted knowledge and remedies handed down over generations have been largely suppressed in the modern age. Yet through his teacher Egelhofer, whom Gertrud characterized as a 'natural philosopher' (SM 31), Sebald was exposed at a formative age to pre-scientific knowledge and practices that would come to inform his thinking and become an important aspect of his later writings.[6]

For example, in the Hebel essay, the specific reference to his grandfather, 'who would every year buy a *Kempter Calender* [Kempten Almanac]' (PC 9/LH 13), seems informed by a nostalgic longing for a well-ordered system such as that of the almanac, with its capacity to integrate the most diverse areas of knowledge and convey the reassuring feeling that 'everything is arranged for the best', as it seemed to have been in his childhood (PC 12–13/ LH 17). Sebald's enduring interest in the writings of Paracelsus (1493–1541) similarly appears to hark back to his grandfather's teachings on the natural world: Paracelsus's nature mysticism and his alchemical instructions represent a whole range of what we would nowadays consider fringe sciences and obscure practices, and Sebald eagerly engages with them (see chapter 22 in this volume).

A passage in Sebald's essay on Gerhard Roth (1942–2022) acquires an almost programmatic character in this context when Sebald describes being a child and witnessing his grandfather tip his hat to an Elder bush, and he expresses his gratitude for having grown up in a village where such superstitions were still alive (UH 161). For Sebald, then, the dignity of writing lies the capacity of literature for safeguarding anachronistic positions and, in particular, thought systems founded in superstition. His writings seek to preserve the trove of knowledge transmitted to him by his grandfather in an act of personal commemoration.

Illustration 3 – Portrait Josef Egelhofer, c. 1940s

Elective Affinities

Under the caring aegis of his grandfather, young Winfried was also initiated into the world of literature: Egelhofer regularly read folk tales from his almanacs to his grandson, who soon knew them by heart. As an adolescent, Sebald came across the familiar diction of Egelhofer, who had learned to read and write in the 1870s, in the writings of Gottfried Keller (1819–1890), Adalbert Stifter (1805–1868), Eduard Mörike (1804–1875) or Johann Peter Hebel (1760–1826). For Sebald, the language he encountered in the works of these authors connected him to a bygone era that had still seemed alive in the figure of his grandfather.

About his own 'native' language, the German dialect spoken in the region where he was born, Sebald remarked: 'I am attached to that language. [. . .] If you have grown up in the kind of environment I grew up in, you can't put it aside just like that' (EM 69). Both aspects – his love for nineteenth-century German and his tendency to use regional expressions – characterize the "sound" of Sebald's literary prose in the original German. However, these crucial features are largely lost in the process of translation, disrupting the hidden connection to the grandfather.

In addition to the stylistic borrowings in Sebald's literary German, which keep the memory of the grandfather alive by conjuring his voice to enable an ongoing dialogue with the deceased, there are several figures in Sebald's writings that correlate with the figure of the grandfather and are sometimes directly, sometimes indirectly connected to Egelhofer. Three of these will be examined in more detail here.

First, the Swiss writer Robert Walser (1878–1956), to whom Sebald pays homage in the essay 'Le promeneur solitaire' by bringing the grandfather into such close proximity to the author that both appear as figurations of the same person. Walser is one of the great solitary figures in German-language literature. A social and cultural outsider all his life, he mostly composed short though highly elegant and ironic texts of an often self-deprecating nature.

In his Walser essay, Sebald states that, whenever he looks at the pictures depicting the elderly Walser, he is struck by how closely the writer resembles Josef Egelhofer in appearance and demeanour: 'Each time I think I see my grandfather before me' (PC 126/LH 136). Sebald's literary portrait of Walser follows the poetics of *Logis in einem Landhaus* (*A Place in the Country*) in its linguistic appropriation of the authorial biography discussed in it. What is more, by mapping the author's story so closely onto his grandfather's, he also effectively adopts Walser and assigns him a key position within his own family history.

The relationship between the fictionalized versions of Walser and Egelhofer ultimately proves reciprocal: the writer, 'the unmistakable figure of the solitary walker just pausing to take in the surroundings' (PC 149/LH 163), not only appears in the essay as 'my grandfather, Josef Egelhofer, with whom as a child I often used to go for walks for hours at a time' (PC 125–126/LH 135), but vice versa, when memories of the grandfather are overlapped with the photographs of Walser:

> Perhaps that is the reason why now, when I think back to my grandfather's death – to which I have never been able to reconcile myself – in my mind's eye I always see him lying on the horn sledge on which Walser's body, after he had been found in the snow and photographed, was taken back to the asylum. (PC 127/LH 137)

Remarkably, Walser is not only assigned a central position within Sebald's own family in the superimposition with Egelhofer, but Sebald himself merges with the writer whom he had admired all his life: 'Walser has been my constant companion. I only need to look up for a moment in my daily work to see him standing somewhere a little apart [. . .] And sometimes I imagine that I see with his eyes' (PC 149/LH 163). More than just an expression of profound identification with a fellow author and predecessor, this also suggests a wishful fantasy of communion with his beloved grandfather, a merging of a holy trinity, as it were.

Another figure in which a poetically transformed Egelhofer manifests himself is the artist and naturalist Alphonso Fitzpatrick in *Austerlitz*. As a paradigmatic teacher of nature, Alphonso assumes the same function for young Austerlitz as Sebald's grandfather did for him as a child. He passes on his botanical and zoological knowledge to Austerlitz, for example, by encouraging him to 'simply gaze' (Ae 128/Ag 136) at the intricate movements of moths in flight at night. Like Egelhofer, and analogous to Walser, Alphonso is a modest, nature-loving person. When working as a watercolour artist, he is equipped only with the bare essentials, painting 'barely sketches of pictures' (Ae 126/Ag 134); a creative approach informed by humble appreciation for the phenomena of the natural world. Thus, in the figure of Alphonso, the practice of art and the study of nature are once again closely connected, exactly as was the case with Egelhofer.

In a very similar way, the Bernese mountain-guide Johannes Naegeli, in the story 'Dr. Henry Selwyn', may be read as an avatar of Egelhofer. The experienced guide died while hiking and, seventy-two years later, his mortal remains are brought to light by the Oberaar glacier; an uncanny event that is emblematic of the 'return of the past' (Ae 261/Ag 269) so often invoked in Sebald's writings and crucial to Sebald's beginnings as a writer.[7] As a projection of Egelhofer, who opened up the world of plants and animals to his grandson and guided him on their shared trails through the alpine landscape, the Naegeli figure is deeply embedded in biographical constellations recalling the relationship between Sebald and Egelhofer: the young Henry Selwyn becomes a pupil and companion to the much older mountain guide, they spend a great deal of time together in the mountains and, in retrospect, the days spent together appear as the happiest of Selwyn's life. He never gets over the loss of Naegeli.

Sebald uses the authentic fate of the mountain-guide, to create a mentor figure who opens up a completely new world for Selwyn. As Richard Gray explains, Naegeli functions 'as a symbolic father-figure'[8] whose death is representative of the unfulfilled promise of a shared future. The real-life model for this paternal figure, however, was not provided by Georg Sebald but by Josef Egelhofer.

Sebald's auto-fictional manoeuvre of constructing family ties that do not actually exist, on the other hand, is a different matter. For example, he claimed a family relation between his grandfather and Rudolf Egelhofer (1896–1919), the 'commander of the Red Army at the time of the Munich Soviet, who was murdered by the right-wing free corps' (SM 257), as he stated in a scholarship application from 2000. The claim was made disingenuously: in the 1980s, Sebald had unsuccessfully tried to find evidence for such a genealogical link in the Munich State Archives. Despite such a link only being wishful thinking on Sebald's part, he maintained its existence until the end of his life.

Though he never translated the genealogical fantasy of a communist family tradition into his literary writings, the motivation was clear: proving that Egelhofer was descended of the "revolutionary line" of German politics that had resisted the rise of Nazism would have allowed him to add a further layer of elective affinity to his literary recreation of the village policeman Josef Egelhofer 'as a marginal, homeless wanderer and societal outsider',[9] as Melissa Etzler succinctly puts it.

Trauma and 'Cult of Remembrance'

Sebald's literary remembrance of Josef Egelhofer finds its Archimedean point in childhood trauma: 'I remember very well how, as a child, I stood for the first time by an open coffin, with the dull sense in my breast that my grandfather, lying there on wood shavings, had suffered a shameful injustice that none of us survivors could make good' (CSe 33/CSg 35). We might think of this feeling of guilt and shame as Sebald's "primal scene".

For the rest of his life, Sebald battled with the problem of how to confront the deeply felt pain caused by this experience. In the literary realm, his efforts were channelled into a poetics aimed at creating 'eine Gemeinschaftsaktion der Lebenden und der Toten' ('a joint enterprise of the living and the dead')[10] – a phrase coined by Sebald in an essay on Herbert Achternbusch (1938–2022). The 'joint enterprise' describes an attempt to ensure the continued existence of a deceased person in a descendant by means of ritualized actions, thus carrying the past forward into the present.

It is exactly this strategy of remembrance and preservation that can be detected in Sebald's creative treatment of Egelhofer: the figure of the grandfather is repeatedly woven into motifs and protagonists in his work.

Yet Josef Egelhofer's presence may even be felt when Sebald proceeds by contrast rather than analogy: just think of the decidedly 'unhappy house' (Ae 61/Ag 69) in which Austerlitz spends his formative years as a child – the backdrop to a bleak adolescence imagined in sharp contradistinction to Sebald's sheltered childhood days in Wertach. Family lore, memory and fiction intertwine in this creative process, and the erstwhile grandson and now author Sebald appears, as Jan Ceuppens puts it, as 'a witness, somebody who is able to continue the story [. . .] in order to preserve its future'.[11]

A prime example of Sebald's interconnection of various characters through the figure of his grandfather can be found in the motif of the hat, that indispensable accessory Egelhofer carried with him all year long. The hat evidently left a lasting impression on young Winfried, for it recurs in multiple contexts: in the meaningful resemblance between Egelhofer and Walser regarding 'the way each had of holding his hat in his hand' (PC 126/LH 137); in the 'narrow-brimmed hat, a kind of trilby' worn by schizophrenic poet Ernst Herbeck, 'which he later took off when it grew too warm for him and carried beside him, just as my grandfather often used to do on summer walks' (V 39/SG 46); in the customary attire of Alphonso, whose straw hat functions as the insignia of a free-spirited, nature-minded artist's existence; and, last but not least, in the various straw hats worn by the writer Sebald, for instance in the photograph adorning the cardboard slipcase of the German-language first edition of *Die Ringe des Saturn* (*The Rings of Saturn*).[12]

Wearing a hat while strolling in nature is the unmistakable mark of walking in Egelhofer's footsteps. Sebald also kept his grandfather's beard brush and often carried it with him, like a fetish, when he left the house, just as the moustache, which Sebald already sported as a young man, was not just an homage to his grandfather but rather an attempt to recreate himself in the ancestor's image. Finally, the narrator of 'Il ritorno in patria' is also keen to stress that a former neighbour remarked to him that 'I reminded him [. . .] of my grandfather who had the same gait and, whenever he stepped out of the house, would pause for a moment to peer up into the sky to see what the weather was doing, just as I always did' (V 210/SG 229–230).

Conclusion

'When my grandfather, whom I loved dearly, lay dying during the first *föhn* storm after the Siberian winter of 1956' (CSe 193/CSg 227–228), this heralded a traumatic loss for Sebald, which he later transmuted artistically into a kind of 'cult of remembrance'[13] in order creatively to confront 'the burden of grief which is probably not imposed on [me] for nothing' (CSe 33/CSg 35). The loss of his grandfather in childhood marks the beginning of Sebald's 'career in mourning' (PC 128/LH 138) that overshadowed his entire life. It stands to reason that the traumatic experience was probably also largely responsible for his melancholic disposition. There has even been some suggestion that the skin rash that Sebald suffered from for most of his life may be explained as a psychosomatic reaction to the loss of Egelhofer.[14]

Egelhofer's death is the original trauma and primal pain to which the mourning work conducted in his literary works must be traced back. The closeness of the bond between grandson and grandfather accounts for the profound significance accorded to ritualized mourning in Sebald's work, which conducts a literary form of *Trauerarbeit* (grief work). It is worth returning to the key quotation in which Sebald retrospectively remembers how he felt as a child when confronted with the corpse of Egelhofer, who, in the boy's mind, 'had suffered a shameful injustice that none of us survivors could make good' (CSe 33/CSg 35).

This is the "survivor guilt" that Sebald was later to encounter again in the clinical study on survivor's syndrome by exiled psychologist William Niederland and in the fates of exile writers such as Paul Celan or Jean Améry. Rather than being primarily an indicator of his engagement with the legacy of the Holocaust, the impulse to write several critical essays on Améry or a prose story on his former schoolteacher (who was forced from his job by the Nazis and committed suicide as a pensioner) is strongly linked to the personal experience of loss.

Regarding the crimes committed during the Nazi regime, Sebald once confessed in an interview: 'While I don't feel any responsibility, I do feel a sense of shame.'[15] Yet it would appear that the experience of shame in the absence of culpability can be traced all the way back to the 'shameful injustice' of young Winfried seeing his beloved grandfather resting in a coffin, his dead body laid out on wood shavings, the smell of which will for ever be evoked for Sebald by his writing paper.

Notes

1. For the wedding portrait of the Egelhofers see Illustration 19 in this volume.
2. U Schütte, *Annäherungen: Sieben Essays zu W.G. Sebald* (Cologne: Böhlau, 2019), p. 46.

3. M Jaggi, Recovered memories, *Guardian*, 22 September 2001.
4. U Schütte, *W.G. Sebald* (Liverpool: Liverpool University Press, 2018), p. 8.
5. Version 1, p. 34; version 2, p. 70 (DLA).
6. Schütte, *Annäherungen*, pp. 46–48.
7. S Bartsch, W.G. Sebald's 'Prose Project'. A Glimpse into the Potting Shed, in: U Schütte (ed.), *Über W.G. Sebald: Beiträge zu einem anderen Bild des Autors* (Berlin/Boston: De Gruyter, 2017), pp. 99–134 (102–104).
8. R Gray, *Ghostwriting: W.G. Sebald's Poetics of History* (London: Bloomsbury, 2019), p. 178.
9. M Etzler, So ein langes Leben. Rebellious Writing and Philosophical Meanderings in W.G. Sebald's Juvenilia, in: Schütte, *Über W.G. Sebald: Beiträge zu einem anderen Bild des Autors*, pp. 29–50 (37).
10. Sebald, Die Kunst der Verwandlung: Achternbuschs theatralische Sendung, in: D James, S Ranawake (eds.), *Patterns of Change: German Drama and the European Tradition: Essays in Honour of Ronald Peacock* (New York: Lang, 1990), pp. 297–306 (303).
11. J Ceuppens, Tracing the Witness in W.G. Sebald, in: A Fuchs, J Long (eds.), *W.G. Sebald and the Writing of History* (Würzburg: Königshausen & Neumann, 2007), pp. 59–72 (72).
12. For a variation of this photograph see Illustration 21 in this volume.
13. M Anderson, Wo die Schrecken der Kindheit verborgen sind: W.G. Sebalds Dilemma der zwei Väter: Biografische Skizzen zu einem Portrait des Dichters als junger Mann, in: *Literaturen* 7/8 (2006), pp. 32–39 (35).
14. C Angier, *Speak, Silence: In Search of W.G. Sebald* (London: Bloomsbury, 2021), p. 12.
15. C Bigsby, *Writers in Conversation with Christopher Bigsby*, vol. 2 (Norwich: EAS, 2001), pp. 140–165 (144).

CHAPTER 3

Manchester

Catherine Annabel

Sebald's literary life began, in a sense, in Manchester. His mature prose fiction would not appear for another twenty-five years, long after he had left Manchester for East Anglia, the autobiographical novel which he wrote in Manchester remains unpublished, and the poetry he wrote there appeared only after his death – and yet, without Manchester, his unique prose works would not have emerged as they did.

Why did Manchester leave such a lasting imprint on his writing? Three aspects are particularly important. Firstly, there is the city itself, which, when Sebald encountered it in 1966, was the archetype of an industrial metropolis. Secondly, his encounter with its long-established and highly visible Jewish community. And, thirdly, Michel Butor's 1956 novel, *L'Emploi du temps*,[1] which Sebald read in his first few months in Manchester and which had a significant and lasting influence on him. I will explore these three elements in the three texts most directly and explicitly inspired by Manchester: the 1967 poem 'Bleston: A Mancunian Cantical' (LWe 18–22/LWg 22–26), the long prose poem *Nach der Natur* (*After Nature*), and the fourth section of *Die Ausgewanderten* (*The Emigrants*), the story 'Max Ferber'.

Sebald, or Max (as he was known from this period onwards) arrived in Manchester in September 1966, having been appointed a *Lektor* (a language teaching assistant) at the University. He stayed in his first accommodation for only a few weeks, before moving to another set of rooms, barely an improvement on the first, but where he would remain until he found much more comfortable and congenial lodgings. These were in the pleasant suburb of Didsbury, in a house owned by the architect Peter Jordan (1923–2020) and his wife Dorothy (1930–2021).

Sebald's new surroundings inspired an early poem (one of his contributions to a *Festschrift* for Idris Parry (1916–2008), Professor of German at the University), which is in stark contrast to his literary portrayals of Manchester as a post-apocalyptic landscape of destruction, as he speaks of church bells, summer hats and chestnut blossoms (LWg 27/LWe 23). Sebald shared the flat with another *Lektor*, Reinbert Tabbert, with whom he had much in common, and with whom he remained in friendly, if occasional, contact for many years. After Tabbert's return to Germany, Sebald moved into an upper-floor flat at the same building, with his new wife, Ute.

Whilst in these new lodgings, Sebald wrote a second version of an autobiographical novel, which was rejected by several publishers at the time (see chapter 8 in this volume). His contract with Manchester was extended, and he was to remain at the University, with an interlude during which he taught English and German at an exclusive international boarding school in St Gallen, Switzerland, until 1970, when he left to take up his appointment as Assistant Lecturer in German Literature and Language at the University of East Anglia (UEA).

During this second period in Manchester, Sebald submitted an MA thesis on the playwright Carl Sternheim (1878–1942), which he then turned into a German book, published in 1969; applied unsuccessfully for a research fellowship at Cambridge on the novelist Alfred Döblin (1878–1957); registered at Manchester to do a part-time PhD on Döblin; and was offered and turned down a post in drama at the University of Bangor (SM 82–85). He then applied successfully for the post at UEA, to which he also transferred his PhD registration. These things suggest that Sebald was uncertain about his future direction. There are even indications that he considered leaving the UK and academia altogether; indeed, he toyed with other ideas, such as becoming a travel writer or moving to southern Europe.[2]

Tabbert recorded some of their conversations in his diary for 1966–67[3] and they convey both lively intellectual debate and introspection, with Sebald repeatedly suggesting that he felt 'close to the limit'. Another fellow lodger, Peter Jonas (1946–2020), then a music student at the University, and later a renowned opera company director, also describes him as 'deeply melancholic'[4] during his time in Manchester. Tabbert recalls Sebald as being lonely in Manchester, and as often going out for long, solitary walks.[5] His early lodgings seem to have contributed to his sense of isolation and depression, although Tabbert does suggest that he 'tended to self-dramatize',[6] and to emphasize the least appealing aspects of his surroundings, the 'scenes of slum clearance and urban decay', the 'desolate leftovers of nineteenth-century Manchester' and the industrial pollution still evident in the city (SM 66). This landscape both echoed and fed his melancholic mood, and his sense of alienation.

Illustration 4 – Manchester, Rochdale Canal, photographed by Sebald

'Bleston. A Mancunian Cantical': Sebald's Encounter with Michel Butor

The impact of the city itself on Sebald was at least in part seen through the lens of Michel Butor's *L'Emploi du temps*, which he read and made notes on during his first months in Manchester. Butor (1926–2016) had himself come to Manchester, in 1951, to work for two years as a *lecteur* (i.e., in the same capacity as Sebald) in the French department of the University. Like Sebald, he experienced a considerable cultural – and climatic – shock upon arrival, and seems to have been somewhat lonely and melancholy.[7] He wrote his first novel, *Passage de Milan*,[8] whilst in Manchester, and later used his experiences in the city to write *L'Emploi du temps*, his first literary success. Manchester here becomes Bleston, which shares Manchester's climate and polluted atmosphere, and many of its landmarks.

Whilst Sebald may have already read the book in its German translation,[9] it was the French edition, now held in the Deutsches Literaturarchiv in Marbach, that was his companion. The pages of the text are full of vigorous underlinings, exclamation marks, and marginal notes, which show not only a very attentive reading, but an identification of his own situation with that of Butor and his protagonist, Jacques Revel.

Just as Butor maps Revel's year in Bleston onto his own first year in Manchester, so Sebald follows Revel's progress in finding congenial lodgings, walking alone on the streets of the city, and struggling with the language, step by step. Richard Sheppard has commented on the way in which this reading may have deepened Sebald's own melancholy (SM 66).

This close reading of *L'Emploi du temps* made itself apparent in Sebald's own writing in the early poem, 'Bleston: A Mancunian Cantical', written in January 1967. The poem describes Manchester in autumn and winter, just after his arrival, the period in which he was reading and making notes on *L'Emploi du temps*. The lyrical voice speaks of the 'snowless lightless month / Of December', with references to 'soot-covered trees', offshore ships 'Waiting in the fog', wasteland and 'pollard willows on snowless fields'. It also refers back to Manchester's earliest history, as a Roman settlement, in a passage that echoes Butor.[10] We find here elements that will re-appear in *After Nature* and *The Emigrants*, where passages from the poem recur in a slightly different form. For example, the description of the starlings who have 'forgotten their old life' (E 157/AW 229), and their migration to warmer climes recurs in *The Emigrants*, while 'Sharon's Full Gospel' church reappears in *After Nature* (NN 86/AN 98).

A labyrinth of intertextual references, with fragments in French, Latin, Aramaic and Yiddish, the poem includes biblical references, allusions to Pythagorean philosophy, a quotation from Pascal as adapted by Adorno, a quotation from Virgil, reference to a novel by Hans Henny Jahnn (1894–1959), and a line from a poem by Heinrich Meiborn (1638–1700). In addition, there are overt and hidden (where the French text has been translated by Sebald into German and thence into English) quotations from Butor as well as more indirect references to *L'Emploi du temps*, along with shared motifs and images such as shadows and phantoms, fire and ash, and the labyrinth.[11]

Such rich intertextuality of course continues to be a feature of Sebald's work, as does the practice of obscuring the origins of quotations. The preoccupations and themes evident here also resonate through his œuvre: trauma and the challenge of speaking about trauma, the threshold between death and life.

Dark Night Sallies Forth: The Shock of Manchester

In the nineteenth century, as Manchester entered into a period of rapid and unplanned growth during the Industrial Revolution, writers such as Hippolyte Taine (1828–1893), Alexis de Tocqueville (1805–1859) and

Friedrich Engels (1820–1895) visited and were shocked by its smoke, dirt, labyrinthine streets and heavily polluted river Irwell. In *After Nature*, Sebald turns to this period of Manchester's history: 'the statesman / Disraeli called Manchester / the most wonderful city of modern times, / a celestial Jerusalem', a reference which illustrates how Manchester's 'boundless growth' impressed even whilst appalling observers such as Engels, Taine and de Tocqueville (AN 95–100/NN 83–87). Sebald's own descriptions are bleak: the narrator takes lodgings 'among the previous century's / ruins', and wonders at the 'work of destruction', the 'traces of smoke, of tar and sulphuric acid', commenting too on the effects of living in such conditions on generations of Mancunians, who later could only be conscripted for military service in 'one of the so-called bantam battalions' (AN 95–96/NN 84).

It has been noted that Sebald's descriptions, which dwell on scenes of desolation and dereliction, may misrepresent the city as it was at the time he lived there.[12] But in the mid-to-late 1960s, whilst progress had been made in reducing pollution from the chimneys through the establishment of smokeless zones (and the decline of some traditional industries), and in rebuilding where bomb damage had created wastelands in the city centre, this work had not yet transformed the city.

Furthermore, nothing in Sebald's life before 1966 had prepared him for Manchester. His upbringing had been rural, and whilst he had encountered war-damaged cities in Germany, he had no experience of a city ravaged in part by war but predominantly by industrialization: 'I was completely unprepared for it. [. . .] I had no concept of what an industrial wasteland was because I hadn't seen that kind of degradation before.'[13]

After Nature not only uses material found in the Bleston poem, but contains sections which are re-used in *The Emigrants*, particularly the references to Liston's Music Hall (AN 98/E 234–235) and Strangeways Prison (AN 98/ E 157).[14] Here too we find an account of his exploration of the old Jewish quarter near the prison, and the names on the derelict shops: 'Goldblatt, Grunspan and Gottgetreu, / Spiegelhalter, Solomon, Waislfish / and Robinsohn' (AN 99/NN 86), which appears in a slightly altered form in *The Emigrants* (E 157/AW 230). We see here the evidence of Sebald's early encounters with Jewish Manchester, primarily in the person of his landlord from January 1967 forward, Peter Jordan, who was later used as a model for Max Ferber in *The Emigrants*.

Manchester for the first time brought Sebald into contact with Jewish individuals and Jewish culture that had been so efficiently excised from his native country. 'When I got to Manchester', Sebald explained, 'I realized that what I had read in the papers and in history books and seen in films wasn't about anonymous victims but that it had concerned real people'.[15] Sebald's first lodgings were owned by a Jewish refugee called van Perlstein, and he fictionalized another Jewish landlord, with whom two other *Lektoren* had lodgings, as his own landlord in *After Nature*. The name, Mr Deutsch, belongs to a real Jewish landlord in Manchester, but the history given to him in *After Nature* does not – there it is stated that he was 'born in Kufstein, had come / to England as a child in nineteen-thirty-eight' (AN 100/NN 87).

Mr Deutsch was not himself a refugee, and is believed to have come to Manchester in the 1920s (SM 100–101). Thus, this first 'emigrant' is, like Max Ferber, Jacques Austerlitz and others, an amalgam and, like those later creations, has caused some confusion amongst readers. However, perhaps more significant than this is the evidence of Sebald's growing preoccupation with the stories these refugees carried with them: 'There were many things he could not / remember; some others he could not erase / from his mind' (AN 100/NN 87).

The Emigrants: Max Ferber and Peter Jordan

There is a whole anthology to be compiled of accounts of the first view of the city – Sebald contributed two, in the 'Max Ferber' section of *The Emigrants*. In preparation for writing *The Emigrants*, Sebald visited his former landlord Peter Jordan and went with him into the Pennines to get a view over the city.[16] Sebald describes Max Ferber's first sight of Manchester, in 1945, thus:

> Over the flatland to the west, a curiously shaped cloud extended to the horizon, and the last rays of sunlight were blazing past its edges, and for a while lit up the entire panorama. [...] Not until this illumination died (said Ferber) did his eye roam, [...] as far as what he took to be the centre of the city, where all seemed one solid mass of utter blackness, bereft of any further distinguishing features. (E 168/AW 246)

The Emigrants gives us a vivid and detailed picture of Manchester, as Sebald encountered it, although, as we have noted, his perceptions tended to emphasize the grimmer aspects of the city. From the opening section, describing the narrator's arrival, there are references to fog and ash, and to a city 'hollow at the core': 'One might have supposed that the city had long since been deserted, and was left now as a necropolis or mausoleum' (E 150–151/AW 220–221). Like Butor's protagonist, he arrives in the early morning, which partly accounts for the fact that no one was about, but this continues – in the wasteland he encounters 'always and only children' and walks amongst 'abandoned depots and warehouses' (E 158/AW 231–232). It is on one of these walks that the narrator encounters Max Ferber, the subject of this fourth section of *The Emigrants*.

This brings us to the most significant of the Jews Sebald met in Manchester, Peter Jordan, who became his landlord after he had suffered in two previous miserable digs. Tabbert suspects that Manchester University paired German staff and students with Jewish landlords as a matter of policy[17] (although the pairing may have been simply based on language). He also suggests that Sebald was uneasy, perhaps conscious not only of his nationality but of being the son of a Wehrmacht officer, and still attempting to process what he had been taught, and what he had learned, of the Holocaust, through watching film footage of the liberation of Belsen whilst at school, and through the Frankfurt Auschwitz trials, which he had followed attentively in 1963–1965.

The story of Max Ferber's escape from Munich is substantially that of Peter Jordan, although Sebald gives Ferber the artistic practice of the painter Frank Auerbach (b. 1931), another Jewish refugee. Jordan/Ferber left Munich in May 1939, leaving his parents behind. Jordan believed for many years that they were deported in 1941 to Riga (the account that Sebald uses) but found out at a much later stage that they were in fact taken to Kaunas,[18] where they were shot, in the notorious Fort 9, which is described in *Austerlitz* (Ag 420–421/Ae 414–415). Ferber's encounter with a hostile customs official in Frankfurt is taken directly from the memories that Jordan shared with Sebald, as is the fact that he then attended a 'very peculiar' public school at Margate.[19]

After this point, Ferber's path diverges from that of Jordan. Ferber comes to Manchester once his schooling has finished, in 1943, is called up in 1944, and volunteers (after basic training at Catterick) for the paratrooper regiment, but is then taken ill and has to stay in a convalescent home in Buxton (AW 245/E 167). On his discharge, he returns to Manchester where he begins his practice as an artist, whereas Jordan studied architecture, and then worked as an interpreter for the army both during and immediately after the war.[20] Clearly, the conversations Sebald had with Jordan during his time in Manchester had a significant impact, such that he decided to base Max Ferber, at least in part, on him. He wrote to Jordan, requesting copies of family memoirs,[21] and then went to stay with the couple, talking for hours, asking many questions but taking no notes.

Whilst Sebald clearly had permission in principle to use this material, Jordan later expressed reservations about the use (without attribution) of his aunt's memoir.[22] Auerbach objected much more vigorously to the use, in the first German editions of the text, of something close to his name (Max Aurach), and of an image of his eye and one of his artworks, and thus Aurach became Ferber and the contentious illustrations were removed.

Short Conclusion

More broadly, we can see that Manchester is present in much more than the obvious texts (the Bleston poem, *The Emigrants* and Part III of *After Nature*). Butor's transformed Manchester was never just Manchester – it was also the dark, dangerous, and violent Paris of the Occupation, the era that haunted Butor throughout his life. And in the same way, Sebald's Manchester is never just Manchester – the Jewish name plates which he sees in the derelict areas of the city speak to him of a more sinister and tragic absence, and the chimneys and ash, of the industrialization of death.

Notes

1. M Butor, *L'Emploi du temps* (Paris: Minuit, 1956); *Passing Time* (Manchester: Pariah Press, 2021).
2. T Honickel, *Curriculum Vitae: Die W.G. Sebald-Interviews* (Würzburg: Königshausen & Neumann, 2021), p. 101.
3. R Tabbert, Max in Manchester, in: *Akzente* 50:1 (2003), pp. 24–25.
4. Honickel, *Curriculum Vitae*, p. 120.
5. Ibid., p. 95.
6. Ibid., p. 97.
7. JB Howitt, Michel Butor and Manchester, in: *Nottingham French Studies* 12:2 (1973), p. 77.
8. M Butor, *Passage de Milan* (Paris: Minuit, 1954).
9. M Butor, *Der Zeitplan* (Munich: DTV, 1964); Honickel, *Curriculum Vitae*, p. 97.
10. Butor, *Passing Time*, pp. 81, 255.
11. Cf. Iain Galbraith's notes on the poem, LWe 176–180.
12. J Wolff, Max Ferber and the Persistence of Pre-Memory in Mancunian Exile, in: *Melilah* 2 (2012), pp. 48–49.
13. C Bigsby, *Writers in Conversation*, vol. 2 (Norwich: EAS, 2001), p. 149.
14. Butor, *Passing Time*, pp. 274–275.
15. Bigsby, *Writers in Conversation*, p. 161.
16. Honickel, *Curriculum Vitae*, p. 106.
17. Ibid., p. 98.

18. Ibid., p. 113.
19. Ibid., pp. 109, 107.
20. Ibid., p. 108.
21. Ibid., p. 106.
22. U Schütte, *W.G. Sebald* (Liverpool: Liverpool University Press, 2018), p. 68.

CHAPTER 4

East Anglia

Jo Catling

Where, or what, is East Anglia? Facing away from the rest of England across the North Sea – or the 'German Ocean', as it was once known (RSg 69; 86; 97; 242/RSe 53; 67; 78, 203), it seems a marginal place, this 'flat expanse of provincial eastern England from which it was once easier to get to Amsterdam than to London and which, even after it had been made more accessible by the advent of the railway, persisted in its eccentric way of life' (SM 321).[1]

For Sebald – who by his own account came from a 'rather peripheral place' in the deep south of Germany, Wertach im Allgäu, 'a rather cut-off place on the Austrian border, about three thousand feet above sea level',[2] – when he arrived there in 1970, via the 'initial culture shock' (G 253) of metropolitan Manchester, the contrast of the legendary flatness of the East Anglian landscape (much of it barely elevated above sea level at all) must have seemed little short of extraordinary. This sense of an exotic, perhaps rather quaint otherness is captured by Sebald in an early article, cited above, 'Die hölzernen Engel von East Anglia: Eine individuelle Bummeltour durch Norfolk und Suffolk' ('The Carved Wooden Angels of East Anglia: A Leisurely Tour through Norfolk and Suffolk'), published in the travel section of the German broadsheet *Die Zeit* in July 1974.

This piece, while initially appearing rather peripheral to Sebald's later academic or literary career, is written somewhat in the manner of a guidebook, complete with a sketch-map of the proposed itinerary, but with the reader addressed directly, in a lightly ironic tone, gently satirizing the "English way of life" while at the same time wholeheartedly recommending the 'strange sights' to be found there. It is, however, prescient in a number of ways. Not only does the route pass through many of the places revisited in the penultimate section of *Nach der Natur* (*After Nature*), such as Woodbridge, Sutton Hoo and Shingle Street (NN 92–95/AN 105–108) and *Die Ringe des Saturn* (*The Rings of Saturn*), as well as a tour of the Norfolk Broads, coast and auction houses; it also passes through places notably lacking from the above texts: Salle church in Norfolk, for example, revisited on a foggy day in *Austerlitz* (Ae 192/Ag 200); or Aldeburgh, with its annual Festival, where Sebald would later give a reading in June 1999.

Its appearance in a newspaper supplement also prefigures Sebald's preference for publishing his "crossover" critical essays in the culture supplements of German-language broadsheets, as well as what he claimed was his plan for writing *The Rings of Saturn*: 'I had this idea of writing a few short pieces for the feuilletons of the German papers in order to pay for this extravagance of a fortnight's rambling tour. That was the plan. But then as you walk along, you find things' (EM 94).

As defined in the 'Wooden Angels' essay, East Anglia stretches from the port of Harwich in Essex (with its ferry link to Hoek van Holland) around the North Sea coast and northwest to Kings Lynn and Sandringham, just skirting Cambridge to the west of the region. In terms of Sebaldian topography, it may be said to extend southwards to Liverpool Street Station in London – famous for its links to the Kindertransport, but also the terminus for trains from Norwich, a journey variously evoked not only by the narrator in *Austerlitz* (Ag 56–57/Ae 48–50) but also at the very end of *Schwindel. Gefühle. (Vertigo)* (SG 284–285/V 259–261) and prefigured in the poem 'Day Return' (LWe 92–95/LWg 57–59).

Similarly, the port of Harwich in the bleak Essex landscape, and the ferry to Hoek van Holland, recur in the poem 'A Galley lies of Helsingborg' (LWe 72)[3] and the later 'I remember' (LWe 164–167), written, unusually, in English; while the flight across the North Sea from Norwich to Schiphol airport near Amsterdam and vice versa is variously evoked (RSg 110–114/RSe 89–92), echoing the topographically accurate dream-flight to Munich at the end of *After Nature* (NN 96–97/AN 109–110). The region is framed by these loci of ingress and egress, routes into and out of what some have termed a voluntary exile or at least emigration.

While Sebald made his home in Norfolk (whose capital, Norwich, he describes as 'the centre of East Anglia', SM 320), it is Suffolk which has the larger presence in Sebald's work, resonating in both *The Rings of Saturn* and the third section of the *After Nature* which in many ways prefigures it. Nonetheless, Sebald's recurring evocations of the Norfolk landscape, 'the vast flatland that stretches southeast to the sea' (RSe 30/RSg 42), does give a sense of the atmosphere and the fascination – and unexpectedly exotic associations – which the region's wide vistas and lack of elevation held for him. While the poem 'Holkham Gap' (LWg 47/LWe 74–75), with its 'camouflaged ornithologists' who recur in *After Nature* (AN 105/NN 92) hints, in its anticipation of an apparently incongruous 'sea lion', at the strategic and historic vulnerability of the coastline, the eponymous poem 'Norfolk', first published in July 1974, the same month as the 'Wooden Angels' piece appeared in *Die Zeit*, seems – in a manner arguably prefiguring *The Rings of Saturn* – to transcend space and time while conveying the unsettling but characteristic impression of boats apparently sailing across fields, a 'landscape populated / by invisible windmillers // Where the Egyptian / in his painted boat / sails between fields' (LWe 76/LWg 48).

There is a striking parallel to this in the 'All'estero' section of *Vertigo*, where the narrator describes 'the county in East Anglia where I live, the great wheatfields [...], the rivers up which the incoming tide drives the sea water, and the times when the land is flooded and one can cross the fields in boats, as the Egyptians did' (V 48/SG 56) Meanwhile, in *The Rings of Saturn* this 'Egyptian' landscape is transposed across the North Sea (which the narrative also criss-crosses) to the topographically similar flatlands of Holland:

> Diderot, in one of his travel journals, described Holland as the Egypt of Europe, where one might cross the fields in a boat and, as far as the eye could see, there would be scarcely anything to break the flooded surface of the plain. In that curious country, he wrote, the most modest rise gave one the loftiest sensation. (RSe 84/RSg 108)

Illustration 5 – 17 Vicar Street, Wymondham, Norfolk

This on the surface unlikely identification of the waterlogged landscapes of, *mutatis mutandis,* Holland and Norfolk with Egypt (and the Nile) already suggests the literary transposition, and characteristic layers of intertextual accretion, the region undergoes in Sebald's work.

Home and Away: Sebald in East Anglia

Sebald moved to Norfolk from Manchester in 1970 to take up a position as Assistant Lecturer in German Language and Literature at the University of East Anglia (UEA), initially renting a flat in a large country house in the small market town of Wymondham, then acquiring a house in a modern development nearby before purchasing and renovating the Old Rectory in Poringland (SM 92–93; 591), a substantial village to the south of Norwich, where he lived until his untimely death in December 2001. As Arthur Lubow suggests, 'he may have felt most comfortable in a place in which he was foreign' (EM 166), and indeed, though he says in an interview: 'I have lived here for thirty years and yet I do not feel in the least at home',[4] Sebald does admit that he felt 'relatively well looked-after' in this 'provisional existence' (G 253), though in his 'Acceptance Speech to the Collegium of the German Academy' in 1997 he notes: 'only a guest in England, I still hover between feelings of familiarity and dislocation there too' (CSe 217/CSg 250).

Nevertheless, the contrast between the rural nature of 1970s Norfolk and both urban Manchester and the German past he had left behind may have had some semblance, at least initially, of an idyllic retreat from the modern world. However, even in 'Wooden Angels' he notes that a visit to Shingle Street, 'a desolate stretch of coast', can give one 'a taste of East Anglian melancholy'(SM 319),[5] a taste reinforced in *After Nature*: 'No, here we can write / no postcards, can't even / get out of the car' (AN 107/NN 94), and reprised in the eighth section of *The Rings of Saturn* (RSg 268–269/RSe 225).

Those parts of his works set in the region frequently reveal the sense of being on the edge, perhaps at 'the end of the world' (AN 107/NN 94): even in such apparently unspoiled landscapes there is, it seems, no escape from the human, history and its 'secret weapons of destruction' (RSe [vi]/RSg [v]). Thus even whereas at Orford Ness, nature is reclaiming the sites of human destruction (RSg 277–283/RSe 232–237), the palimpsestic awareness of the region's strategic involvement in history is never far beneath the surface. An extract from *Luftkrieg und Literatur* (*On the Natural History of Destruction*) makes this historical dimension very clear:

Many of the more than seventy airfields from which the war of annihilation was waged against Germany were in the county of Norfolk. [. . .] most were abandoned after the war. Grass has grown over the runways, and the dilapidated control towers, bunkers, and corrugated iron huts stand in an often eerie landscape where you sense the dead souls of the men who never came back from their missions, and of those who perished in the vast fires. I live very close to Seething airfield. I sometimes walk my dog there, and imagine what the place was like when the aircraft took off with their heavy freight and flew out over the sea, making for Germany. (NHD 77–78/LL 83–84)

The same Seething airfield reappears in the second draft of the Corsica Project where one of the many 'dilapidated country houses' of which Sebald is so fond, 'Andromeda Lodge' (which in *Austerlitz* is situated on the west coast of Wales), is located 'in the immediate vicinity' of the airfield (KP 159–164).

'Imaginary Locations': Sebald's East Anglia

As is well known, Sebald admits – or rather explains – in various interviews that writing involves a 'sleight of hand', pointing out the deliberate ambiguity in the German title of *Vertigo, Schwindel. Gefühle.*:

> the German title, Schwindelgefühle, does mean vertigo, but Schwindel on its own also means legerdemain, conjuring or confidence trick. The text is a sort of confidence trick by the writer who is able to pull the wool over the reader's eyes and who is [. . .] engaged in a morally dubious exercise, particularly perhaps when that exercise is executed with a great deal of virtuosity.[6]

Notwithstanding such caveats, Sebald's consistent use of a first-person narrator who shares his name, occupation and birthday has led to considerable curiosity as to the whereabouts and veracity of the locales and persons represented in his books. And while readers may and do derive a certain satisfaction from the "unmasking" of "true identities" and locales, such blurring of fact and fiction is not a practice unique to Sebald but rather, as he points out, a general characteristic of fiction. 'It isn't anything new', he explains in conversation with his colleague Chris Bigsby.

> If you read a novel by Thomas Mann, the vast majority of the characters are based on people he knew and observed closely, or he collated a character out of two people he knew. For those who knew the Mann family and their social surroundings, these novels were romans-à-clef.[7]

Examples of such blurring in his own work may readily be found in, for example, the 'Dr. Henry Selwyn' story in *Die Ausgewanderten* (*The Emigrants*), set in 'Hingham' (a small town to the west of Norwich); yet while the flat rented by the narrator may indeed resemble Sebald's first East Anglian domicile, the latter was located in a different town, Wymondham, where he resided in a flat in a house on Vicar Street; the story's opening photograph of a yew tree in a churchyard does not represent either place. His original books were, of course, conceived for a German-speaking, rather than local, audience, and it is worth noting that several of the names in this story are also changed in the English translation: 'Hedi' and 'Aileen' become 'Elli' and 'Elaine', while 'Edward Ellis' (E 21) (i.e., Ted Ellis, a well-known local naturalist and author still living at the time) becomes the 'well-known botanist and entomologist' Edwin Elliot (E 12).

Similarly, in *The Rings of Saturn* 'Alec Garrard', the architect of the model of the Temple of Jerusalem at 'Moat Farm' (RSg 286–287) becomes 'Thomas Abrams' at 'Chestnut Tree Farm' (RSe 242) – for which reason, presumably (although possibly at the request of Garrard) the photograph with the monkey-puzzle tree (RSg 287) is absent in the English version. An unexplained photograph of a sweet chestnut tree, found in Sebald's papers after his death and prepared for reproduction, may well have been intended as a possible replacement.

Illustration 6 – Sweet chestnut tree, photographed by Sebald, c. 1998

As Sebald comments to Bigsby with regard to the final section of *Vertigo*, 'places have more of a symbolic significance than anything. I wanted to avoid the trap of [their] being identified and the text being seen as a realistic and faithful portrayal of these places, when in the texts they are in fact imaginary locations.'[8] While *The Rings of Saturn* – with parts of the Ordinance Survey maps of Suffolk reproduced as endpapers in the first German edition – on the surface appears topographically accurate, a similar principle also applies to the representations of East Anglian localities: factual accuracy is subordinated to the 'patterns of association' and 'veracity'[9] of the fictional text.

For example, one cannot alight from the train to Lowestoft at the aptly named Herringfleet (RSg 42–43/RSe 30–31); while in a later section the 'Eccles church tower' (RSe 156/RSg 188–189) shown in the (genuine) photograph – being, as the narrator points out, 'probably built on sand' (surely a clue for the attentive reader, as well as an example of Sebald's self-referential ironic humour) – did not, as the narrative suggests, descend miraculously intact from the cliffs of Dunwich, but was overcome by sand as the sea encroached upon the no less erosion-prone north-east corner of Norfolk, eventually collapsing in a storm in 1895. Those who, 'walking . . . and stalking Sebald',[10] wish to follow in Sebald's footsteps on their own literary pilgrimage around Suffolk are thus led a merry dance.[11]

This is, however, not to suggest that the places, and the events that occurred in them, are not meticulously researched; nor that the narrative and the characters portrayed are not largely authentic. 'The fictional changes', Sebald notes, 'are on the margins, [. . .] largely of a stylistic nature, adding a touch here and there'.[12] Thus in the section of *The Rings of Saturn* where the narrator visits the house of the narrator's *alter ego*, Sebald's friend and colleague Michael Hamburger (1924–2007) – one goal of the 'English pilgrimage' ('Eine englische Wallfahrt') which forms the subtitle of the original German (though not the English) text – this sense of both identification and disorientation is underpinned by an intricate web of intertextual allusion, both to Hamburger's own 'intermittent memoirs'[13] and to his poems and translations of Hölderlin;[14] just one of many examples of 'the conjuring that goes on' in the production of what Sebald calls his 'prose fiction'.[15]

East Anglia's Sebald: The 'Eeyore of the East'?

Unsurprisingly, Sebald and his writings have generated considerable local interest in academic and creative circles alike. UEA's first conference on his work, 'W.G. Sebald and the European Tradition', took place in June 2007, coinciding fortuitously with the *Waterlog* exhibition at Norwich Castle Museum and the Sainsbury Centre for Visual Arts (SCVA), 'invoking the digressive literary journeys of the writer WGS through East Anglia' (SM 657); this was followed by 'W.G. Sebald: An International and Interdisciplinary Conference' in September 2008. In Suffolk, events included Michael Hamburger reading from his translation of *After Nature* at the Aldeburgh Festival in June 2002, and the world premiere at Snape Maltings in January 2011 of Grant Gee's film *Patience* – inspired by and retracing *The Rings of Saturn* – at the weekend tribute, 'After Sebald: Place and Re-Enchantment', also featuring a tribute concert by Patti Smith.[16]

In May 2019, the seventy-fifth year of Sebald's birth was marked by a symposium hosted by the British Centre for Literary Translation (BCLT), 'Sebald. Image. Translation', and two parallel exhibitions curated by Nick Warr: at SCVA, the exhibition *Far away but from where* focussed on Sebald's photographs for *Austerlitz* alongside responses by Tacita Dean, Tess Jaray and Julie Mehretu, while at Norwich Castle, *Lines of Sight* sought to discover and document the visual sources and local East Anglian connections and materials underlying *The Rings of Saturn*.

Visual artists locally continue to find inspiration in *The Rings of Saturn*, for example the 'Cley 2018' summer exhibition on the theme 'The greater the distance the clearer the view'[17] – quoted from the section on that 'good Norwich figure'[18] Sir Thomas Browne (RSe 19/ RSg 30). In Suffolk, Orford Ness, that 'island of secrets that is its own work of art', continues to host a series of art and writing projects,[19] while undertakings like the 2017 Arca Project[20] respond to the perceived 'bleakness' of Sebald's work and of the scenes, with their grainy accompanying images, where 'to landward, there is nothing but grey water, mudflats and emptiness' (RSe 138/RSg 165–166), echoing the evocative resonance of passages such as these:

> Dunwich, with its towers, and many thousand souls, has dissolved into water, sand and thin air. If you look out from the cliff-top across the sea towards where the town must once have been, you can sense the immense power of emptiness. (RSe 159/ RSg 192)

haracteristically, though, this passage is immediately tempered by a typical moment of self-referential irony as the narrator muses that 'perhaps it was for this reason that [it] became a place of pilgrimage for melancholy poets in the Victorian age' (RSe 159/ RSg 192). In reality, neither Sebald, nor the

East Anglian landscapes described, are quite as bleak as the narrator of *The Rings of Saturn*, on his 'melancholy journey through landscapes of transience',[21] would have us believe.

Notes

1. Sebald, 'Die hölzernen Engel von East Anglia: Eine individuelle Bummeltour durch Norfolk und Suffolk'. First published in *Die Zeit*, 26 July 1974, reprinted in SM 319–324; translated with detailed annotations by Richard Sheppard in: *Journal of European Studies* 41 3–4 (2011), pp. 243–254 (243).
2. C Bigsby, *Writers in Conversation with Christopher Bigsby*, vol.2 (Norwich: EAS, 2001), pp. 140–165 (144, 142, 140).
3. Sebald, Liegt eine Galeere bei Helsingborg, in: Gedichte aus dem Nachlaß, in: *Akzente* 58:6 (2011), pp. 494–518 (508–509).
4. Qtd. in: J Mühling, The Permanent Exile of W.G. Sebald, in: *Pretext* 7 (2003), pp. 15–26 (16).
5. Cf. also RSg 268–269/RSe 225 and NN 94/AN 107.
6. Bigsby, *Writers in Conversation*, p. 157.
7. Ibid., p. 153.
8. Ibid., p. 141.
9. Ibid., pp. 155, 157.
10. P Smith, *On Walking ... and Stalking Sebald: A Guide to Going Beyond Wandering Around Looking at Stuff* (Axminster: Triarchy, 2014).
11. For example, the film *Patience (After Sebald)*, dir. Grant Gee (2011); J Noel-Tod, Dog Days, in: *Slightly Foxed* 18 (2008), pp. 43–49; also C Brown, Diary: W.G. Sebald, in: *Private Eye* 958, 4 September 1998.
12. Bigsby, *Writers in Conversation*, p. 155.
13. M Hamburger, *String of Beginnings: Intermittent Memoirs 1924–1954* (London: Carcanet, 1993).
14. For a detailed discussion of intertextuality in this and the preceding section of *The Rings of Saturn*, J Catling, W.G. Sebald: ein 'England-Deutscher'? Identität – Topographie – Intertextualität, in: I Heidelberger-Leonard, M Tabah (eds.), *W.G. Sebald: Intertextualität und Topographie* (Berlin: LIT, 2008), pp. 25–53 (27–29; 37–49).
15. Bigsby, *Writers in Conversation*, pp. 158, 156.
16. www.artevents.info/latest/2010-2011/an-artevents-weekend.
17. On the Cley 18 exhibition see https://livinggeography.blogspot.com/2018/08/cley-contemporary-art-18.html.
18. Bigsby, *Writers in Conversation*, p. 159.
19. L Cummings, Artangel: Afterness, in: *Observer*, 27 June 2021, R Macfarlane, S Donwood, *Ness* (London: Hamish Hamilton, 2019).

20. On the Arca Project: www.artlyst.com/previews/artists-writers-explore-arca-project-new-payne-shurvell-exhibition.

21. J Pieldner, A Melancholy Journey through Landscapes of Transience: W.G. Sebald ›The Rings of Saturn‹, in: *Acta Universitatis Sapientiae: Philologica* 7:1 (2015), pp. 65–72.

CHAPTER 5

Academia

Florian Radvan

Among the myths that came to characterize the profile of W.G. Sebald as a writer looms large the perception that he was a latecomer to the literary scene. His literary career stretched from his debut in 1988 with *Nach der Natur* (*After Nature*) to his final novel, *Austerlitz*, published thirteen years later. His international notoriety only emerged from around 1996 with *The Emigrants*, so his track record as an author was reduced to a mere five years in anglophone countries – until it was abruptly abbreviated by his untimely death.

Such a view of Sebald as a sort of writer *manqué* overlooks the fact that he spent all of his life as a Germanist and as a literary critic. His literary-critical output continues to be overshadowed by his fictional writings. This is especially true in an anglophone context as, so far, only a fraction of his essays and none of his monographs have been translated. However, his late works of literature are based substantially on the academic texts (see chapter 17 in this volume).

The world of academia, rather than literature, was the intellectual habitat where Sebald spent more than thirty years after he entered the field of German studies with his controversial study about Carl Sternheim in 1969. The focus of this essay is therefore on Sebald's day job as an academic and as an *Auslandsgermanist* – that is, as a Germanist working outside Germany. Furthermore, special attention is paid to his role as an academic tutor from my personal perspective.

Going Abroad: Studies in Freiburg, Fribourg and Manchester

After graduating from secondary school in Oberstdorf in July 1963 with his *Abitur* – a qualification that grants university admission – Sebald registered for the winter semester at the University of Freiburg, which is a distance of about 150 miles from his home in Sonthofen. His chosen subjects were English language and literature and German studies. However, he departed from the university after only four semesters, primarily due to his disillusionment with the course content as well as with the conservative attitude of the professors.

In retrospect, Sebald was frustrated because he felt that the past had been 'swept under the carpet'. He was looking for a fresh appraisal of German literature, such as he gleaned from the works of Walter Benjamin and Critical Theory whose critical and outside (Jewish) perspective he appreciated:

> When I commenced my studies in Freiburg in 1963, all that had only just been swept under the carpet, and since then I have often wondered how dismal and distorted our appreciation of literature might have remained had not the gradually appearing writings of Walter Benjamin and the Frankfurt School – which was, in effect, a Jewish school for the investigation of bourgeois social and intellectual history – provided an alternative perspective. (PC 8/LH 12)

The upsurge of political awareness in the second half of the 1960s also swept Sebald along with it. However, he kept away from the street skirmishes in Germany and did not become a political campaigner. Instead, he diverted any rebellious tendencies to the world of academia and began 'a decades-long partisan war with the techniques of literary-criticism to remain at logger-heads with the established academics of German studies whom he considered as a politically suspect clique in general'.[1]

Sebald's transfer in 1965 to the Université de Fribourg in French-speaking Switzerland also marked his turning away from the domain of the German university system and confirmed his situation as an *Auslandsgermanist*. After several months in Switzerland he submitted a polemical dissertation about the playwright Carl Sternheim, for which he was awarded the degree of *licence ès lettres*. The next stage of his academic and personal emigration followed at the University of Manchester where he began his job as a language assistant (*Lektor*) in 1966. Here, Sebald expanded his Fribourg thesis to an MA dissertation. This was further revised and published three years later as his first book. Its controversial theories consciously sought to antagonize and led to a wide-ranging debate in the German-language context that identified Sebald as an academic *enfant terrible*.

This dissident attitude was sustained by Sebald, aged thirty, as an early career researcher who published a series of academic reviews in the University of East Anglia's (UEA) *Journal of European Studies*: 'Consisting mainly of scathing critiques, the PhD candidate criticised books by leading German scholars for all sorts of inexcusable mistakes.'[2] His rebellious behaviour thus obstructed him from moving back into the fold of German studies in Germany and other German-language countries. However, at the same time he regarded his protest stance as important as his secure career as an academic in England made him independent from the job market in Germany.

An appraisal of Sebald's career as a student already indicates how far he was ready to explore beyond traditionally mainstream ideas and theories. Early on he indicated dissatisfaction with the approach of German studies as it was currently being taught, due to the conservatism both of its methods and of the discipline's academic figureheads. He was a vocal critic. One of Sebald's radical was to relocate abroad – an unusual step back then – although the reasons for this were primarily pragmatic and economic. In Switzerland at first, and in England later on, he could complete his studies in a shorter time and finish an academic degree more quickly. Besides, people abroad showed greater tolerance for his unorthodox academic methods.

After the compulsory exile of many Jewish scholars who fled to the United Kingdom, Sebald thus was one of the pioneers among Germanists of the next generation who chose voluntary emigration in search of a new academic home there. Even in the early 1970s this step amounted to self-imposed exile because – the corporatist Germanists working in Germany had a tendency to view their academic colleagues who taught abroad as outsiders and even, perhaps, as intellectually inferior.

Arriving Home: University of East Anglia, Norwich

The University of East Anglia (UEA) was founded in 1963. Its modernist architecture, influenced by the British brutalist contemporary style, reflected its progressive academic philosophy. The newly established schools incorporated several interdisciplinary fields of study. In 1970, Sebald accepted a job at the UEA as Assistant Lecturer in the German Department, which was part of the School of Modern Languages and European History. It was here that he submitted his PhD thesis, *Revival of Myth: A Study of Döblin's Novels*, for which he was awarded his doctoral qualification in 1973. The UEA was to remain Sebald's academic home for over three decades until his death in 2001.

Following his promotion to Senior Lecturer in October 1985, a full fifteen years after he had joined the institution as Lecturer, he then progressed quickly to Reader in October 1987 and was awarded a chair in European Literature in 1988. It seems likely that an academic career in the British higher education system had not always been his goal, as his attempt to break away in 1976 demonstrates: he spent several months at the Goethe-Institut in Munich where he joined an advanced training course as a German teacher. However, when it transpired that he would probably be posted to developing countries he decided to return to Norwich.

After a promising early career period, Sebald's academic life in England was gradually accompanied by increasing frustration as circumstances changed. Under the neo-liberal policy for higher education from the late 1970s onwards there was a growing pressure for rationalization that eventually culminated in the introduction of university tuition fees in 1998 under the Labour government of Tony Blair. On a local level, Sebald had to cope with a steep rise in the volume of administrative work as well as the strategic decisions laid out by the university administration, which he mostly regarded as an interference.

Once more, he sought to secure a potential escape route. In 1986, he undertook his second doctorate (*Habilitation*) at the University of Hamburg; this entitled him to apply for professorships in Germany and keep a foot in the door in German academia. He hoped that this would give him a back-up option to withdraw from the English university system in case the conditions deteriorated further.[3]

However, the way out of his academic disillusionment turned out to be not a return to his native country but – at the latest from early to mid-1980s – a greater concentration on his literary writing. It was in his "potting shed" that he found the freedom and satisfaction that his academic profession offered him less and less. It is true that in 1993 he still declared: 'Yes, I like my profession. I like the contact with people, with the students, and it is an honest way to make a living' (G 103–104). However, by the late 1990s, at the latest, Sebald was obviously frustrated with the day-to-day business of his profession: he complained about the effort involved in teaching due to the increasingly poor standards of school education and the lack of intellectual curiosity among the students.[4]

The departmental faculties at UEA underwent a reorganization in 1999. This culminated in the winding up, not only of the German Sector, but of the whole School of Modern Languages and European Studies (EUR). Along with colleagues from other departments of language and literature, Sebald was integrated into the School of English and American Studies (EAS). From the year 2000, Sebald was obliged to teach courses for the Creative Writing programme that was set up by academics and writers such as Malcolm Bradbury and Angus Wilson.

Until his international success with *The Emigrants* in 1996, Sebald had still been secretive about his literary writing; he maintained a level of discretion about this activity to the point of a denial of his personal achievements. However, there was no hiding after *The Rings of Saturn* and *Vertigo* were published in English to wide acclaim. Sebald held the opinion that one cannot actually teach the art of writing, so initially he had misgivings. However, eventually he thoroughly enjoyed teaching the subject.

It was soon obvious to the students in his last seminar – (that ended three days before Sebald's death) – that he did not hold himself and his successful books up as a standard: 'When discussing students' work he was anecdotal and associative, more storyteller than technician. He had weary eyes that made it tempting to identify him with the melancholy narrators of his books, but had also had a gentle amiability and wry sense of humour. We were in his thrall.'[5]

One legacy of his work on the Creative Writing programme is the numerous aphorisms that Sebald recited in the seminars and that were compiled posthumously by the students. They may be read as an expression of his understanding of literature as well as of his idiosyncratic approach to writing. 'Oddities are interesting', ran one of the pieces of advice he gave; another said: 'Write about obscure things but don't write obscurely.'[6] Sebald's fascination for the minor figures of great history was reflected in this maxim: 'It's hard to write something original about Napoleon, but one of his minor aides is another matter.'[7] However, paradigmatic for Sebald's self-understanding as an academic, author and creative writing teacher is this recommendation: 'Don't listen to anyone. Not us, either. It's fatal.'[8]

Do Different: Sebald in the Classroom

'Do Different', the University of East Anglia's motto, can be applied to Sebald's organization of seminars or his teaching philosophy. At the beginning of his career, he was actively involved in planning new study and teaching programmes (that at the relatively new university were primarily delivered in the form of seminars, rather than tutorials or lectures). A close colleague remembered him as: 'Fizzing with ideas and radiating considerable energy at all turns, he contributed easily and without inhibition to discussions of the Germans and European literature programmes and, to a lesser extent, to the German Honours Language programme' (SM 109).

On the basis of the memories submitted by many UEA students after Sebald's death, often elaborated with anecdotal incidents (SM 109–142), it is possible to put together a profile – an insight into how Sebald came across as a teacher and also some sense of his educational approach. For example, frequent comments were made about Sebald's reserved manner in seminar discussions and, accompanying this, his resistance towards adopting a dominant or instructive teaching role: 'He was so quiet and unassuming that it was easy to forget he was there' (SM 113).

This went along with a conversational culture that is reminiscent of the Socratic method: 'He was a very calm and relaxed teacher, of course, of great intellect – a teacher who extracted great responses from his students and who knew how to stimulate them without putting direct pressure on them' (SM 112). An open exchange of opinions and ideas evolved in the seminars, at times based on just a few pointers from Sebald. A strongly discursive approach had an emancipatory effect on his students.

I personally experienced this motivational approach which supported the individual abilities of every student. From autumn 1996 to early 2001, I was a PhD student working on a thesis about the actuality of politically critical theatre post-1945, with Sebald as my supervisor. I believe that his educational approach only worked because he sought a special intellectual curiosity from the students. This went hand in hand with his encouragement of an independent analysis of texts and the formulation of positions going beyond just regurgitating the secondary literature.

Many students perceived this autonomy in the formation of opinions, which he demanded and promoted, as motivating or almost liberating: 'To be given the confidence to approach these things!', 'Max created within us a hunger to think and look and look again.' Or: 'He truly was the first person in my life who listened and then looked at the landscape of what I had to say' (SM 114). The students' reading impressions were at the heart of things and the springboard to the encouragement of an individual ability to engage in discourse and to be self-confident about forming a personal judgment.

Nonetheless, it must be noted that Sebald always knew how to lead diverse and even uninformed opinions back to the texts under discussion, as well as to their inner core and their thematic focus. He particularly excelled at this in the case of texts that were freely interpretable. A case in point is Kafka's prose fragment *Der Jäger Gracchus* (*The Hunter Gracchus*). The central motif is a person who is perpetually in a state of transition between life and death. The key point for Sebald during the seminar discussion of this text, which features of course prominently in his prose book *Schwindel. Gefühle.* (*Vertigo*), was to heighten one's sensitivity for Kafka's play with the mysterious, the irresolvable, the enigmatic and not, for instance, any (supposed) resolution of the puzzle.

Sebald put into practice in his courses the interdisciplinary approach that is a hallmark of UEA. It constituted the design and implementation of his seminars: 'Max wove in so many other aspects to expand the study of literary texts – politics, philosophy, new ideas in theology or psychology' (SM 113). Similarly: 'Max made literature accessible and fascinating, drawing parallels with art, film, psychology etc' (SM 113). All the while his digressions often incorporated personal reminiscences, including anecdotes about travel experiences or, later, biting notes about the literature business: 'I loved the way classes were interspersed with little anecdotes or the way that he would even lapse into French in order to express himself better in certain contexts' (SM 110).

Early in his time at UEA, Sebald set out the thematic focus of his seminars on German literature of the nineteenth and twentieth century. Later on, courses were added on comparative subjects such as 'European Autobiographical Writing', in which texts by Günter Grass (1927–2015) and Elias Canetti (1905–1994) featured on the reading list as well as works by Primo Levi (1919–1987). Perhaps it was only surprising for those who, like me, came to Norwich from Germany that his seminars dealt with literary texts, and occasionally also essays, yet virtually no literary theory (see chapter 22 in this volume).

As for his use of teaching media, he relied on formats like television or slide shows only for selective instruction in class. A straightforward method which might have appeared boring and uninspired from another tutor, I experienced with Sebald as natural or – to adopt the educational jargon – as 'authentic'. It was the special appeal of his teaching and, in any case, was in keeping with his otherwise hostile attitude towards technology.

For instance, he refused to install a computer in his office. Up to his death, he only communicated with students in person, sometimes by telephone or else by putting written notes into student pigeonholes. Sebald's essay corrections were always in pencil and his notes were only short, summary appraisals. He indicated his approval with a few ticks in the margin: 'Max's marking was firm but fair, and his comments minimal, which meant they were valued all the more. [...] If he judged it an "intelligent, well-constructed essay" you were simply overwhelmed' (SM 118).

Among the pieces of advice given by Sebald was the recommendation to restrict the citation of secondary literature and only to refer to it where it was relevant for one's personal line of argument. His feedback about one of my essays on Kafka's short story *Ein Bericht für eine Akademie* (*A Report to an Academy*) is also to be understood in this context:

> An extremely well-researched, very comprehensive essay. You do have a tendency though (in this piece at any rate) to restrict yourself to reporting the work of other scholars & to refrain from direct engagement with the text. Perhaps you should have tried to identify (against & across existing interpretations) the story's case which is (as one can say with hindsight) a lament about the foundering of the hopes which four or so generations had invested in the idea & practice of 'integration'. In other words, I would urge to pursue a bolder line of argument.

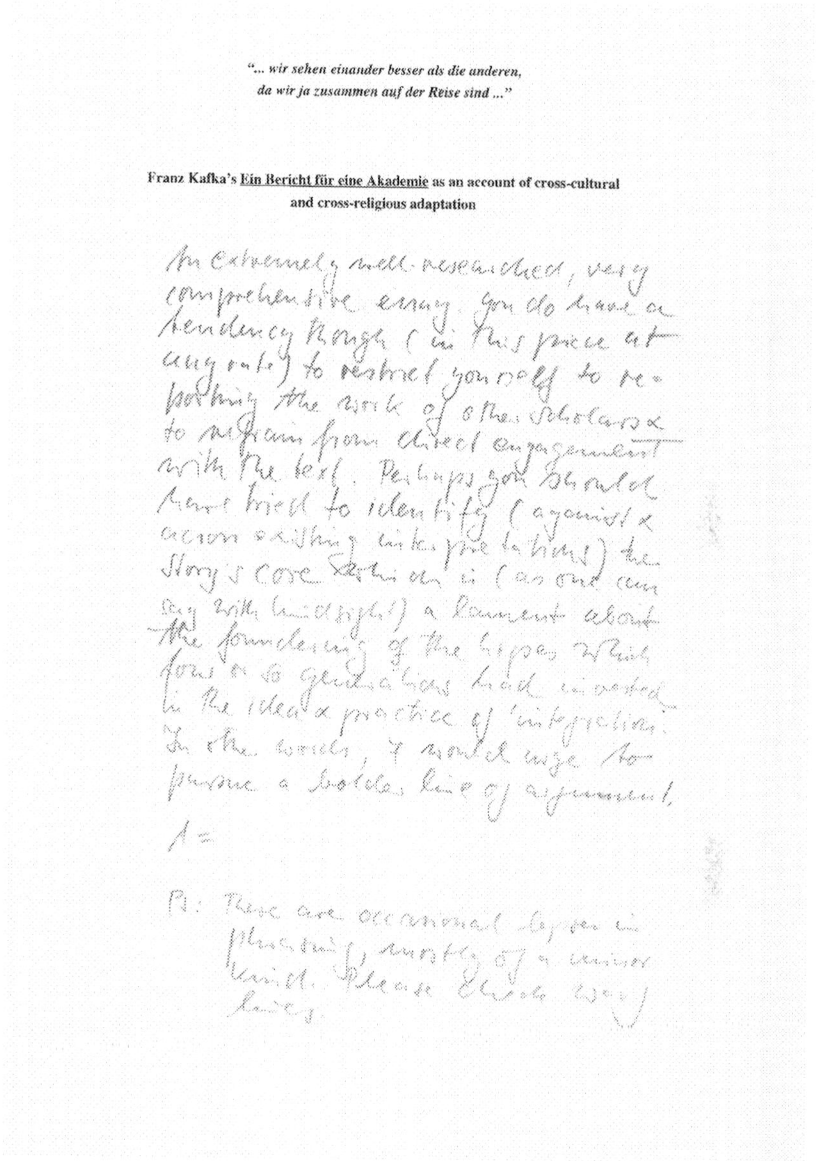

"... *wir sehen einander besser als die anderen,*
da wir ja zusammen auf der Reise sind ..."

Franz Kafka's Ein Bericht für eine Akademie as an account of cross-cultural
and cross-religious adaptation

[Handwritten note reproduced as an image.]

Illustration 7 – Sebald's feedback to Radvan

Meeting Sebald

Our supervisory meetings were often characterized by anecdotes and digressions. They involved an experience that Sebald's other PhD students – Ralf Jeutter[9] and Uwe Schütte[10] – also confirmed. Schütte recalled his tutorials as follows:

> Sebald would sit patiently, listening to me, normally with a wry smile [. . .]. Then he would embark on an impromptu lecture that ignored all other critics' opinions. Rather, he would come up with an overall assessment of a writer that hugely differed from the generally approved opinion. Or he would identify a certain flaw or easily overlooked detail in a book and base his disregard or approval of the text on this.[11]

My conversations with Sebald always started with only a brief summary of how my research was progressing. It's fair to say that its advancement was based on a mutual understanding and trusting that the project would turn out alright. Instead, anecdotes about the literary business in England and Germany were discussed at our meetings as well as personal travel reflections that were often interspersed with discourses on literature.

Therefore, and not just with hindsight, I can confirm that interactions with Sebald always became especially enthralling when the conversation moved to topics outside the limitations of one's own project. Since the mid-1990s such other topics often involved the international literary scene where he played an increasingly influential role as a personality and as a writer.

In reflecting on the memory of Sebald as a university professor, it is striking how many students had such a profound emotional attachment to him. Of course, posthumously composed snippets of reminiscences about departed academic teachers are perhaps predisposed to forms of idealizing and stylizing. By the same token, I think that it is to be fair to Sebald to describe him as an exceptional and particularly charismatic academic teacher. Yet his charisma came from being the kind of person who did not make a grand appearance and who was a master of the sublime punchline, of empathy and of understatement.

Notes

1. U Schütte, Wissenschaftliche Biographie, in: M Niehaus, C Öhlschläger (eds.), *W.G. Sebald-Handbuch* (Stuttgart: Metzler, 2017), pp. 2–5 (2).
2. U Schütte, Out of the Shadows, in: *Times Higher Education*, 22 September 2011, pp. 44–47 (46).

3. U Schütte, *Annäherungen: Sieben Essays zu W.G. Sebald* (Cologne: Böhlau), 2019), pp. 126–128.
4. E Battersby, Man from the Margins [Interview], in: *Irish Times*, 27 November 1999.
5. D Lambert, R McGill, The Collected 'Maxims', in: *Five Dials* 5 (2014), pp. 8–9 (8).
6. Ibid.
7. Ibid.
8. Ibid., p. 5.
9. R Jeutter, Some Memories and Reflections: W.G. 'Max' Sebald, Man and Writer, in: U Schütte (ed.), *Über W.G. Sebald: Beiträge zu einem anderen Bild des Autors* (Berlin/Boston: De Gruyter, 2017), pp. 303–308.
10. Schütte [interview], in: *T Honickel, Curriculum Vitae: Die W.G. Sebald Interviews*, ed. by U Schütte, K Wolfinger (Würzburg: Königshausen & Neumann, 2021) pp. 147–155 (147–151).
11. U Schütte, Teaching by Example, in: *Five Dials* 5 (2014), pp. 42–43 (42).

CHAPTER 6

The British Centre for Literary Translation

Duncan Large

W.G. Sebald did not spend much time translating the work of others, but he was nonetheless greatly interested in the art of literary translation.[1] He had close personal friendships with a number of translators – foremost among them Michael Hamburger, whom he nominated for an honorary doctorate at the University of East Anglia (SM 346–348) – and worked closely with translators of his own work, especially his English translators Michael Hulse and Anthea Bell.[2] Ulrich von Bülow describes how 'he worked over his translators' manuscripts so extensively [...] as to be considered a co-translator at the very least' (SM 255). The most lasting testament to Sebald's 'militant dedication to the art and practice of literary translation'[3] – and one of the most significant aspects of his legacy *tout court* – is the British Centre for Literary Translation (BCLT), which he founded at UEA in 1989.

Founding and Funding the BCLT

By the late 1980s Sebald was in his mid-forties, and his career as a university academic was reaching its high point. In recognition of his prolific publishing of academic articles throughout the 1970s and 1980s he was promoted in quick succession to Senior Lecturer in October 1985, Reader in October 1987 and finally, in October 1988, to Professor of European Literature (SM 632–635).

The security of establishing his academic position allowed him to devote his energies in two new directions. Firstly, he could turn his attention more to developing his own writing: a few weeks before his promotion to professor came into effect, his first book-length literary work was published in late summer 1988, the long poem *Nach der Natur* (*After Nature*), and this was followed eighteen months later by his second, the prose fiction *Schwindel. Gefühle.* (*Vertigo*) in March 1990. The other new direction was to follow through on a plan he had been formulating already for a number of years, to establish a translation centre at UEA.

Sebald founded BCLT in the spring of 1989 with a grant from the Arts Council of Great Britain. BCLT was unlike anything that existed in the UK at the time, and from the beginning its outlook was thoroughly international: it was to be 'British' not in the sense of a national as opposed to a regional centre, but rather as a UK equivalent of existing European models. This was acknowledged by the Arts Council in its annual report for 1989: 'We were also able to support the establishment of a British Centre for Literary Translation, based on models which have been success-fully launched in France and West Germany.'[4] (The references here are, respectively, to the Collège International des Traducteurs Littéraires, founded in 1987 at Arles in southern France, and the Europäisches Übersetzer-Kollegium Nordrhein-Westfalen (European College of Translators) in Straelen, West Germany, which was founded in 1978 by Elmar Tophoven and Klaus Birkenhauer as the first literary translators' college worldwide.)

Sebald visited the latter in April 1988 (SM 634), and Birkenhauer paid a return visit to UEA at the end of May 1989 to effectively baptize Straelen's new British equivalent.[5] It took a little while for BCLT's branding to take hold: earlier in May, Sebald's colleagues Christopher Smith and Holger Klein had organized 'The Second Bite: A Conference on Translations and on Re-Translations' which was described as 'under the aegis of the BCLA [British Comparative Literature Association] and the University of East Anglia Centre for Literary Translation',[6] but by July 1989 Sebald was advertising residential bursaries for translators in the *Times Literary Supplement* (*TLS*) on behalf of 'The British Centre for Literary Translation, newly established at the University of East Anglia, Norwich, with the support of the Arts Council of Great Britain'.[7]

The *TLS* advertisement, one of the first published appearances of the BCLT name, is notable in a number of respects. First, it gives a sense of the remit of the fledgling Centre and of Sebald's understanding of the field of 'literary translation'. The advert continued: 'The British Centre for Literary Translation [...] is offering bursaries for translators engaged in projects of a literary or scholarly nature who wish to avail themselves of the University's excellent library and other resources.' It demonstrates, in other words (and not surprisingly, given the hybrid nature of his own literary writing), that Sebald's understanding of 'literary translation' exceeded the confines of a narrow definition of *belles-lettres* and included the full range of humanistic endeavour.

Second, the reference to 'projects of a [...] scholarly nature' was at the same time also a recognition that BCLT was from the outset a branch of the University of East Anglia, and its distinctive appeal would remain the interface between the literary translation profession and academia. In the case of UEA, moreover, 'academia' offered its own distinctive blend combining literary scholarship, the teaching of creative writing (UEA is home to the UK's longest-standing creative writing programme, founded by Malcolm Bradbury in 1970) and, subsequently, the training of literary translators (an MA in Literary Translation was set up in October 1993 by Sebald's colleague Jean Boase-Beier).

What the BCLT's advertisement for residential translator bursaries in 1989 also demonstrates, is that in line with his European models Sebald's first priority with BCLT would be bringing visiting translators to UEA and providing a conducive atmosphere to promote high-quality literary translation work. As literary editor Bill Swainson put it: 'Initially, BCLT offered 4-week bursaries for translators translating from any European language into any other European language, and provided accommodation, the use of a library and, perhaps most important of all, a community of fellow translators and academics.'[8]

The first translator in residence was Michael Wynne-Ellis, who came from Helsinki to spend the first half of August 1989 in Norwich, translating nineteenth-century Finnish dramatist Aleksis Kivi's comedy *Nummisuutarit* (*The Village Cobblers*). There were three other visiting translators in 1989, but the scheme really took off in 1990 with at least eighteen visitors. Resident translators were given accommodation on campus and looked after by the German Sector Secretary, Beryl Ranwell.[9]

Sebald served as Director of BCLT for five years, with Ranwell as BCLT Secretary. In the early years Sebald threw himself into fundraising. Uwe Schütte comments:

> Setting up the centre involved numerous trips to London to obtain funding for bursaries and staff, not to mention endless meetings with university officials who needed to be convinced of the inherent value of such a decidedly unprofitable enterprise. After the centre was successfully established, Sebald's role was to ensure its financial stability – something that would prove to be a constant struggle and meant endless fishing for external funding.[10]

Sebald's efforts in this regard certainly bore fruit. Initial funding from the Arts Council in 1989 was relatively modest, although the £3,115 awarded was still the highest of the twenty-three grants made from its recently established fund for translations.[11] In successive years, Arts Council funding increased to £14,000 (1990–1991), £49,470 (1991–1992) and £50,000 (1992–1993), and from 1993–1994 the Arts Council agreed to support BCLT on an annual basis, initially at £50,000.[12] Furthermore, already by 1991 Sebald had secured funding for BCLT not just from the Arts Council but also the British Council, European Commission and Council of Europe among other sources.[13]

Sebald's colleague Christopher Smith recalled: 'Despite some frustrations, [he] clearly enjoyed the business of setting up the BCLT from 1989 onwards, dealing directly with UEA's Vice-Chancellor [Derek Burke] and the Arts Council, and then maintaining the Centre as something of a private fief.'[14] Sebald also gathered a small team round him as the operation of the Centre intensified and diversified. His former colleague Richard Sheppard lists the 'supporting cast' of colleagues who worked with Sebald at the BCLT in the early years, in addition to Ranwell: 'George Hyde is Deputy Director and Adam Czerniawski first Translator in Residence; Czerniawski later becomes Associate Director; Anthony Vivis becomes Translator in Residence (1992–1993)' (SM 635). The work of the Centre was also overseen by an Advisory Panel.

BCLT's Aims and Activities under Sebald's Leadership

Sebald's broad goals in setting up BCLT are summarized by Schütte: 'The BCLT was an idealistic enterprise, an attempt to accord more recognition to the undervalued profession of literary translation as well as a contribution to cultural exchange between an often isolationist Britain and the rest of the world.'[15] In its early years the Centre hosted dozens of visiting translators working on their own projects, but BCLT also initiated a number of its own activities, as detailed in this description from 1991:

> Among the Centre's main aims are the provision of bursaries for literary translators both from the UK and from abroad; organizing conferences and seminars on aspects of translation; creating a resource centre for literary translators; collecting data relevant to the business of translation.[16]

In the service of the latter two goals Sebald recruited a BCLT Research Secretary, Jeanne Sheriff, who worked one day per week for three years from July 1991. Sheriff wrote to a range of publishers asking for a) information on their translators for a database of translators in the UK; b) information on their fiction translations for a bibliography of translations published in the UK and the USA since 1970; c) copies of all translations already published and published in future for a 'Library of Translations'. Over three decades the 'Library of Translations' became the BCLT Library which currently runs to several thousand volumes; the *Directory of Literary Translators* was the most significant of BCLT's early projects and an important contribution to raising the profile of translators in the UK.

Not all these plans came to fruition, of course. In September 1989 Geoffrey Kingscott reported: 'The British Centre for Literary Translation which has recently been founded at the University of East Anglia is considering undertaking research on lexicographic work for translators, and the idea of a multilingual thesaurus has already been mooted as a possible project.'[17] Under Sebald's (technophobic) management BCLT was never going to emerge as a centre for research into translation and the computer, although Duncan Large's research has moved BCLT in this direction more recently.[18]

Significant BCLT events in the early years included a symposium on 'Shakespeare in German / Shakespeare auf Deutsch' organized by Holger Klein in December 1990, a substantial series of seminars on 'Writing in the Shadow of the Shoah' spanning two years 1990–1992 (SM 187–188), and in December 1992 the European Writers' Forum. Swainson describes the latter as 'perhaps the highpoint of BCLT's public-facing work in its early years': 'The writers, who read their work and spoke in the discussions that December weekend, were Marie Cardinal, Cees Nooteboom, Lars Gustafsson, Jaan Kaplinski, Gianni Celati, Julian Ríos, Hans Magnus Enzensberger, Ryszard Kapuściński and Max Sebald himself.'[19] Swainson omits to mention that the European Writers' Forum also featured a host of leading translators, including Peter Bush (eventually one of Sebald's successors as BCLT Director), Czerniawski, Hamburger, Suzanne Jill Levine, Antonia Lloyd-Jones and Christopher Middleton (SM 190).

All this activity and grant capture did not go unappreciated within the university. Confirming internal funding for the translator database project in April 1992, Sebald's Dean of School commented: 'The British Centre for Literary Translation is perhaps the most successful applied humanities venture the university has known.'[20] Sebald was able to capitalize on the goodwill that he had accrued within the university the following year, when his concern for the broader welfare of translators came to the fore. In 1993 he heard of the plight of Croatian translator and academic Mario Suško, a former BCLT translation bursary holder who was caught up in the siege of Sarajevo. Sebald successfully arranged internal funding for Suško to return to UEA with his family on a year-long visiting fellowship with free accommodation, and he launched a public appeal for additional funds which led to *The Sunday Times* paying for Suško's transport to the UK.

By 1994 Sebald's reputation as a writer had grown so substantial (especially after the publication of *Die Ausgewanderten* (*The Emigrants*) in September 1992) that he needed to step down as BCLT Director. The last major initiative Sebald undertook on behalf of BCLT before stepping down was to inaugurate an annual public lecture series, known initially as the St Jerome Lecture. The first of these was given by George Steiner, doyen of British translation studies, on 26 April 1994 at UEA's Sainsbury Centre for the Visual Arts.[21]

Sebald's Legacy at BCLT

Sebald handed over the reins of the day-to-day running of BCLT on the appointment of a new Director (Terry Hale) and Administrator (Christine Wilson), who both started work in April 1994. Sebald left BCLT in good health, both financially (it was still offering twenty-five translator bursaries per year) and culturally. Even after stepping down as Director, he continued as a member of the BCLT Advisory Board, and his association with the Centre continued until his death.

In March 1995, Sebald took part in a meeting at the Goethe-Institut in London, organized by BCLT, to discuss recognition of literary translation as a research activity by the forthcoming Research Assessment Exercise in UK higher education (SM 642). In the late 1990s he tried in vain to persuade the university to acquire for BCLT a dedicated home in the shape of Earlham Lodge, a Grade II listed building near the student village.[22] Sebald attended the inaugural BCLT Summer School in 2000, then shortly before his death, in late September 2001, he gave the St Jerome Lecture in London.[23]

Sebald's successor as BCLT Director, Terry Hale, would go on to inaugurate in his own ways: he liaised with the Charles Wallace India Trust (CWIT) to establish an annual visiting translator fellowship in 1996, which recently celebrated a quarter century of bringing Indian translators to Norwich. Hale also placed an emphasis on the acquisition of translator archives, which now form the core of the Literary Translation collection in the British Archive for Contemporary Writing, based at the UEA Library. Hale was succeeded in January 1998 by Peter Bush, who introduced the annual Summer School in 2000 and brought *In Other Words*, the journal of the Translators Association, to BCLT. Bush was succeeded in March 2004 by Amanda Hopkinson, Hopkinson in January 2010 by

Valerie Henitiuk, then in July 2014 the current head of BCLT, Duncan Large, took over.

Each of Sebald's successors has taken BCLT in new directions, but a surprising amount of the original impetus and vision behind Sebald's BCLT remains. BCLT has continued to be funded by Arts Council England, now (since 2015) via a collaboration agreement with the National Centre for Writing (also in Norwich), which partners with BCLT on a wide variety of initiatives such as the annual Summer School. Sebald's initial focus on hosting visiting translators is now less pronounced, as BCLT's primary role is now as a research centre, but the Centre continues to host visiting Indian translators under the CWIT scheme and, since 2021, has funded two further three-month translation residencies annually. BCLT was a founder member of RECIT, the European Network of International Literary Translation Centres set up in 2000, and it continues to play a leading role in the organization with current BCLT Manager Anna Goode serving as its Secretary since 2017. The PhD in Literary Translation which Sebald tried unsuccessfully to introduce was later approved and now forms part of UEA's suite of 'creative-critical' PhDs.[24]

The St Jerome Lecture was renamed the Sebald Lecture in 2003 to commemorate BCLT's illustrious founder, and it continues to be given annually by a prominent cultural figure. Over the years, these have included Margaret Atwood, Hans Magnus Enzensberger, Carlos Fuentes, Seamus Heaney, Arundhati Roy and Susan Sontag. Most have at least referred to Sebald's own work during their lecture, and in one notable case the 2009–2010 Sebald Lecture was entirely devoted to its namesake.[25] A volume of Sebald Lectures, edited by former BCLT National Programme Director Daniel Hahn, is forthcoming in the series Routledge Studies in Literary Translation which is co-edited by Duncan Large.

For someone who was not himself a very prolific translator, Sebald showed a true dedication to promoting literary translation through BCLT. He was not a natural administrator or founder of institutions, but BCLT proved the great exception to this rule. BCLT has outlived him by over two decades (and counting) and represents an important legacy by means of which he continues to help translators, to enrich the intellectual life of UEA, and to represent a beacon of internationalism in the barren post-Brexit cultural landscape of the UK.

Notes

1. J Catling et al., Among Translators: W.G. Sebald and Translation, in: *In Other Words* 38 (2011), pp. 111–120.
2. M Hulse, Englishing Max (SM 95–208) and A Bell, Translating W.G. Sebald: With and Without the Author (SM 209–215).
3. S Rahmani, Words, Not Bombs: W.G. Sebald and the Global Valences of the Critical, in: *Boundary 2* 47:3 (2020), pp. 1–20 (16).
4. *Arts Council: 44th Annual Report and Accounts, 1988–89* (London: Arts Council, 1989), p. 17.
5. Handwritten note in BCLT archive, UEA.
6. Printed flyer in BCLT archive.
7. *The Times Literary Supplement* 4504 (1989), p. 836.
8. B Swainson, Excitement and Possibility, in: D Large et al. (eds.), *My BCLT: Celebrating 30 Years of the British Centre for Literary Translation* (Norwich: BCLT, 2019), pp. 8–10 (8).
9. On Ranwell's role, cf. C Angier, *Speak, Silence: In Search of W.G. Sebald* (London: Bloomsbury, 2021), p. 336.
10. U Schütte, *W.G. Sebald* (Liverpool: Liverpool University Press, 2018), pp. 26–27.
11. *Arts Council: 45th Annual Report and Accounts*, 1989–90 (London: Arts Council, 1990), p. 68.
12. Cf. Arts Council annual reports 46 (1990–1991), p. 64; 47 (1991–1992), p. 64; 48 (1992–1993), p. 67; 49 (1993–1994), pp. 18, 69.
13. Advertisement for appointment of an Administrator, 1991 (BCLT archive).
14. C Smith, W.G. 'Max' Sebald as I Knew Him: A Memoir, in: *Journal of European Studies* 41:3–4 (2011), pp. 255–265 (262).
15. Schütte, *Sebald*, p. 26.
16. Letter to publishers, BCLT archive.
17. G Kingscott, *Applications of Machine Translation: Study for the Commission of the European Communities* (Nottingham: Praetorius, 1989), p. 47.
18. D Large, Could Google Translate Shakespeare?, in: *In Other Words* 52 (2018/19), pp. 79–94.
19. Swainson, Excitement and Possibility, p. 8.
20. Funding application, BCLT archive.
21. Subsequently published as G Steiner, An Exact Art, in: *No Passion Spent: Essays, 1978–1996* (London: Faber & Faber, 1996), pp. 267–289.
22. C Wilson, Working with Max at BCLT, in: Catling et al. (eds.), *Among Translators*, p. 115.
23. St. Jerome Lecture 2001: W.G. Sebald in Conversation with Maya Jaggi and Anthea Bell, in: *In Other Words* 21 (2003), pp. 5–18.
24. Schütte, *Sebald*, p. 27.
25. W Self, Absent Jews and Invisible Executioners: W.G. Sebald and the Holocaust, in: *In Other Words* 35 (2010), pp. 60–76.

CHAPTER 7

Between Germany and Britain

Rüdiger Görner

Being in-between is a precarious comfort zone, as illustrated by the life and work of W.G. Sebald. Almost any comment on Sebald, whether in journalistic, essayistic or academic form, testifies to this.[1] Sebald's work is an ideal example assemblage of cultural transfers communicated in accomplished translations of his works by Michael Hulse, Anthea Bell,[2] Michael Hamburger and Jo Catling, and confirmed by his "arrival" in the works of numerous anglophone writers ranging from Susan Sontag to Will Self, Geoff Dyer, Rachel Cusk and Ben Lerner.

Inhabiting the no man's land of the in-between can make us accept mental homelessness as our first domicile. For some, acquiring a "settled status" has something of an officially certified illusion. At the same time, as an in-between, one can become a waverer between cultures, but also a weaver who works in different threads from divergent traditions and values and creates a new fabric with distinctive patterns – as Sebald did in his best prose.

Sebald only wrote the occasional academic article and poem in English, perhaps most poignantly the poem 'I remember'. Not surprisingly, it concerns a transfer, in this case a voyage from Harwich to Hoek van Holland, during which the speaker encounters a truck driver from Wolverhampton who – a transfer within a transfer – is transporting old lorries to post-Soviet Russia. The poem ends with the German Sebald wishing the driver 'the best of British' (LWe 167).[3]

Über das Land und das Wasser (*Across the Land and the Water*), the title Sebald chose for a collection of poetry that was only published after his death, could not have been more appropriate, creating as it does an impression of perpetual transitoriness. That said, although many aspects of British and German culture, mentality and heritage seem deceptively similar, their common ground often turns out to be treacherous.

Leaving one's country of origin voluntarily to experience "difference" may imply a desire for a substitute identity, and such a desire for self-transformation may even be the reason for leaving one's own culture in the first place, particularly if it is burdened by a traumatic history. However, such a personal decision is an intellectual luxury compared to that of the refugee forced to flee political turmoil, economic hardship or social deprivation. Both the voluntary and involuntary emigrant, though, share a fundamental similarity: they become uprooted.

In addition, both types of emigrants must sooner or later realize that they still carry with them what they thought they had left behind. Even the physical and mental point of departure tends to remain with us; it continues to be part of the baggage we carry through our lives. Some leave home perhaps in the subconscious hope of receiving a warm welcome one day as the returning prodigal son. Others venture into the wide world with "great expectations". However, a most unexpected sentiment may catch up with them at a much later stage: nostalgia in the shape of deceiving memories and illusions about a culture one thought one had left behind, which are in turn matched by the illusions one had entertained about the country of one's choice, in socio-speak "the target culture". By the same token, we need to ask how much of this "target culture" can be appropriated and by what means?

On the Move

Sebald was not prone to, or plagued by, nostalgia, illusions or a true desire to return to German-speaking lands, even though the deeply sobering, if not disturbing, experience of (post-)Thatcherite Britain, with its devastating effect on the country's academic culture, left him profoundly unsettled in England as well. For Sebald and others in his situation, it was a matter of assessing scars and traumata, living conditions, present demands and the "remembrance of things past" in relation to English and German cultures. Fundamentally, any writer must consider where they can work most effectively. Sebald chose the status of a writer in the in-between, simulating the experience of an exile who would continue to write mostly in his mother tongue.

It is a truism that one learns most about one's own language in a foreign language culture. This will naturally depend on when in one's life such an exposure takes place. It is different for those who had to leave their cultural contexts in early childhood, that is before language had become an object of reflective consciousness.

In Sebald we encounter the wanderer between cultures and spheres of consciousness of German, English and French denomination. Writers who walk so deliberately as Sebald did are pathfinders who are constantly *unterwegs* or *en route* since that is a prerequisite for their work. Even if he sometimes took wrong turns, as he did on Dunwich Heath in the chapter on the emigré poet Michael Hamburger in *Die Ringe des Saturn* (*The Rings of Saturn*), it is not surprising that Sebald excelled in a style and compositional method suitable to his 'English Pilgrimage'.

Sebald's actual "pilgrimage" through Norfolk and Suffolk took the form of a series of walks between August 1992 and spring 1993,[4] but the narrative relates a single, long walk through a historically charged physical landscape that is turned into literature step by step. It brings together seemingly unrelated phenomena, such as the tomb of Saint Sebaldus and the Berlin childhood of Michael Hamburger, who now lives in Middleton in Suffolk. The narrator's elective affinity with Hamburger is a symbol for the affinity Sebald felt, not only with Hamburger, but also with all emigrants or exiles.

However, Sebald's 'English Pilgrimage' is more than a presentation of elective affinities between protagonists in real or simulated exile: it is the only volume of critical essays on English writers we will ever have since Sebald never produced an English equivalent to his essays on Austrian writers.[5] It makes clear that he was attracted to English writers such as Thomas Browne, Edward FitzGerald, Samuel Pepys and indeed Michael Hamburger[6] – in other words, as always, he tended to gravitate towards the periphery.

European Peripheries

In 1992, Sebald wrote a seemingly marginal text entitled 'Europäische Peripherien' ('European Peripheries') that summarized the basic British view of Europe.[7] However, this short essay is a remarkable document in more ways than one because, in it, Sebald at once sympathizes with and questions the credibility of English apprehensions about the European project. In contrast to Thomas Carlyle, who attempted to Germanize English syntax, Sebald kept his syntax and style stubbornly German while making a very English argument.

As are all of Sebald's texts, 'Europäische Perspektiven' is carefully woven and provides an intriguing reason for his insistence on syntactical complexity. Literature, according to Sebald, is not to assimilate or imitate the 'babble of daily communication', or the 'isotope of information speech' as is all too often the case with contemporary fiction. In his mind, differentiation, remembering things past, and past-tense narratives should be the hallmarks of literature.[8]

This text stands out in Sebald's œuvre as it combines Anglo-German concerns regarding Europe, political positioning and economic analysis, with statements on regional infrastructure, and does so in relatively direct terms, something Sebald otherwise only did in a few critical essays, for example that on Alfred Andersch and in his controversial essay on the failure of German post-war literature to adequately address the Allied air war against Germany, *Luftkrieg und Literatur* (*On The Natural History of Destruction*).

Sebald opens his reflections on European peripheries, an interest he shared with, amongst others, Hans Magnus Enzensberger and Karl-Markus Gauß, by quoting a slogan criticizing Britain's attitude towards Europe: 'The British Isles as the Scilly Isles of the European Continent', a motto more relevant to the present Brexit-situation than to the time of the Maastricht Treaty. As a German burdened with the unbearable baggage of recent history, Sebald seeks to understand the British attitude by arguing that Britain's eccentric self-positioning has led to valuable advantages in the past. He speculates that the English may have internalized and cultivated this geographical and political eccentricity 'in collective rituals and individual attitudes'.[9]

In characteristic Sebaldian fashion, he turns to a particular object that symbolized the conscious effort a few British politicians made to demonstrate their connection with the European continent: the then Foreign Secretary's distinctly continental-looking Loden coat, which he sported on appearances in Brussels and elsewhere in Europe. Wearing a Loden coat, Sebald muses, was Douglas Hurd's 'quasi diplomatic gesture, an anticipated expression of loyalty and a denial of his otherwise decidedly English bearings and way of thinking'.[10] The choice of this iconic garment must have struck Sebald since the Loden coat is typically worn in the Alpine region from which he came.[11]

Yet, Sebald in his essay did not allow himself to enter the sphere of a "philosophy of clothes" as Thomas Carlyle and Gottfried Keller did; instead, he moved from the English scepticism of the European project to comments on the economic 'colonization of European backwaters' turning landscapes into satellite cityscapes, the 'auto-proliferation of economic development', and random, unplannable development, towards his main concern: that society will soon exist only in the present and people will no longer be autonomous individuals but mere networkers with no memory.

Interfaces

A German-British interface conditioned much of Sebald's work, although the fragmentary Corsica Project seems to have been a conscious attempt on his part to break through this pattern, at least geographically. This interface took the shape of a literary, transformative engagement with exiles, most prominently in *Die Ausgewanderten* (*The Emigrants*)[12] and in *Austerlitz*, where he specifically engaged with H.G. Adler.[13] However, Sebald most poetically summarized this Anglo-German engagement in the third section of *Nach der Natur* (*After Nature*).

The lyrical subject of the poem remembers his arrival 'Half a life ago now' in Manchester, once called by Disraeli 'the most wonderful city of modern times, / a celestial Jerusalem' of technology and industry. But what the lyrical speaker found there was dereliction, the ruins of industrialization, deprivation and desolation, in short: a post-industrial "waste land" with one peculiar trace of German culture. Outside Liston's Music Hall 'where a radiantly blue-eyed, / down-and-out heroic tenor, / who always wore a winter coat / too long for him and a Homburg hat, / sang Tannhäuser arias, accompanied / by a Wurlitzer organ' (AN 98/NN 85–86).

This is followed by an allusion to Kafka's fragment *Amerika* and, most poignantly, by an encounter with a former emigrant, 'Mr Deutsch, / born in Kufstein', who had come to England in 1938: 'There were many things he could not / remember; some others he could not erase / from his mind. He had never / mastered the English language', even though he had followed for years, day in and day out 'the entire television schedule, as if / at any moment he expected / a message that would / change his whole life' (AN 100/NN 87). This may be one Sebald's finest endings, a closing and opening at the same time, symbolically enough for someone who is waiting for a definitive sign from each of his cultures with the ability to wait being the curious mode of their mediation.

It appears that Sebald deliberately confronted himself with the fate of German emigrants to England so as to turn their stories into narrative paradigms of life as an outsider, no matter how successful their respective acculturation had been. This confrontation made him even more acutely aware of the German past because as an author he selectively personalized the otherwise shapeless clutter of historical facts and data. This narrative method of measured selectivity enabled Sebald to penetrate the past without being overwhelmed by it. Thus, on his wanderings, he used his pen as a compass to find his way through time.

Coda: A Report to an Academy

Sebald's definitive statement regarding his in-between status came in 1999 in his address to the German Academy of Language and Literature upon being elected a corresponding fellow. Given its significance for this topic, the following statement must be quoted in full:

> Only when I went to Switzerland in 1965, and a year later to England, did ideas of my native country begin to form from a distance in my head, and these ideas, in the thirty years and more that I have now lived abroad, have grown and multiplied. To me, the whole [Federal] Republic has something curiously unreal about it, rather like a never-ending déjà vu. Only a guest in England, I still hover between feelings of familiarity and dislocation there too. Once I dreamed, and like Hebel I had my dream in Paris, that I was unmasked as a traitor to my country and a fraud. (CSe 208/CSg 250)

He concludes on a slight ironical note by saying that he welcomed the election to the German Academy as 'an unhoped-for form of justification' (CSe 208/CSg 250). Is the sphere of the in-between a territory inhabited by fraudsters, or is this simply a space where cultures blend or hybridize? Sebald did not elaborate on his alleged 'dream', instead, he remained firmly on the grounds of memory with all its productively painful hallmarks.

Notes

1. W Self, Incidents along the Road, in: *Guardian*, 7 February 2009, pp. 2–4.
2. A Bell, On Translating W.G. Sebald, in: Görner (ed.), *The Anatomist of Melancholy: Essays in Memory of W.G. Sebald* (Munich: Iudicium, 2003), pp. 11–18.
3. U Schütte, *Figurationen: Zum lyrischen Werk von W.G. Sebald* (Eggingen: Isele, 2014), pp. 11–12.
4. Schütte, *W.G. Sebald: Leben und literarisches Werk* (Berlin/Boston: De Gruyter, 2020), p. 224.
5. R Robertson, W.G. Sebald as a critic of Austrian Literature, in: *Journal of European Studies* 41:3–4 (2011), pp. 305 322.
6. B Hutchinson, *W.G. Sebald: Die dialektische Imagination* (Berlin/New York: De Gruyter, 2009), pp. 124–144.
7. Sebald, Europäische Peripherien, in: J Wertheimer (ed.), *Suchbild Europa: Künstlerische Konzepte der Moderne* (Amsterdam: Rodopi, 1995), pp. 65–67.
8. Ibid., p. 67.
9. Ibid., p. 66
10. Ibid., p. 65. On the essay, cf. Schütte, Europäische Peripherien: Sebald, Tübingen, Bertaux, in: *Weimarer Beiträge* 2 (2022), pp. 300–311.

11. This is an interesting example of what has been described as Sebald's adherence to "Romantic items", in: M Jacobus, *Romantic Things: A Tree, a Rock, a Cloud* (Chicago: Chicago University Press, 2012), esp. pp. 128–149.

12. P Schlesinger, W.G. Sebald and the Condition of Exile, in: *Theory, Culture & Society* 21:2 (2004), pp. 43–67.

13. M Atze, W.G. Sebald und H.G. Adler: Eine Begegnung in Texten, in: *Recherches Germaniques. Hors Série* 2 (2005), pp. 87–97.

PART II

The Literary Works

CHAPTER 8

Unpublished Juvenilia

Melissa Etzler

'If you are once on the track for symbols, you find them everywhere' – this handwritten sentence across the bottom of the first type-written page of W.G. Sebald's 1967 unpublished and untitled book-length work is so striking that the reader's eye is unavoidably drawn to it. While this sentence could be interpreted as a challenge to his readers or as tongue-in-cheek mockery of his anticipated reader's approach to his prose, the statement is accurate in considering how readers interact with his works of prose fiction published over twenty years after he set this text aside.

Sebald's juvenilia is fragmentary, immature and unpolished, yet worthy of attention as a contributing factor in his literary development. The primary symbols, themes and even, to a mild extent in his first novel, the literary style for which Sebald is now known have their genesis in these early texts. This essay will present instances of congruity between Sebald's juvenilia and his major works of prose fiction to reveal a portrait of a budding artist who ultimately never wandered far from his personal and literary origins. However, it equally emerges that the mature prose writer had clearly learned his lessons from youthful ventures into writing, avoiding the mistakes of his first attempts at literature.

Between 1961 and 1965, Sebald contributed a number of texts to school magazines and newspapers. There are twelve confirmed articles for *Der Wecker* (*The Alarm Clock*), published by the Oberrealschule (grammar school) in Oberstdorf between 1961 and 1963. Most are reviews but a few are first attempts at literary prose. For the *Freiburger Studenten-Zeitung* (*Freiburg Student Newspaper*), Sebald contributed the poems that now open *Über das Land und das Wasser* (*Across the Land and the Water*), as well as five short prose pieces and one review.

Sebald's juvenilia remains under-researched, which is not surprising considering its inaccessibility. In order to read Sebald's unpublished literary writings, one must seek out these documents, which are catalogued under 'Prosa 1968' (1968 Prose) in his literary estate at the Deutsches

Literaturarchiv in Marbach (DLA). Despite his early interest in writing, few texts have survived and so some pieces may have been lost. The folder in the DLA thus includes only one short play along with various brief prose texts and two versions of a novel. The brief prose texts introduced here are the four-page narrative 'Wartend' ('Waiting'), the one-page untitled story about Herr G. (Mr G.) and the six-page play *Der Traum ein Leben oder die Geschichte des Fr. v. Sch.* (*The Dream A Life, Or The Story of Fr. v. Sch.*).

Throughout all the prose texts, the narrator maintains a detached voice and yet the reader clearly recognizes Sebald's opinions and points of view regarding what he observes, records and recollects. While the short texts and play are quite literary and could appeal to a broad audience, the novel at times reads like an inside joke intended for friends and at other times like a solipsistic exploration in identity formation, devoid of the ties to socio-historical events found in his melancholy, self-reflective, mature prose fiction. Nonetheless, these texts shed light on the writer Sebald would become.

'Wartend' ('Waiting'): Consumer Culture and Devolution

'Wartend' ('Waiting') from 1968 most hints at characteristics of Sebald's later published prose. The plot of this four-page tale is simple: The first-person narrator drops off his friend P. at a hospital in Hampstead, North London, and waits, either in the Tosca café or driving around the city, until he can return to the hospital for visiting hours. The time the narrator spends with P. at the hospital comprises only a few sentences; otherwise, the narrative contains descriptions of eclectic customers in Tosca, his overnight stay at a friend's house and his reflections on the appearance of Hampstead locals walking by his car.

While the narrator's observations of the people of Hampstead provide him with a distraction, at one point his thoughts turn to the activity that gave the text its title – waiting – and he notes: 'waiting becomes the sacrifice one makes for a desired change and it is almost a sin to leave the place to which one has banished oneself earlier than agreed' (3).[1] The narrator thus views the process of waiting as banishment.

While the narrator is temporarily paralysed by waiting, the people of Hampstead are also immobile, yet more negatively so, as this is the result of either self-elected or biological regression. Most of them have become lethargic after giving into the temptations of capitalism and either eating too many baked goods in the Tosca café or canned foods in front of their television sets. Sebald's critique of capitalism by way of literal consumption

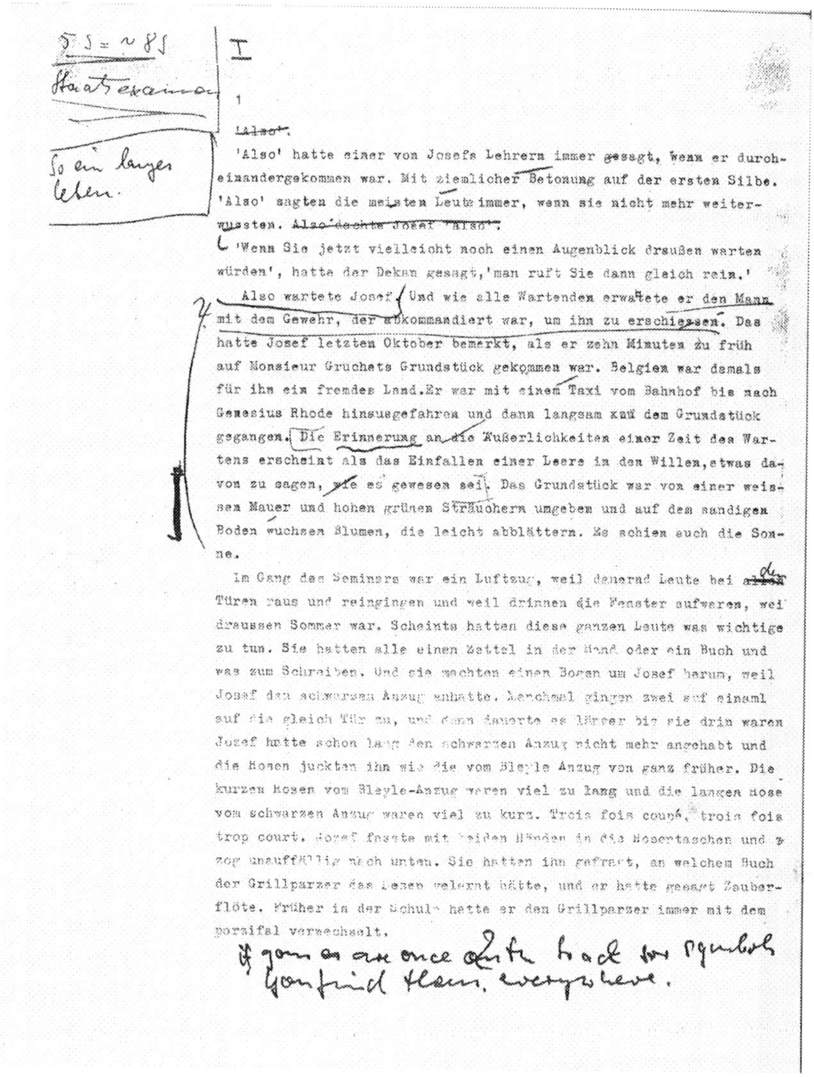

I

1

'Also'.

'Also' hatte einer von Josefs Lehrern immer gesagt, wenn er durcheinandergekommen war. Mit ziemlicher Betonung auf der ersten Silbe. 'Also' sagten die meisten Leute immer, wenn sie nicht mehr weiterwussten. Also dachte Josef 'also'.

'Wenn Sie jetzt vielleicht noch einen Augenblick draußen warten würden', hatte der Dekan gesagt, 'man ruft Sie dann gleich rein.'

Also wartete Josef. Und wie alle Wartenden erwartete er den Mann mit dem Gewehr, der abkommandiert war, um ihn zu erschiessen. Das hatte Josef letzten Oktober bemerkt, als er zehn Minuten zu früh auf Monsieur Gruchets Grundstück gekommen war. Belgien war damals für ihn ein fremdes Land. Er war mit einem Taxi vom Bahnhof bis nach Genesius Rhode hinausgefahren und dann langsam zu dem Grundstück gegangen. Die Erinnerung an die Äußerlichkeiten einer Zeit des Wartens erscheint als das Einfallen einer Leere in den Willen, etwas davon zu sagen, wie es gewesen sei. Das Grundstück war von einer weissen Mauer und hohen grünen Sträuchern umgeben und auf dem sandigen Boden wuchsen Blumen, die leicht abblättern. Es schien auch die Sonne.

Im Gang des Seminars war ein Luftzug, weil dauernd Leute bei allen Türen raus und reingingen und weil drinnen die Fenster aufwaren, weil draussen Sommer war. Scheints hatten diese ganzen Leute was wichtiges zu tun. Sie hatten alle einen Zettel in der Hand oder ein Buch und was zum Schreiben. Und sie machten einen Bogen um Josef herum, weil Josef den schwarzen Anzug anhatte. Manchmal gingen zwei auf einmal auf die gleich Tür zu, und dann dauerte es länger bis sie drin waren. Josef hatte schon lang den schwarzen Anzug nicht mehr angehabt und die Hosen juckten ihn wie die vom Bleyle Anzug von ganz früher. Die kurzen Hosen vom Bleyle-Anzug waren viel zu lang und die langen Hose vom schwarzen Anzug waren viel zu kurz. Trois fois coupé, trois fois trop court. Josef fasste mit beiden Händen in die Hosentaschen und zog unauffällig nach unten. Sie hatten ihn gefragt, an welchem Buch der Grillparzer das Lesen gelernt hätte, und er hatte gesagt Zauberflöte. Früher in der Schule hatte er den Grillparzer immer mit dem Parsifal verwechselt.

So ein langes leben.

Illustration 8 – First page of typescript of first novel

is pervasive; for example, as the narrator of *Die Ringe des Saturn* (*The Rings of Saturn*) notes: 'I bought a carton of chips at McDonald's, where I felt like a criminal wanted worldwide as I stood at the brightly lit counter' (RSe 81/ RSg 101).

Regarding biological regression, the narrator of 'Waiting' claims it is 'as if the whole of society had entered into a decisive phase of mutation' (3). Similarly, in Sebald's *The Rings of Saturn* when the narrator spies a couple on the beach, their entwined bodies are 'misshapen, like some great mollusc washed ashore [...] a many limbed, two-headed monster [...] the last of a prodigious species' (RSe 68/RSg 88). This is an example of a tendency the narrator noted earlier on, namely for evolution to repeat 'its earlier conceits with a certain sense of irony' (RSe 32/RSg 44).

Pierre Bertaux's *La mutation humaine* (*Human Mutation*, 1960) probably inspired Sebald to include the concept of mutation so early on.[2] Bertaux (1907–1986) argues that the regression of reason, as illustrated by our industrializing of nature and mechanization of humankind, is a literal devolution reflected in our corporeal structure. He claims the regressive tendency of humans will result in both further physical malformations and in the origination of an entirely new species, assuming we do not destroy ourselves first.[3]

'Waiting' and Material Objects

The narrator's observations from Hampstead in 'Waiting' are often underscored by a summative, philosophical thought, much as in Sebald's published prose. For example, as the narrator wanders through the cemetery at Golders Green, he passes the final resting place of Sigmund Freud (1856–1939) and thinks: 'His ashes repose there in one of his favourite Grecian urns' (2). Intertextually, the narrator's observation provokes a consideration of the relevance of Freud or perhaps of John Keats' poem 'Ode on a Grecian Urn' (1819) in which the material object itself is an actant instigating analysis.

From the cemetery, the narrator goes to what is clearly a friend's house to spend the night and nevertheless claims it is difficult to sleep and dream in the rooms of 'strangers' ('fremde Leute'; 2). This is compounded by the fact that 'the uncanny shadows and contours of the furniture fully come to life' (2). The rhetoric alludes to Freud's essay 'Das Unheimliche' ('The Uncanny', 1919) in which objects and people that should be intimately familiar suddenly become strange/*fremd* and the inanimate becomes alive/*lebendig*.[4]

Sebald recorded similar thoughts on the power of objects in the second version of his novel. While gazing at a country road and bridge, the narrator claims that there is 'a mutual astonishment between himself and objects', but that there is 'a demand within the object which surpasses the abilities of the individual' (17). Later in the novel, as the narrator prepares to leave his university room, he claims the furniture is 'waiting for him to leave', and he asks 'would it move if I turned by back on it?' (85).

Sebald explains what is most uncanny about the liveliness of objects thirty years later in *Austerlitz*. While photographing a column in Pilsen, Austerlitz claims that 'the idea, ridiculous in itself, that this cast-iron column, which with its scaly surface seemed almost to approach the nature of a living being, might remember me and was [. . .] a witness to what I could no longer recollect for myself' (Ae 311/Ag 319–320). Objects are the prime recorders of history and, long after we have passed, they will remember that which we already during our lifetimes, as Freud would say, repress.

Ending on another example of the impact of material things, 'Waiting' concludes with air raids and rubble. Waiting in his car for another round of visiting hours, the narrator hears planes and, looking up to the sky, imagines the planes 'are loaded with bombs. In such a large city, the thought that there is a war raging naturally occurs' (4). This relates to Sebald's own period of waiting for a train in Munich as a child and seeing the rubble that he assumed was 'an element of the natural history of larger cities' (G 177). This is the only reference to World War Two, but since it occurs at the end, it underscores the general malaise of the text while pointing to a theme crucial to Sebald's mature prose: the 'natural history of destruction'.

Der Traum ein Leben oder die Geschichte des Fr. v. Sch. (The Dream a Life or the Story of Fr. v. Sch.): A Commentary on a Totalitarian Personality

In 'The Dream A Life', a 'Monologue in One Act', the character Fritz von Schiegl is arguably the most peculiar to take centre stage in Sebald's works, and yet he is consistent with Sebald's concern regarding the rise of totalitarian leaders and ignoring the horrors of the past. The script is based on an encounter Sebald claimed to have had while on holiday in summer 1968, and was written later that autumn in St Gallen, Switzerland. Sebald sent the monologue to the Austrian satirist Helmut Qualtinger (1928–1986) since the *raconteur* Schiegl bears an evident similarity to Qualtinger's famous character Herr Karl, a Viennese petty-bourgeois Everyman, whose ramblings showed him as opportunist supporter of Hitler's regime. Qualtinger, however, never replied (SM 82).

The script features a couple, Max and Marika, making it into the first text in which Sebald used the name he chose for himself for one of his characters. The couple sits at one of many 'fake marble tables' (*Kunstmarmortische*) in the winter garden at the Hotel Belle Vue and speak in hushed tones as Fritz von Schiegl walks in. The specificity of the tables is important since they serve as material extensions of Schiegl. The German term refers to an artful imitation of marble and, not uncoincidentally, Schiegl has a flamboyant, artful appearance: he wears many ornate rings, flower-print mauve braces and clown shoes. He is also guilty of artificial narration – that is, lying.

His biography reveals his misogyny and violent tendencies, and his alleged professions include everything from selling silks, to working in gastronomy, to selling diamonds, to championship weightlifting. The 73-year-old Schiegl seems aware of the implausible nature of his experiences as he punctuates most accomplishments with commentaries such as this one on his ability to lift hundreds of kilos 'thanks to my monstrous power, which you perhaps don't recognize in my physique' (6).

The fact that Schiegl has a 'Führer moustache' makes the monologue a commentary on post-war reactions to Hitler, ranging from horror and fascination (seen in the couple Max and Marika, respectively) to numb acceptance (seen in the two silent women accompanying Schiegl). The play ends with a commentary on unspeakable violence by returning to the marble tables. Schiegl is so angered during his retelling of a story in which he'd become a laughingstock, that he begins shattering all the marble tables with his bare fists before turning to attack the audience.

The megalomaniacal nature of Schiegl and the deep-seeded paranoia of becoming a laughingstock (regardless of his clown shoes) culminates in unwarranted violence enacted on a group of scapegoats. This outbreak of destructive aggression serves as an allegorical warning that – despite the lip service paid to coming to terms with the past – the tradition of fascist violence continued to thrive in the Catholic culture of Austria and southern Germany in which Sebald was brought up.

Mr G. and the Artist's Dilemma

Sebald's one-page long, untitled short story about the painter Mr G. offers a commentary on the problematic position of the artist, marking out the engagement with visual art that proved so crucial to his mature prose. The narrative consists primarily of a detailed description of the expression on Mr G.'s face and his clothing that appears to be made by a man analysing himself in the mirror but turns out to be the artist Mr G. observing his self-portrait in a London art gallery.

It is not clear whether Sebald had a specific artist in mind as a model; however, the themes in the text (such as mirrors and distorted reflections) hint at the art of Francis Bacon. In any case, artist figures and the motif of artistic self-reflection pervades Sebald's later works, ranging from Grünewald and Max Ferber/Max Aurach to the work of Jan Peter Tripp.

For Mr G, there is little hope the message in his self-portrait will be recognized by the public. Although many people study the painting and whisper about it, 'they don't understand it' (1). Towards the end, Mr G. experiences an existential crisis which prefigures many of Sebald's later artist figures. Mr G. recognizes that art is an exercise in futility and will not only be misunderstood but also be, as the character Paolo says in Sebald's unpublished novel, neglected on a shelf. Paolo claims of novels: 'one doesn't even know where to begin with them, other than to dust them off from time to time' (76). Sebald probably did not anticipate at the time he wrote this that Paolo was describing the fate of his 1967 novel, minus the occasional dusting.

Such a Long Life: Sebald's Unpublished Novel

Sebald's first attempts at a novel are located in the archival folder ambiguously labelled 'W.G. Sebald?' Sebald began composing the text in autumn 1966 and completed it in March 1967 but it was inspired by the four semesters he spent in Freiburg im Breisgau between autumn 1963 and summer 1965, as well as additional experiences prior to his move to Manchester in autumn 1966 (SM 45, 70). The novel features the malaise, world-weariness and accentuated introspection of the semi-autobiographical narrator, Josef. Sebald's impetus for writing this seems to lie in chronicling events, impressions and relationships from his college years. Commonly known about the novel is that Sebald put it in a drawer, claiming that, when he 'read it out to [his] girlfriend, she fell asleep' (SM 350).

The drafts – version one is just over one hundred and version two is one hundred and fifteen pages long – are primarily an embellished and fictionalized record of Sebald's personal experiences. Josef is preparing for an extended journey abroad having passed his university exams and, before leaving, returns to home to visit his parents. There are also scenes with joking dialogue and various shenanigans inspired by Sebald's circle of friends from his student residence, the Max-Heim, at university in Freiburg im Breisgau, many of whom are recognizable in the novel.[5] Additionally, Josef spends time in his girlfriend's apartment, makes small outings with her and travels with her to Brussels, pointing to later mentions of Belgium in *Die Ringe des Saturn* (*The Rings of Saturn*) and the opening of *Austerlitz*.

Clearly, though, the most meaningful relationship is the one between Josef and his grandfather (see chapter 2 in this volume). The scenes involving Josef's grandfather change little between the two drafts, in which the narrator tends to express emotion via changes in the weather rather than rhetoric. This is in stark opposition to the narrator's relationship with his parents, which is distanced to the point where he imagines their deaths.

Scattered throughout the novel are introspective moments that connect images and history's more violent moments. In the second draft, Josef recalls lying sick in bed as a young child and flipping through the pages of a book with images of Hitler. His mother nonchalantly returns the book to the night table, exchanging it for a cup of tea. At another point, the narrator sees an image of the Duke of Reichstadt (Napoleon II) in a magazine and offers personal impressions not inherent within the image itself, as is typical of Sebald's descriptions of photographs in his published prose, such as that 'he has an average, if somewhat insane expression' (49).

This prepares the reader for Josef's feelings when he visits the Lion Monument memorializing the Battle of Waterloo and the end of the Napoleonic wars. This episode pre-empts the corresponding passage in *The Rings of Saturn*, where the narrator philosophizes about the 'falsification of perspective' (RSe 124–125/RSg 151–152) inherent in historical monuments. In the novel, Josef merely claims: 'I was afraid of losing my balance' (104). If an encounter with historical locations impacted by violence can induce vertigo, perhaps images that record and allow us to interpret history can keep us grounded, if not sane.

Conclusion

Even cursory exposure to Sebald's juvenilia makes clear that they foreshadow the philosophical, historical and sociological considerations in his mature prose fiction. Doubt regarding teleological progress, affirmation of the agency of objects, the crisis of the artist, the horrors of the past, the destruction wrought by nature: these and other later themes are already found in his juvenilia. His early prose shows that his struggle to express the more inexplicable tendencies of humankind and of nature had already begun in the 1960s.

Notes

1. In this essay, quotations from the unpublished material held at the DLA are referenced by the page numbers of the respective typescripts.
2. On Sebald and Bertaux, cf. U Schütte, Europäische Peripherien: Sebald, Tübingen, Bertaux, in: *Weimarer Beiträge* 2 (2022), pp. 300–311.
3. P Bertaux, *Mutation der Menschheit: Zukunft und Lebenssinn* (Frankfurt: Suhrkamp, 1979), pp. 11–15.
4. For a study on the impact of Freud's 'The Uncanny', see the editors' introduction in: JJ Long, A Whitehead (eds.), *W.G. Sebald: A Critical Companion* (Edinburgh: Edinburgh University Press, 2004), pp. 3–15 (8).
5. For further information on the sequence of events in the novel and its autobiographical connections, see C Angier, *Speak, Silence: In Search of W.G. Sebald* (London: Bloomsbury, 2021), pp. 219–224.

CHAPTER 9

Film Scripts

Michael Hutchins

Despite growing interest in W.G. Sebald's early work, today, two decades after his death, many readers remain unaware that among his first serious literary efforts were two screenplay projects. In the early- and mid-1980s, at least a decade before Sebald's prose works gained attention in the English-speaking world, he toiled on these two experimental film scripts. The first, *Jetzund kömpt die Nacht herbey: Ansichten aus dem Leben und Sterben Immanuel Kants* (*Night Now Draweth Nigh: Scenes from the Life and Dying of Immanuel Kant*) concerns, as the title suggests, the biography of the philosopher Immanuel Kant (1724–1804). The other project, *Leben Ws* (*The Life of W*) traces the life of another philosopher, Ludwig Wittgenstein (1889–1951).

Literary Beginnings

Despite the questions these projects raise, and their potential to revise understanding of his development as an author, they have scarcely been discussed in Sebald scholarship. There are at least two reasons for this. First, these projects represent failures. They were not produced as films and only the Wittgenstein Project was published.[1] A shortened version of the Kant Project was eventually broadcast as a radio play by Westdeutscher Rundfunk (WDR) radio 3 in July 2015. This has meant that, at least in the case of the Kant Project, the text itself remained available only to scholars willing to do archival work. A second reason for their continued obscurity is that, as incomplete, unfinished works, they present unique interpretive challenges to readers accustomed to Sebald's published writings, and for whom the definitive versions of these two texts remains unclear.

The Kant Project consists of three drafts of roughly forty to fifty pages of typescript each and an exposé. The final, most complete version is typed in two columns with input from Berlin filmmaker Jan Franksen. In this professional version, the left-hand column features technical directions

Max SEBALD
The Old Rectory
22 Upgate
Poringland
Norwich NR14 7SH
England

Exposé für einen Fernsehfilm mit dem

Arbeitstitel:

Jetzund kömpt die Nacht herbey —

Ansichten aus dem Leben und Sterben

des Immanuel Kant.

But it is only since I have ceased
to live that I think of these things.
It is in the tranquillity of decompo-
sition that I remember the long confused emotion which was my life and
that I judge it, as it is said that
God will judge me, and with no less
impertinence. To decompose is to live
too, I know I know, don't torment me,
but one sometimes forgets.

Samuel Beckett, *Molloy*

Illustration 9 – Cover sheet Kant Project

such as camera angles and set descriptions, and the right-hand column contains dialogue and minor stage directions. Sprinkled throughout the text are handwritten annotations and corrections; clearly, the last draft remained a work in progress. In total, this last version contains twenty-three chronologically organized scenes that present episodes from the philosopher's life, ranging from 1715 to his death in 1804, with special emphasis on Kant's physical decline at the end of his life.

By contrast, the Wittgenstein text was less developed. Sebald composed two drafts of an eleven-page list, cryptically describing sixty-two scenes he planned to write, with a handful of camera angles and stage directions. The second draft of the list is interspersed with twelve photocopied images taken from a biography of Wittgenstein by Michael Nedo and Michele Ranchetti.[2] Sebald planned to incorporate these images into the film, but they were omitted from the published version of the script. He also typed an exposé to send out to potential producers but apparently never developed an actual workable script.

Instead, only a few dialogue exchanges, both typed and handwritten, are included in the same archival folder as the scene list. Because of this fragmentary quality, it is difficult to discern whether certain passages refer to scenes Sebald intended to write or to images. On page five, for example, we read 'Brother Hans' boat. Apparently rudderless'. It is unclear whether Sebald intended such snippets to constitute actual action sequences, reproduced still photographs, or camera shots.

In their construction, both projects are unmistakably different from Sebald's other work, though the inclusion of uncaptioned images in the Wittgenstein Project is reminiscent of the author's later prose narratives. Nevertheless, these two projects represent important intermediate phases in Sebald's development as an author. Although imperfect, unfinished works, they bear the same thematic and aesthetic imprint as his later work, above all the focus on biographical aspects, the intertextual incorporation of marked and unmarked pre-texts and the intermedial practice of combining text and image.

Origins of the Screenplays

Sebald had been writing poetry and fiction since his university days, but the origins of his mature literary efforts coincided with his growing disenchantment with academic life and German Studies. Thus, his literary turn should largely be understood as an attempt to secure a future outside the academy. Beginning in the early 1980s, the newly elected conservative

Thatcher government had begun to pressure British academic institutions to curtail what the conservatives saw as inefficient and irrelevant public expenditures. Sebald therefore found himself in an increasingly managed, bureaucratic environment at the University of East Anglia (UEA). As he would later observe, life in the British university became 'extremely unpleasant'.[3]

At the same time, Sebald continued to be at odds with the accepted practice of German Studies both in Britain and on the continent. From his earliest days as a scholar, Sebald had staked out a contrarian position, engaged in polemics and questioned the received wisdom on figures at the centre of scholarly discourse, focusing instead on individuals from the periphery.

It was within this context that he began to work on film projects in an attempt to transition from academic to literary author. Philippa Comber conservatively locates the beginning of the Kant Project in autumn 1981,[4] which is when she first encountered it, and when Sebald received the first of many rejection letters.[5] Uwe Schütte dates the Kant Project to the end of 1980 or beginning of 1981.[6] This means that Sebald began composing his Kant script shortly after meeting influential colleagues and figures in the filmmaking world. The film historian Thomas Elsaesser (1943–2019) had founded the Film Studies programme at UEA in 1976 and was co-teaching a seminar on the cinema of the Weimar Republic with Sebald by 1980 (though Sebald kept his screenwriting ambitions from his colleague).[7]

Sebald had developed an important working relationship with the experimental filmmaker Jan Franksen, whom he met in 1976, and with whose help he secured provisional approval from Sender Freies Berlin (SFB) in May 1983.[8] However, this approval was suddenly reversed the following October. Sebald may never have completely forgotten the project – there is a newspaper clipping about Kant from 1992 among the project papers in his literary estate – but, though he continued to submit the scripts to producers, theatrical companies, and publishers for several more years, by late 1982 he had moved on to poetry, namely 'Über das Land und das Wasser' ('Across the Land and the Water') and *Nach der Natur* (*After Nature*).

In spring 1986, a few months after completing *After Nature*, Sebald began research on his Wittgenstein Project, which he finished and sent off to the German Federal Film Fund on 25 August 1986. They rejected it in a letter dated 27 January 1987 and Sebald never submitted it anywhere else prior to placing it with the *Frankfurter Rundschau*, which published it on 22 April 1989, the philosopher's centenary. However, by then, Sebald had

long since abandoned all hope of producing a film from this material. Since
the Kant and Wittgenstein Projects were highly experimental, they would
have been difficult to produce, but Sebald was unwilling to attempt to get
them accepted by compromising his vision.

Understanding the timeline of these projects, and the conditions under
which they emerged, should help to correct the misconception, especially
prevalent among his anglophone audience, that Sebald burst upon the
literary scene fully formed in the 1990s when his prose works gained
international acclaim. His transition to literary writing began much earlier
in the early 1980s. Although his early efforts were rejected, he carried on,
undeterred.

Approaches to the Texts: Kant

The Kant and Wittgenstein Projects are at odds with what readers have
come to expect from Sebald. Unlike the rhizomatic, intricate prose of *Die
Ringe des Saturn* (*The Rings of Saturn*) and *Austerlitz*, these scripts have
short, often cryptic sentences sprinkled with set and camera directions.
The Kant Project also has dialogue, which is quite rare in Sebald's œuvre,
but therefore lacks the distinctive sound of his narrative prose.
Nevertheless, they have some continuity with the rest of Sebald's work.
Here, two scholarly interpretations are especially noteworthy: Schütte's
2017 study of the Kant scripts and Richard Gray's 2017 examination of the
Wittgenstein project.

Both point to Sebald's practice of, as Schütte terms it, 'periscopic
intertextuality',[9] which ties these early projects stylistically to
Sebald's later work. However, as both Schütte and Gray point out,
Sebald chose secondary works – biographies of the philosophers
rather than their primary texts – as intertexts since he was more
concerned with their respective life stories than with their work.
Comber, who read the first draft of the Kant script, observes that it
does not directly engage with the philosopher's work or thoughts,
but instead presents a view of him as a fragile, eccentric human.[10]
Less sympathetically, Mario Gotterbarm states that Sebald problem-
atically instrumentalizes Kant by reducing him to his biography.[11]
This echoes the sentiments of many publishers and producers who
rejected those scripts.

In his introduction to the Kant Project, Sebald admits as much, writing
that the excerpts from Kant's life, thought, wishes and fears illustrate 'the
irrevocability with which we as individuals succumb to entropy' and

wondering 'whether the small traverse of our ontogenetic existence does not allow certain conclusions to be drawn about our species-historical prospects'.[12] In other words, Kant's life, and in particular his decline, serve only as examples of entropy and Sebald's bleak view of the future of the human species.

Sebald intentionally refused to engage with Kant's philosophy and, instead, used it as mere set dressing, as he stated in a letter from 4 November 1983 to Jürgen Tomm, then a television editor at Sender Freies Berlin (SFB), which had cancelled plans to produce the film. He wrote that the editorial board should reconsider its decision to reject his project due to a preference for science programming over "culture" since his script 'concerns itself much less with Kant's philosophy than with the problem of nature and natural science'.[13]

Kant's thought was, however, not irrelevant to Sebald in that, in those scripts, he critiqued the belief in progress and view of nature that was based on the Enlightenment tradition Kant represented and had resulted in exploitation of the natural world. The central scenes of the project trace a narrative arc that takes Sebald's Kant from scepticism about human progress to a more affirmative position. This arc parallels the scripts' portrayal of Kant's mental decay and is consistent with Sebald's other work.

The sense of dread about the chances of human survival Sebald expresses in his Kant Project is again found in a scholarly article he wrote about Kafka's 'evolution stories' in 1983, with the former being a literary exploration of the thesis expounded in the latter.[14] Thematically, the Kant Project was a preliminary strike of a melancholic tuning fork, which would resonate throughout the rest of Sebald's work, especially in *The Rings of Saturn*.

Approaches to the Texts: Wittgenstein

The Wittgenstein Project is more clearly indebted to the insights of its title character. Rather than merely deploying an instrumentalized version of the philosopher, the style of 'The Life of W.' is similar to the philosopher's practice, or, as Gray puts it, 'a visually translated replication of the aphoristic model Wittgenstein himself employed'.[15] Sebald's introduction to the Wittgenstein Project also indicates that he used the philosopher's insights to structure his script. After explaining that the film should not be merely a documentary or

illustrated biography but rather images that constituted
Wittgenstein's life, Sebald continues:

> Corresponding to the nature of pure images, [the film] is about the con-
> struction of an achronological, asyntactic 'sentence' that is to 'express' the
> things about which W. was mostly silent during his life. The counterpoint
> according to which one might proceed is the concept of death Wittgenstein
> alluded to now and again. (SM 324)

As Gray points out, this sense of showing, rather than telling, corresponds to the
insight in Wittgenstein's *Tractatus* that, 'by limiting oneself to this act of saying
the sayable, [...] one simultaneously also shows what is unsayable'.[16]
Nevertheless, it is striking that here, as in the Kant Project, Sebald did not
actually engage with Wittgenstein's philosophical works in this script – not
even, as he did elsewhere, through veiled quotation. For example, in the
project's thirty-seventh scene Sebald had planned to include 'a passage from
the *Tractatus*' (SM 329) but did not indicate which passage he had in mind or its
relevance to his project.

Instead, the Wittgenstein Project, motivated as it was, in part, by
biographical similarities between Sebald and the philosopher, evinces
what Gray has described as a 'haunting'[17] reminiscent of the way in
which Wittgenstein surfaces in the rest of Sebald's work. Wittgenstein's
'life, thought and language [...] course through Sebald's fictions like
a rhythmic thorough-bass'.[18] There are, for example, the various characters
in Sebald's prose works who resemble Wittgenstein, or have characteristics
drawn from his biography, such as Paul Bereyter in *Die Ausgewanderten*
(*The Emigrants*), and the eponymous character of *Austerlitz*, who bears, as
the narrator puts it in the novel, a 'striking likeness' (Ae 41/Ag 64) to the
philosopher.

Furthermore, certain of Wittgenstein's ideas continued to resonate with
Sebald and make their way into his fiction. Tea Lobo reveals a similarity
between the aesthetic philosophies of Wittgenstein and Sebald, pointing to
Austerlitz as an example of Sebald's understanding of Wittgenstein's notion of
language. In Lobo's reading, Sebald constructs in *Austerlitz* an 'outside perspective on the totality of facts that is the world (to use Wittgenstein's expression in
the *Tractatus*, 1.1), and therefore scope for reflection on real-world events and
people'.[19] Images from the Wittgenstein Project also reappeared in Sebald's
later work. As Gray points out, Kafka's Hunter Gracchus, whom Sebald
invokes in *Schwindel. Gefühle. (Vertigo)*, contains an echo of the aforementioned sailboat in Sebald's Wittgenstein Project, drifting aimlessly on the water
after Wittgenstein's brother Hans drowned himself.[20]

Conclusion

Sebald's Kant and Wittgenstein scripts give us a better understanding of his development as an author. In a secondary literature largely calcified around now-familiar themes and texts, Sebald's abandoned film projects offer an opportunity to expand our horizons and revise assumptions. They show the author in a transitional phase, seeking literary expression for notions he had addressed in critical essays in the 1970s and 1980s, and they should be read together with that body of work.

The scripts evidence his frustration with academic life and rebellious focus on what scholars of Kant and Wittgenstein would consider mere biography. They also experiment with elements and themes of Sebald's later style, such as his incorporation of images and his alarm at the trajectory of human progress. As Gray puts it, they were an 'incubator'[21] for his later ideas and practices.

Perhaps the most important point of continuity with his mature style is the loose connection between the scenes and images in these texts; the reader must extrapolate relationships from the juxtaposition of seemingly disparate parts. Although the Kant and Wittgenstein Projects demonstrate that he had not yet found his most effective medium, their aesthetics and themes are already unmistakably Sebaldian.

Notes

1. Leben Ws. Skizze einer möglichen Szenenreihe für einen nichtrealisierten Film, in: *Frankfurter Rundschau*, 22 April 1989 (SM 324–333).
2. M Nedo, M Ranchetti (eds.), *Ludwig Wittgenstein: Sein Leben in Bildern und Texten* (Frankfurt: Suhrkamp, 1983).
3. R McCrum, Characters, plot, dialogue? That's not really my style [interview], in: *Observer*, 7 June 1998.
4. P Comber, Autorbiographie, in: C Öhlschläger, M Niehaus (eds.), *W.G. Sebald Handbuch: Leben – Werk – Wirkung* (Stuttgart: Metzler, 2017), pp. 5–9 (6).
5. Filmverlag der Autoren to W.G. Sebald, 7 September 1981 (DLA).
6. U Schütte, Durch die Hintertür: Zu W.G. Sebalds unveröffentlichter Szenenreihe über das Leben und Sterben des Immanuel Kant, in: Schütte (ed.) *Über W.G. Sebald: Beiträge zu einem anderen Bild des Autors* (Berlin/Boston: De Gruyter, 2017), pp. 63–98 (74).
7. Ibid.
8. On Franksen's unique work in TV, cf. Christoph Rosenthal, ›*Die Wirklichkeit des Filmes ist fiktiv*‹: *Der Berliner Filmessayist Jan Franksen* (Marburg: Tectum, 2018).

9. Schütte, *Durch die Hintertür*, p. 83.
10. P Comber, *Ariadne's Thread: In Memory of W.G. Sebald* (Norwich: Propolis, 2014), p. 116.
11. M Gotterbarm, *Die Gewalt des Moralisten: Zum Verhältnis von Ethik und Ästhetik bei W.G. Sebald* (Paderborn: Fink, 2016), p. 492.
12. Vorbemerkung p. 1 (DLA).
13. Sebald to Jürgen Tomm, 4 November 1983 (DLA).
14. M Hutchins, *Tikkun: W.G. Sebald's Melancholy Messianism* (PhD thesis: Cincinnati, 2011), pp. 149–153.
15. R Gray, *Ghostwriting: W.G. Sebald's Poetics of History* (London: Bloomsbury, 2017), p. 38.
16. L Wittgenstein, *Tractatus Logico-Philosophicus* (London: Routledge, 1981), 4.113–4.1212.
17. Gray, *Ghostwriting*, p. 29.
18. Ibid.
19. T Lobo, *A Picture Held Us Captive: On Aisthesis and Interiority in Ludwig Wittgenstein, Fyodor Dostoevsky and W.G. Sebald* (Berlin/Boston: De Gruyter, 2019), p. 200.
20. Gray, *Ghostwriting*, p. 41.
21. Ibid., p. 32.

CHAPTER 10

The Prose Project

Paul Whitehead

Between mid-1981 and late August 1986, W.G. Sebald – alongside writing a string of critical essays, mainly on Austrian literature, which culminated in *Die Beschreibung des Unglücks* (*Describing Disaster*), as well as his teaching and administrative duties at the University of East Anglia – worked on a number of literary projects: experimental scripts on Im- ma- nuel Kant (1724–1804) and Ludwig Wittgenstein (1889–1951), a collection of poetry titled *Über das Land und das Wasser* (*Across the Land and the Water*) and three long prose poems that eventually formed *Nach der Natur* (*After Nature*).

Autumn 1986 marked a fresh and decisive departure in Sebald's œuvre. He had temporarily stopped writing poetry in late 1985, and permanently renounced scriptwriting after August 1986, in order to turn his attention to a pioneering form of lyrical, highly stylized prose fiction that incorporated black-and-white images such as photographs and reproductions of drawings, advertisements and paintings. The 'iconotext' has, of course, since become his 'trademark'.[1] From approximately July 1986 to early 1988, he then worked on a first collection of literary prose that had no official working title and was simply referred to as his 'prose book', 'prose work', or 'prose project'.[2]

A New Departure

The single most-important document relating to Sebald's then-new undertaking is a 'Project Description' that formed part of a funding application dated 28 February 1987 to the German Literature Fund (Deutscher Literaturfonds, DLF), Germany's main public source of financial support for writers.

In this five-page submission, which is extant in his literary papers at the German Literature Archive in Marbach (Deutsches Literaturarchiv, DLA), he defines *After Nature* as 'a preliminary exercise and test piece', and states that he is embarking on a project 'far more extensive than his previous literary endeavours' (DLA). His description of the project – 'a prose work with images' (DLA) – makes clear that it was the common origin of two collections later published separately thirty months apart: *Schwindel. Gefühle.* (*Vertigo*), in March 1990, and *Die Ausgewanderten* (*The Emigrants*), in September 1992.

The Project Description mentions three prose pieces: two already-completed biographical texts – on the writers Stendhal (1783–1842) and Franz Kafka (1883–1924) – with which we are now familiar as 'Beyle oder das merckwürdige Faktum der Liebe' ('Beyle, or Love is a Madness Most Discreet') and 'Dr. K.s Badereise nach Riva' ('Dr. K. Takes the Waters at Riva'), respectively, and a third, autobiographical text designated by the rudimentary itinerary 'Vienna–Venice–Verona–Riva' (later to become 'All'estero') that also included a more structured account of a journey from Riva to the village W. 'on the northern fringes of the Alps' – easily identifiable as Sebald's childhood home, Wertach (the later 'Il ritorno in patria'). The Prose Project thus mirrors *After Nature* in that it is a triptych structured in accordance with chronological patterns and the sequence biography–biography–autobiography.

The Project Description also alludes to recurring themes such as exile, teaching and learning, suicide in old age and the history of socialism in Germany. It identifies protagonists such as the Hunter Gracchus from Kafka's eponymous short story (1917), the Seelos family from W., Armin (later Paul) Bereyter, the 'hut warden' Johannes Naegeli and political radical Rudolf Egelhofer (1896–1919). While both Gracchus – along with the double-bind of hunting and being hunted – and Mathild Seelos are to be found in *Vertigo*, we encounter Naegeli, Bereyter and William Seelos, alias Ambros Adelwarth in *The Emigrants*.

Sebald had been conducting research on Rudolf Egelhofer – the revolutionary sailor who, in April 1919, was the military commander of the short-lived Munich Soviet Republic – since the mid-1980s. Although Egelhofer was later omitted from the Prose Project and does not appear in either *Vertigo* or *The Emigrants*, he was scheduled to reappear in Sebald's planned follow-up to *Austerlitz*, provisionally titled the World War Project (see chapter 15 in this volume). Thus, the Project Description not only provides insight into Sebald's creative process in 1987 but also into the long gestation period of another project he worked on nearly fifteen years later.

The Project Description indicates that, in the Prose Project, both 'Ambros Adelwarth' and 'Paul Bereyter' were to be woven into the third, travelogue section mentioned above, which was, in February 1987, still conceived as one continuous story. Thus, 'Il ritorno in patria'. was not meant to end effectively, as it does in *Vertigo*, in mid-December 1952 with the Sebald family's relocation from Wertach to Sonthofen (SG 233/V 214), but was to encompass the young Winfried's experiences under the tutelage of primary school teacher Armin Müller in 1953/54 and, by definition, the year in which Ambros Adelwarth, here still referred to as William Seelos, would later die. Furthermore, the Naegeli episode, which now features prominently in 'Dr. Henry Selwyn', was to be included to underscore the vagaries of individual and collective memory: 'And, above all, memory. How everything is buried and then nonetheless resurfaces' (DLA).

It is difficult to determine the point at which the third section of the Prose Project outgrew its original narrative confines and was divided into two separate stories. It is likely, however, that an invitation to contribute to the one-hundredth issue of Graz-based literary magazine *Manuskripte*, in which Sebald had previously published critical essays on Austrian literature and early versions of the three long poems forming *After Nature*, played a major role. The theme of the centenary edition was, appropriately, 'Growing Older'. Although the relevant correspondence is no longer extant, the magazine's founder and editor, Alfred Kolleritsch, would have invited Sebald to submit a previously unpublished story in mid-January 1988 for a deadline in mid-May.

Faced with writing a new piece within such a short period of time, Sebald combined elements of a story by Karl Emil Franzos (1848–1904), 'Das Christusbild' ('The Painting of Christ', 1869), with the biography of his former landlord in Wymondham, Dr Philip Rhoades Buckton, and the Naegeli episode.[3] This led to the story now known as 'Dr. Henry Selwyn', which was originally published in *Manuskripte* in June 1988 under the title 'Verzehret das letzte selbst die Erinnerung nicht?' ('And the last remnants memory destroys', now the motto of 'Dr. Henry Selwyn' in *The Emigrants*). It is probable that, no later than at that time, Sebald realized the Prose Project had outgrown itself and split it into two separate collections: *Vertigo* and *The Emigrants*.

Structural Principles and Poetological Permutations

Temporal and geographical coincidences are the Prose Project's 'structural principle' (DLA) and narrative motor. The births of Stendhal and Kafka, the subjects of the first two biographical pieces, were separated by one hundred years – 1783 and 1883, respectively – as were the dates of their respective visits to Lake Garda – 1813 and 1913.[4] And, to complete the triptych, Sebald added 1983 – the year in which the Bereyter character was to die and the remains of Naegeli's body were initially to be recovered from the glacier – and 2013, the year in which the original German text closes (SG 287).

In *Vertigo* as published, the year 1983 has no significance whatever; it is only when one is able to consult Sebald's literary archive that its implications within the framework of his cross-references become clear. These so-called coincidences, which Sebald ranked among the 'most inexplicable things of all' (DLA), may be defined metaphysical epiphanies to which he assigned a degree of importance that is impossible to overstate.[5] Closely associated with this are Sebald's ethics of perception, concisely summarized in *Vertigo* by Major General Ludwig von Koch, a character Sebald took from a 1987 article by Anthony Northey:[6] 'Tiny details imperceptible to us decide everything!' (V 156/SG 171).

Sebald's psychogrammatical experiment (G 50–51) entails the capacity to discern traces of past suffering in objects and lived spaces, and the coincidences and synchronisms in his 'system of "commemorative days"' (DLA) inform his poetics of remembrance. *Vertigo*, for example, highlights a genealogy of catastrophe via repetitions of the number thirteen: 1813, a year out of Napoleon's campaigns to unite Europe under French rule, which, in Sebald's view of history, contributed to the virulent nationalism that, by 1913, had brought us to the brink of World War One. Finally, as the German original of *Vertigo* makes clear, the ineluctable process of destruction continues into the future and culminates in an apocalypse in 2013. In an interview with Dutch literary critic Piet de Moor, Sebald expounded on this bleak worldview: 'Of course, I don't know what 2013 will bring, but whether we shall carry on for that long, either individually or collectively, is uncertain' (SM 350–351).

The Prose Project sheds light on the development of Sebald's intermedial aesthetics. Inspired by the works of Klaus Theweleit (b. 1942), Alexander Kluge (b. 1932), Roland Barthes (1915–1980), John Berger (1926–2017) and Susan Sontag (1933–2004), Sebald had been engaging productively with (photographic) images as a means of artistic expression since the early 1980s and, in the February 1987 Project Description, he was at pains to point out that images were to form an integral part of his texts and not be understood as 'mere illustrations' (DLA). Indeed, *Vertigo*, which grew out of the Prose Project, has rightly been described as a 'text with a view'[7] since, in it, text and image enter into a reciprocal relationship.[8]

Images were to be such a crucial part of the Prose Project that Sebald included two of them in his Project Description: one showing Bereyter's classroom (AW 70/E 47), and another showing William Seelos, the future

4

zig Jahren wieder 'entlassen' wurde. D.h. es war nicht mehr viel übrig
von ihm, nur die Leder- und Metallteile seiner Ausrüstung und der Geld-
beutel mit den 28 Franken aus der Hüttenkasse, von denen gelglaubt worden
war, dass er sie veruntreut habe.

Usw. Usf. Sie können sich denken, dass ein Projekt dieser Art in viele
Richtungen wachsen, ja auswachsen kann. Es wird auch notwendig sein, das
heterogene Material durch motivische Verbindungen, sowie vermittels einer
ganz spezifischen Topographie und über eine System von 'Gedenktagen' immer
wieder aufeinander zu beziehen. Die Logik ist zuletzt die, dass, wenn man
nur genau hinschaut, wirklich alles mit allem verbunden ist, und dass man,
wenn man nur an einem Faden zieht, bald schon eine ganze Decke aufgedröselt
hat.

Von Vorbildern will ich nicht reden. Am liebsten wäre es mir, es würden
sich sowas wie Kalendergeschichten ergeben, an denen ich, oder auch sonst
wer, später nach Belieben fortschreiben kann.

Zuletzt noch zwei Bilder. Das erste zeigt den Lehrer A.B., 21jährig als
Lehramtskandidat in seiner ersten Klasse. Kurz vor der Auswanderung nach
Frankreich. Viele seiner Gewohnheiten und Lehrmethoden waren, wie ich
natürlich jetzt erst sehe, denen des Volksschullehrers Wittgenstein sehr
ähnlich.

Illustration 10 – Application to Deutscher Literaturfonds, excerpt, 1987

Ambros Adelwarth, in Arab costume (AW 137/E 94). Under the latter, as if they were a caption, Sebald closes his Project Description with the words: 'Perhaps such fragments are the best way to convey an impression of the planned project' (DLA). In other words, far from attempting to sweep it under the rug, Sebald proudly highlighted the heterogeneous nature of his material. It is no surprise that the DLF, which could not possibly have known what he would make of it, rejected it.

The Prose Project also demonstrates that Sebald's œuvre did not develop consistently but rather was the result of constant reworking of (auto)biographical material in accordance with Sebald's unique commitment to authenticity. In the aforementioned interview with de Moor, Sebald had this to say about his journey through northern Italy in 1980: 'I wrote an account of that trip in the long story "All'estero", which ended up as a part of a triptych in between the stories about Stendhal and Kafka. That is how the book structured itself' (SM 350). Sebald's turns-of-phrase are telling: 'ended up' and 'structured itself' indicate, at once, an unshakeable faith in contingency and an implicit trust that his material would structure and order itself.

Sebald states as much in the Project Description, with a nod to Johann Peter Hebel (1760–1826): 'I would like to see calendar stories emerge, which could later be expanded upon, by myself, or by anyone so inclined' (DLA). Whilst the emancipation of material from the author is an idea Sebald ultimately dismissed (G 68), the Prose Project was to contain a form of depersonalized narration from a 'bird's-eye perspective' (DLA). As stated in the Project Description, in 1987 he specifically intended to use it to write brief biographies of members of the Seelos family. Having already explored a 'synoptic' technique with impressive results in the final section of *After Nature*, Sebald would go on to fully realize this in the detached, self-reflexive and ironic mode of narration adopted in *Die Ringe des Saturn* (*The Rings of Saturn*) (G 115) and *Austerlitz*.[9]

A Brief Stay in the 'Potting Shed'

When Thatcherism arrived in British universities in the early 1980s, Sebald sought to mitigate the frustrations of his professional life by making creative writing his refuge, one which he repeatedly referred to as a 'potting shed' (EM 61). However, it was not until he conceived the Prose Project in 1986, after unsuccessful attempts at scriptwriting and poetry, that he truly entered his potting shed – and, as he himself stated, his very success ensured that he did not long remain there.[10] Indeed, the Prose Project represents an intermediary phase in Sebald's literary work, coming as it did after decades of poetry and prior to the book-length prose narratives *The Rings of Saturn* and *Austerlitz*.

Nevertheless, the Prose Project reveals the common roots of the two – apparently – diverse collections that came out of it: *Vertigo* and *The Emigrants*. The personal treatment of the related *topoi* of exile, expatriation and self-expatriation in *Vertigo* are elaborated upon in *The Emigrants* in the context of German–Jewish relations (G 93). Geographical and psychological alienation and displacement in fact run through Sebald's body of work from *After Nature* to *The Emigrants*, and are again taken up in *Austerlitz*, whose main character may be viewed as Sebald's unofficial fifth *émigré* (G 119).[11] In any case, as he noted in his day planner (DLA), Sebald completed the final story to have, at one point, inhabited the Prose Project – 'Ambros Adelwarth' – on 7 February 1992, five years after he wrote the Project Description in which it was first outlined.

The DLF's Rejections of Sebald's Funding Applications

We now know that, having thus finished *The Emigrants*, Sebald was less than a year from a literary breakthrough in Germany, and only five years from a meteoric rise internationally. However, this cannot justify regarding the rejection of his 1987 funding application as evidence that his work was not sufficiently appreciated in Germany. Given the heterogeneous nature of his Prose Project, and his Project Description's meandering sentences, colloquial tone and seemingly wilful disregard of formal conventions, the DLF could not have deemed him eligible for financial support at the time.

However, this is far less true of a second application he submitted to the DLF on 7 May 1991. It concerned *The Emigrants* in essentially the form we know it today and, although perhaps too brief, was far more carefully written. Nevertheless, it too was rejected. Might the DLF, in retrospect, now regret this decision? The only indication we have is a brief handwritten note on the form rejection letter from its then-secretary: 'Tut mir leid!' ('Sorry!') (DLA).

Illustration 11 – Detail from rejection letter, Deutscher Literaturfonds, 1991

Notes

1. U Schütte, *W.G. Sebald: Leben und literarisches Werk* (Berlin/Boston: De Gruyter, 2020), p. 48.
2. S Bartsch, W.G. Sebald's ›Prose Project‹: A Glimpse into the Potting Shed, in: U Schütte (ed.), *Über W.G. Sebald: Beiträge zu einem anderen Bild des Autors* (Berlin/Boston: De Gruyter, 2017), pp. 99–134. This essay is deeply indebted to Bartsch's work, which is still the most in-depth exploration of the Prose Project.
3. S Bartsch, Eine Passage nach Amerikum: Die Entstehung von ›Henry Selwyn‹, in: R Felberbaum et al. (eds.), *Nebelflecken und das Unbeobachtete: Neue Forschungsansätze zum Werk W.G. Sebalds* (Würzburg: Königshausen & Neumann, 2022), pp. 31–51.
4. In Stendhal's case the visit to Lake Garda is a Sebaldian invention; Stendhal was in Italy in 1813 – but demonstrably did not then visit Lake Garda.
5. P Whitehead, *Im Abseits: W.G. Sebalds Ästhetik des Marginalen* (Bielefeld: Aisthesis, 2019), pp. 21–78, and E Santner, *On Creaturely Life: Rilke, Benjamin, Sebald* (Chicago: Chicago University Press, 2006), pp. 52–58.
6. A Northey, Kafka in Riva, 1913, in: *Neue Zürcher Zeitung*, 24 April 1987.
7. R Gray, *Ghostwriting: W.G. Sebald's Poetics of History* (London: Bloomsbury, 2017), p. 75.
8. Whitehead, *Im Abseits*, pp. 23–24.
9. On the comical aspects of this narrative strategy, see P Whitehead, ›Schön ist das Leben‹: Witz und Komik im Werk W.G. Sebalds, in: Felberbaum et al. (eds.), *Nebelflecken und das Unbeobachtete*, pp. 215–230.
10. C Bigsby, *Writers in Conversation with Christopher Bigsby*, vol. 2 (Norwich: EAS, 2001), pp. 139–165 (165).
11. D Anderson, *Landscape and Subjectivity in the Work of Patrick Keiller, W.G. Sebald, and Iain Sinclair* (Oxford: Oxford University Press, 2020), p. 165.

CHAPTER II

Auto-/Biography

Christoph Singer

In winter 2021, on the occasion of the twentieth anniversary of W.G. Sebald's death on 14 December, commentators were mostly concerned with the (auto-)biographical dimensions of Sebald's work. Of particular interest were the porous dichotomy between fact and fiction and the ethical dimension of Sebald's transposition and synthesis of real biographies into literary figures. Regardless of one's position in these debates, a recurring denominator of Sebald's writing was expressed with Max Norman of *The New Yorker* as follows: 'If you stand far back enough, though, you could also call Sebald's work biography. [. . .] He was a biographer in the literal sense: a life writer.'[1]

Standing far back allows a broader perspective on the minute details and wide range of literary techniques used by Sebald to (de-)construct biographies. Sebald, who wrote an unpublished autobiographical novel as a student, uses *bricolage*, intermedial montage and (un-)marked quotations to compose a multimodal, periscopic palimpsest of texts and voices. He merges fact and fiction, author- and narrative personas, memory and history, past and present. These biographies firstly, uncover the life-stories of those silenced by historical catastrophe; secondly, they highlight individual and communicative memory as process rather than product; and thirdly, they alert readers to the inexplicable, the forgotten or the repressed.

Sebald's literary landscapes – psycho-geographies of space – are devoid of people. Yet, his writings are filled with the biographies of writers, artists, scholars, explorers and teachers. Alongside persona of historic renown, such as Matthias Grünewald (1478–1528), Georg Wilhelm Steller (1709–1746), Franz Kafka (1883–1924), to name just a few, Sebald transposes the biographies of relatives, friends and acquaintances on to literary figures. These allow him to relate histories "from below". A third group consists of those who are beyond biography, the deindividualized subjects of the industrial and military masses, as illustrated in *Schwindel.*

Gefühle. (*Vertigo*) by the Napoleonic army of '36,000 men [...] an interminable column' (V 3/SG 7), the 'obscure crowds' (AN 98/NN 95) of industrialized Manchester or the 'some sixty thousand people [who] were crammed together' in Theresienstadt (Ae 331/Ag 339).

Additionally, these biographies merge with or mirror the narrative persona and thus partake in the characterization of the auto-fictional narrator. Sebald has a penchant for combining biographical detail and uses literary texts as epiphenomena, thus dissolving the boundaries between life and work, as Ruth Klüger has pointed out.[2] This approach transcends the genre of biography beyond merely chronicling dates and the emplotment of events and rather complicates biographical writing as seen in the 'Paul Bereyter' episode in *Die Ausgewanderten* (*The Emigrants*) where the search for Bereyter's past achieves the opposite: 'such attempts did not bring me closer to Paul' (E 29/AW 45).

Triple Portrait: *After Nature*

Nach der Natur (*After Nature*) introduces some of Sebald's biographical concerns, while differing in two aspects from later literary texts: the debut is a prose poem and, despite extensive ekphrasis, devoid of illustrations. *After Nature*'s three poems focus on one biography each: the medieval artist Matthias Grünewald, the explorer Georg Wilhelm Steller and an evidently autobiographical speaker, appearing to be Sebald himself.

The first poem – 'Wie der Schnee in den Alpen' ('As the Snow on the Alps') – claims that 'little is known of the life of / Matthaeus Grünewald of Aschaffenburg' (AN 9/NN 13) despite employing sources by Joachim von Sandrart (1675), Wilhelm Fraenger as well as Walther Karl Zülch's *Der historische Grünewald* (*The Historical Grünewald*, 1938) and Wolf Lücking's *Mathis: Nachforschungen über Grünewald* (*Mathis: Research on Grünewald*, 1985).

Some sources remain unmarked, requiring careful reading. The narrative persona uses an inquit-formula ('the author knows not', AN 9/NN 13) to introduce a quotation by Sandrart. This quotation, however, is marked by code-switching rather than inverted commas: the antiquated expression 'bey leben' (NN 13) linguistically marks the transition from narrator to Sandrart. The narrator then claims 'that we may trust that report', which is hardly the case, since biography does not preclude poetic licence. Sebald, for example, includes Lücking's hardly substantiated claim that Grünewald was homosexual. Ultimately, Grünewald's biography dissolves his identity when Grünewald is assumed to be identical with the painter Mathis Nithart and both turn into initials: 'M.N.', 'M.G.', 'N.' (AN 18/NN 17).

The second poem 'Und blieb ich am äußersten Meer' ('And if I Remained by the Outermost Sea') follows the German scientist Georg Wilhelm Steller on an expedition to Alaska in 1741. The poem, again, relies on sources from Steller's diary, Adelbert von Chamisso's *Reise um die Welt* (*Journey Around the World*, 1818) and Corey Ford's *Where the Sea Breaks Its Back* (1966). Sebald provides Steller with a biography, but does so by altering some of the sources. When Steller speaks, one hears quotations by Paracelsus (1457–1534).[3]

The final poem 'Die Dunkle Nacht fährt aus' ('Dark Night Sallies Forth') questions the intersections of home, identity and biography by relating memories of the speaker's (grand-)parents and his moving to Manchester in 1966. This poem shows time, space and memory as non-linear. Spaces overlap, such as the panoptic star-shaped Strangeways Prison recalling the walls of Jericho. And whereas the speaker's parents cannot remember the bombing of Nuremberg (1943) and Dresden (1945) he claims to do so, despite having been an embryo at the time of the Nuremberg bombing.

After Nature introduces Sebald's poetic of coincidences, whereby the accidental appears deterministic: Similar initials connect different persons, such as Steller's G.W.S. mirroring Sebald's W.G.S. Similar dates connect events. On 18 May 1525, Grünewald is informed of the Battle of Frankenhausen, while Sebald is born on 18 May 1944. And a single space turns into a biographical nexus across time: in 1525, Grünewald passes through Windsheim where, in 1709, Steller is being born and, in 1943, the autobiographical speaker's mother realizes she is pregnant.

Biographical Mirrors: *Vertigo*

The ambiguous German title of Sebald's next publication *Schwindel. Gefühle.* (*Vertigo*) is programmatic in that it opens up a variety of meanings and possible interpretations in how it refers to the content of the book. *Vertigo* is a travel-narrative with elements of a thriller and consists of four biographies two of which are based on Sebald. 'Biographical cameos' include writers from Dante (1265–1321), Stendhal (1783–1842), Kafka (1883–1924) to Ariosto (1474–1533), Casanova (1725–1798), Werfel (1890–1945) and Sciascia (1921–1989). The narrative voice emerges as a character who obsessively connects coincidences and the biographical lives of others with his own.

Already the first paragraphs combine various media to create a poly-chronic palimpsest. Where *After Nature* ends with an ekphrasis of the Battle of Alexander, *Vertigo* begins with an illustration of Napoleon's army. This illustration by Carle Vernet is taken from the autobiography by Stendhal. His younger self, the seventeen-year-old Marie Henri Beyle, was – as opposed to the other soldiers – 'not lost in nameless oblivion' (V 4/SG 8). Still, Beyle questions his memories: the past either consists of 'grey patches' (V 5 /SG 8–9) or appears too vivid to be true. Sebald follows Stendhal's auto-biography fairly closely, only to suddenly include an invented and impossible encounter with Kafka's dead, fictional Hunter Gracchus. This literary figure marks the line between reality and fiction.

The second episode – 'All'estero' – connects two Sebaldian Italian journeys, including the murder-plot surrounding the so-called 'Organizzazione Ludwig', and further undermines the boundary between reality and fiction. This is illustrated by the inclusion of a copy of an identity-card, issued by the German Consulate in 1984 (SG 114/V 114). The photo simultaneously verifies and undermines the identification of author, narrative persona and the related events. A black bar dissects the head-shot and renders the authorial position as fragile as will the photos of a hardly recognizable Sebald dwarfed by a Lebanese Cedar in *The Rings of Saturn* (RSg 313/RSe 263) or Sebald's blurry yet discernible reflection in a shop-window in *Austerlitz* (Ag 284/Ae 216).

Kafka returns in the third episode entitled 'Dr. K's Badreise nach Riva' ('Dr. K. Takes the Waters at Riva'), an interpretation of Kafka's travel-diary which is echoed by Sebald's own travel-narrative. The alignment of Kafka and the narrator is symbolically presented in a scene set in an Italian urinal. The narrator wonders whether the urinal's mirror could have reflected Kafka in the past. The final narrative 'Il ritorno in patria' continues the theme of mirroring biographies. The narrator returns to his birthplace Wertach, referred to only as W., where he observes the river at night – recalling K., the protagonist from Kafka's *Process* (*The Trial*). Ultimately, however, *Vertigo*'s pervasive melancholia highlights the impossibility of returning to a home and to one's biographical past.

Damaged Biographies: *The Emigrants*

The publication of *Die Ausgewanderten* (*The Emigrants*) in 1992 marks a turning point. Sebald's sudden international prominence generated inter-est in the author's biography and those of his characters. *The Emigrants* was perceived, Uwe Schütte argues, as an 'empathic reconstruction of damaged biographies.'[4] The biographical details of writers such as Vladimir Nabokov (1899–1977) or Jean Améry (1912–1978) are now used in the service of four emigrants' biographies. These – Dr. Henry Selwyn, Paul Bereyter, Ambros Adelwarth and Max Ferber – are based on but not identical with models taken from Sebald's group of family-members, friends and acquaintances.

The book's first protagonist, Dr. Henry Selwyn, is modelled after Sebald's landlord Philip Rhoades Buckton, but simultaneously imbued with characteristics of Nabokov. The setting, such as the decaying tennis court, the housemaid, or Buckton's pastime of lying in the grass are taken from life. Buckton, however, was not Jewish, as claimed by Sebald. To infer as much from Sebald's biographical transposition would mean to misread the biographical project of *The Emigrants* which is set against simplistic forms of categorization. *The Emigrants* is about biographies of exile in general, rather than Jewish-German biographies in particular: Adelwarth's heritage is not Jewish and only Bereyter's grandfather was so; and Dr. Selwyn is not from Germany.

The second episode about the pedagogically passionate and politically disillusioned Paul Bereyter is – alongside references to Jean Améry and Ludwig Wittgenstein (1889–1951) – based on Sebald's third-grade teacher Armin Müller from Sonthofen. His suicide in 1983 sets off a cascade of memories and an attempt to re-constitute fragments, voices and sources into a biography. The Ambros Adelwarth narrative depicts a relative of Sebald and equally employs a form of periscopic narration by combining testimonials of relatives who also emigrated. While the narrator's aunts, Theres and Fini, and his uncle Kasimir are based on reality, their names are changed. Sebald's mother Rosa, who remained in Germany, is the only one to retain her real name, as if to stress that emigration leads to a loss of identity.

The final episode takes Sebald's biographical work one step further and foreshadows *Austerlitz*. 'Max Ferber' synthesizes two models: the artist Frank Auerbach (b. 1931), who left Berlin for London on a Kin- dertransport; and the architect Peter Jordan (1923–2020) who in 1939 fled Munich for Manchester.

Sebald's intra-textual plots maybe inevitably inspired an extra-textual search for the biographical sources, which similar to Carole Angier's contested biography of Sebald himself has been framed as detective-work.[5] Some of Sebald's models and their relatives find themselves identi-fied and interviewed. Buckton's relatives, for instance, express dismay about their relative's detailed biographical transposition without their consent. Frank Auerbach, whose fictional name Max Aurach bears the closest resemblance of a character to model, was equally angered. And while Auerbach is a public persona, Sebald's lengthy excerpts from a diary of Peter Jordan's aunt used in the Luisa Lanzberg's section, raise questions concerning the ethics of transposing lives into literature and the importance of consent.

Biographical Bricolage: *The Rings of Saturn*

Sebald's *Die Ringe des Saturn* (*The Rings of Saturn*) provides an autobiographical frame-narrative which connects biographies and historical observations. Yet a realist or truthful representation of (auto-)biographical detail is not intended. While this secular 'English Pilgrimage' along the coastal towns of Suffolk did happen, it actually did consist of a series of separate walks rather than one journey. The narrator's stay at the hospital in Norwich, however, is factual. *The Rings of Saturn* may be considered a biographical bricolage including biographies of Thomas Browne (1605–1682), Algernon Charles Swinburne (1837–1909), Edward FitzGerald (1809–1883), the Vicomte Chateaubriand (1768–1848), Roger Casement (1864–1916), Joseph Conrad (1857–1924) or the Chinese Emperor Hsien-feng (1831–1861). The book also features one of the few female biographical figures in Sebald's œuvre, the Chinese Empress Tz'u-hsi (1835–1908).

These historical figures appear alongside Sebald's friends and colleagues such as Michael Hamburger (1924–2007), Michael Parkinson (1945–1994), Janine Rosalind Dakyns (1939–1994) or a biographical account of Sebald's neighbour Frederick Farrar (1906–1994). This "mini-biography" alludes in particular to John Aubrey's collection of biographies, the *Brief Lives* from the late seventeenth century. Sebald's "brief lives" are equally short as exemplified in a biographical vignette in chapter nine. This biographical account of an aristocratic visitor to the home of Reverend Ives identifies the visitor only towards the end: François-René de Chateaubriand (1768–1848). The decidedly short fragment is implicitly contrasted with its source-material, Chateaubriand's biography *Mémoires d'Outre-Tombe* (1848) which prior to publication consisted of a staggering forty-two volumes.

Yet the brevity of Sebald's biographies does not equal superficiality. The brevity is counteracted by aligning separate biographies into a biographical network. By means of specific details, repetition, coincidences and parallelism, such as similar spaces (e.g. Manchester) or dates (e.g., 14 April), these biographies are connected: 14 April is wrongly given as the date of the liberation of Bergen-Belsen, which actually happened one day later. The date, however, gains significance considering this is the death-date of Sebald's beloved grandfather (see chapter 2 in this volume). Additionally, this date marks the illustration of a signature, supposedly by Roger Casement.

(Semi-)Fictional Biography: *Austerlitz*

Sebald's final prose work, the novel *Austerlitz*, can be understood either as a repetition of motifs, symbols and techniques or as their being brought to perfection. Regardless of the question as to what Sebald would have achieved had he lived on, *Austerlitz* repeats and combines various literary features. As Lynn Wolff argues, 'the multiplicity of genres – biography, autobiography, travelogue, even crime story (detective story) – is a defining aspect of Sebald's prose. Nevertheless, one could argue that *Austerlitz* is first and foremost a biography, albeit fictional'.[6]

The anonymous narrator turns into a listener to Jacques Austerlitz. With every encounter Austerlitz's biography evolves, the biographical project that cannot be completed, as highlighted by the book's open ending. *Austerlitz* is more concerned with the process of writing an (auto-)biography than the resulting product. The public, however, was more interested in the "story" than in the "discourse", and a search for the "real" Austerlitz ensued. In an interview with *Der Spiegel*, Sebald claims that Austerlitz was the combination of two-and-a-half life stories, including a colleague who taught in London (G 196–197). While the scholar has never been identified, the photo of Austerlitz's office (Ae 43/ Ag 51) was confirmed to be that of a colleague at UEA. And while biographical elements of the poet Franz Wurm (1926–2010) and Saul Friedländer (b. 1932) are discernible, the childhood photo of Austerlitz on the cover was lifted from a random postcard which adds an ironic dimension to Austerlitz's statement that 'pictures had a memory of their own' (Ae 258/Ag 266).

The central model for Jacques Austerlitz was Susi Bechhöfer (1936–2018). In 1939, she and her twin-sister Lotte left Munich on a Kindertransport. In 1991, Bechhöfer related her past in a TV programme on Channel 4, which Sebald saw. And in 1996, Bechhöfer published a book called *Rosa's Child*.[7] When Bechhöfer's German editor alerts her to the similarities found in *Austerlitz*, she expresses her frustration with this biographical transposition in an article in *The Sunday Times* (2002) entitled 'Stripped of My Tragic Past by a Bestselling Author'. Simultaneously, Sebald's hagiographic machine largely neglects this aspect, despite Martin Modlinger showing that the similarities are not coincidental.[8] Bechhöfer's correspondence with Sebald was cut short by the author's death. And her wish to see her life acknowledged as an inspiration for Austerlitz's life-story remained unfulfilled.

Conclusion

Sebald's (auto-)biographies must not be misunderstood as post-modern language games. Rather they evoke a sense of reality without naturalistic modes of storytelling. For Sebald, the forgotten, the coincidental and the repressed are not detrimental to biographical storytelling but essential to it. Characters like Ferber, Beyle or Casement may result from painstaking research. Yet Sebald is less interested in these as documents but in their being metonymical representations of experiences untold or forgotten. These biographies are intended to make history, in Sebald's own words, 'empathically accessible'.[9] Empathy, however, must not be mistaken for sentimentalism. Sebald's form of *bricolage* and 'non-mimetic biography'[10] may be complex, but it is also transparent in its layering of voices, temporalities, written and visual documents.

Critics have been reminded of Brecht's form of 'epic theatre' which similarly espouses sentimentalism and invites audiences to be critical readers.[11] The resulting distance between narrative voice, reader and protagonists is an ethical concern of Sebald. With Susan Sontag one may ask: 'Is the narrator Sebald? Or a fictional character to whom the author has lent his name, and selected elements of his biography?'[12] In Sebald's words one can identify his work as 'pseudo-biographical' (EM 168). For one, it precludes the danger of speaking for other people. Secondly, it counters inappropriate sentimentalism. Thirdly, Sebald highlights the complicated production of biographical narratives as an ongoing process rather than finite product.

Notes

1. M Norman, W.G. Sebald, The Trickster, in: *The New Yorker*, 20 November 2021.
2. R Klüger, Wanderer zwischen falschen Leben, in: *Text + Kritik* 158 (2003), pp. 95–102.
3. T Hoorn, Auch eine Dialektik der Aufklärung: Wie W.G. Sebald Georg Wilhelm Steller zwischen Kabbala und magischer Medizin verortet, in: *Zeitschrift für Germanistik* 19:1 (2009), pp. 108–120.

4. U Schütte, *W.G. Sebald: Leben und literarisches Werk* (Berlin/Boston: De Gruyter, 2020), p. 171.

5. E Shaffer, W.G. Sebald's Photographic Narrative, in: R Görner (ed.), *The Anatomist of Melancholy: Essays in Memory of W.G. Sebald* (Munich: Iudicium, 2003), pp. 51–62 (57).

6. L Wolff, Literary Historiography: W.G. Sebald's Fiction, in: G Fischer (ed.), *W.G. Sebald: Schreiben ex patria / Expatriate Writing* (Amsterdam/New York: Rodopi, 2009), pp. 317–330 (329).

7. J Josephs, S Bechhöfer, *Rosa's Child: One Woman's Search for her Past* (London: Tauris, 1999).

8. M Modlinger, ›You can't change names and feel the same‹: The Kindertransport Experience of Susi Bechhöfer in W.G. Sebalds ›Austerlitz‹, in: A Hammel, B. Lewkowicz (eds.), *The Kindertransport to Britain 1938/39: New Perspectives* (Amsterdam: Rodopi, 2012), pp. 219–232.

9. S Löffler, Wildes Denken: Gespräch mit W.G. Sebald, in: F Loquai (ed.), *W.G. Sebald* (Eggingen: Ed. Isele, 1997), pp. 135–137 (137).

10. A Fuchs, *Schmerzensspuren der Geschichte: Zur Poetik der Erinnerung in W.G. Sebalds Prosa* (Vienna: Böhlau, 2004), p. 122.

11. L Wolff, *W.G. Sebald's Hybrid Poetics: Literature as Historiography* (Berlin/Boston: De Gruyter, 2014), p. 70.

12. S Sontag, Mourning Sickness, in: *Times Literary Supplement*, 25 February 2000.

CHAPTER 12

Natural History and the Anthropocene

Bernhard Malkmus

In an interview shortly before his death in December 2001, Sebald rumin-ates on the multiple concentric circles with which history envelops our biographies, concluding that, ultimately, our lives are circumscribed by 'natural history' and 'the history of the human species' (G 259–260). One of the enduring intellectual appeals of his work twenty years after his untimely death is related to the rigour with which he renders ecological degradation as a literary theme. He pre-empts Amitav Ghosh's critique of the western novelistic tradition for having succumbed to a 'probabilistic' world view that subjects every aspect of life – our biosphere as much as the stirrings of our souls – to a shopkeeper's cost-benefit analysis.[1]

This probabilism of incremental individual self-advancement and techno-logical progress blinkers our perception of the world and hampers our ability to comprehend the magnitude of the ecological crisis. Sebald's work is a reaction to this failure of Western imagination Ghosh critiques – and an attempt to reframe inherited social imaginaries with socio-ecological ones that acknowledge human embeddedness in natural environments. This is most evident in a recurring reference that permeates his œuvre: the concept of *Naturgeschichte* (natural history). Yet, natural history is not simply an added layer of environmental awareness that Sebald weaves into his geneal-ogy of modernity. It is rather a bundle of different threads connected to different conceptual sources; they do not always mix very well and partially obscure his avowed political ecology.

Broadly speaking, he uses the term 'natural history' in seven ways: a) in the historical sense of the term; b) as a synonym for the history of life (evolution); c) as a synonym for the history of matter (entropy); d) as a reference to Walter Benjamin and Theodor W. Adorno's philosophy of history; e) as an integral part of his engagement with the 'natural history of destruction' of modern warfare; f) as a reflection on 'creaturely life', as defined by Eric Santner; and g) an alias for the death-drive in human history.

By merging all of the above layers of meaning into his natural history framework, Sebald forges a powerful analytical tool in thinking about the past through the prism of the present – and at the present through the prism of the future perfect. However, it also exposes his narratives to the risk of mythologizing destruction and transience as historical agencies (an aesthetic and ethical flaw he, incidentally, chastised in his book on Alfred Döblin).

Historia naturalis, Evolution, Entropy

In its most basic sense, "natural history" is derived from the Latin *historia naturalis*, which refers to the study of the natural world in the broadest sense. Contrary to what the term seems to imply, "natural history" is related to an ahistorical concept of nature that only morphed into the "history of life" in the course of the nineteenth century.[2] The term today survives in three partly related meanings: first, as a synonym for evolution; second, as a historical term denoting the taxonomical approach to nature in the Enlightenment as well as the convention of combining empirical observations with cultural histories in early modern times; and, third, as a reference to the amateur scientist's approach to the natural world, which is guided primarily by an interest in the form and structure of organisms and has recently undergone a reappraisal as "citizen science".

Points two and three are obliquely present throughout Sebald's work: as an appreciation of nature that he shares with naturalist-collectors and as premodern cultural practices. For Sebald, these practices form a bridge to the early modern coexistence of empiricism and metaphysics he sees embodied in figures such as Paracelsus (1493–1541) and Thomas Browne (1605–1682) or, indeed, in a central work for Renaissance scholarship: Lucretius' *De rerum natura*.

Evolutionary history is generally imagined as devoid of telos and orientation in Sebald. Balance is absent in nature, the speaker of *Nach der Natur* (*After Nature*) declares, 'which blindly makes one experiment after another / and like a senseless botcher / undoes the thing it has only just achieved' (AN 27/NN 24). The convulsions of the suffering bodies in Matthias Grünewald's Isenheim Altarpiece manifest an indiscriminate evolutionary force that works its machinations 'inside us also and through us and through / the machines sprung from our heads' (AN 27/NN 24). This is a reductionist version of the evolutionary theories as proposed for example in the concept of non-teleological complexity in Stephen Jay Gould or in the adaptionism popularized by Richard Dawkins.

Sebald equates individual development of life-forms, marked by mortality, with the collective development of a species – an operation unmoored from a systems-biological understanding of life. He does not acknowledge the life-engendering and life-preserving dimensions of this blind 'experiment': from the perspective of biology, however, the genetic code's subjection to the workings of a 'senseless botcher' (mutation and adaptive selection) is precisely what ensures the survival of life. Life is defined by its ability to resist, through the genetic code, the entropy inherent in matter. Death plays a crucial part in this ability.

The history of life is in fact a history of 'dissipative structures' (Ilya Prigogine) – that is, of co-evolving organisms weaving the web of life and thus shielding the latter from entropy.[3] From this perspective, the equation of biological death and entropy in Sebald's pessimistic view of history marked by 'the gradual dissolution of life' (RSe 160/RSg 193) lacks scientific foundation. Sebald short-circuits this reductive understanding of life with Pierre Bertaux's (1907–1986) reflections on biological manipulation and nascent AI,[4] the theory of aberrant evolutionism in Stanisław Lem (1921–2006),[5] the progressive homogeneity in Jorge Luis Borges' (1899–1986) world of Tlön and the pessimism of Thomas Bernhard's (1931–1989) Gnostic world view.

Yet, on an important level Sebald's radical coalescence of all historical dimensions in one cosmic history of disintegration is clairvoyant. His eclecticism enables him to envision something that has only recently been conceptualized within earth-systems sciences: the anthropogenic technosphere is following its own independent development and, in so doing, instils a rapidly accelerating entropic agency into the biosphere.[6] Maybe Homo sapiens is indeed unravelling the macrosystemic stability that has allowed life to flourish on earth; maybe we humans are the Trojan horse of entropy in the midst of the web of life. Sebald's "natural histories" break free of the strictures of our Holocene imagination and engage with the human condition in the Anthropocene.

Naturgeschichte in Critical Theory

One of the central frames of reference for Sebald is the concept of *Naturgeschichte* in Benjamin and Adorno.[7] The term played a major role in Benjamin's study *Ursprung des deutschen Trauerspiels* (*The Origin of German Tragic Drama*, 1928), which was the focus of a lecture series Adorno gave in 1931. Their correspondence on the concept and its ramifications forms the basis of Adorno's lecture 'Die Idee der Naturgeschichte'

('The Idea of Natural History', 1932), central arguments of which recur in Adorno's *Negative Dialektik* (*Negative Dialectics*, 1966).[8]

Benjamin endorses the power of allegory to render history as 'petrified, primal landscape' and thus represent it as a history of suffering.[9] Allegory, he claims, has the potential to make us see how human artefacts 'acquire an aspect of mute, natural being at the point when they begin to lose their place in a viable form of life'.[10] It is this dissociation from the historical constellations they denote that Benjamin refers to with his idiosyncratic use of the term *Naturgeschichte*.

He thus ascribes a dual uncanniness to our experience of history. We often encounter historical remnants without being able to endow them with meaning or, vice versa, find ourselves enmeshed in inherited modes of signification without being aware of their original genesis: 'Natural history transpires against the background of this space between real and symbolic death, this space of the "undead".'[11] The experience of undeadness marks the moment when – as Benjamin sees it – an epistemic formation sinks back into an overarching natural history.

Adorno is interested in this radical revision of the idealistic dichotomy of nature versus history, which he then develops further, with Max Horkheimer, in *Dialektik der Aufklärung* (*Dialectics of the Enlightenment*, 1944). They emphasize that an increasing domination of nature inadvertently leads to an increasing entanglement in the vicissitudes of nature. Sebald integrates this aspect of Critical Theory into his narrative meditations on history and the human condition, in particular in *After Nature, Die Ringe des Saturn* (*The Rings of Saturn*) and the abandoned Corsica Project.

However, he often does so without employing the dialectical method of Critical Theory, with which he shares an interest in the spectral nature of capitalism and imperialism. The ruins the narrator of *The Rings of Saturn* encounters during his journeys are commodities of high capitalism, bereft of their original symbolic nexus and thus, in Benjamin's sense, prone to falling back into natural history. This links back to the mythic violence inherent in the commodified object: its modes of production, commodification and consumption perpetually unravel all social relations.

The undeadness of what the narrator encounters in the British landscape results from the uncanny perpetuation of capitalist epistemes while the architecture representative of these epistemes is disintegrating. The narrator views this ruinscape as a premonition of our civilization's demise; he walks in the past as much as in the future perfect: 'the closer I came to these ruins, [...] the more I imagined myself amidst the remains of our own civilization after its extinction in some future catastrophe' (RSe 237/RSg 282).

The Creaturely and the Inorganic

Eric Santner has inserted Sebald in a predominantly German-Jewish tradition of reflecting on creaturely life as 'the peculiar proximity of the human to the animal at the very point of their radical difference' (see chapter 30 in this volume).[12] This tradition, associated with names such as Franz Rosenzweig (1886–1929) and Martin Buber (1878–1965), also influenced Benjamin. It emphasizes solidarity as a form of testifying to the other's creaturely expressivity. Practising neighbourly love becomes an ambivalent act of bearing witness to that expressivity: for the one who witnesses, it is an experience of alterity; for the one being witnessed, it is an experience of self-estrangement.

This tradition formulates an ethics based on the mutual recognition of creatureliness as our being subjected to political and social power that can be described as traumatic. Humans appear more creaturely than non-human creatures, since they have to compensate for their indeterminate nature by an excess of signification in the political sphere. This excess leads to a contradictory overdetermination of humans, which makes them prone to regressing into "natural history", resulting in the undeadness referred to above (and epitomized by many characters in Kafka). Human sexuality, Santner adds with reference to Freud and Lacan, is also marked by such an excess, provoked by the experience of absence, lack and self-estrangement in the other – and of our 'traumatic [...] overproximity to the mysterious desire of the other'.[13] Attending to this 'desire' – the other being subjected to his or her enigmas – is an ethical act; but it is also tied up with the intrinsically human ability to feel pleasure in pain and become addicted to it.

What, then, does it mean to be exposed to the world 'under the dual impact of historical violence and the structural dislocations generated by capitalist modernity'?[14] In Sebald, the answer is ambivalent: The ethos of bearing witness is, of course, an attempt to restore dignity to the victims of history; but it is also marked by an enjoyment beyond the pleasure principle that furnishes a private mythology with traumata of others. The narrator of *The Rings of Saturn*, for example, is enamoured with the ruinscape of capitalism he traverses. As much as he feels depressed by it, he is also drawn to it; he brilliantly analyses it but also succumbs to the morbid fascination with the psychopathology of capitalism – the suppression of the human consciousness of mortality through the compulsion to produce, consume and accumulate. The fear of death is overcompensated in the violence inherent in geographical and economic expansion.

The Rings of Saturn sketches a realm of death inhabited by undead life; it also monitors the narrator's obsession with the death-prone remnants of high capitalism and his own enjoyment in subsuming their emerging *Naturgeschichte* in a cosmology of decline. In so doing, he also reveals an affinity to the concept of the 'death-drive' that Freud formulated in the wake of World War One in *Jenseits des Lustprinzips* (*Beyond the Pleasure Principle*, 1920). Its most concrete manifestation can be found in the yearning for the inorganic that marks the three protagonists in *After Nature*: all of them feel the pull of landscapes shaped by ice and snow.

The Anthropocene

Sebald's narrative use of natural history unites different elements: the tension between the idea of a universal history of decline and his eclectic array of natural histories 'breaks out of the novel form that owes its allegiance to bourgeois concepts' (CSe 89/CSg 88). In so doing, it suspends the grip probabilism and individualism have had on the social imaginaries in the Western tradition, as Ghosh has noted. The simultaneity of these non-simultaneous natural histories pries open our impoverished sense of time, reinstates narrative art as a mode of embracing our embeddedness in wider socio-ecological imaginaries beyond progress and growth.

Sebald's narrator intuits the moribund nature of our culture in the future perfect, which is, according to the geologist Jan Zalasiewicz, the tense in which our age of human geological agency beckons to be narrated: we are projecting ourselves into the position of future archaeologists reading the fossil record of our present culture.[15] In fact, Sebald's natural history of human civilization can be mapped onto the various time frames that are discussed for the Anthropocene: the idea that anthropogenic changes to Earth systems start as early as human adaptation to sedentary agricultural lifestyles (the 'early Anthropocene' theory) sets the tone of 'The Alps in the Sea' from the Corsica Project.

The connection between early modern colonialism and its detrimental impact on the biosphere is frequently spelt out in *The Rings of Saturn* – a connection that can be related to the more recent 'Orbis spike' theory, that relates the beginning of the Anthropocene to 'ecological imperialism'.[16] *Schwindel. Gefühle.* (*Vertigo*) spells this out in the context of modern warfare and inner-European imperialism in the wake of the French Revolution, whereas *The Rings of Saturn* can be read as a compelling aesthetic engagement with the radical transformations germane to any history of the Anthropocene, the Industrial Revolution. Here we read about mechanical revolutions in which humans are 'strapped to looms [. . .] reminiscent of instruments of torture or cages' (RSe 282/RSg 334), the nascent fossil-fuel age, in which combustion forms 'the hidden principle behind every artefact we create' (RSe 170/RSg 202) and an accelerated globalization, for which silk production forms the central allegory.

Most importantly, however, Sebald also engages with the legacy of the Great Acceleration – that is, the explosion of industrial production and consumerism 1945–1975, which many scholars now regard as the decisive Anthropocene moment. While the Corsica Project opens up the deep history of deforestation and *The Rings of Saturn* presents dialectical images, in Benjamin's sense, for the self-destruction of industrial capitalism, they point at something that is spelt out in the third part of *After Nature*, the utter moral confusion of the human becoming a destructive force. If we extend these dynamics into the future, we understand the central Anthropocene momentum: The technosphere will have ushered in a new dimension of entropy that life will have to resist. This perspective is best encapsulated in this passage – an eagle's-eye view on the technosphere, which is in fact a technoscopic one from an aeroplane:

> No matter whether one is flying over Newfoundland or the sea of lights that stretches from Boston to Philadelphia after nightfall, over the Arabian deserts which gleam like mother-of-pearl, over the Ruhr or the city of Frankfurt, it is as though there were no people, only the things they have made in which they are hiding. (RSe 91/RSg 113)

Little has happened since Sebald died that would give us licence to dismiss his view as paranoid. In fact, there is an unsettling and thought-provoking Anthropocene realism to his luminescent prose:

> In Brazil, to this very day, whole provinces die down like fires when the land is exhausted by overcropping and new areas to the west are opened up. In North America, too, countless settlements of various kinds, complete with gas stations, motels and shopping malls, move west along the turnpikes, and along that axis affluence and squalor are unfailingly polarized. (RSe 159/RSg 191)

Notes

1. A Ghosh, *The Great Derangement: Climate Change and the Unthinkable* (Chicago: University of Chicago Press, 2016), pp. 16–17.

2. W Lepenies, *Das Ende der Naturgeschichte* (Munich: Hanser, 1976).

3. I Prigogine, *The End of Certainty: Time, Chaos, and the New Laws of Nature* (New York: Free Press, 1997), pp. 9–56.

4. U Schütte, Europäische Peripherien: Sebald, Tübingen, Bertaux, in: *Weimarer Beiträge* 2 (2022), pp. 300–311.

5. U Schütte, Negative Evolution. Zur Rezeption von Stanisław Lem bei W.G. Sebald, in: *Prace Literaturoznawcze* 10 (2022), pp. 23–48.

6. PK Haff, Technology as a Geological Phenomenon: Implications for Human Well-Being, in: *Geological Society of London* 395 (2014), pp. 301–309.

7. B Malkmus, Das Naturtheater des W.G. Sebald: Die ökologischen Aporien eines ›poeta doctus‹, in: *Gegenwartsliteratur* 10 (2011), pp. 210–233.

8. Adorno, Die Idee der Naturgeschichte, in: *Gesammelte Schriften*, vol. 1 (Frankfurt: Suhrkamp, 1973), pp. 345–365.

9. Benjamin, *Origin of the German Trauerspiel* (Cambridge, MA: Harvard University Press, 2019), p. 174.

10. E Santner, *On Creaturely Life: Rilke, Benjamin, Sebald* (Chicago: University of Chicago Press, 2006), p. 16.

11. Ibid., p. 17.

12. Ibid., p. 12.

13. Ibid., p. 31.

14. Ibid., p. 49.

15. J Zalasiewicz, *The Earth After Us: What Legacy Will Humans Leave in the Rocks?* (Oxford: Oxford University Press 2009), pp. 1–6. For a philosophy of time in the Anthropocene cf. D Chakrabarty, *The Climate of History in a Planetary Age* (Chicago: University of Chicago Press, 2021).

16. S Lewis, M Maslin, *The Human Planet: How We Created the Anthropocene* (London: Penguin, 2018), chapter 5.

CHAPTER 13

The Corsica Project

Lisa Kunze

Sebald published four of his major works during a seven-year period between 1988 and 1995. Then, more than half a decade elapsed between the publication of *Die Ringe des Saturn* (*The Rings of Saturn*) in October 1995 and *Austerlitz* in February 2001. He travelled on exploratory research trips to Corsica in September 1995, soon after the publication of *The Rings of Saturn*, and again in 1996. Yet, later that December, he declared that his plans for the Corsica Project had come to nothing.

From the outside, it seemed his intensive production of prose works had stalled during this interim period from 1995 to 2001.[1] In fact, Sebald was absorbed with various activities: he cooperated closely with Michael Hulse on the English translations of his books; he worked on an essay collection of Alemannic literature authors, published in September 1998 as *Logis in einem Landhaus* (*A Place in the Country*); he also compiled the poetry lectures, delivered in Zurich in winter 1997, culminating in his book *Luftkrieg und Literatur* (*On the Natural History of Destruction*). Nonetheless, the main literary text of this phase was the Corsica Project, a fragmentary work preserved in two versions under the working title of *Aufzeichnungen aus Korsika: Zur Natur- & Menschenkunde* (*Notes from Corsica: On its Natural History & Anthropology*).

Sebald published two extracts from this project: 'Kleine Exkursion nach Ajaccio' ('A Little Excursion to Ajaccio') and 'Die Alpen im Meer' ('The Alps in the Sea'). They were both reprinted later in *Campo Santo* together with an unpublished section from the manuscript, 'Campo Santo'. The complete manuscript portfolio was published in the catalogue *Wandernde Schatten* (*Wandering Shadows*), which was issued to mark the Sebald exhibition at the German Literature Archive (Deutsches Literaturarchiv), Marbach, in autumn 2008.

The two versions of the Corsica Project differ markedly: the first version is largely a diary format; the second, longer text is in the form of a travelogue like *The Rings of Saturn*. The second version introduces new characters, scenes are added or deleted and motifs are developed that link with Sebald's other works. There are also more abundant intertextual references, which align the second version more closely with Sebald's published literary output. However, both versions have the same underlying concept – and this concept is not only fundamental for the Corsica Project but for the entire creative period after 1995: namely, the concept of a 'natural history of destruction'.

Under the Omen of the 'Natural History of Destruction'

Sebald's pessimistic concept derives from two forms of aggression: on the one hand, the auto-aggression of nature; and on the other hand, human aggression directed against nature. At the forefront of the Corsica Project is the aggression of the island's inhabitants – yet its origin lies in nature itself.

Sebald takes his starting point and basic premise from the Corsicans, who live in constant fear of death, their 'thinking pervaded through & through by the fear of death' (KP 141). The rationale for this fear is firstly that, on Corsica, the landscape is steeped in the reality of nature's formidable force. The narrator becomes personally aware of this on his repeated hiking excursions across the island: it is the 'fear of abandonment in the world' and the 'suspicion that one cannot do the slightest thing against the unknown quality of nature' (KP 141). There is no need here for any unprecedented event or natural disaster to be able to talk about the 'mighty force of nature':

> During each of the excursions, [. . .] despite the truly astonishing beauty of the vistas, which were laid out before me, I felt a dull discomfort in my heart, gradually deadening the senses, a kind of feeling of being lost in the world that, as I believe, originates from the mighty force of nature reflected everywhere around me, and increasingly leaving me in a speechless state. (KP 191)

It is such an awesome sight to behold the natural beauty of the landscape that the narrator feels oppressed by an overwhelming force that is stultifying for his senses and deprives him of the capacity for words. How are the native Corsicans to fare, who spend their lives here? The fact of Corsica's island existence only adds to the inhabitants' feelings of negativity, since they are at the mercy of nature and 'as good as condemned to life-long captivity' (KP 141). The narrator attributes the behaviour of the Corsicans to

Illustration 12 – Corsica, photographed by Sebald, c. 1996

their much-lauded desire for freedom, the blind fury with which they
defend their property and honour against the tiniest encroachment – is
this not an unhealthy reaction to the fear that they could be driven from
their beleaguered position, by a neighbour or by their eternal enemy, nature
itself. (KP 142)

The destructive customs of the local people are based on the ferocity of
nature that they are faced with day after day, so somehow holding up
a mirror image to them. Since they know nothing else than always living
with the fear of death, the Corsicans, according to the narrator, vent their
feelings of aggression in hunting, vendettas, deforestation and pyromania.

Self-Destructive Reflexes

Sebald devotes meticulous attention to the hunting traditions in 'The Alps
in the Sea' and in the second version of *Notes From Corsica*. His method is
mainly to refer to works by other writers: a Corsican travelogue of 1852 by
Ferdinand Gregorovius (1821–1891) and 'La Legende de Saint Julien
l'Hospitalier' ('The Legend of Saint Julian the Hospitalier', 1877) by
Gustave Flaubert (1821–1880).

Gregorovius' text clearly demonstrates that man's destructive rage during the past century led to damage on an irreversible scale. Even in the mid-nineteenth century, it was clear 'that the island struck him as a paradise garden [. . .] particularly because of the small size of its fauna species' (CSe 40/CSg 43). It was still possible to come across animals that even then were relatively rare, for instance, the Tyrrhenian red deer, 'an animal of dwarfish stature with a head much too large for the rest of its body', whose physiognomy is already engrained with the dread of its impending fate in its 'eyes wide with fear in constant expectation of death' (CSe 40/CSg 43).

Gregorovius met this deer several times. Yet, for the narrator of the Corsica Project such encounters are only fantastic tales from distant times. In the meantime, the red deer has also vanished from Corsican forests – in other words, it has not simply died out but like everything else, 'the game that once lived in such abundance in the forests of the island has been eradicated almost without trace today' (CSe 40/CSg 43). Besides, the deer were also hunted down and killed by humans.

Although hardly any wild game is found and the hunters generally return empty-handed, the fever of the chase breaks out on Corsica every year. The narrator exposes this "fever" as a kind of disease, which is neither mitigated by statistics of the decline in the wild game population, nor by the experiences of past unsuccessful hunting expeditions: 'During my excursions into the interior of the island, I repeatedly felt as if the entire male population were participating in a ritual of destruction, which became pointless long ago' (CSe 40–41/CSg 43). The narrator shows that this behaviour is an urge for destruction that humans are naturally born with, which is why rational arguments have no calming influence.

The narrator finds affirmation of this thought in Flaubert's 'Legend of Saint Julian'. Here, the aimlessness of the destructive urge is carried too far as, in the course of one day, Julian shoots down every animal that he sees. The narrator again accentuates the animalistic urge: 'As soon as he has learned the art of the chase from his father, the urge comes over him to go out into the wilderness'(CSe 44–45/CSg 47). The urge *possesses* him – it is not rational action, but rather a far deeper instinct that he is created with. So, for as long as the slaughter lasts, Julian is in a kind of state of frenzy, in which he conceives not one thought but carries out merely what his nature compels him to. When not a single creature stirs around him anymore, he only looks 'at the vast extent of the slaughter and wondering how he can have done it' (CSe 45/CSg 47). It seems as if it wasn't his doing, but the compulsive urge that overcame him.

Finally, the narrator shows that each person is naturally born with this destructive urge. He gives an example of his own action after he stumbles across a column of processionary caterpillars:

> After I had observed these peculiar creatures for a while, probably out of one of the destructive urges that most of us carry in our hearts from early childhood, I pulled one of the caterpillars out of the procession, which only resulted in its remaining lying as though lifeless, evidently incapable of returning to its place, which was hardly any distance from its current position. The caterpillar, which was removed from the column, was not only frozen – the entire procession did not stir, making no efforts to close the gap created by my aggressive intervention, but simply stopping in its tracks. (KP 195)

This makes it especially obvious that the natural world has an inherent, all-pervasive tendency towards self-destruction because it is simultaneously unleashed from two sides. On the one hand, it emerges from man's innate appetite for destruction felt from an early age, 'one of the destructive urges that most of us carry in our hearts'. On the other hand, it is due to the reflex of the caterpillars and their 'unquestionably self-destructive reaction going against every vital interest of the caterpillars' (KP 196) and in their paralysis anticipating their own death.

However, man's innate aggression and appetite for destruction is not directed purely against animals, but equally against fellow humans. The vendetta is an exemplary case and has been practised for centuries on Corsica. In this context, it is significant which particular vocabulary Sebald uses to discuss this phenomenon in the text. He remarks that the vendetta was 'endemic' on Corsica and that the acute awareness of family, which was intensified because of endogamous marrying among their own group, was a 'hotbed [...] of collective paranoia' (KP 135). Thus, the terms of biology and medicine are used to describe a sociological phenomenon.

This further underlines the narrator's assumption that the aggressive behaviour of the Corsicans is down to their nature and to the feeling of being at its mercy and held captive by it: 'The pallid hatred, murder, revenge, carried on from generation to generation, in that respect, a kind of prison syndrome, a permanent rebellion of prisoners against themselves' (KP 142). The innate urge for destruction doesn't even stop at those of its own kind. Man's self-decimation due to the vendetta is reminiscent of the self-destructive reflex of the processionary caterpillars – everything always amounts to one thing: the reduction of life.

Pyromania and the Destruction of the Forests

The decimation of the forests is a prime example of man's destructive rage. Here, Sebald again reverts to historical nature descriptions. They provide the means to evoke the grandeur, tranquillity and beauty of the forests in past centuries, thus allowing the effects of the destruction to appear all the more fatal.

In the nineteenth-century travelogues, the Corsican forest is 'described with awe' (CSe 36/CSg 39). Its beauty is repeatedly accentuated, as no one 'has ever seen a more beautiful forest' with such 'magnificent, [. . .] fascinating views' (CSe 41/CSg 41). However, the narrator points out in the present day that 'nothing is now as it once must have been': man has accomplished such comprehensive destruction that only pitiful remnants of the vast forests have been left behind. Where trees once stood 'growing to a height of almost sixty metres', now only 'meagre pines' grow, and the forest floor is 'largely bare' (CSe 39/CSg 42).

Gilloch also highlights this contrasting description of the forests as they are today with the paradise gardens of the past:

> In the stark and repeated contrasts made between the lush landscapes of the recent past, and the present ruinous condition of the island, a process of degradation whose modern intensification he dates to around the 1870s, [. . .] Sebald makes clear that we today are left with the residues and remnants of once-majestic panoramas and abundant wildlife.[2]

Sebald again cites our fear of nature, by adopting an idea of Rudolf Bilz (see chapter 18 in this volume), to explain this unprecedented destruction: 'who knows, perhaps larger and larger species would have evolved, trees reaching to the sky, if the first settlers had not appeared and if, with the typical fear felt by their own kind for its place of origin, they had not steadily forced the forest back again' (CSe 36/CSg 39). Pyromania is the most exponential form of the destructive rage wreaked on the forests. Fire is the symbol for man-made destruction both in the Corsica Project and in Sebald's other books: 'Fire and flames, infernos and ashes, smoke and pyromania comprise a group of motifs that pervade the work in many forms.'[3]

In the second version of *Notes from Corsica*, this theme is introduced in a gradual progression. On the flight to Corsica, the first 'glow' that the narrator is aware of are the lights of the towns beneath him, 'a single, ever-onwards spinning pattern of illumination' (KP 168). This is man-made smouldering. On the plane's approach to the island, the mountains seem to burn against the sunrise: 'While we drew our circles & loops, the highest summits, soaring two-and-a-half to three-thousand metres above sea level, glowed purple & fire red, as though they had been set alight' (KP 174). What actually lies at the heart of this comparison quickly emerges: during his hiking excursions across the island the narrator repeatedly encounters 'land charred & ravaged by fires' (KP 175) and 'scorched hillsides reaching from the road all the way to the horizon' (KP 208).

On Corsica, the forests are repeatedly set ablaze, and arson is the cause of a high number of fires. The narrator regards this as a confirmation of his theory that the inhabitants' appetite for destruction is caused by the landscape that they live in fear of. Therefore, for him, pyromania is the defining human characteristic:

> There is plenty to indicate that we are strangers in the forests, that there is nothing that we fear deep in our hearts as much as the perennial flora, & we only know we are at home where the fire is, where we can light a fire & sense smoke in the nostrils. Pyromania is more typical than any other characteristic of our species from the very beginning. We could only advance with the help of fire against the wilderness, where we also once lived, & from where we were banished and fell into a spurt of evolution in a hopelessly loss-ridden existence. (KP 209)

By describing pyromania as a 'characteristic of our species', once again man's urge towards destructive behaviour is presented as something he is born with and that he has no power to resist. Hence, the narrator also notes the futility of all measures to tackle arson: 'the attempts to halt the process of disintegration, now increasingly accelerating to its final stage, are doomed to failure from the start, indeed, if one looks carefully, they are themselves symptoms of the collapse' (KP 208).

Human aggression is merely one element of the all-embracing natural history of destruction. 'It is in line with the dialectic of man's turning against nature, to which he permanently belongs, that precisely because of this behaviour he accelerates the process of self-destruction that is created from the beginning in nature.'[4] The vision that the narrator describes at the end of 'The Alps in the Sea' has the impact in this context of a tribunal that humans prepare for themselves as co-participants in the natural history of destruction. Just as was the case for his arrival on the island, the setting sun casts a red glow over the cliffs, and the narrator thinks he identifies silhouettes in the rock formations: 'Sometimes I thought I saw the outlines of plants and animals burning in that flickering light, or the shapes of a whole race of people stacked into a great pyre' (CSe 47/CSg 49).

The Concept of a Natural History of Destruction

The vision of the people going up in flames seems to revert back to a core concept that Sebald had already formulated in *The Rings of Saturn*: 'From the earliest times, human civilization has been no more than a strange luminescence growing more intense by the hour, of which no one can say when it will begin to wane and when it will fade away' (RSe 170/RSg 203). This central motif not only closely aligns the Corsica Project with *The Rings of Saturn*, it also intimately connects it with the theme of the self-destruction of flora and fauna, by nature itself and, particularly, by man's actions. Perhaps it was this proximity, which makes the Corsica Project appear to flow organically from the previous book, that motivated Sebald to discontinue his work on it.

At the same time, the Corsica Project anticipates the essay collection *On the Natural History of Destruction*. This title clearly reflects how the concept of the natural history of destruction, especially during the years from 1995 to 2001, forms the common ground for Sebald's works. In *On the Natural History of Destruction* a change is initiated that widens the scope of natural history to contemporary history: the destruction of nature by man is no longer centre stage, but rather the destruction of cities in the inferno of aerial bombardment during World War Two. The conclusion of *Notes From Corsica* already hints at this when the narrator asks: 'Have we not even incinerated entire peoples, have we not seen our cities burnt to the ground in mile-high firestorms?' (KP 209).

In *On the Natural History of Destruction*, Sebald refers to the term originally deriving from an (unwritten) report by Solly Zuckerman (1904–1993). During World War Two, Zuckerman was an advisor to the British Government about the Allied aerial bombing campaign. Upon his return from bombed German cities, he intended to publish his thoughts and observations under the heading *On the Natural History of Destruction*.

It is true that Sebald never explicitly formulated or even defined his concept of a natural history of destruction. At best, we can reconstruct it using the main outlines of his literary as well as essay compositions. In the Corsica Project, pyromania appears as a symbol of the natural history of destruction with far-reaching, exponential effects. Similarly, in *On the Natural History of Destruction* he focuses on the extreme phenomenon of the firestorms in the aerial bombing campaign. We can read the harrowing passage, which describes the air raid on 27 July 1943 and the ensuing devastating ferocity of the firestorm, as an example of the disastrous effect of the natural history of destruction.

Just as the aerial bombardment is exposed as a mechanism of total warfare, man's destructive actions are part of the superordinate, natural self-decomposition. Hence, they mark 'the point at which we shall drop out of what we have thought for so long to be our autonomous history and back into the history of nature' (NHD 67/LL 72–73). Sebald's deterministic cultural pessimism raises a whole gamut of questions, not least the question about whether, if we have a naturally inherited urge for destruction, we can be pronounced guilty for our human action.

Notes

1. On the "interim period" cf. U Schütte, *W.G. Sebald: Leben und literarisches Werk* (Berlin/Boston: De Gruyter, 2020), pp. 313–384.
2. G Gilloch, The ›Arca Project‹ : W.G. Sebald's Corsica, in: J Baxter et al. (eds.), *A Literature of Restitution: Critical Essays on W.G. Sebald* (Manchester: Manchester University Press, 2013), pp. 126–148 (138).
3. U Schütte, *Annäherungen: Sieben Essays zu W.G. Sebald* (Cologne: Böhlau, 2019), p. 180.
4. P Schmucker, *Grenzübertretungen: Intertextualität im Werk von W.G. Sebald* (Berlin/Boston: De Gruyter, 2012), p. 244.

CHAPTER 14

Poetry

Iain Galbraith

'How far [...] must one go back / to find the beginning?' (AN 81/NN 71), asks the speaker of 'Die dunkle Nacht fahrt aus' ('Dark Night Sallies Forth') – the third part of W.G. Sebald's triptych of poems *Nach der Natur* (*After Nature*) – before proceeding to insert, as if according to a 'system of bricolage' (G 84), particles of the author's own biography and previously unpublished poems into the evocation of a 'silent catastrophe' rolling across the centuries 'almost unperceived' (AN 87/NN 77).

Sebald's work has frequently been described as dark or melancholic. If his diagnosis of the *condition humaine* gives more weight to despondency than lightness of heart, that is neither particularly surprising nor always true. The shards of hope may not amount to a whole, but his writing can suggest that civilization's disasters are sometimes a consequence of choice. In the second part of *After Nature* the naturalist and explorer Georg Wilhelm Steller (1709–1746) finds a coastland that is undisturbed by human civilization, where 'unperturbed / [...] black / and red foxes, magpies too, jays and / crows went with him on his way'. There is an emblematic scene in which Steller rejects his inclination to embrace this natural state, instead following the 'constructs of science in his head', which, 'directed towards a diminution / of disorder in our world, / ran counter to that need' (AN 61–62/NN 54).

Similarly, in an earlier passage, the poet and botanist Adelbert von Chamisso (1781–1838) cannot simply marvel at the 'spectacular sight' of a whale without pondering its transformation into a working 'water-elephant', subservient to the needs of Man (AN 59–60/NN 52). Such moments transmit foreboding, but they also suggest how the wrong choice can lead to calamity. 'Melancholy', Sebald writes, 'is a form of resistance.[...] The description of misfortune implies the possibility of overcoming it' (BU 12).

The story of Sebald's poetry has many beginnings (indeed some poems themselves are sketches for later prose works).[1] We could start with the poems he published in a magazine when he was a student and signed off as *Winfried Sebald*. Or with *After Nature*, the tripartite poem mentioned above, which was rejected by at least five publishers before appearing with the small press Greno in 1988. Or we could begin towards the end, with the gnomic poems Sebald published in *For Years Now*, days before his death in 2001. He had written some of these in English, others he translated from his own German. In an era of intense climate awareness, this might catch our eye: 'In Scipio's days // one could walk / all the way / through the north / of Africa in / the shade' (FYN 27).

Meanwhile, the posthumous anthologies *Über das Land und das Wasser: Ausgewählte Gedichte, 1964–2001* and *Across the Land and the Water: Selected Poems, 1964–2001* offer further portals to the author's poetry. Combining fresh perspectives with hindsight, they collect not only poems published in his lifetime, but many unpublished poems found after his death.

What of the themes of his poems? These differ little from his concerns elsewhere: history, nature, destruction, the Holocaust, landscapes, time, the gaze, memory, surfaces, texts, borders, journeys (mostly by train), half-way or inconclusive states, concealed orders, hearsay, astrology, arcane signs and symbols, myth and legend, and, perhaps most conspicuous of all, absences. Such absences can be more or less palpable. In the poem 'Somewhere' (LWe 135),[2] probably written in the 1990s, little happens. There is a winter scene, possibly the view from a train window. The seemingly casual mention of a place name, however, places the poem, as research reveals, in a landscape of enforced labour and concentration camps from the Nazi period (LWe xix–xxii).

In an interview Sebald asserted that he 'always felt that it was necessary above all to write about the history of persecution, of vilification of minorities, of the attempt, well-nigh achieved, to eradicate a whole people'. He added that he could only view such subjects 'tangentially, by reference rather than direct confrontation' (EM 80). By mention of an object or name, absence can be translated into a ghostly presence: for his interviewer, such obliquity seems to culminate in 'the poem of an invisible subject' (EM 82). In one of the 'miniatures' collected in the posthumously published volume *Unerzählt* (*Unrecounted*) Sebald refers to such indirectness as a gaze that is 'almost averted', like that of 'a dog' (Ue 51/Ug 45).

If we are looking for a typical Sebald poem, the first, and earliest poem in *Across the Land and the Water* might qualify: 'For how hard it is / to understand the landscape / as you pass on a train / from here to there / and mutely it / watches you vanish' (LWe 3/LWg 7). While addressing several of the themes listed above (e.g., history, landscapes, time, the gaze, surfaces, journeys, absence and, by implication, the Holocaust), the poem suggests that the repressive German landscape of the 1960s invites an almost heroic cognitive effort of engagement, which nevertheless will be in vain. The repellent surface refuses to return the alienated gaze or answer the interrogator's questions. Sebald writes: 'The longer I look at the paintings of Jan Peter Tripp, the better I understand that behind the illusions of the surface a dread-inspiring depth is concealed. It is the metaphysical lining of reality, so to speak' (Ue 86/LH 181). The poem was written shortly after the second Auschwitz trials began at the end of 1963. 'I read these reports every day', Sebald said in an interview in 2001, 'and they suddenly shifted my vision [. . .] I understood that I had to find my own way through that maze of the German past'.[3] The task has shaped his poems no less than his prose.

Non-simultaneous Receptions

Few would dispute that the strength of Sebald's reputation rests on the compelling qualities of his prose rather than on his poetry. However, not everyone who agrees with this assessment will be aware that Sebald's writing career both began and ended with poetry. The first five poems in *Across the Land and the Water* appeared in a literary magazine in 1964. Together with a book review and a short prose piece in the same magazine that year, they were Sebald's first published works. *Austerlitz* is often assumed to be Sebald's last book. However, a slim volume entitled *For Years Now*, a collaboration with the artist Tess Jaray containing twenty-three short poems (or 'micropoems', as Sebald called them in a letter to Jaray[4]), was launched in London on 3 December 2001, less than two weeks before the author's death.

Furthermore *Unrecounted* (2003), a collaboration with the artist Jan Peter Tripp, contains thirty-three 'micropoems' written by Sebald between 1999 and December 2001. Published a decade later in 2011, the English-language selection and translation *Across the Land and the Water: Selected Poems*, leaving *After Nature*, *For Years Now* and *Unrecounted* aside, brings together a further ninety poems written between 1964 and 2001. Many of these were published during Sebald's lifetime; others, discovered among the author's papers, were posthumously deposited in the Deutsches Literaturarchiv (German Literature Archive) in Marbach.

Attention has not always been paid to the order in which Sebald's books were published, nor to the importance of the author's poetry to the development of his early writing or in bridging his turn towards narrative forms. While scholars have elucidated chronological divergencies relating to the publication and reception of Sebald's prose works in German and English, the effect of such divergency on the reception of his poetry is rarely singled out for mention.

Sebald's long poem *After Nature*, for example, published in German in 1988, is generally referred to by German critics as his literary debut. When an English translation was published in 2002, however, *After Nature* became the sixth of Sebald's books to appear in English. Consequently, with Sebald's literary reputation already secure in the English-speaking world, enhanced by acclaim from Susan Sontag, Gabriel Josipovici, A.S. Byatt, Will Self and other leading writers, *After Nature* garnered better-informed attention on its appearance in English than it had in German, with only three German reviews for *Nach der Natur* in 1988, while twenty-two are recorded for *After Nature* in 2002 (SM 556).

Moreover, readers could now compare three books of Sebald's poetry published in English in swift succession within a period of four years, with *After Nature* appearing between the two volumes *For Years Now* and *Unrecounted*. For German readers, by contrast, the temporal gap between the two books of 'micropoems' and *After Nature* amounted to some fifteen years. Appearances suggested to German readers that Sebald had unexpectedly turned to poetry at the end of his life, an illusion dispelled only when Sven Meyer's 2008 German edition of the author's poems showed he had written a substantial number of poems before *After Nature* and had continued to write and publish poetry throughout the 1990s.

Prose or Prosody?

Critics have called Sebald's prose fiction 'poetic', while *After Nature* has been described as a 'prose poem'. When the English translation of *Die Ausgewanderten* (*The Emigrants*) received an enthusiastic welcome in the British and American press in 1996, excitement was accompanied by astonishment at this startling "debut" by an unknown lecturer from the University of East Anglia, the engaging rhythms of whose unfamiliar style had apparently sprung from nowhere.

By this time, however, not only had *After Nature* and, in 1990, *Schwindel. Gefühle.* (*Vertigo*), as well as *The Emigrants* appeared in German, but German readers could access two significant volumes of Sebald's essays published in 1985 and 1991. These, together with a third essay volume, *Logis in einem Landhaus* (*A Place in the Country*), which came out in 1998, revealed Sebald's profound sympathy for writers who had attained, as he explained in an interview, 'a very, very high intensity in their prose' and who 'hailed from the periphery of the German-speaking lands', in other words from the Southern German, Austrian and Swiss traditions in which Sebald located the cradle of his own sensibility.

In the same interview Sebald was asked whether the influence of German poetry might explain the 'breaths and cadences' of his prose. His answer was revealing. It was 'not at all' poetry, he replied, but these Southern writers' prosodic rhythms that had strongly influenced his style and paved the way to his prioritizing the 'carefully composed page of prose over the mechanisms of the novel' (EM 77–78). While attributing the idiosyncrasies of his prose to any single source risks circumscribing the author's voice too narrowly, one may nonetheless wonder whether that melodious solemnity, sometimes referred to as the 'Sebald sound', or the unusually overarching structures of his sentences, seemed as outlandish to German readers who knew their Adalbert Stifter (1805–1868) or Thomas Bernhard (1931–1989) as they did to readers of his work in English.

Sebald referenced conspicuously few poets in his essays and interviews, nor did he contribute directly to the vitally discursive contemporary German poetry scene. While his exposure to the self-reflective and frequently monological hypotactic prose of Stifter, Handke, Bernhard and others was, at least in his own perception, foundational for his own prose style, the prosodic timbre and leisurely complexity of their writing may also have influenced the intonation and syntax of his poems.

This is palpable in *After Nature*, in which a main clause may weave its way through a proliferation of subordinating clauses and adjectivally inserted participial constructions across some twenty lines, delaying conclusive meaning and stimulating reflection (e.g., AN 44/NN 38). The composition of the third part of *After Nature*, 'Dark Night Sallies Forth' differs from that of the first two parts, however. The reason for this will become clear in the ensuing discussion of the development of Sebald's earlier poetry as a whole, and of its relation to the predominantly narrative triptych.

Lyrical Workshop and Narrative Turn

Prior to Meyer's 2008 edition of Sebald's poetry in *Über das Land und das Wasser*, or the present writer's expanded and translated edition, *Across the Land and the Water* (2011), neither German nor English readers could have elicited poetry's role in Sebald's early development as a writer. Far from appearing out of the blue, Sebald's German literary "debut" *After Nature* had emerged from two decades of writing – albeit not always publishing – mainly lyrical poems. To illustrate this development, it will be necessary to mention material held by the German Literature Archive in Marbach (LWe xii–xvi).[5]

Sebald kept his earliest poems in a folder on which he inscribed a working title: 'Poemtrees: Lyrisches Lesebuch für Fortgeschrittene und Zurückgebliebene' ('Poemtrees: Lyrical Reader for Advanced and Backward Pupils'). The folder contains some fifty poems, amongst them many that remain unpublished, or have found their way into the German and English editions of his *Selected Poems*. It is clear that poetry was his chosen mode of literary expression at this time. So much so that between 1971 and 1975, while living in Wymondham, near Norwich, and apparently with publication in mind, the author compiled and paginated a manuscript of forty-seven poems including several from 'Poemtrees', entitled 'Schullatein' ('School Latin'). Nine appeared in the artists' and writers' magazine *ZET* (*Das Zeichenheft für Literatur und Grafik*) in 1974 and 1975.

After moving to the Old Rectory in Poringland in 1976, where he lived until his death, Sebald then began work on a new project: 'Über das Land und das Wasser' ('Across the Land and the Water'). This manuscript inherited seventeen poems from 'School Latin', and again, Sebald ordered and paginated the forty-four poem manuscript as if for publication. The final poem is longest of all, recounting the life, observations, discoveries and sufferings of the botanist and traveller Georg Wilhelm Steller during his voyage with Vitus Bering (1681–1741) through the Northern Pacific to Alaska. This poem, entitled 'Und blieb ich am äussersten Meer' ('And if I Remained by the Outermost Sea'), would become the second part of *After Nature*.

Sebald sent this narrative poem to the Austrian magazine *Manuskripte*, where it appeared in October 1984, to be followed in June 1986 by the first part of *After Nature*, 'Wie der Schnee auf den Alpen' ('As the Snow on the Alps'), the author's reflections on the life and work of the sixteenth-century painter Matthaeus Grünewald (1480–1530), who, in Sebald's exquisite and extended description of the Isenheim Altarpiece, 'silently wielding his paintbrush, / rendered the scream, the wailing, the gurgling / and the shrieking of a pathological spectacle / to which he and his art, as he must have known, / themselves belong' (AN 26–27/NN 24). Meanwhile a note in the archive reveals that Sebald had started sending the manuscript of *After Nature* to book publishers by November 1985, suggesting that he had not only written the first two parts of the book by that time, but had also already assembled 'Dark Night Sallies Forth', the third part of the *After Nature*, which would appear in *Manuskripte* in March 1987.

'Dark Night Sallies Forth' inserts details of the author's own biography into the grand historical context that gives *After Nature* its narrative structure. It also documents Sebald's decision to excise at least eighteen poems from the unpublished manuscript of 'Across the Land and the Water' and reassemble them instead in the final part of *After Nature*. Some of these poems have not otherwise been published in German or translated into English. 'Lend me a looking Glass – Notes on a Sunday Excursion' (original English), for example, forms almost the entire sixth subsection of 'Dark Night Sallies Forth', whose second subsection contains an assemblage of eight poems, six of which have since appeared in the German or English *Selected Poems*. Because of its textual hybridity, much of 'Dark Night Sallies Forth' has a more lyrical texture than the preceding two narrative parts of the book. The movement of Sebald's poetic work across 'Poemtrees', 'School Latin' and 'Across the Land and the Water' resembles a cascade flowing from manuscript to manuscript, culminating in *After Nature*.

Integrating such a large part of the 'Across the Land and the Water' manuscript into *After Nature* had two important consequences: it paved the way for publication of *After Nature*, but scuttled his chances of publishing 'Across the Land and the Water' as a separate volume. At the same time, this period in his writing career demonstrates Sebald's turn from predominantly lyrical poetry in the 1960s and 1970s to more narrative forms of his poetry in the 1980s and 1990s, and ultimately to the prose fiction that followed *After Nature*.

With the benefit of hindsight, Sebald cannot be portrayed as a writer who gave up writing poems after turning to prose following the publication of *After Nature*, nor as a prose writer who returned to poetry at the end of his life. It is clear that his medium was prose, but as manuscripts consulted at the Marbach Archive as well as bibliographies of his published work confirm (SM 484–485), he wrote and published poetry from his early twenties until shortly before his death. It is not unthinkable that W.G. Sebald would have published other poetry volumes had he lived longer.

Notes

1. L Wolff, *W.G. Sebald's Hybrid Poetics: Literature as Historiography* (Berlin/Boston: De Gruyter, 2014), pp. 241–244.
2. 'Irgendwo', the original German version of this poem, appeared in: *Akzente* 58:6, p. 516.

3. C Bigsby, *Writers in Conversation with Christopher Bigsby*, vol. 2 (Norwich: EAS, 2001), pp. 146–147.
4. U Schütte, *Figurationen: Zum lyrischen Werk von W.G. Sebald* (Eggingen: Ed. Isele, 2014), p. 113.
5. For more on the unpublished poetry cf. Galbraith, Im Archiv: Zu den nachgelassenen Gedichten von W.G. Sebald, in: *Akzente* 58:6 (2011), pp. 519–522.

CHAPTER 15

The World War Project

Richard Hibbitt

In January 2000, with intercession on the part of his old colleague Richard J Evans, then Professor of Modern History at Cambridge, W.G. Sebald was invited to apply for a NESTA Fellowship.[1] The National Endowment for Science, Technology and the Arts had been set up by the UK Government in 1998 to support outstanding creative talent and innovation in the arts and sciences. That summer, around the same time that he sent his manuscript of *Austerlitz* to Anthea Bell, his new English translator, Sebald applied to NESTA to spend four consecutive spring semesters from 2001 to 2004 working on a new writing project, with the plan being to teach each autumn semester at UEA.

When Sebald's application was accepted in October, Evans became Sebald's NESTA mentor. Thanks to the fellowship, Sebald was able to take study leave in the spring semester of 2001, during which he travelled to France and Germany to undertake research for what he referred to as his 'W. W.' (World War) Project. The notes he made are held in the Deutsches Literaturarchiv in Marbach (German Literature Archive). They consist of two box files of assorted materials and most of the papers left on Sebald's desk in December 2001. Taken together, these encompass two short drafts, preliminary studies, extracts from historical accounts and copies of archival documents.[2] It is a great pity that the project could not be completed.

The NESTA application form provides a tantalizing insight into Sebald's plans:

> My intention is to research for and begin with the drawing of an extensive narrative which will encompass the period 1900–1950. Several of my forebears will pass review, among them Rudolf Egelhofer, commander of the Red Army at the time of the Munich Soviet, who was murdered in 1919 by the right-wing free corps. The 'éducation sentimentale', under the fascist regime, of the social class to which my parents belonged will be another prominent topic, as will be my father's progress during the war and the post-war years which were the

years of my childhood. I should point out that the form this will take is *not* that of (auto)biography: it will be more like the 'semi-documentary prose fiction' for which I have become known. Accounts of the process of research will also be included as integral parts of the narrative. (SM 257–259)

In fact, the project notes themselves show that, although the planned focus had been on the first half of the twentieth century, Sebald's research quickly expanded to include the Franco-German conflicts from the Franco-Prussian War in 1870 until the end of World War Two. In both 2000 and 2001, Sebald visited the area around the northern French town of Saint-Quentin, taking photographs of battlefields and making notes. In the Franco-Prussian War, Saint-Quentin initially repelled the Prussian army before falling in October 1870. During World War One, the town was occupied and integrated into the Hindenburg Line by the German army, then later evacuated and largely destroyed.

One of the two extant drafts for the project shows how Sebald planned to use Saint-Quentin as one of the settings for his work: Sebald's narrator visits a close French friend named Sophie in a mill at Berthenicourt, outside Saint-Quentin, where he is able to read her grandfather's diary from the Great War (SM 259). At the same time, the narrator is researching his own ancestors, which involves a trip to the German War Archive in Munich. Sebald himself visited this archive on 31 May 2001, where he copied a large number of documents relating to the history of the First Bavarian Infantry Regiment in World War One.

This dual narrative suggests a comparative consideration of the experiences of French and German soldiers and their families. Much of the other material in Sebald's notes consists of eyewitness accounts of World War One in English, French and German. It is this combination of real and fictional narratives which illustrates Sebald's claim that the work is 'semi-documentary prose fiction'.

One of the loose papers in the World War Project is a page where a 'real' and a 'fictional' family tree are juxtaposed. Here we see how Sebald was beginning to sketch out the parallel lives of actual and invented members of the paternal side of his family, a technique he used to create fictional biographies. Other notes on this sheet – such as a reference to a photograph of the silver wedding anniversary of his great-grandparents – show how he planned his characteristic juxtapositions of text and image.

The sheet also includes a list of different professions, including cottagers, weavers and glass grinders, which gives a sense of how he intended to see history through the prism of the landless working class from which

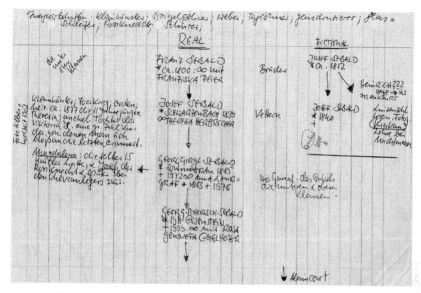

Illustration 13 – Draft concept showing real and fictional family trees

he came. In an interview with Arthur Lubow in August 2001, he referred to his ancestors as 'lower class', commenting on the difficulty in ascertaining their biographical details: 'As they all came from the lower classes, there are often not even exact dates of birth or places of residence [...] This uncertainty begins two generations back' (EM 163).

Lubow's interview with Sebald also contains several other insights into the World War Project. For example, the aforementioned diary was based on twenty-three volumes of an actual diary, kept from 1905 to 1950 by the grandfather of his French friend Marie. Although, as he told Lubow, Sebald had not established a family link between the Red Army Commander of the Munich Soviet Republic, Rudolf Egelhofer, and his mother's family, the fact that he had the same last name had caught his attention and he was pursuing the coincidence (EM 163–164). Another part of his NESTA application explains how he wanted to research his own personal family history, which was to include trips to the southern German town of Sonthofen:

> where I grew up and where the Nazis, soon after seizing power, built the *Ordensburg*, a school designated to promote the formation of a new fascist elite. Further, I intend to visit places through which my father passed between the so-called Polish campaign and his time as a prisoner of war in France. (SM 259)

In 2001, Sebald visited his mother in Sonthofen on several occasions, sometimes in conjunction with his research trips. Although he wanted to avoid a conventional approach to (auto)biographical writing, his initial research and plans indicate that the World War Project would have contained a considerable amount of personal material. In addition, his intention to include metatextual reflections on his research process suggests that the (auto)biographical element would not have been limited to members of his family and his own experience growing up in the immediate aftermath of World War Two. We can therefore surmise that the finished work would have fused (auto)biography, history, fiction and criticism, and would have been a variation on the hybrid poetics for which he is known.

It is also possible to gain a sense of Sebald's plans from the memories of conversations which he had with various friends and colleagues at the time, particularly with two of his old schoolfriends, Ursula Liebsch and Heidemarie Nowak. In interviews conducted by the film maker Thomas Honickel for his film portrait on Sebald,[3] both refer to Sebald's interest in the story of another of their schoolfriends, Barbara Aenderl, who had died from cancer a few years earlier. Her papers included letters revealing a hidden love affair in her family, which Sebald consulted during his visits to Sonthofen.[4] He also read her diaries, which related various expeditions in different parts of the world, including a winter spent in Spitzbergen with a trapper.[5]

Sebald had visited Aenderl shortly before her death, discussing both her travels and her illness. According to their friends, he was fascinated by the way in which she balanced new experiences in her travelling with periods spent back in the calmness of home. It seems as if the story of her life may have formed part of the parallel German strand to the French parts of the narrative.

A State of Self-Examination

It is of course impossible to know exactly what the World War Project would have led to. The drafts and preliminary sketches point initially to a continuation of the technique employed in *Austerlitz*, where his narrator encounters fictional characters, some of which are clearly composites of real people. The projected geographical scope of the novel, with sections in northern France and southern Germany, is similarly reminiscent of the narrative trajectory in *Austerlitz* from Belgium and Wales to London, Prague and Paris, among other places. Although the autobiographical elements recall not only *Die Ringe des Saturn* (*The Rings of Saturn*, 1995) but also parts of *Schwindel. Gefühle.* (*Vertigo*, 1990) and *Die Ausgewanderten* (*The Emigrants*, 1992), there is a sense that autobiography would have played a greater role: here the narrator was to confront his own past, not just those of others.

A further difference is the temporal range: the project hints at a sustained engagement with late-nineteenth and early-twentieth-century history, as opposed to the aftermath of the Shoah, as in *Austerlitz* and *The Emigrants*, and it may have had a more linear approach than the discrete treatment of isolated episodes from Stendhal's and Kafka's lives in *Vertigo* or the kaleidoscopic approach to different periods of history in *The Rings of Saturn*.

It is also interesting to consider how the World War Project might have differed in structure from preceding works. *Vertigo* and *The Emigrants* are each divided into four parts; *The Rings of Saturn* into ten sections; and *Austerlitz* is a continuous narrative. Sebald might have used one or a combination of these previous structures, or perhaps experimented with parallel narratives in different fonts, as in Georges Perec's *W ou le souvenir de l'enfance* (*W, or the Memory of Childhood*, 1975) or with different page layouts, as in Claude Simon's *Le Jardin des Plantes* (*Jardin des Plantes*, 1997), two books he admired (SM 264).

Yet, despite an interest in more experimental approaches, the drafts indicate that his starting point was the semi-autobiographical first-person narration that had served him so well before. In the interview with Lubow, he commented on his suspicion of omniscient narration: 'Very often you don't know who the narrator is, which I find unacceptable. The story comes through someone's mind. I feel I have the right to know who that person is and what his credentials are' (EM 169). Sebald's suspicion of conventional narrative techniques was part of his general reluctance to call his prose works 'novels', keeping in mind that Germans make a sharper distinction between prose fiction and the novel.

Sebald addressed classification of his writings in several interviews. In a conversation with his colleague Jon Cook in 1999, he gave the following appraisal of his own approach to writing:

> But I am simply unable, I think, to write, in another way; I think it would be quite difficult for me to write a proper novel which has a plot and, as it were, free-moving independent characters who are directed by an authorial narrator, because I think I would be incapable of doing this. (SM 362)

This interview came while Sebald was writing *Austerlitz*, which is closer to a conventional novel than his other prose fictions in terms of both plot and characterization. We might interpret this self-appraisal as a challenge: Sebald clearly set himself the task of writing the biography of a fictional character, even though all the required information is ostensibly relayed to the narrator in improbable chance meetings. Lubow gives an interesting critique of this development in Sebald's technique:

> In *Austerlitz*, he tried to cleave more closely to the structure of a traditional novel, propelling the narrative forward with the saga of a man's search for his parents, and you could feel the author's unconventional mind creaking against the walls of convention. The new book promised to return to the free-ranging, more musical structure of the earlier ones, as seemed natural for someone who deprecated the ability of the old-fashioned novel to function in modern times. (EM 169)

However, we can also see this 'creaking against the walls of convention' as productive friction: Sebald using his idiosyncratic approach to the novel in order to push prose fiction onto new ground. Lubow may of course be right about the putative structure of the World War Project, but Sebald might also have continued his experimentation with the conventions of the traditional novel, in this instance in a wider geographical and temporal context.

James Wood also has an astute opinion on Sebald's writing as a new variation on literary realism: 'Here was the first contemporary writer since Beckett to have found a way to protest the good government of the conventional novel-form and to harass realism into a state of self-examination.'[6] Although we can never be certain, it seems safe to assume that the World War Project would have continued this process of self-examination, not only for realism but also for the book's narrator, characters and eventual readers.

War and Peace: A Speculation

From the extant notes and drafts, we know that the World War Project would have explored the effect of war and peace on civilian lives. The use of the family trees also suggests an intergenerational focus on individuals caught up in tumultuous periods of history, including the insidious influence of fascism on everyday lives. The envisaged work may therefore have approximated more to two particular types of prose fiction: the historical novel and the family novel. To this we can add the *Bildungsroman*, but not in the conventional sense of the education and personal development of a single protagonist: Sebald's reference in his NESTA application to the 'éducation sentimentale' of a social class under the fascist regime alludes to Flaubert's novel *L'Éducation sentimentale* (*Sentimental Education*, 1869), which traces the experience of a young man during the 1848 Revolution. Sebald would no doubt have approached these three concentric elements of the nineteenth-century novel – individual, family, and history – in a non-traditional way.

In fact, the novel which his inchoate World War Project most nearly resembles is Tolstoy's *Voyna i mir* (*War and Peace*, 1869), which also fuses real events and generations of fictional characters with reflections on a recent period of history (in this case the Napoleonic Wars and their aftermath, spanning from 1805 to 1820). But the similarities between the two projects go beyond setting and construction. Tolstoy also cast doubts on the generic status of his work, writing: 'What is *War and Peace*? It is not a novel, even less is it an epic poem, and still less an historical chronicle.'[7] Tolstoy's novel is similarly hybrid, encompassing conventional fictional passages and critical reflections on philosophy and historiography, which are in turn based on eyewitness accounts and other historical sources.

With regard to the difference between the work of the artist and the work of the historian, Tolstoy writes:

> Studying so tragic an epoch, so rich in the importance of its events, so near to our own time, and regarding which so many varied traditions survive, I arrived at the evident fact that the causes of historical events when they take place cannot be grasped by our intelligence.[8]

Although it may be hard to imagine such a hyperbolic and categorical sentence occurring in one of Sebald's interviews, there seems to be an underlying consensus here regarding historiography and the difficulty of grasping the past. Tolstoy's view of history is also the subject of Isaiah's Berlin's 1953 essay *The Hedgehog and the Fox*, which analyses the reasons for Tolstoy's rejection of the "great man" theory of history. Berlin's appraisal of Tolstoy's view of history anticipates Sebald's own approach:

> How would an ideal historical science operate? By using a kind of calculus whereby this 'differential', the infinitesimals – the infinitely small human and non-human actions and events – would be integrated, and this way the continuum of history would no longer be distorted by being broken up into arbitrary segments.[9]

This comparison between *War and Peace* and the World War Project is not meant to imply that Sebald would have simply applied Tolstoy's techniques to his planned 'extensive narrative'. It seems fanciful to suggest that there would have been an omniscient narrator describing a battle, or large sections of carefully constructed dialogue between fictional characters.

However, since they both wanted to harass realism into self-examination, the analogy seems credible with regard to their shared desire to write plausible prose fiction about history from multiple perspectives. In addition, both writers were interested in the role of chance in human activity and rejected a neat, causal view of history. Sebald's World War Project might also have been multilingual, with sections of French text retained verbatim. Although we can only speculate on what form the book might have taken, it would surely have given us a different view of the continuum of history and added immeasurably to his existing work on human relationships and the natural history of destruction.

Notes

1. The biographical information in this essay draws mainly on R Sheppard, W.G. Sebald – A Chronology, in: SM 619–658.
2. U Bülow, The Disappearance of the Author in the Work: Some Reflections on W.G. Sebald's Nachlass in the Deutsches Literaturarchiv Marbach, in: SM 257–259.
3. T Honickel, *Curriculum Vitae: Die W.G. Sebald-Interviews*, ed. U Schütte, K Wolfinger (Würzburg: Königshausen & Neumann, 2021), pp. 39–53, 69–74.
4. Ibid., p. 49.
5. Ibid., pp. 69–74.
6. J Wood, W.G. Sebald's Uncertainty, in: *The Broken Estate. Essays on Literature and Belief* (London: Cape, 1999), pp. 273–284 (273).
7. L Tolstoy, Some Words about War and Peace, in: *War and Peace* (Oxford: Oxford University Press, 2010), pp. 1308–1317 (1308).
8. Ibid., p. 1314.
9. I Berlin, *The Hedgehog and the Fox: An Essay on Tolstoy's View of History* (London: Weidenfeld & Nicolson, 2013), p. 34.

CHAPTER 16

Interviews

Torsten Hoffmann

Although the cliché of the melancholy loner still follows him today, W.G. Sebald is a writer of conversation. He once stated in 1993 in an interview his belief 'that literature to a considerable degree consists of conversations with the departed' (G 81). This applies at least to his own prose writings that typically incorporate long passages of reported speech. In many cases, Sebald based his texts on conversations that he held during his meticulous process of research.

Furthermore, he appeared in multiple public (or recorded) panel discussions as an academic and as a writer between 1971 and 2001. From the early 1970s until the 1990s, he discussed other writers (especially Austrian writers such as Adalbert Stifter (1805–1868), Joseph Roth (1894–1939) and Peter Handke (b. 1942)). During the 1970s he led interviews with distinguished guests of the University of East Anglia (UEA) – for example Reiner Kunze (b. 1933) or Franz Reichert (1908–1998) – that he recorded at the university's film studio (SM 587).

From 1990 onwards, he was a willing interviewee and, as a writer, gave over eighty interviews for television, radio, journals and newspapers in both German and English. Nine English interviews are included in *The Emergence of Memory* (published in 2007). The Sebald handbook, *Saturn's Moons*, contains three more interviews in English (SM 349–375), and a compilation was published in 2014 with a further three conversations in English.[1] A collection of twenty interviews has been available in German since 2011. Although the secondary material on Sebald often utilizes his interviews extensively, they are only rarely the primary subject of analyses in literary studies.

The Development and Poetics of Sebald's Works

The interviews granted by Sebald stand apart from many other writers' interviews for three reasons. Firstly, in the interviews Sebald

Illustration 14 – Sebald, interviewed by literary critic Sigrid Löffler, UEA

expresses his opinion very candidly and goes into great detail about his own writing. Secondly, Sebald's prose creates a desire in the reader to determine and differentiate the mix of facts and fictions within the narrator through the format of the interview. Thirdly, Sebald appears in the interviews not only as a commentator of his own work but also repeatedly falls into storytelling (also with an air of fictionality). This begs the question whether the interviews are a source of biographical facts or whether they belong to literary fiction.

Sebald's interviews describe the creative development process of his texts as a combination of meticulous research – that he recommends for all writers (G 196) – and intuition. He attributes his collection of material for his books, which is associated with numerous trips, as highly rewarding in its own right; indeed, compared with the increasing effort involved in writing each book, Sebald values his research activity as the greatest personal bonus of writing (G 213). However, his concern consistently is to present these explorations as unsystematic and to separate them from academic working methods. Sebald tends to refer at this point to the motif of dogs whose inquisitive activity he suggests as exemplary for his own approach to the collection of material.[2] In an interview with *The New Yorker* he stated:

> I never liked doing things systematically. Not even my Ph.D. research was done systematically. It was done in a random, haphazard fashion. The more I got on, the more I felt that, really, one can find something only in that way—in the same way in which, say, a dog runs through a field. If you look at a dog following the advice of his nose, he traverses a patch of land in a completely unplottable manner. And he invariably finds what he is looking for. I think that, as I've always had dogs, I've learned from them how to do this. (EM 94)

On the other hand, on many occasions Sebald summarizes his work as a kind of 'private archaeology' (G 176). The sign of smooth progress within research and the writing process is when things spontaneously take on their own momentum: 'if things come in from the sides to offer themselves, then you're going in the right direction' (EM 72).

Sebald dismisses the 'novel' as a genre label for his fictional prose (G 85, 199) and instead brings into play 'documentary fiction' as a generic term (EM 39). He speaks of a 'juncture where documentary and fictional worlds coincide' and describes his approach as a 'kind of zipping together' of these worlds in his fictional narratives (G 198, 56), where he finds modern literature at its most convincing both in aesthetic as well as ethical terms. This is supposed to provoke the reader into a 'feeling of continual irritation' (G 141) that Sebald came to appreciate in the literature of Alexander Kluge (b. 1932), whose name is mentioned in several interviews as a literary role model (as well as Franz Kafka (1883–1924), Vladimir Nabokov (1899–1977) and Thomas Bernhard (1931–1989)).

Sebald cites realism as the predominant literary-historical reference point for his writing, yet in his case it 'must transcend at some periphery into the realm of fantasies or the mysterious' (G 98). Although he is always scrupulously insistent about emphasizing his distance from religious certainties, Sebald regularly expresses his interest in metaphysics. He credits black-and-white photographs as especially productive for his writing mainly because they reveal a grey zone where the boundary is blurred between the living and the departed (G 174).

In a typically defensive mode about this subject Sebald explains his metaphysical assumption that 'somewhere there is a form of existence that is secondary, adjunctive, superordinate or subordinate to us' (G 168), and whose trail he is following as a writer. Sebald's interviews admittedly express just as few real certainties about this topic as his fictional texts; he asks the question about the transcendent realm, although he has no truths to declare (EM 165).

Holocaust and Self-Representation

The subjects of National Socialism and the Holocaust emerge in numerous conversations, especially because the anglophone interviewers present Sebald as a writer whose primary interest is in this subject field. The focus of attention is directed above all (just as in Sebald's books) to the aftermath: on the one hand, for the victims; on the other hand, for the Germans and the question of how, and at what psychological cost, they were able to keep silent about this period of their own biography in the post-war era. Sebald recounts several instances of how, at school, he was shown a film without any further comment about the liberation of the Bergen-Belsen concentration camp.

He also cites the silence of his parents' generation as another important biographical context for his intense literary interest in the Holocaust, describing this as a 'conspiracy of silence' and also as a 'huge taboo zone' (EM 44, 105). Sebald talks more often of the feeling, which gradually intensifies in retrospect, about the 'injustice' (G 138) of his own sheltered childhood when the killing of the Jews happened at the same time. The Frankfurt Auschwitz trials of 1964/65 were the important impetus for his own in-depth research on the Holocaust: 'I realized that there were subjects of much greater urgency than the writings of the German Romantics.'[3]

Sebald has voiced some contradictory opinions about the prospect of generalizing the task of remembrance. On the one hand, he complained of a dwindling awareness of the past among his students and considered it an absurd call from Martin Walser (b. 1927) to, as it were, draw a line under 'coming to terms with the past' (G 220, 259). On the other hand, all practical forms of facing up to the reality of the Holocaust in Germany are treated by him as 'certainly something very German' (G 92) and dismissed as inadequate – from the Holocaust memorial to anti-fascist city tours to inviting Jewish survivors to visit schools. Great Britain provides a positive alternative image, for Sebald it is 'a place where history is hugely present',[4] yet to its detriment it resembles Germany more and more.

Sebald's anti-German resentment is combined in many interviews with his noticeable fixation on his place of origin. Like many of his literary protagonists, Sebald presents himself as someone who – despite living abroad for the greatest part of his life – is deeply influenced by the places and experiences of his childhood in the Allgäu (see chapter 1 in this volume). He had no permanent feelings of home either for England or for Germany, yet his early childhood years from 1944 to 1950 gave him a sense of 'temporary *Heimat*', as 'identity' and as a place of origin 'from where one writes one's story' (G 177) – in especially personal interview passages Sebald regularly switches to the use of the impersonal 'one' (see chapter 7 in this volume). Almost the entire field of Sebald's thematic material and writing processes is derived in the interviews from his early childhood, including his preoccupation with the departed, his love of photographs, his working technique of *bricolage*, his interest in Austrian writers and generally his reasons for becoming a writer.[5]

In an interview for the *Jewish Quarterly*, when Sebald insisted that his interest in Jewish biographies was not mainly for philo-Semitic or ethical reasons, but merely to have shed light on a secret from his childhood (EM 167), such statements also serve the purpose of correcting his image. Sebald was attempting at that time to distance himself from a certain image as a writer that was gradually gaining ground, especially in America, and styling him as a model German and as "the nation's conscience" or as the "good German". On more than one occasion, particularly in the American interviews, comic effects emerge when the interviewer elevates Sebald to a global literary star who had written 'some of the most important prose writing of the century' (EM 77), whereas Sebald in the interview ostentatiously presents himself as a provincial Allgäu poet.

By treating his writing as an outcome of a random biographical constellation and, therefore, as unplanned, as an enigma to himself and at times even as a pathological compulsive act, he projects his own image more strongly as an object than as a free subject of his craft: 'I don't even know what thinking is [. . .]. It is a completely random process.'[6] This also counteracts the expectation of dealing with a rational *poeta doctus*, a swift and calculating writer. Anyone who anticipates a writer under the guidance of clear moral principles and effortlessly handling literary motifs and processes is about to learn another thing from the interviews: 'I'm out of control' (EM 117) is the essential message. Sebald projects this idea of himself as a person and as an author at the height of his fame at the time of his 2001 interview in New York.

The interviews indirectly make it clear which authorship models Sebald rejects. At times this also applies to the image of the man with a bout of melancholia. In some interviews, he comments about this ironically and dismisses it (of course, in other contexts he drops this into the conversations, while distancing himself from any form of unproductive depression).

'In person', remarks Arthur Lubow, as well as other interviewers, 'Sebald was funnier than his lugubrious narrators' (EM 170).

Sebald's relationship to his personal as well as collective past appears ambivalent not least due to his opinion that the present is 'one single incredible disaster, everywhere' (G 72). Moreover, he consistently glances at the future with a culturally pessimistic outlook. Even though he dismisses the attitude of a prophet of the apocalypse (G 150), what comes to the fore in so many interviews are misanthropic characteristics – man is a 'perverse species, a species that has lost its common sense as an animal' (G 151). In this context nostalgic elements are also blended with Sebald's talk of the past: it 'at least is nothing like our present' and to that extent is 'a safe terrain where I gladly linger for a while' (G 65). The slightest glance at old family photos causes him to experience a shock of impermanence, which resembles a 'negative epiphany' (G 169), and so he becomes aware 'that we are constantly treading on an incredibly thin layer of ice [...] that the whole thing has a fragility that makes it almost impossible for someone to make it from one day to the next' (G 170).

Following this line of argument, the intense fascination with the past can be read as an attempt at the aesthetic suspension of time. This is consistent with earlier comments that the aim of his writing is 'to create tiny lagoons that are separated from time' (G 75). The use of visual material also has a function in this context because Sebald treats the fine arts as timeless and grants them the capacity 'at least momentarily of countering the inevitability of the end with one thing or the other' (G 140). In several sporadic phases the writer, whose reputation was built on his treatment of historical subjects, at least warms to the idea of an ahistorical aesthetics.

Literariness and Fictionality of the Interviews

Not only Sebald's essays gradually became more and more attuned to the intonation and fictionality of his prose works but so do his interviews.[7] For instance, the interviews dealing with thematic aspects and not referring to his most recent book published at the time, incorporate passages of a "literary" narrative. The subordinative description and interpretation of a Kafka photo from the detailed conversation in 1997 with the photographer, Christian Scholz, would also fit in Sebald's prose writings (G 174). In the same interview the writer drafts a miniature prose study about a night that he spent, unintentionally, at Schiphol airport in Amsterdam: the travellers who were camping in this 'extremely ghostly scenario' appeared to him like 'human beings that, laid out like the dead, were lying curled up on their side or very rigidly on their back'. An alternative fictionalized version of the experience, with different nuances, is in the posthumously published poem 'In der Nacht auf' ('On the Eve Of') (LWg 100–101/Lwe 157–158).

In a radio interview in 2001 Sebald describes at length the ghostly and claustrophobic impression that the Parisian underground made on him with the names of its stations steeped in history. Here, one gets

> the feeling in fact that these Metro travellers are somehow the departed who must continue to live down here, riding on these trains back and forth. In other words, all of the fallen, the devastated, all of these people are still down below in the underworld. (G 240)

This passage easily highlights a characteristic style and an imaginary world that is reminiscent of Hades and that obviously influenced the corresponding passages in his book *Austerlitz* (Ag 187/Ae 179, Ag 362–363/Ae 355). The interviews also give a valuable source of information about those two book projects that Sebald did not complete, namely the Corsica Project (see chapter 13 in this volume) and his research for the World War Project (see chapter 15 in this volume), which he was working on at the time of his death (EM 163–165; G 212–213, 219, 263).

The habitual unreliability of the interviews is yet another mark of their literariness. Sebald often defends the 'secret of fiction' (G 181) and only appears to dissolve the relationship of facts and fictions existing in his texts. It is true that he supplies, for example, precise answers to the question about the authenticity of the visual content-material in his books yet, depending on the interview, there are serious discrepancies between the versions. At a reading in Los Angeles in 2001 he provides the detail that 'perhaps four or five percent' (SM 366) of the photos in *Austerlitz* were 'fakes', while a few months beforehand in his interview with *Spiegel* magazine he mentioned about half of them (G 204).

After Sebald's death there was some controversy about the interview passages in which he granted a Jewish background to the real-life role model for his character, Henry Selwyn, when this was contrary to the facts.[8] Moreover, there are ethical issues relating to his inaccurate assertion that he had been granted permission by the Holocaust survivor, Susi Bechhöfer, to use her Kindertransport-biography for *Austerlitz* (G 198). Richard Sheppard refers to other false statements in interviews and draws the conclusion: 'never believe Sebald the interviewee when he is solemnly stating facts rather than expressing opinions, and even then be sceptical'.[9] For Sebald, interviews are also a central component of his auto-fictional work that he described as a 'morally questionable business' 'because one appropriates and manipulates the lives of others for certain ends. [. . .] Most writers have a splinter of ice in their heart.'[10]

Although the responses in the interviews give the appearance of being an illuminating secondary contribution, one should read them very carefully and with the same serious approach as the prose texts. The person we meet in the interviews is not the man whose friends called him Max (and whose private and family life is largely undisclosed), not the writer or academic W. G. Sebald and not the anonymous narrator of his books, but rather a linguistic self-projection, a version in which – either intentionally or unplanned – the different expressive forms blend together. The self-enactments of Thomas Bernhard present a recognizable role model.

On the one hand, the complex image emerges of a person who seems to understand himself as a moral authority. Thus, with echoes of the familiar polemical overtones from Sebald's essays, the novels of Alfred Andersch (1914–1980) are discredited, or Steven Spielberg's celebrated film *Schindler's List* (1993) is deemed a fundamentally wrong approach to coming to terms with the Holocaust. On the other hand, the self-portrayals are marked by insight into the unstable and questionable nature of the personal life and literary work. Sebald concedes much more openly than in his essays that he, too, (like the writer Andersch whom he criticized) is engaged in his texts in an ethical balancing act, and he was uncertain about its success.

Sebald would be the last person to know whether the basic impetus of his writing was an ethical or rather financial one, or possibly 'glory, imposture' (G 79). He mentioned his emotional instability ('I have felt for some considerable time to be close to the edge of my reason', G 92) as well as his fundamental conviction that 'territories in one's own life are indefensible and that, in fact, one cannot live an honest life with this indefensibility' (G 80). This smart avowal of not being sophisticated at all is often revealed in the interviews in incidental remarks, which make a relative or ironic comment out of what has just been said. The interrogatives posed in the interviews therefore meet a writer – and this is generally by no means the case in all writers' interviews – who repeatedly calls himself into question. A different version of this essay was published as T Hoffmann, Interviews, in: M Niehaus, C Öhlschläger (eds.), *W.G. Sebald-Handbuch: Leben – Werk – Wirkung* (Stuttgart: Metzler, 2017), pp. 108–112.

Notes

1. R Sheppard, Three Encounters with W.G. Sebald (February 1992–July 2013), in: *Journal of European Studies* 44 (2014), pp. 378–414.

2. T Hoffmann, Das Interview als Kunstwerk: Plädoyer für die Analyse von Schriftstellerinterviews am Beispiel W.G. Sebalds, in: *Weimarer Beiträge* 55 (2009), pp. 276–292 (289–290).
3. C Bigsby, In Conversation with W.G. Sebald, in: C Bigsby (ed.), *Writers in Conversation*, vol. 2 (Norwich: EAS, 2001), pp. 139–165 (147).
4. P Morgan, Living Among the English [interview], in: *Welsh Internationalist* 158:2 (2003), pp. 13–18 (14).
5. T Hoffmann, Die Ausschaltung der Einschaltung des Autors: Autorkritische Selbstinszenierungen in Interviews von Heiner Müller und W.G. Sebald, in: C Jürgensen, G Kaiser (eds.), *Schriftstellerische Inszenierungspraktiken: Typologie und Geschichte* (Heidelberg: Winter, 2011), pp. 313–340 (338–339).
6. Bigsby, In Conversation with Sebald, p. 148.
7. R Klüger, Wanderer zwischen falschen Leben: Über W.G. Sebald, in: *Text +Kritik* 158 (2003), pp. 95–102 (96).
8. C Angier, *Speak, Silence: In Search of W.G. Sebald* (London: Bloomsbury, 2021), pp. 15–26.
9. R Sheppard, Woods, Trees and the Spaces In Between: A Report on Work Published on W.G. Sebald 2005–2008, in: *Journal of European Studies* 39 (2009), pp. 79–128 (97).
10. Bigsby, In Conversation with Sebald, p. 153.

PART III

Themes and Influences

CHAPTER 17

Critical Writings

Sven Meyer

W.G. Sebald was forty-four years of age when he made his literary debut with *Nach der Natur* (*After Nature*) in 1988. Nonetheless, his literary critical debut dates much earlier: in 1969, the twenty-five-year-old junior academic published the revised version of his MA dissertation entitled *Carl Sternheim: Kritiker und Opfer der Wilhelminischen Ära* (*CS: Critic and Victim of the Wilhelminan Era*).

The notably polemical analysis of the German-Jewish playwright Carl Sternheim (1878–1942) is characterized by two aspects. Firstly, it fiercely attacks German Studies as a discipline. Secondly, it openly vilifies the dramatist, Sternheim, in an endeavour to discredit him on moral, literary and political grounds.

Sebald's study attempts nothing short of a total destruction and, in turn, it serves as a blueprint for a series of subsequent rigorous polemics in the 1990s when he attempts to correct the positive image established in German literary studies of writers such as Alfred Andersch (1914–1980) or Jurek Becker (1937–1997). His critical outbursts against the authors also implicitly attack *Germanistik* that, in Sebald's opinion, were simply incapable of recognizing their compromised position both politically and morally. In Sebald's view, this position was the result of a discipline afflicted by a variety of intellectual shortcomings (see chapter 24 in this volume).

Sebald's polemical tendency is revealed once again in an exemplary fashion in his 1980 study on *Der Mythus der Zerstörung im Werk Döblins* (*The Myth of Destruction in the Work of Döblin*). This book is the German version of his PhD thesis submitted in 1973 on *The Revival of Myth: A Study of Alfred Döblin's Novels*. The dissertation had no appreciable effect as a contribution to research on Alfred Döblin (1878–1957). However, it is immensely important for Sebald's own genesis as a literary writer.

Here, Sebald heavily focuses on the representation of violence in Döblin's writing and summarizes: 'The artistic reproduction of pain contributes nothing to its redemption. It merely displaces it to another level' (MZ 159). Sebald was convinced that the shock effect, to which Döblin commits himself, results in a 'paralysis of consciousness' for the reader (MZ 159) and ultimately amounts to 'intellectual terror' (MZ 160). Adopting an idea of Adorno, Sebald sums up: 'The act of violence of the intellect does not stand beyond the violence of political practice' (MZ 160).

This is the nucleus of Sebald's principle of poetics that is elaborated in an exemplary way in *Die Ausgewanderten* (*The Emigrants*). The key point is not to portray violence itself as this equates to revitalizing it. Instead, Sebald repeatedly advocated indirect representation of violence as the only possible approach to deal aesthetically with the enormity of the Holocaust: 'So the only way in which one can approach these things, in my view, is obliquely, tangentially, by reference rather than by direct confrontation' (EM 80).

The subtitle of Sebald's thesis – *A Study of Alfred Döblin's Novels* – offers another telling insight into what he understands by the generic term of 'novel'. This carries a negative connotation in the Döblin analysis because Sebald determines the reasons for the inadequacy of the explicit representation of violence in Döblin's writing as being equally inherent to the genre rules: novels demand a plot, an arc of suspense and dialogues (G 235).

Sebald defines his writings in contrast to these literary features: 'My medium is prose, not the novel' (G 85). The fact that Sebald's prose writings deny any classification along the lines of traditional genres – that he even rejects "novel" as a term for his prose text *Austerlitz*, which according to the acknowledged criteria is hardly to be classified as anything else – stems from his early interest in Döblin's works.

Critical Essays: The 'Case Study' Approach

Sebald's two scholarly monographs about German writers from Jewish backgrounds are followed by two collections of essays about Austrian literature, *Die Beschreibung des Unglücks* (*Describing Disaster*, 1985) and *Unheimliche Heimat* (*Strange Homeland*, 1991). In the latter's introduction, Sebald explains that the collection of essays 'pursues a case study approach that changes its analytical method depending on the difficulties that arise' (BU 9). Sebald was not only to retain the flexible, non-theoretical and often unorthodox working method in his subsequent essay collections (his output no longer included monographs) but also the 'case study approach', since his literary work comprises volumes of fictional narratives consisting of correlated case materials.

In both of his essay collections on Austrian literature, Sebald devotes himself to writers such as Adalbert Stifter (1805–1868), Franz Kafka (1883–1924), Elias Canetti (1905–1994), Jean Améry (1912–1978), Thomas Bernhard (1931–1989), Gerhard Roth (1942–2022) and Peter Handke (b. 1942). In other words, he deals with literary authors whose influence on his work was repeatedly emphasized. The essays often show at least as much interest in the personal circumstances of the writers and their lives as their literary contribution. Hence, they already suggest an interest in the biographical search for clues, which equally characterizes all of Sebald's narrative writings, because they always recount personal biographies as well.

There is an evolving tendency in Sebald's work from a pronounced idiosyncratic, yet nonetheless conventional, scholarship in the critical writings of the 1970s and 1980s towards a much freer form from approximately the 1990s. These essays of the later years 'finally dispense with footnotes, throw the ballast of scholarly references overboard and instead strike the typically Sebaldian note'.[1]

This is especially obvious in *Logis in einem Landhaus* (*A Place in the Country*), which is a compilation of essays about writers from the Alemannic cultural background. Here, Sebald devotes his attention to such like-minded writers as Johann Peter Hebel (1760–1826), Gottfried Keller (1819–1890) or Robert Walser (1878–1956) in a notably empathetic manner. He writes about authors with whom he feels an emotional connection and whose life paths and traces of their work he comprehends empathetically.

In this way, the critical discourse mixes time and again with autobiographical reminiscences, such as is most noticeable in superimposing the writers Hebel and Walser on Sebald's grandfather Josef Egelhofer (see chapter 2 in this volume). Here, Sebald not only dispenses completely with footnotes, but also the language of his late essays is differentiated from the characteristic style of his earlier works and resembles the tone of his fictional narratives. In *A Place in the Country*, he also relies on the integration of visual images – a technique that became his trademark from *Schwindel. Gefühle.* (*Vertigo*) onwards – although this does not depict conventional illustration. Accordingly, in his late essays Sebald creates a genre *sui generis* that integrates into his literary work.

Typically, again, there are the notorious invectives against German Studies. While Sebald is no longer bound by its scholarly rules, he evidently still needs such attacks on his own academic discipline to confirm his personal position as an outsider and as a dissident. In this respect the attacks underline Sebald's personal positioning as a wanderer between the worlds of academia and literature, never quite wanting to belong to either one.

Sebald continues his series of polemical studies with *Luftkrieg und Literatur* (*On the Natural History of Destruction*). None of Sebald's other critical works came anywhere close to producing such a strong international reaction. Sebald now accuses the whole of German post-war literature of having been a total moral and aesthetic failure, because it largely avoided tackling the immense importance of the aerial bombardment of German cities during World War Two for the collective psyche of the German population in post-war society. Furthermore, wherever post-war literature addressed the terror unleashed by the Allied bombing campaign, it failed to culminate in any appropriate literary form for the representation of total destruction.

In addition to these four essay collections, there are still dozens of essays, mostly in German, though with some versions already in English, which were circulated largely in a disparate pattern over three decades. These mostly consist of critical essays that discuss literary topics, but they also include forewords to exhibition catalogues, extensive review essays, keynote speeches for literary events or obituaries. Their heterogeneity gives rise to a veritable treasure trove of essayistic contributions where quite a few amazing discoveries can be made.

The posthumous volume *Campo Santo* (2003), in which I gathered together essays that were published between 1975 and 2001, offers a representative cross-section of such materials. Similarly, *On the Natural History of Destruction* (unlike its German companion piece) contains three essays about Alfred Andersch, Jean Améry and Peter Weiss (1916–1982) that are central for understanding Sebald's literary work. Nevertheless, this leaves numerous essays that, for the most part, are still untranslated into English, as well as unpublished essayistic texts from Sebald's literary estate that give informative insights into his thinking and literary writing.[2]

Topics, Motifs and Approaches: Essay and Prose

Many topics that significantly define Sebald's narrative prose are already dealt with in the critical writings, such as the loss of *Heimat* and exile or melancholia as 'a form of resistance' (BU 12), memory and remembering, the connection of ethics and aesthetics, the history of humanity as a sequence of war and aggression as well as man's destruction of nature.

In addition to these topics, the essays also focus on a variety of motifs that define Sebald's literary writing. Special attention is reserved, on the one hand, for trees,[3] and on the other hand for a group of motifs related to birds, flight and levitation, which convey the sense of a 'poetic over-view' (UH 86). Sebald identifies in Handke's *Die Lehre der Sainte Victoire* (*The Lesson of Mont Sainte-Victoire*) 'bird images emblematically inserted into the text' (BU 180). They anticipate the importance that birds also have for Sebald's literary writing.

Sebald illustrates this in an essay, published in 1996, with reference to the example of Vladimir Nabokov, 'whose work contains many passages written from a kind of bird's-eye-view' (CSe 150/CSg 188). According to Sebald, Nabokov's literary approach is based on the possibility 'to see the world through the eye of the crane' so that 'the landscapes of time that have already sunk below the horizon can be seen once again in a synoptic view' (CSe 151/CSg 188–189). However, in an analogous way, the metaphor of the crane's-eye-view is already evident in his 1988 literary debut *After Nature*:

> Now I know, as with a crane's eye / one surveys [Altdorfer's] far-flung realm, / a truly Asiatic spectacle, / and slowly learns, from the tininess / of the figures and the / incomprehensible / beauty of nature that vaults over them / to see that side of life that / one could not see before. (AN 112/NN 98)

Bird descriptions and 'the art of levitation' (CSe 18/CSg 21) form a network of motifs that runs like a golden thread through all of Sebald's narrative (as well as poetic) texts. For example, the narrator of *Die Ringe des Saturn* (*The Rings of Saturn*) recalls as follows: 'At earlier times, in the summer evenings during my childhood when I had watched from the valley as swallows circled in the last light, still in great numbers in those days, I would imagine that the world was held together by the courses they flew through the air' (RSe 67/RSg 87).

Birds are also omnipresent in Sebald's poetry and – for example, as 'our brothers the ducks' (LWe 93/LWg 58) – they frequently denote the interface of human civilization and nature. Hence in the fluent passages between essay and prose the subsequent hybridizing of academic and literary writing methods is already under preparation in a 'poetic form of literary criticism'[4] in *A Place in the Country*.

In his essays, Sebald refers to Claude Lévi-Strauss (1908–2009); his concepts of *bricolage* and mytho-poetically 'wild thought' (*pensée sauvage*) have a significant influence on Sebald's own writing (see chapter 22 in this volume). Lévi-Strauss states that, in the best case, preliminarily valid diminutive experiments denoting the analogous thinking in the *pensée sauvage* are equivalent to scientific and quantifiable thought. However, such thinking also influences our cultural standards of values: 'The ideal-typical work of our culture still flaunts itself in the format of monumental greatness' (UH 160).

Sebald discusses a form of 'irregular' literature, which is a striking contrast to the prevailing aesthetic, by referring to the exemplary paradigm of the schizophrenic poet Ernst Herbeck (1920–1991). In this case, he also clearly takes sides with the social outsider. Sebald paid repeated visits to the patient at the clinic and, for instance, joined him on an excursion that was included as an episode in *Vertigo*. Sebald's aesthetic of the insignificant and marginal individual in general has its roots here.[5]

Scholarly research has consistently affirmed the importance of intertextual references and approaches for Sebald's narrative prose. Sebald's intertextual working method is basically prepared via the essays. Quotations and intertextual references are primarily directed at those writers to whom Sebald dedicated his scholarly output. For example, in one essay Sebald is concerned with Jean Améry's 'Über die Tortur' ('On Torture') and in *Austerlitz* he returns to 'the tortures [Améry] suffered in Breendonk' (Ae 34/Ag 42), where the narrator in the torture chamber simultaneously recalls aspects of his childhood biography.

However, favourite authors whose texts Sebald repeatedly quotes in his critical as well as literary writings not only come from the field of literature: for example, Walter Benjamin (1892–1940), whose angel of history is repeatedly invoked by Sebald; Roland Barthes (1915–1980), Michel Foucault (1926–1984) or John Berger (1926–2017). The sources quoted in the essays later appear once again in his narrative prose so that 'the quotations also serve to some extent to transport the imputed meanings they are given in the essays into the newly constituted text'.[6]

'Of the Same Order': A Poetics of Connection

In the late essay 'Ein Versuch der Restitution' ('An Attempt at Restitution'), Sebald pointedly illustrates more clearly than ever before the question of the function and purpose of literature: 'So what is literature good for?' (CSe 247/CSg 214). He continues: 'There are many forms of writing; only in literature, however, can there be an attempt at restitution over and above the mere recital of facts and over and above scholarship' (CSe 215/CSg 248). The resulting poetics of restitution, the idea that fictional writing can redeem what has been lost, or at least do it justice, as well as the possibility of self-healing through writing, was already indicated at an earlier point.

Hence, Sebald had already described, in *Strange Homeland*, 'the bridge of letters between misfortune and solace' (UH 13), and so emphasizes the redeeming dimension of literature. Sebald explicitly formulates these poetics in his essay on Joseph Roth, where the focus is on a childhood memory of visits to a clockmaker's workshop. The clockmaker's activity involves a messianic connotation in which Sebald recognizes an ideal for the artisan and the writer that is inherent to both Roth and himself: 'The hope of the clockmaker as well as of the prose writer is that a tiny intervention has the capacity to bring everything back into the right order, as it was intended from the beginning' (UH 114).

That is to say the focus is on creating connections and thus finding restitution for what is lost. In *A Place in The Country* Sebald writes how he grasped, when reading Robert Walser, 'how everything is connected across space and time' (PC 149/LH 162). This 'poetics of connection'[7] or 'poetics of coincidence'[8] is prepared in Sebald's critical writings and defines his narrative prose. Their structuring principles are elective affinities, correspondences and analogy formations.

In *Vertigo*, Sebald finds this image: 'I sat at a table near the open terrace door, my papers and notes spread out around me, drawing connections between events that lay far apart but which seemed to me to be of the same order. I wrote with an ease that astonished me' (V 94/SG 107). In *Austerlitz*, on the other hand, the adopted term is 'family likeness' (Ae 44/Ag 52) and connections are created while arranging the pictures in a game of patience 'depending on their family resemblances' (Ae 168/Ag 176). Sebald's prose texts repeatedly explain this literary programme.

Two Sides of the Same Coin

In 1990, after he was awarded his first literary prize for *After Nature*, Sebald commented that he had 'two writing rooms: one for literature and one for scholarship.'[9] However, these two categories cannot be separated for Sebald. Indeed, one can hardly overestimate the influence of his scholarly writings on the genesis of his literary texts. The critical writings turn out to be a testing ground to check and elaborate those principles of poetics that later will strongly influence his literary work and even define some of its central features. Thus, the critical writings precede the literature – and at the same time seep into it. Due to this decidedly critical scholarship, the essays cultivate the emergence of a negative poetics that finally form the determining principle of Sebald's literary texts.

There are hardly any significant tensions between Sebald's academic and literary œuvre. They appear as two sides of the same coin. For instance, what the critical writings incriminate in the texts of other writers (such as the inappropriate representations of violence) becomes the guiding principle for the production of his own texts. Similarly, those authors that Sebald positively appraised beforehand in the critical writings are intertwined with his narrative texts by means of quotations and intertextual references.

These findings can be confirmed time and again with numerous references to passages in the texts. However, this fact comes at the risk of substantiating and deriving Sebald's poetics primarily based on his critical approach. That would leave a circular argument – and perhaps it provides one of the reasons for the tremendous success that Sebald enjoys in German Studies internationally. Academics make rich findings in Sebald's texts because he orders his texts according to the principles that he creates through his own poetics. Therefore, one frequently interprets "Sebald with Sebald".

However, it would be more rewarding to establish productive tensions and thus to compile a more differentiated picture of the writer. Because Sebald's literary criticism is 'also always disguised autobiography and mirroring of the self in the other',[10] it allows the reader generally to learn more about the author of the critical writings than about the subjects in their own right.

Notes

1. S Meyer, Foreword, in: Sebald, *Campo Santo* (London: Penguin, 2006), pp. ix–xii (xi).
2. Uwe Schütte is the editor of a forthcoming volume that collects the large part of these disparate texts with unpublished pieces from W.G. Sebald's literary estate.
3. U Schütte, *Annäherungen. Sieben Essays zu W.G. Sebald* (Cologne: Böhlau, 2019), pp. 77–104.
4. U Schütte, *Interventionen: Literaturkritik als Widerspruch bei W.G. Sebald* (Munich: Ed. Text + Kritik, 2014), p. 534.
5. P Whitehead, *Im Abseits: W.G. Sebalds Ästhetik des Marginalen* (Bielefeld: Transcript, 2019).
6. P Schmucker, Die Beschreibung des Unglücks, in: M Niehaus, C Öhlschläger (eds.), *W.G. Sebald Handbuch. Leben – Werk – Wirkung* (Stuttgart: Metzler, 2017).

7. S Meyer, Keine Kausallogik: Zum Zusammenhang in W.G. Sebalds Schreiben, in: U Schütte (ed.), *Über W.G. Sebald: Beiträge zu einem anderen Bild des Autors* (Berlin/Boston: De Gruyter, 2017), pp. 19–28 (26).
8. M Atze, Koinzidenz und Intertextualität: Der Einsatz von Prätexten in W.G. Sebalds Erzählung ›All'estero‹, in: F Loquai (ed.), *W.G. Sebald* (Eggingen: Ed. Isele, 1997), pp. 151–175 (152).
9. S Meyer, Der Kopf, der auftaucht: Zu W.G. Sebalds ›'Nach der Natur', in: M Atze, F Loquai (eds.), *Sebald. Lektüren.* (Eggingen: Ed. Isele, 2005), pp. 67–77 (69).
10. Schütte, *Interventionen*, p. 17.

CHAPTER 18

Minor Writing

Uwe Schütte

Sebald appreciated eccentrics, oddballs and obscurantists of all kinds, but he had a particular soft spot for amateurs and dilettantes whose non-conformist positions resisted being integrated into an enlightened, empirical view of the world. Therein also lay their relevance for Sebald's own work, for he rightly suspected scientifically discredited hypotheses and idiosyncratic theories of having the potential to yield a rich vein of untapped insights for his writing. As early as his 1973 PhD thesis, he stated with programmatic force: 'It is precisely the aprofessional dilettantism which sometimes affords a prospect undreamed of by professional criticism' (RM 213–214), thus overturning the hierarchy of professional and amateur on which academia founds its claim to superiority.

Sebald's own disposition duly tended towards non-conformity. His critical writings often disregarded scholarly convention, and his literary work was similarly informed by a predilection for the discredited and the heterodox. Rather than to the literary greats and tradition, he turned to whatever lay outside the established canon as a benchmark, broadly orienting himself by a view of literature as 'minor writing'.

Amateurs, Eccentrics, Obsessives

Lifestyles and conduct that defied social norms and convention were fascinating to Sebald and he found, at least from a German's point of view, a rich tapestry of these in 1960s England. The members of Manchester's German Department had already been aware of Sebald's 'preference for the oddities and eccentricities of English life' (SM 82). Ending up in East Anglia in the 1970s, then still a remote backwater where eccentricity seemed to flourish, gave him ample opportunity for indulging that preference. By contrast, towards the end of the 1990s, he lamented being the only one of his kind still remaining:

> I am now the only person in the university not to have a computer, and that is regarded as quixotic. It is the only sort of eccentricity that is left. But when I first came here, almost every other colleague was slightly eccentric. [. . .] They have all been eliminated.[1]

In the short travelogue Sebald wrote in 1974 about a walking tour of East Anglia (SM 319–323), he praised the area for stubbornly 'persist-[ing] in its eccentric way of life'.[2] The travel essay, which was written for the German newspaper *Die Zeit*, might be read as a prelude to *Die Ringe des Saturn* (*The Rings of Saturn*) and its assortment of eccentric East Anglian figures, including poets Algernon Charles Swinburne (1837–1909) and Edward FitzGerald (1809–1883). Sebald was drawn to their unconventional biographies, but above all to their distinctly idiosyncratic approach to literature, as displayed, for instance, in Fitzgerald's elaborate project of 'making notes towards a dictionary of commonplaces, with compiling a complete glossary of all words and phrases relating to the sea and to seafaring and with pasting up scrap books of every conceivable description' (RSe 199–200/RSg 237).

Another East Anglian oddity to catch Sebald's attention was farmer Thomas Abrams (recte: Alec Garrard), who had been 'working on a model of the Temple of Jerusalem for a good twenty years' (RSe 242/RSg 286). Garrard/Abrams was a quintessential amateur in Sebald's eyes, whose meticulous undertaking points to the Latin root of the word: *amare*, to love. He was obsessively devoted to his intricate hobby because it consti-tuted a profound, personal passion.

This is also how Sebald viewed the craft of literature, as informed by Garrardian dedication: 'I don't consider myself a writer', he explained, likening his work to 'someone who builds a model of the Eiffel Tower out of matchsticks. It's a devotional work. Obsessive' (EM 169). Sebald has in mind here the endless hours spent in the metaphorical 'potting shed' (EM 61) of his dingy upstairs study at the Old Rectory, where he did his writing. Just as Garrard/Abrams once told a visitor enquiring about the secret of his work, Sebald, too, might have said: 'it's research really and work, endless hours of work' (RSe 245/RSg 291).

Illustration 15 – Sebald, presenting homegrown asparagus

'Toward a Minor Literature'

What characterizes devotees such as Garrard/Abrams is that they approach their projects 'with a combination of curiosity and authority that retains the amateur's conception of his or her labour as a personal endeavour'.[3] Not only do amateurs and eccentrics abound in Sebald's books but, as Ruth Franklin further observes, 'the books themselves both depict and embody an almost anti-academic [...] approach to study and contemplation'.[4] This becomes particularly apparent in figures close to the narrators' hearts, as in the fictional teacher André Hilary in *Austerlitz* or the fictionalized versions of Sebald's real-life colleagues Michael Parkinson and Janine Dakyns in *The Rings of Saturn*.

As well as to eccentrics and amateurs, Sebald was drawn to disciplines and schools of thought considered outmoded and past it. Prime among these was metaphysics:

> Certainly, one of the things that has interested me most is the much-despised discipline of metaphysics, which was relegated from philosophy proper generations ago. I always thought that metaphysics was by far the most interesting branch of philosophy and anything to do with it always held my attention.[5]

Precisely because 'it has become almost taboo to speak of metaphysics today' (G 74), Sebald wrote about it with a passion that made his focus on insignificant and discarded items read as a 'meditation on the detritus, the curiosities and the forgotten objects of history'.[6] Hence, for instance, the curious *teas-maid*, which in the 'Max Ferber' chapter seems to the narrator to operate as a guardian angel of sorts, a magical device with metaphysical properties, requiring for its use an 'initiation into the mysteries of what Gracie called an *electrical miracle*' (E 155/AW 226).

Sebald harboured a special fascination for lesser, "poorer" substances for their capacity to acquire a metaphysical substrate: 'I admire ash very much', he observed. 'The very last product of combustion, with no resistance in it. The borderline between being and nothingness. Ash is a redeemed substance, like dust.'[7] And it is this 'borderline between being and nothingness' that Sebald attempted to travel and traverse in his writing. His devotion was to the insubstantial and obscure, rather than the durable and monumental.

A similar inclination towards the lesser and seemingly negligible informed where Sebald sought cultural or environmental inspiration. Rather than to any symbolically overdetermined sites at the heart of high culture, he was drawn to more peripheral retreats such as the Sailors' Reading Room in Southwold: 'by far my favourite haunt', as the narrator of *The Rings of Saturn* puts it (RSe 93/RSg 115).

Correspondingly, it was not the hallowed monuments of high culture that inspired Sebald to write but their opposite: while Thomas Mann's creativity was ignited by the opulent compositions of Richard Wagner, to Sebald, it was the carnival music of a down-at-heel travelling circus orchestra with its slightly out-of-tune instruments that embodied transcendental art: an 'extraordinarily foreign nocturnal music conjured out of thin air' that made it impossible for Austerlitz to say 'whether my heart was contracting in pain or expanding with happiness for the first time in my life' (Ae 383/Ag 389–390).

Against the backdrop outlined above, this essay will put forward a reading of Sebald as a "minor author", in acknowledgment of Sebald's own explicit 'commitment to a lesser form of literature' (G 118). The significance of this devotion to an unsanctioned, self-authorized, autodidactic practice of art at the periphery, or outside of, the canon, for Sebald's own critical and literary writings cannot be overestimated, and yet it's a significance that risks being obscured by the ironic centrality his œuvre has been accorded in the literary canon.

Academic Outlaws

Given his self-perception as an academic nonconformist (see chapter 24 in this volume), Sebald's interests naturally tended beyond standard authorities such as Walter Benjamin and the rest of the Frankfurt School to ideas and theories outside the normative academic canon. One example is the controversial work of anthropologist Gregory Bateson (1904–1980) on patterns of connection, in which Bateson disputes the coincidentality of coincidence and argues for an underlying consonance that remains to be discovered. In this, Bateson appears as a successor of sorts to Thomas Browne (1605–1682) and his writings on the geometrical arrangement of the quincunx as the key to a metaphysical view of the world, thus also providing further inspiration for Sebald's own 'poetics of coincidence'.

As Sebald once stated in an interview: 'When we're faced with disconcerting coincidences, it is hard to shake the feeling that there must be some deeper meaning to them. And yet we don't know what that meaning is' (G 74). A major driving force behind his writing was the desire to seek this meaning in the disparate and draw 'connections between events that lay far apart but which seemed to me to be of the same order' (V 84/SG 107).

Sven Meyer has pointed out the 'airbrushing of undesired elements'[8] from the image of Sebald, citing as an example the heretical natural scientist Rupert Sheldrake (b. 1942), who had a recognizable influence on Sebald's thinking. Sheldrake's theory of morphic resonance, dismissed by the scientific community as esotericism, offers a perfectly coherent explanation for what Sebald raises as the crucial question in his essay on Robert Walser (1878–1956), namely 'how everything is connected across space and time, [...] Robert Walser's long walks with my own travels, dates of birth with dates of death, happiness with misfortune, natural history and the history of our industries, that of *Heimat* with that of exile' (PC 149/LH 162–163).

Another marginal academic figure of significance to Sebald is the now-forgotten anthropologist Rudolf Bilz (1898–1976), who sought to explain irrational conduct as phylogenetic atavisms. Bilz's explanatory models, which, in their merging of objective science with subjective conjecture, far exceeded what could be empirically proven, appealed to Sebald, and his critical essays from the 1970s and 1980s – from Kafka to Handke to Ernst Herbeck – contain numerous explicit and implicit references to Bilz's ideas.

Thus Sebald's third essay on Kafka adopts Bilz's idea that humankind experienced the prehistoric migration from the forests to the plains as a primal catastrophic loss. And when the narrator of the Corsica Project confesses that, in dense forests, he can feel 'how the fear of being lost in the world constricts your heart & overwhelms you with the suspicion that you are at the mercy of nature in its hostile alienness' (KP 141), he is putting into words precisely that atavistic, uncanny fear Bilz postulated as humankind's reason for leaving the primeval forests.

In keeping with Bilz's contention that migrating from the forests to the plains marked the beginning of our species' separation from nature, Sebald suggests: 'Nature is the context in which we originally belonged and from which, unrelentingly, [. . .] we have been driven. Our physical bodies may still contain a memory of nature, but it is just a memory' (G 94). Over decades, ideas that can be traced back to Bilz have surfaced in essays and prose narratives by Sebald. However, because Bilz's speculative writings have so long been considered outdated and have been marginalized from academic discourse, this has been comprehensively overlooked by Sebald scholarship.

Minor Writers: Herbert Achternbusch and Ernst Herbeck

Sebald was particularly interested in outsiders who, like himself, had succeeded in writing their 'way out of anonymity' (UH 15). His essays singing the praises of Herbert Achternbusch (1938–2022) and Ernst Herbeck (1920–1991) mark a protest against German studies: an impassioned intervention in support of authors who fall below or outside of what is conventionally considered as literature.

Anarchist, autodidact, filmmaker, actor, painter, playwright, author and eccentric celebrator of the absurd and scurrilous, Herbert Achternbusch, is a perfect case in point. His literary and painterly work often closely resembles that of artists grouped under the category of *art brut*, so 'the work of the insane, prisoners, children, and primitive artists'.[9] Sebald defines the distinction between normal and non-normative artistic practice as a dichotomy between engineering and tinkering: 'In contrast to a literary engineer, a tinkerer-writer such as Achternbusch produces linguistic constructions and images that a professional author wouldn't dream of.'[10]

Drawing on Lévi-Strauss's *La pensée sauvage* (*The Savage Mind*, 1962), Sebald regards Achternbusch's uncultivated prose as a form of "wild writing": a comparison of his texts 'with the artfully crafted syntax of accredited major writers, brings home the remarkable accuracy with which they capture the increasingly uncanny reality of our times'.[11] In particular, Sebald is referring here to Achternbusch's recurring emphasis on the marginalized and 'the suffering of our interned comrades':[12] those excommunicated from society into homes, asylums or reservations.

Sebald also appreciated Achternbusch's identificatory solidarity with imprisoned or exploited animals. For both Sebald and Achternbusch, zoos and abattoirs epitomize power in their unvarnished display of mechanisms of exclusion and control. And both men responded polemically, as in their provocative analogy between slaughterhouses and concentration camps, both governed by ruthless instrumentalizing reason.[13]

Finally, Sebald admired about Achternbusch's prose the fact that 'not many have come closer to the language of schizophrenia without themselves losing their mind'.[14] Sebald himself was well aware of the particularities of psychopathological writing. Since 1966, informed by the writings of Austrian psychiatrist Leo Navratil, he had been engaging with poetry by institutionalized schizophrenics, chief among them the poet Ernst Herbeck: 'I first came upon [his] eccentric figures of speech in 1966 [...] sitting in the Ryland's Library in Manchester [...] and found myself amazed by the brilliance of the riddling verbal images' (CSe 130/CSg 171).

This was a watershed moment for Sebald: 'The magnetism of [Herbeck's poems] kept Sebald enthralled as a young academic and continued to exert a force over roughly the next three decades.'[15] In 1980, he visited Herbeck in his care home near Vienna and later incorporated a (semi-fictional) account of an outing the two of them took together in his work (SG 44–57/V 38–49). The passage includes a reproduction of the short-form poetry Herbeck was fond of jotting down spontaneously. What *Germanistik* would dismiss as a form of writing therapy, Sebald took seriously as poetry.

What is more, to Sebald, schizophrenic poetry felt like a paradigm of minor literature, for it 'indicates what we aspire to more precisely than rational discourse ever could. [...] The more administered culture, like science before it, becomes, the greater the potential significance of minor literature, of which Herbeck should be considered an ambassador' (BU 161).

However, Sebald does not just situate Herbeck's writing in the context of Deleuze and Guattari's *littérature mineure*. Lévi-Strauss, and especially the idea of *bricolage*, are again just as important to him. As well as representing a fundamentally non-professional 'tinkering' with language, Herbeck's approach, to Sebald's mind, constitutes a form of 'wild thinking', by dint of the fact that 'schizophrenia enables the re-emergence of more primal forms of human expression' (BU 135). 'Following "twisted" paths', Herbeck would 'approach unerring insights' in the course of his writing (BU 135).

Sebald considers two aspects of Herbeck's poetry to be crucial: For one, as in the case of Achternbusch, his pronounced empathy with animals and, in particular, his identificatory solidarity with small, captive or exploited creatures. Caged zoo animals or pets (such as a rhino, mouse or bird) repeatedly serve as overt symbols of his own near-lifelong psychiatric institutionalization. In a Deleuzoguattarian sense, such a poetic becoming-animal constitutes a line of flight as an escape from heteronomous, marginalized living.

Above all others, according to Sebald, it is the hare that 'is undoubtedly the totem animal in which the writer sees himself' (CSe 135/CSg 175). Herbeck had a cleft palate, a 'harelip', which compounded his social marginalization and caused him great pain. In his essay 'Des Häschens Kind, der kleine Has' ('The Little Hare, Child of the Hare'), Sebald analyses an autobiographical prose text by Herbeck about a family meal in the course of which a hare is consumed. Sebald reads the text as an accusatory parable on the harmful impact of dysfunctional family dynamics and the individual's forced inclusion in a system of power relations in which everyone is at once victim and perpetrator. 'This victim-perpetrator position is universal and yet the majority of people in society', according to Sebald, 'are blind to this state.'[16]

The second crucial aspect of Herbeck's writing for Sebald was its commitment to a becoming-minoritarian, for there is a 'correlation between the experience of suffering and the dream of becoming smaller' (BU 147). Accordingly, one of Herbeck's maxims was: 'The greater the pain / The smaller the poet.'[17] Sebald read this idealization of self-shrinkage as a form of resistance against, and withdrawal from, contemporary society's obsession with progress and expansion.

In his commitment to both lines of flight, becoming-animal and becoming-minoritarian, Herbeck recalls other authors of importance for Sebald, including Franz Kafka or Elias Canetti, making him a further admired exponent of minor writing in the eyes of the German academic and writer.

Robert Walser: Mastery in a Minor Key

A devaluation of the monumental in favour of the diminutive and modest runs like a thread through Sebald's whole œuvre. It sees him, for instance, have his architectural historian Austerlitz reject 'a vast edifice such as the

Palace of Justice' and praise 'domestic buildings of *less* than normal size –
the little cottage in the fields, the hermitage, the lockkeeper's lodge, the
pavilion for viewing the landscape, the children's bothy in the garden', for
their ability to 'offer us at least a semblance of peace' (Ae 23/Ag 31).

It is therefore hardly surprising that Sebald held in particularly high
esteem a German-language author who like no other stands for mastery of
the minor: Robert Walser. 'Le promeneur solitaire', Sebald's great essay on
the author of microgarms, is more literature than literary criticism, and less
homage than hagiography: the canonization of a literary saint.

Sebald transfigures Walser into a 'legend' (PC 122/LH 132) whose
biography bears all the signs of a holy vocation: renunciation of the
world, reclusiveness, and an asceticism encompassing self-sacrifice, morti-
fication and martyrdom. Sebald even ascribed to Walser the ability to
perform miracles with his minor writing: Walser always 'refused the grand
gesture' (PC 146/LH 159), but he can bring about a state change from
'something very dense to something almost weightless. His ideal was to
overcome the force of gravity' (PC 130/LH 141). In Sebald's aesthetic frame
of reference, there was no higher accolade than to be attributed the ability
to achieve levitation through literature.

In keeping with his 'natural inclination [...] for the most radical
minimization and brevity' (PC 130/LH 142), Walser's focus was trained
on the negligible, ephemeral and evanescent. This manifested itself materi-
ally in the medium of his handwriting, which progressively decreased in
size to where the pencilled letters of his late manuscripts were barely more
than a millimetre tall. Sebald described these microgarms, which tended
towards illegibility, as a 'work of fortifications and defences, unique in the
history of literature, by means of which the smallest and most innocent
things might be saved from destruction' (PC 141/LH 154). They were, in
Sebald's reading, a form of subversive writing, the 'coded messages of
someone forced into illegitimacy' (PC 141/LH 154), even as their development (from the mid-1920s, if not before) significantly preceded Walser's
first admission to a psychiatric hospital in 1929.

The culmination of Walser's life in the social margins of psychiatric
institutionalization is just one reason for Sebald's close association of his
minor literature with that of Herbeck. In *Vertigo*, he merges both authors
by having a photograph of Walser, cropped at the neck, purportedly
represent Herbeck (SG 46/V 39).

In his Walser essay, he also, again through the medium of photographs,
connects the Swiss writer with his own grandfather Josef Egelhofer,
because 'it was not only in their appearance that my grandfather and

Walser resembled each other, but also in their general bearing' (PC 126/LH 136). Beyond any physical resemblance, Walser and Egelhofer are linked by the coincidence of having died in the same year, in 1956. By so closely aligning the most important figure of his childhood (see chapter 2 in this volume) with 'Saint Robert', Sebald is at the same time apotheosizing his own grandfather, with whose death 'I have never been able to reconcile myself' (PC 127/LH 137).

Thus positioned in close proximity to two important persons in Sebald's own life, Walser also acquires a special significance for Sebald himself. Apostrophizing him as a 'departed colleague', Sebald says of his 'strangely close relationship' (PC 128/LH 139) with the Swiss author:

> Walser has been my constant companion. I only need to look up for a moment in my daily work to see him standing somewhere a little apart, the unmistakable figure of the solitary walker just pausing to take in the surroundings. And sometimes I imagine that I see with his eyes. (PC 149/ LH 163)

Here Sebald imagines himself not just physically merging with Walser but even taking on the role of his *ghost writer*, seeing what he sees, and thinking as he thinks when, with reference to the 'Ambros Adelwarth' chapter of *Die Ausgewanderten (The Emigrants)*, he claims the neologism 'Trauerlaufbahn' ('career in mourning'), initially taken to be his own, had in fact been prompted to him by Walser from beyond the grave (LH 138–139/PC 127–128).

While we may take his miracle story with a grain of salt, there can be no doubt that Sebald identified deeply with authors whose life and works mark them out as minor writers. It is not least this commitment to the minor that makes him great.

Conclusion

As has become apparent, Sebald's conception of minor writing should be understood in relation to, but by no means as dependent on, the idea of *littérature mineure* as developed by Deleuze and Guattari on the basis of Kafka's work. Privileging literary theory over practice was not how he operated. Yet there is no doubt that Sebald would have included Kafka in the canon of minor writing. And just as Kafka wrote in a minority language in Prague, Sebald not only continued to write in German in England but also employed a markedly antiquated version of it, informed with Southern German vernacular, thus further minoritizing what, in the context, was already a minority language.

Sebald as a representative of minor literature deserves greater attention, as seemingly incidental sources or passing references reveal themselves to be important influences. For instance, Sebald repeatedly consulted the extensive *Handwörterbuch des deutschen Aberglaubens* (*Dictionary of German Superstition*, 1927–1942) as a source of forgotten knowledge, and *Nach der Natur* (*After Nature*) contains several unmarked inclusions of apocalyptic visions by the eighteenth-century Bavarian 'forest prophet' Mühlhiasl.

Not least, there is an important moral and ethical dimension to Sebald's predilection for discredited, minor positions. In his essay on Gerhard Roth's *Landläufiger Tod* (*Common Death*, 1984), Sebald explicitly praises Roth for 'restoring to the art of writing much of its dignity, a dignity which consists in steadfastly preserving lost perspectives and refusing to surrender one's superstitions, since there is no less wisdom in superstition than there is credulity in science' (UH 161).

Notes

1. T Green, The Questionable Business of Writing [interview], in: Three Encounters with W.G. Sebald, in: *Journal of European Studies* 44:4 (2014), pp. 378–414 (388–389).
2. Sebald, The Carved Wooden Angels of East Anglia: Travelogue 1974, in: *Journal of European Studies* 41:3–4, pp. 243–254 (243).
3. R Franklin, Sebald's Amateurs, in: S Denham, M McCulloh (eds.), *W.G. Sebald: History – Memory – Trauma* (Berlin/New York: De Gruyter, 2006), pp. 127–138 (137).
4. Ibid., p. 128.
5. C Bigsby, *Writers in Conversation with Christopher Bigsby*, vol. 2 (Norwich: EAS, 2001), pp. 139–165 (159).
6. P Whitehead, *Im Abseits: W.G. Sebalds Ästhetik des Marginalen* (Bielefeld: Aisthesis, 2019), p. 41.
7. S Katafou, An Interview with W.G. Sebald, in: *Harvard Review* 15 (1998), pp. 31–35 (32).
8. S Meyer, Keine Kausallogik: Zum Zusammenhang in W.G. Sebalds Schreiben, in: U Schütte (ed.), *Über W.G. Sebald: Beiträge zu einem anderen Bild des Autors* (Berlin/Boston: De Gruyter, 2017), pp. 19–28 (26).
9. www.tate.org.uk/art/art-terms/a/art-brut.
10. Sebald, Die weiße Adlerfeder am Kopf: Versuch über den Indianer Herbert Achternbusch, in: *Manuskripte* 79 (1983), pp. 75–79 (77).
11. Ibid., p. 78.
12. Ibid.

13. Sebald, The Art of Transformation: Herbert Achternbusch's Theatrical Mission, in: Sebald (ed.), *A Radical Stage: Theatre in Germany in the 1970s, and 1980s* (Oxford: Berg, 1990), pp. 174–184 (184).

14. Sebald, Die weiße Adlerfeder am Kopf, p. 77.

15. M Etzler, Peripheral Writing: Psychosis and Prose from Ernst Herbeck to W. G. Sebald, in: Ö Çakırtaş (ed.), *Literature and Psychology: Writing, Trauma and the Self* (Newcastle: Cambridge Scholars, 2019), pp. 18–48 (19).

16. Ibid., p. 35.

17. E Herbeck, *Im Herbst da reiht der Feenwind: Gesammelte Texte 1960–1991* (Salzburg: Residenz, 1999), p. 68.

CHAPTER 19

Franz Kafka

Ritchie Robertson

Sebald's fascination with Franz Kafka (1883–1924) extended beyond admiration to identification. Richard Sheppard maintains that 'Kafka was probably the foremost of [Sebald]'s numerous alter egos'.[1] Such identification is apparent from Sebald's critical writing, which includes two major essays and several shorter pieces on Kafka, and from his narrative prose: *Schwindel. Gefühle.* (*Vertigo*), above all, is dominated by motifs from Kafka's personal and fictional writings. Sebald's technique throughout is to create a richly suggestive web of associations.

Sebald as Kafka Critic

Sebald's two substantial essays, published in the early 1970s, deal with *Das Schloss* (*The Castle*).[2] Though packed with material, they aim at suggestion and stimulus rather than conclusiveness. Sebald later denounced the speculative and tedious nature of most academic Kafka commentary, except for some historical and biographical studies which enable us to reconstruct the image of the author in his time (CSg 196/CSe 159). For the latter his model is clearly Walter Benjamin (1892–1940), whom Sebald constantly cited, particularly his essay on Kafka.[3] Like Benjamin, Sebald seeks to illuminate Kafka by juxtaposing textual passages with other literary texts, myths and folktales.

Conventional academic commentary is rarely cited, though Ronald Gray's *Kafka's Castle* (1956) is drawn on, and an article by Klaus Wagenbach relating the fictional Castle to a real castle in the southern Bohemian village of Osek (Wossek) is mentioned without a reference.[4] By largely ignoring the critical literature on Kafka, Sebald keeps the literary text in the foreground and enables the reader to encounter it freshly. This hands-on approach also characterized his teaching, to the surprise and pleasure of German students accustomed to the theory-heavy approach of literary studies as practised in Germany (see chapter 5 in this volume).

The earlier essay from 1972, 'Das unentdeckte Land: Zur Motivstruktur in Kafkas ›Schloss‹' ('The Undiscover'd Country: The Death Motif in Kafka's ›The Castle‹', BU 78–92), offers an alternative to the broadly 'existentialist' readings of Kafka current in the 1950s and 1960s. Sebald declares his allegiance to the Frankfurt School by quoting from an essay by Theodor W. Adorno (1903–1969) on Franz Schubert (1797–1828) and Benjamin's study of Charles Baudelaire (1821–1867). Benjamin's essay on Kafka is cited when Kafka's female figures are related to the primeval phase that Benjamin, borrowing from the Swiss classical scholar Johann Jakob Bachofen (1815–1887), calls 'hetaeric'.[5] It is also evoked, though not specified, when Sebald speaks of the famous photograph showing Kafka as a sad-looking five-year-old.[6]

Like his mentors, Sebald also draws eclectically on psychoanalysis. Discussing K.'s recollection of climbing a wall and planting a flag in *The Castle*, Sebald rejects the 'crude psychology' which would interpret this as a sexual triumph and finds rather the ambivalence seen in 'Freud's theory, developed in his later years, of the identity of the life and the death wish', both of which, according to Freud, sought an escape from individuation.[7] In *Jenseits des Lustprinzips* (*Beyond the Pleasure Principle*, 1920), Sigmund Freud (1856–1939) certainly assigns the death-drive great power as 'an urge inherent in organic life to restore an earlier state of things'.[8] However, it does not dominate the life-instinct as Sebald suggests, seeking support for his thesis that death is omnipresent in *The Castle*. Although Sebald interprets many textual details as symbolizing death, he is perhaps more convincing when he intuitively associates *The Castle* with Schubert's *Winterreise*: there is no genetic connection between Schubert and Kafka (who professed to be completely unmusical), but the association strengthens one's sense of the poetic depth of Kafka's novel.

Here Sebald also introduces the theme of messianism, noting that other characters regard K. as a potential deliverer. Hence the schoolboy Hans prophesies that 'K. might be in a low, humiliating position at the moment, but in an admittedly almost unimaginably distant future he would still triumph over everyone'.[9] K. has a 'latent messianic mission to invade the realm of the dead as a living saviour'.[10] Here Sebald may be recalling the Christian tradition that Christ descended into hell and granted salvation to the righteous among the dead. However, since K. is only human, his limited strength gives out when he falls asleep on Bürgel's bed: he is a failed messiah.

The original German essay of 'Das unentdeckte Land' opens with a reference to Kafka's childhood photograph that is absent in Sebald's

English translation and adaption of the essay; also, death-imagery is pursued less relentlessly, and the material on messianism is much briefer.[11] The essay is brilliantly wayward, expressing 'a powerful, idiosyncratic vision, ostensibly trained on Kafka's text [. . .] but ultimately shooting past it'.[12]

The later essay, 'The Law of Ignominy', 1974/1976 (translated and adapted by Sebald as 'Das Gesetz der Schande: Macht, Messianismus und Exil in Kafkas ›Schloss‹', 1975, UH 87–103) develops the messianic theme further. It begins with reflections on power, exemplified by the power that the Castle wields over the villagers and, despite his efforts, over K., the alleged land-surveyor. The power of the Castle is sterile, aiming only to perpetuate itself. It is parasitic, in that it depends on reducing other people to impotence and creating ugliness and deformity. The statement in the text that Castle officials leave their rooms filthy prompts Sebald to maintain that power rejects whatever it cannot use and turns it into filth and excrement: order generates ordure. Although there is no reference, the ahistorical assertions about power also recall Elias Canetti's *Masse und Macht* (*Crowds and Power*, 1960), a book that left traces in many of Sebald's writings.[13]

Sebald then links power with messianism by asserting that power, thus described, demands a revolutionary upheaval, yet renders such an upheaval impossible. The only way one can imagine transcending this impasse is by a messianic transformation. Sebald now speaks of the Jewish tradition of Messianism, in which the messiah is often pictured as emerging from among the downtrodden. He finds this tradition alluded to in *The Castle*, where 'the Hebrew word for land-surveyor, *moshoakh*, is but one unwritten vowel removed from *mashiakh*, the Hebrew word for messiah'.[14]

Since writing the earlier essay, he seems to have read the Kafka study by Evelyn Torton Beck, who reports this pun without exploring its implications for the novel.[15] Sebald, who often ignored academic niceties, does not reference her work. He understands Kafka's K. as a messianic figure who seeks a confrontation with the Castle in order to overthrow its power. The members of the Barnabas family, ostracized by the other villagers, represent Jewish life in exile and look to K. for redemption. However, K.'s strength gives out. Humankind may just not to be strong enough for such a liberating deed. However, this need not matter, for 'what is important in messianic thought is solely the viability of what Ernst Bloch called *das Prinzip Hoffnung*, "the Hope Principle"'.[16]

As an interpretation of *The Castle*, this is broadly tenable. Besides staying close to the text, it provides a historico-religious context for the novel and

presents it with sharper outlines than the many fuzzy metaphysical readings then current. Sebald does not tell us where his knowledge of Jewish
tradition comes from, apart from citing Martin Buber's (1878–1965) retell-
ings of Hasidic tales. Throughout, one feels Benjamin's presence, especially
his 'Theses on the Philosophy of History', where Benjamin hints at the
messianic hope implicit in revolutionary moments.

In his later essay, 'Tiere, Menschen, Maschinen: Zu Kafkas
Evolutionsgeschichten' ('Animals, Humans, Machines: On Kafka's Stories
of Evolution, 1986),[17] Sebald uses Kafka as a pretext for a meditation on
cultural decline. Drawing heavily on writings by Stanisław Lem (1921–2006)
and Pierre Bertaux (1907–1986) (see chapter 18 in this volume), Sebald cites
contemporary predictions that humanity will mutate, perhaps soon, into
mechanical entities or cyborgs, and relates them to Kafka's 'Ein Bericht für
eine Akademie' ('A Report to an Academy', 1917) in which the captive ape
Rotpeter reports on his (alleged) accelerated evolution into a human being.

This is interpreted as a critique not only of Darwin's theory of evolution
but of all doctrines of progress based on it. Rotpeter is still a captive,
submitting to the demands of civilization, while the academicians who
hear his report in silence may, for all we know, already be the inorganic
beings of the post-human future. This is hardly an interpretation of Kafka,
but it again shows how Sebald incorporated Kafka's texts into his thought
processes.[18]

The essays in the posthumously published *Campo Santo* include two
shorter pieces on Kafka. In 'Via Schweiz ins Bordell: Zu den
Reisetagebüchern Kafkas' ('To the Brothel by Way of Switzerland',
1995), Sebald reads Kafka's 1911 travel diary and confirms his identification
with Kafka by recalling journeys in his own childhood (CSg 140–145/CSe
179–183,). The other essay, 'Kafka im Kino' ('Kafka Goes to the Movies',
1996), originated as a review of Hanns Zischler's book on Kafka's filmgoing (CSg 193–209/CSe 156–73).[19]

The version in *Campo Santo*, based on Sebald's manuscript, works
associatively. It moves from cinema to Kafka's well-attested unease about
photographs, which seemed to be 'Doppelgänger' of their subjects. Sebald
then wonders whether Kafka saw the film *Der Student von Prag* (*The
Student of Prague*, 1913) about a student pursued by his double (see chapter
34 in this volume). Zischler's information that Kafka saw a documentary
film about the settlements in Palestine, *Schiwat Zion* (*Return to Zion*, 1921),
leads Sebald to reflect on the Jewish people, the reluctance of post-
Holocaust Germanists to acknowledge the importance for Kafka of his
Jewish background and Leni Riefenstahl's Nazi propaganda film *Triumph*

des Willens (*Triumph of the Will*, 1935). These related themes would later resurface in *Austerlitz* (Ag 243/Ae 239).

Kafka's Presence in *Vertigo*

In *Schwindel. Gefühle.* (*Vertigo*, 1990), one Kafka text is pervasively present: the fragment, extant in several versions, known as 'Der Jäger Gracchus' ('The Huntsman Gracchus', 1917). Set in Riva on Lake Garda, where Kafka stayed from 12 September to about 13 October 1913, it tells how a barque arrives in the harbour at Riva; from it two men carry a bier on which a man is lying; the Mayor of Riva lifts the pall and converses with the man, who says that he is the Huntsman Gracchus. When hunting in the Black Forest, he fell into a ravine and was killed. However, the boat carrying him to the land of the dead missed its way, and since then the huntsman, like the Flying Dutchman, has travelled on all earthly waters, unable to die. Kafka gave this story a personal subtext by calling the huntsman 'Gracchus', which means jackdaw in Latin, as did Kafka's last name in Czech (*kavka*).

Three of the four sections of *Vertigo* recount journeys through Northern Italy to Riva. The first was made by Henri Beyle (1783–1842, better known as the novelist Stendhal). Sebald follows the details of Beyle's biography until, at Riva, he and his companion see an old, weather-beaten boat from which two men are carrying a bier on land (SG 30–31/V 25). The next section, 'All'estero', recounts two journeys made by Sebald's narrator in Northern Italy, one in 1980, the other in 1987. Kafka is explicitly present in the narrator's second journey. On leaving Venice, the narrator travels via Verona – where Kafka, as is recalled in 'Dr. K.', spent an unhappy afternoon – to Desenzano on Lake Garda and then to Limone, which lies just south of Riva, where Kafka spent three weeks in a sanatorium. Twin boys he sees on the bus ride to Limone remind him uncannily of the young Kafka (SG 105/V 88). In a public lavatory he notices a graffito reading *il cacciatore* (the huntsman), recalling Gracchus, and later he has a mental image of two men carrying a bier (SG 147/V 125).

These relatively random reminiscences of Kafka lead to the third narrative, 'Dr. K.s Badereise nach Riva' ('Dr. K Takes the Waters at Riva').[20] Sebald's text, however, opens in a drily factual manner, recounting Dr. K.'s activities in Vienna (where Kafka, in his professional capacity, attended a conference on insurance) and his further travels from there to Trieste, thence by steamer to Venice, by rail via Verona to Desenzano, and, finally, by steamer to the sanatorium at Riva.[21] Sebald works in all the available, though still scanty, material from Kafka's diary and letters. He also includes a dream about an angel descending from the ceiling which Kafka noted in his diary much later, on 25 June 1914.

What interests Sebald is Dr. K's state of mind. Kafka was depressed and unwell, in particular since he was unhappy about his relationship with Felice Bauer. They would become officially engaged in May 1914, but the engagement would be acrimoniously dissolved on 12 July of that year. In 1913, however, he felt unable to contemplate life either with or without a wife. In Riva he was strongly attracted to an eighteen-year-old Swiss woman, with whom he managed to have a relaxed, friendly relationship. They went rowing together, told each other their medical histories, and vowed that neither would ever reveal the other's identity. In his diary, Kafka calls her only 'G. W.' and Sebald, who must have been struck by the similarity of her initials to his, stylizes her into a folk-tale figure, an 'Undine' or mermaid, and evokes Dr. K.'s emotions as he watches her depart on the steamer and leave his life for ever.

A sombre event, the suicide and funeral of an elderly general staying at t"e sanatorium, leads Sebald into exploring the theme of death. He re-tells the story of the huntsman Gracchus. Suggesting that Gracchus' wanderings are a penance for Kafka's own yearning for love, Sebald continues probing this personal dimension by retelling a story Kafka had told Felice in a letter, namely how he had become inexplicably fascinated by the forty-year-old son of a Jewish bookshop owner and followed him down the street. Sebald surmises that, here, Kafka was implicitly acknowledging an unfulfilled – presumably homosexual – yearning. Sebald had in fact already hinted at homosexuality when he had Dr. K. take note of an iron *angel* in Trieste, for it was in that city that the homosexual art historian Johann Jakob Winckelmann (1717–1768) was murdered by a criminal named Arcangeli ('arch*angel*' in Italian).[22]

Ostensibly a narrative, 'Dr. K.' is a richly textured composition which starts from the factual details of Kafka's Italian journey and interweaves them with supernatural intimations of unearthly love, death, life-in-death and angelic visitations. It also hints at inadmissible desires for sexual happiness – with a water nixie or a man – that contrast sharply with the bourgeois misery promised by Kafka's – or Dr. K.'s – engagement to Felice.

Gracchus appears briefly in the fourth narrative, 'Il ritorno in patria'. The narrator recalls that the drinkers in the bar included one Hans Schlag, a huntsman from the Black Forest, and that Schlag fell to his death in a ravine (like Kafka's figure). At the autopsy, it is noticed that the corpse has a small barque tattooed on one arm (SG 283/V 249).

Sebald's obsession with Kafka appears not only in such interpolations, but in the very texture of his prose. When, for example, the narrator of 'Il ritorno' pauses on the bridge before entering his home town, the sentence recalls the opening of *The Castle*, where K. too pauses on the bridge leading to the village (SG 209/V 183). And in *Austerlitz*, Agáta receives a visit from two messengers wearing 'jackets furnished with assorted pleats, pockets, button facings and a belt, garments which looked especially versatile though it was not clear what purpose they served' (Ae 250/Ag 258), a clear – and disconcerting – quotation from *Der Process* (*The Trial*, 1925).²³

Sebald's fascination with Kafka is all the more noteworthy since he otherwise ignores the conventional classics of German literature from Goethe (1749–1832) to Thomas Mann (1875–1955) or Bertold Brecht (1898–1956). Instead, Sebald focuses mainly on writers commonly judged "minor", such as Johann Peter Hebel (1760–1826) and Robert Walser (1878–1956). Hence Kafka's originality emerges even more strongly, and much of Sebald's œuvre can be read as a homage to his work.

Notes

1. R Sheppard, Dexter – Sinister: Some Observations on Decrypting the Mors Code in the Work of W.G. Sebald, in: *Journal of European Studies* 35 (2005), pp. 419–463 (443).
2. Sebald, The Undiscover'd Country: The Death Motif in Kafka's ›Castle‹, in: *Journal of European Studies* 2 (1972), pp. 22–34; The Law of Ignominy: Authority, Messianism and Exile in ›The Castle‹, in F Kuna (ed.), *Franz Kafka: Semi-Centenary Perspectives* (London: Elek, 1976), pp. 42–58. Both exist also in German versions, cf. SM 461.
3. W Benjamin, Franz Kafka: On the Tenth Anniversary of his Death, in: *Illuminations* (London: Fontana, 1992), pp. 108–235.
4. Sebald, Undiscover'd Country, p. 32; K Wagenbach, Wo liegt Kafkas Schloß?, in: J Born et al., *Kafka-Symposion* (Berlin: Wagenbach, 1965), pp. 161–180.
5. Benjamin, Franz Kafka, p. 126. The term comes from Bachofen's *Das Mutterrecht* (1861). The 'hetairic' period was supposed to be one of primitive promiscuity preceding that of matriarchy.
6. Benjamin, Franz Kafka, p. 115. The photograph has often been reproduced: e.g., in J Adler, *Franz Kafka* (London: Penguin, 2001), p. 25.
7. Sebald, Undiscover'd Country, p. 28.
8. J Strachey (ed.), *The Standard Edition of the Complete Psychological Works of Sigmund Freud*, 24 vols. (London: Hogarth Press, 1953–1974), p. xviii.
9. F Kafka, *The Castle* (Oxford: Oxford University Press, 2009), p. 133. Sebald quotes the earlier translation by Willa and Edwin Muir.
10. Sebald, Undiscover'd Country, p. 31.

11. D Medin, *Three Sons: Franz Kafka and the Fiction of J.M. Coetzee, Philip Roth and W.G. Sebald* (Evanston: Northwestern University Press, 2010), pp. 82–91; U Schütte, *Interventionen: Literaturkritik als Widerspruch bei W.G. Sebald* (Munich: Ed. Text+Kritik, 2014), p. 211.

12. Medin, *Three Sons*, p. 89.

13. Sebald, Summa Scientiae: System und Systemkritik bei Elias Canetti, in: BU 93–102.

14. Sebald, The Law of Ignominy, p. 47.

15. E Beck, *Kafka and the Yiddish Theater* (Madison: Wisconsin University Press, 1971), p. 195.

16. Sebald, The Law of Ignominy, p. 53.

17. Sebald, Tiere, Menschen, Maschinen: Zu Kafkas Evolutionsgeschichten, in: *Literatur und Kritik* 21:205–206 (1986), pp. 194–201.

18. For a more sustained reading of the essay cf. Schütte, *Interventionen*, pp. 220–227.

19. H Zischler, *Kafka geht ins Kino* (Reinbek: Rowohlt, 1996).

20. The original title, 'Dr. K.s Badereise nach Riva', playfully evokes two narratives by Jean Paul, *Dr. Katzenbergers Badereise* and *Des Feldpredigers Schmelzle Reise nach Flätz* (both 1809).

21. For biographical data, cf. R Stach, *Kafka: Die Jahre der Entscheidungen* (Frankfurt: Fischer, 2002), pp. 417–427.

22. P Schmucker, *Grenzübertretungen: Intertextualität im Werk von W.G. Sebald* (Berlin/Boston: De Gruyter, 2012), p. 178.

23. F Kafka, *The Trial* (Oxford: Oxford University Press, 2009), p. 5.

CHAPTER 20

Literary Predecessors

Ben Hutchinson

Few major writers of recent years have been as saturated in the literary canon as W.G. Sebald. Partly this is a function of temperament and training: a professor of European literature, Sebald spent much of his life teaching and writing about the German-language tradition. It is also, however, a constituent element of his aim, as expressed across all his major works from *Nach der Natur* (*After Nature*) to *Austerlitz*, to understand the historically constructed condition of "culture". The canon, in this regard, plays a double role in Sebald's work, as an expression both of our complicity – in the exploitation of non-Western cultures, in the collapse of European culture in the Holocaust – and our resistance to this complicity. Literature, as an example of "high" culture, both perpetuates and repudiates the 'marks of pain' ('Schmerzensspuren') left by history (Ae 16/Ag 20).

Given that it is beyond the scope of this brief essay to trace Sebald's every engagement with his literary predecessors, my focus will be on the causes and consequences of this engagement. From Thomas Browne (1605–1682) to Joseph Conrad (1857–1924), from Thomas Bernhard (1931–1989) to Vladimir Nabokov (1899–1977), it would be easy to enumerate a list of Sebald's major influences. Beyond the impact of specific individuals on his work, however, I want to consider why the *idea* of a literary tradition was so important to Sebald's creative project, and how his intertextual engagement with this tradition – through allusion, echo and quotation – helped shape the very terms of his writing. What does it mean, to quote Susan Sontag's review of *Vertigo*, to be 'a European at the end of European civilization'?

Towards a Literature of Restitution

Like everyone else, Sebald was shaped by his formative years as a student and young adult. Where his story differs from that of other generations, however, is in the time and place in which he reached maturity. Born in

1944, Sebald came of age in the West Germany of the 1960s, an increasingly radicalized environment which saw the first generation of post-war Germans start to question the role played by their parents during the Nazi period. Such questions related not just to the events themselves, but to the culture that had made them possible in the first place. The great German tradition of *Dichter und Denker*, from Goethe (1749–1832) and Kant (1724–1804) to Thomas Mann (1875–1955) and Gottfried Benn (1886–1956), was suddenly suspect, seen at best as powerless to prevent, or at worst as aiding and abetting, the atrocities of the Third Reich.

Sebald's engagement with his literary predecessors cannot be understood without acknowledging this formative period in his life, since it shaped his view of culture as an instrument of both repression and resistance. On the one hand, he learned from the so-called Frankfurt School – a group of thinkers centred around Max Horkheimer (1895–1973) and Theodor W. Adorno (1903–1969) and including such luminaries as Walter Benjamin (1892–1940) – that every document of culture is also a document of barbarity, to cite the latter's famous formulation.[2]

On the other hand, he also came to see that culture – which for Sebald meant, first and foremost, literature – can promote what the German author Peter Weiss (1916–1982) called, in a three-volume novel of this name, an 'aesthetic of resistance'. From his earliest exposure to the Frankfurt School to his very last lecture on what he termed a 'literature of restitution' – with its attempt to find an answer to Hölderlin's (1770–1843) seminal question 'what are poets for in a destitute time?' – Sebald always understood his own place in the literary tradition in relation to his predecessors. Literature, for Sebald, was a way of gesturing towards an alternative metaphysics of history (Ae 14/Ag 23).

Reflections from Damaged Life

What this means for how Sebald's writing works may be exemplified by his final work, *Austerlitz*. The book begins with the narrator arriving in Antwerp, feeling uneasy; his view of Belgium, it will later become clear, encapsulates his rejection of Europe's colonial exploitation of other continents. The story opens, however, on a smaller scale, in the so-called nocturama behind the train station. The only animal that the narrator explicitly remembers from his visit to this twilight world is a raccoon, manically washing the same slice of apple over and over 'as if it hoped that all this washing, which went far beyond any reasonable thoroughness, would help it to escape the unreal world ('falsche Welt') in which it had arrived' (Ae 3/Ag

11). As the first creature encountered in the book – immediately followed by
pictures of the eyes of a monkey and an owl juxtaposed with those of the
painter Jan Peter Tripp and the philosopher Ludwig Wittgenstein – the
raccoon has symbolic value: placed under its sign, the book is to constitute
an attempt 'to penetrate the darkness which surrounds us' (Ae 3/Ag 11).

Yet the extent to which the raccoon functions as an anticipation of
Austerlitz himself only becomes fully clear once one hears the echo of
Adorno's celebrated claim, in his autobiographical fragments *Minima
Moralia* (1951): 'There is no right life in the wrong *(falsch)* one'.[3] Just as
the raccoon is living in a false world, so it will become apparent – not least
through the recurrence of the phrase 'false world' throughout the book (Ag
247, 302, 357)[4] – that Austerlitz has also been living in false consciousness:
brought up as a little Welsh boy, he is in fact a Czech Jew who narrowly
escaped the Nazis on one of the Kindertransport. Austerlitz has spent
decades washing the wrong slice of the apple.

The point for our purposes is that this is as much a matter of technique
as of topic. Not only does Sebald anticipate the fate of Austerlitz by
piercing, with his enlightened gaze, the 'sombrous life' (Ae 2/Ag 10) of
the raccoon – thereby creating what the great comparatist Erich Auerbach,
writing about anticipations of the messiah, would call a *figura* or fore-
shadowing of Austerlitz's subsequent awakening[5] – but he does so through
reference to someone else writing about (and from) exile.

The very act of making an unacknowledged allusion to Adorno thus
mirrors the act of recovery that Austerlitz will undergo when his
unacknowledged identity suddenly surges back to him upon hearing
a discussion about Kindertransport on the radio. Literature, in other
words, can show us that modernity took a false turn even before the
Holocaust – the many references to Kafka, if to no one else, demonstrate
this – while at the same time helping us to recover its prelapsarian
plenitude, by forming a subterranean echo-chamber out of which "true
life" comes surging back to us.

It would not be hard to adduce further examples of this technique in Sebald's œuvre. The many damaged lives chronicled in his
books – 'Reflections from Damaged Life', the subtitle of *Minima
Moralia*, would surely be a fitting title for Sebald's collected works – are
juxtaposed with moments in which history seems to slow down and
reverse; to cohere, if only momentarily, into something more meaningful.
References to literature are the glue that holds these exiled lives together:
Sebald does not so much shore fragments against his ruin as ruins against

his fragments, using the European tradition as a way of suggesting a better, truer life beneath the false one.

What are *Die Ringe des Saturn* (*The Rings of Saturn*) if not reflections and refractions of damaged life – and an indictment of the Western mind? What is Austerlitz's first breakdown in 1992 if not a microcosm of the central European catastrophe, with its passing references to the Viennese figures of Wittgenstein ('language may be regarded as an old city full of streets and squares', Ae 174/Ag 183) is lifted straight from *Philosophische Untersuchungen* (*Philosophical Investigations*, 1953)[6] and Hugo von Hofmannsthal (1874–1929) ('I could see no connections any more, the sentences resolved themselves into a series of separate words' (Ae 175/Ag 185) is taken directly from the so-called 'Chandos Letter'). The dizzying, dazzling nature of the "Sebald sound" suggests nothing so much as an over-educated professor trying – and largely failing – to escape the burden of his own, all-too-literary consciousness.

Butterflies and Periscopes

We can gain greater purchase on this consciousness by focusing, by way of case studies, on two of Sebald's most important predecessors. The Russian-born writer Vladimir Nabokov exerted an evident attraction for him both biographically and aesthetically. Like Sebald, Nabokov emigrated from one country and language to another; like Sebald, he was both writer and professor; like Sebald, he wrote a highly stylised prose, polished to the point of being mannered. If the two authors part ways in Sebald's enduring refusal to write in the language of his adopted country, this in itself tells us much about his sense of being rooted in a (largely nineteenth-century) Germanic idiom.

Where the parallels become particularly instructive, however, is in their shared approach to how we remember. Sebald was interested in the metaphysics not just of history but also of memory, and Nabokov played a central role in showing how this metaphysics could be explored through literature. The two most common models for literary memory, Proustian *mémoire involontaire* and Freudian *Nachträglichkeit*, were less important to Sebald than the Nabokovian model of aesthetic pleasure. Nabokov's autobiography *Speak, Memory* (1951/1966) evokes the lost world of his pre-Revolutionary youth, meditating movingly on the ways in which we try, in vain, to recapture the past even as we describe it.

The fleeting, evanescent nature of such an undertaking is expressed nowhere more beautifully than in the figure of the butterfly catcher who

recurs throughout *Die Ausgewanderten* (*The Emigrants*), most notably in
a photograph of Nabokov (E 16/AW 27), a figure who combines the
Russian author's gossamer-light prose style with his status as a leading
collector of butterflies. Beauty and levity, time and memory: they can all be
arrested, but only if they are killed. Nabokov's butterfly plays a similar role,
for Sebald, as Proust's madeleine, an icon of remembrance that is consumed as it is captured.

Beyond the butterflies, Nabokov exerted a significant influence on
Sebald's vision of the possibilities of literature as a vehicle for memory.
In the matter of literary style, however, undoubtedly the greatest influence
on Sebald's prose – at least if we set Kafka aside (see chapter 19 in this
volume) – was the Austrian author Thomas Bernhard. Bernhard is noted
for two main things: his unrelenting misanthropy and his mesmerizing
prose style. If Sebald, with his much gentler, melancholic temperament,
did not share the former characteristic – his work is closer, in this regard, to
the 'gentle law' ('sanftes Gesetz') of another great Austrian writer, Adalbert
Stifter (1805–1868) – he learned a considerable amount from the latter.

The great cascading sentences and blocks of prose, the (almost) single
paragraph in which *Austerlitz* is composed: such stylistic markers are easy
enough to identify as post-Bernhardian, at least in the original German
version of his works. Perhaps the true measure of the Austrian author's
influence, however, is the extent to which his style informs not just Sebald's
aesthetics, but also his metaphysics. That the two are indelibly linked is the
signal achievement of Sebald's work, and for all their differences in
temperament this achievement owes an obvious debt to Bernhard's
example.

What does Sebald take from his Austrian predecessor? Above all, he
borrows the technique of multi-layered narration, a technique that defines
Bernhard's writing to the point of caricature. In Sebald's own words,
Bernhard 'invented, as it were, a kind of periscopic form of narrative.
You're always sure what he tells you is related at one remove, at two
removes, at two or three' (EM 83). If Bernhard is a virtuoso of this kind
of writing, Sebald makes no less compelling use of the periscope, contriv-
ing to suggest, through 'the [narrative] passing on of his knowledge [...]
a kind of historical metaphysic, bringing remembered events back to life'
(Ae 14/Ag 22–23).

Examples of this technique accrue over the course of Sebald's writing,
culminating in his most Bernhardian work, *Austerlitz*, which evokes the
layers of history – 'so I think Věra began, said Austerlitz, your mother
Agáta ...' (Ae 235/Ag 243) – in the very structures of the narrative style. It

also functions as a form of ethical tact, as a way of looking at the past – and at the Holocaust, in particular – akin to how one must look at the Gorgon: indirectly, reflected, with great respect. It's not just the stories that Sebald tells, in other words; it's the way, informed by his literary predecessors, that he tells them.

Allusion as Excavation

What I am trying to suggest is that Sebald uses these literary predecessors as a means of adding depth to his explorations of history. The Bernhardian periscope provides a good example: by looking through it, Sebald not only sees above the surface of his own present moment, but he also deploys a self-consciously literary technique that places him in a particular narrative tradition. His saturnine rings work in similar terms, unspooling the history of English country houses and European colonial atrocities via predecessors such as Joseph Conrad or Edward FitzGerald (1809–1883), while at the same time meditating on the very nature of this unspooling by bracketing *The Rings of Saturn*, in its opening and closing chapters, with references to the history of silk-weaving. That these, in turn, are mediated via the presiding spirit of Thomas Browne – an obvious ancestor for a Norwich-based, metaphysically inclined writer – merely confirms Sebald's circular vision of history. The past is always already mediated, always already buried under layers of literary and historical accretion.

As such, one might plausibly describe Sebald as a kind of embedded novelist – embedded, that is, in the structures of history. His relationship to the literary canon provides the loam out of which the past re-emerges: time and again in his books, images of the re-emergence of memory are tied, if only implicitly, to writers whom he admires. The poetic realists of the nineteenth century on whom so much of Sebald's critical work focuses – mostly, for political reasons, Austrian and Swiss writers such as Stifter or Gottfried Keller – provide numerous instances of this process. The *locus classicus* is perhaps the conclusion to the first story in *The Emigrants*, 'Dr. Henry Selwyn', in which the frozen body of the mountain guide Johannes Naegeli is recovered from an Alpine glacier seventy-two years after he disappeared.

Sebald's description of this moment – 'And so they are ever returning to us, the dead' (E 23/AW 36) – carefully but unmistakeably echoes the celebrated short story *Unverhofftes Wiedersehen* (*Unexpected Reunion*, 1811) by the Alemannic writer Johann Peter Hebel (1760–1826), in which a bridegroom disappears into a mine just before his wedding and is only rediscovered half a century later. The phrase recurs, in variation, in the passage in *Austerlitz* describing the excavation of Liverpool Street Station, where the image of unearthed skeletons is juxtaposed with the plan of Bishopsgate that looks like an anatomical stetch, 'as if the dead were returning from their exile' (Ae 188/Ag 194–195).

And it also recurs, at least conceptually, in the pivotal moment in Prague when Austerlitz is given the photograph of himself as a child (the cover image of the book), which Věra pointedly finds in an edition of Balzac's *Le Colonel Chabert* (1832) – a story that tells of Chabert's return from having been presumed dead at the Battle of Eylau (1807).

Beyond the thematic similarity between Hebel's, Balzac's and Sebald's stories, it is the structural echo, crucially, that makes the point: in excavating meaning from the mineshaft of literary history, Sebald enriches time present with time past. 'Only in the books written in earlier times', says Austerlitz of Věra, 'did she sometimes think she found some faint idea of what it might be like to be alive' (Ae 288/Ag 296–297). Like a glacier – like a mine, like a battlefield – literature holds hidden depths.

Sebald's constant recourse to literary predecessors, then, functions as a structuring principle throughout his work. Even the very titles of his books – *Vertigo, The Emigrants, The Rings of Saturn* – can be read as a response to literary as well as to actual history. As noted in *Schwindel. Gefühle.* (*Vertigo*), Sebald's methodology consists of 'drawing connections between events that lay far apart but which seemed to me to be of the same order' (V 94/SG 107), and his constant recourse to literature – as in the two chapters of that book on Stendhal and Kafka – ratchet up the resonance.

A Quixotic Mind

In some ways, indeed, Sebald is a kind of tragic version of Don Quixote: having read too much, he projects his imagination onto reality, producing a kind of professorial paranoia in which 'everything becomes confused in my head: my experiences of that time, what I have read, memories surfacing then sinking out of sight again' (Ae 319/Ag 327). Time and again, literary predecessors are evoked to suggest both constriction (the two men hunting the narrator in *Vertigo*, reminiscent of the two guards who arrest Josef K. at the start of *Der Process* (*The Trial*)) and escape (the moments of levitation that recur throughout Sebald's work, redolent of any number of forebears from Stifter to Nabokov).

The allusions imply a kind of double consciousness, a hinterland of history just waiting to be explored if only we have eyes to see and ears to hear. Beyond the obvious references, moreover, lies a whole network of winks and nudges: for every explicit allusion to Kafka or Flaubert, to Browne or Nabokov, there is an implicit allusion to Giorgio Bassani (1916–2000) or Claude Lévi-Strauss (1808–2009), to Heinrich von Kleist (1777–1811) or Hugo von Hofmannsthal. After twenty years of ever-expanding research, we are still sounding the depths of Sebald's haunting, haunted, quixotic consciousness.

Notes

1. S Sontag, A Mind in Mourning, in: *Times Literary Supplement*, 25 February 2000, p. 14.
2. For discussion of Sebald and the Frankfurt School, cf. B Hutchinson, The Shadow of Resistance: W.G. Sebald and the Frankfurt School, in: *Journal of European Studies* 41:3–4 (2011), pp. 263–280.
3. Theodor W Adorno, *Minima Moralia* (Frankfurt: Suhrkamp, 2003), p. 43.
4. In the English version, these phrases are not always faithfully rendered: 'a world turned upside down' (Ae 243); 'the wrong life' (Ae 298); 'the false pretences of his English life' (Ae 354).
5. E Auerbach, Figura (1938), in: *Time, History, and Literature: Selected Essays of Erich Auerbach* (Princeton: Princeton University Press, 2014), pp. 65–113.
6. L Wittgenstein, *Philosophische Untersuchungen* (Frankfurt: Suhrkamp, 1977), p. 24.

CHAPTER 21

Walter Benjamin

Luisa Banki

The singular significance of Walter Benjamin's (1892–1940) philosophy for Sebald is indicated in an essay on Johann Peter Hebel (1760–1826), where Sebald traces Hebel's reception as 'a piece of German intellectual history' (PC 7/LH 11). Even after the defeat of National Socialism, which had laid claim to Hebel, Sebald argues, the 'false neo-Germanic manner of speaking' continued and German literary scholarship of the 1950s and beyond 'did not differ at all from what was proffered during the fascist regime' (PC 8/LH 12).

By mentioning Benjamin approvingly in the opening sentence of his Hebel essay, Sebald had already assigned him a quasi-timeless authority outside the chronological history of Hebel's reception. He then goes on to refer to Benjamin as the representative of *another* mode of reading:

> When I commenced my studies in Freiburg in 1963, all that had only just been swept under the carpet, and I have often wondered since how dismal and distorted our understanding of literature might have remained, had not [. . .] Benjamin's writings as well as those of the Frankfurt School – which was, in effect, a Jewish School for the investigation of bourgeois social and intellectual history – provided an alternative perspective. (PC 8/LH 12)

It is striking that Sebald here describes the Frankfurt School's influence as allowing for 'alternative perspectives' and quite literally enabling him to see differently. This helps explain an issue often raised by scholars attempting to define Sebald's relation to Benjamin: 'There are some authors, whose influence can be felt everywhere in Sebald's work although their names are hardly ever mentioned. Adorno and Benjamin are obvious examples: their style, their ideas are ubiquitous in Sebald's prose, however he never dedicated independent essays to them.'[1]

If, however, Benjamin and the Frankfurt School, as Sebald's own description suggests, function as the medium or, as it were, the glasses through which he views literature (and society), then it stands to reason that he would not focus on the glasses themselves but rather look through them in his reading and writing. In this sense, Judith Ryan's assessment that Sebald engages with Surrealism 'through the prism of his reading of Walter Benjamin'[2] can be generalized to encompass Sebald's Benjaminian view of history as well as the possibilities of its literary representation. Thus, Benjamin can be seen as the most important – albeit not always the most explicit – philosophical influence on his writing.

Although scholarship has long routinely mentioned a Benjaminian quality in Sebald's literary representation of melancholia, history and remembrance, the question of exactly how Benjamin influenced Sebald and his writings has only recently been systematically discussed.[3] Sebald's private reference library and notes, as preserved in his literary estate in the Deutsches Literaturarchiv, provide insights into his reception of and thoughts on Benjamin. As the markings and annotations in his copies of Benjamin's works show, Sebald continuously read and reread Benjamin throughout his academic and literary career, and regularly quoted or paraphrased Benjamin in his notes on other authors.[4]

Sebald's literary and literary critical works resonate with Benjaminian theorems and reflections in direct quotations and allusions, in a shared imagery and preoccupation with certain themes and in a similar method of engaging with history and literature. While Benjamin is the author probably most often quoted in Sebald's essays, his influence becomes more indirect in the literary works. Because of the complexity and often the indirectness of these resonances, tracing, analysing and interpreting Sebald's relation to Benjamin methodically demands a both philological and philosophical reconstruction of what Peter Schmucker convincingly termed 'poetic paraphrase',[5] the rendering of philosophical concepts in literature.

Natural History

The fundamental influence of Benjamin's conception of history is discernible in Sebald's literary preoccupation with remembrance, especially the way in which those born after an event remember it. His narrator's conflicted attempt to understand his own position in history is expressed in *Die Ringe des Saturn* (*The Rings of Saturn*):

> This then, I thought, as I looked round about me, is the representation of history. It requires a falsification of perspective. We, the survivors, see everything from above, see everything at once, and still we do not know how it was. [...] Are we standing on a mountain of death? Is that our ultimate vantage point? Does one really have the much-vaunted historical overview from such a position? (RSe 125/RSg 151–152)

An alternative to the 'historical overview' – again: another perspective – is found in Benjamin's understanding of history as natural history (see chapter 12 in this volume).

To understand history as natural history means to focus on the convergence of the historical and the natural in the process of decaying: in an overgrown ruin for example or, conversely, in an artefact that seems out of place or "denaturalized" because the life form it had belonged to has ceased to exist.[6] Sebald's literary works abound in descriptions of loci where nature and history are inseparable in their decay. Somerleyton Hall, for instance, which the narrator visits early on in *The Rings of Saturn* is 'imperceptibly nearing the brink of dissolution and silent ruin' (RSe 36/ RSg 50), but situated within grounds that 'were now at their evolutionary peak' (RSe 37/RSg 51). The 'evolutionary peak', however, already implies the descent into decay: 'It was easy to imagine this species of plane tree spreading over the country, just as concentric circles ripple across water [. . .], and while so conquering the land slowly becoming weaker and dying off from within' (RSe 37/RSg 51).

These and similar descriptions of decay call to mind Benjamin's reflections on natural history in his *Ursprung des deutschen Trauerspiels* (*The Origin of German Tragic Drama*, 1928), where he describes ruins as sites where 'history has physically merged into the setting. And in this guise history does not assume the form of the process of an eternal life so much as that of irresistible decay.'[7] The ruin assumes this signifying power because it can be read: 'When [. . .] history becomes part of the setting, it does so as script. The word 'history' stands written on the countenance of nature in the characters of transience. The allegorical physiognomy of natural history [. . .] is present in reality in the form of the ruin.'[8] Thus, the ruin becomes the rune, the script to be deciphered, the allegory to be read. Such a reading, however, is based on a special sort of perception, which Benjamin terms the 'melancholy gaze'.[9] Here, melancholia – which is the intellectual attitude most often associated with both Benjamin and Sebald – is less an affective state but rather a specific stance of perception and ultimately of knowledge.

Melancholia and the Skandalon of Remembrance

Sebald's conception of melancholia owes little to Sigmund Freud's (1856– 1939) psychological differentiation between mourning and melancholia and almost everything to Benjamin's epistemological functionalization.

(That Sebald was nevertheless aware of both his own and Benjamin's indebtedness to Freud is evidenced by the only long annotation in his copy of Benjamin's *Origin of German Tragic Drama*: a quotation from *Totem und Tabu* (*Totem and Taboo*).[10]) Benjamin focuses on the functionality of melancholia and sees it at work in the perception of things: melancholics 'ponder over signs'[11] while their contemplative gaze alienates objects from their everyday function and endows them with a new allegorical meaning so that 'the most simple object appears to be a symbol of some enigmatic wisdom'.[12]

The mode of perception that is the melancholy gaze blurs the distinction between past and present, the living and the dead, and recognizes the simultaneity of the non-simultaneous. Whereas successful mourning, according to Freud, results in detachment from the lost object, melancholia refuses to break with it. The literary figure who best exemplifies the refusal to break faith with the dead is Hamlet, whom Benjamin views as the embodiment of the Baroque melancholic.[13] Building on this characterization, Sebald has Hamlet figure centrally in his essay 'Konstruktionen der Trauer' ('Constructs of Mourning') in the context of memory politics and 'the difficulty of post-war writing'. This difficulty, Sebald argues, lay 'in the fact that memory was shameful ('ein Skandalon') and that anyone who did remember would, like Hamlet, be admonished by the new men in power' (CSe 105/CSg 104). Here, Hamlet appears as the ideal typical embodiment of melancholic resistance; he resists the politics of forgetting propagated by the living and opposes it with his own melancholy knowledge that the past and its dead live on.

In the same vein, in the preface to his collection of essays on Austrian literature, *Die Beschreibung des Unglücks* (*Describing Disaster*), Sebald defines melancholia as 'thinking over misfortune as it unfolds' and insists that it 'has nothing in common with a desire for death. It is a form of resistance' (BU 12). Herein lies Sebald's functionalization of melancholia as a form of resistance that – in keeping with Benjamin's conception – aims for knowledge: 'Melancholy betrays the world for the sake of knowledge. But in its tenacious self-absorption it embraces dead objects in its contemplation, in order to rescue them.'[14] This is why Sebald can conclude that 'the motivity of disconsolateness and of knowledge are identical executives' (BU 12).

The question of how far Sebald seamlessly follows Benjamin's conceptions of history and melancholia has led to some controversy amongst scholars, in particular with regard to the political dimension of Benjamin's philosophy.[15] The question, in Eric Santner's words, concerns 'the nature of the relation between the saturnine gaze that informs [Sebald's] work and the dimension of the act, between melancholic immersion into the past [...] and the sphere of ethical and political agency and production'.[16] Benjamin's fundamentally political conception of history becomes explicit for instance in *Das Passagen-Werk* (*The Arcades Project*, written 1927–1940, published 1982), where he explains the 'Copernican revolution in historical perception':

> Formerly it was thought that a fixed point had been found in 'what has been,' and one saw the present engaged in tentatively concentrating the forces of knowledge on this ground. Now this relation is to be overturned, and what has been is to become the dialectical reversal – the flash of awakened consciousness. Politics attains primacy over history. The facts become something that just now first happened to us, first struck us; to establish them is the affair of memory.[17]

If the past reveals itself to be founded in the present, the dialectical reversal of the "Copernican revolution" demands the replacement of continuous temporal relations with constellations, and entails the subversion of the conventional separation of the subject and object of historical perception. Status and function of memory are hereby radically revalued and their importance enhanced. In Benjamin's thinking, this valuation of remembrance does not lead to phantasmatic arbitrariness, but rather memory remains bound to and anchored in material repositories.

Sebald adopts Benjamin's materialist understanding of memory, placing an emphasis on material remnants as catalysts in his prose works. He therefore shares, if not Benjamin's materialist politics as such, the underlying epistemological significance of a historical perception that sees the present and the past in constellation and in 'secret agreement', as Benjamin wrote in 'Über den Begriff der Geschichte' ('Theses on the Philosophy of History', 1940).[18]

Rescue and Restitution

A characteristic and decidedly Benjaminian stance that Sebald adopts in all his writings is an attention to marginalized or overlooked persons and things. In his literary criticism, Sebald tends to focus on non-canonical authors, while his literary imagination is preoccupied with material remnants and outsiders. In his essay 'Le promeneur solitaire' on Robert Walser (1878–1956) – whom both Sebald and Benjamin admired greatly – Sebald references Benjamin to characterize the fleetingness of Walser's prose (LH

148/PC 117). He connects the thematic and poetological significance of the ephemeral, small and marginal in Walser's writing with the famously miniscule handwriting in his 'Bleistiftgebiet' ('pencil regions', PC 124/ LH 133) and explains it as a defence strategy whereby 'the smallest and most innocent things should be rescued from perishing in the "great times" then looming on the horizon' (PC 141/LH 154). Here, Sebald is drawing on Benjamin's method of literary criticism as rescuing forgotten or marginalized authors and texts – a method that includes juxtaposing the rescuing critique with mainstream interpretations: 'The attitude of a rehabilitating engagement with ignored texts and at the same time the resistance against common models of interpretation is characteristic of Sebald's literary criticism.'[19]

The rescuing critique sheds new light on its object of inquiry by opposing conventional criticism; herein lies both its literary and political impetus because it comments not only on the text and its previous reception, but also on its own present time of rereading: rescuing critique looks to the past to understand the present. The methodical and ethical stance herein is a Benjaminian 'devotion to the insignificant',[20] a philological diligence that Sebald revered in his own literary criticism and adapted in his literary writings into an attitude of turning to, listening to and giving a voice to marginalized persons and objects. In a manner reminiscent of Benjamin's cultural archaeology in his *The Arcade's Project*, Sebald blends out or calls into question official historiography while focusing his literary imagination on overlooked persons and objects, aiming to rescue 'bygone paraphernalia' (RSe 35/RSg 48).

If in *Austerlitz*, for instance, the 'ornaments, utensils, and mementoes stranded in the Terezín bazaar, objects that for reasons one could never know had outlived their former owners and survived the process of destruction', are 'timeless' (Ae 276/Ag 285), they appear as traces, as present markers of an absence. Austerlitz perceives them in constellation, which endows them with significance even though they have lost their original function and meaning:

> But even these four still lifes obviously composed entirely at random [. . .] exerted such a power of attraction on me that it was a long time before I could tear myself away from staring at the hundreds of different objects [. . .], as if one of them or their relationship with each other must provide an unequivocal answer to the many questions I found it impossible to ask in my mind. (Ae 274–275/Ag 282–283)

Austerlitz's inconceivable questions refer to the dimension of trauma that he and his interlocutor, the narrator, reconstruct by way of their dialogical search for his life story. That Austerlitz here gazes at a small statue of a rider 'turning to look back' (Ae 276/Ag 284) and rescue a girl, references Benjamin's famous 'angel of history', whose 'face is turned toward the past. Where we perceive a chain of events, he sees one single catastrophe which keeps piling wreckage upon wreckage and hurls it in front of his feet.'[21] The common aim of Benjamin's philosophy of history and Sebald's stories of the past lives of persons and things is to assemble these wreckages, and thereby do justice to those who are not on the side of the 'victors' of history and therefore do not figure in their historiography.[22]

At the core of the 'elective affinity' between Sebald and Benjamin lies a philosophical – that is, aesthetical as well as ethical – dimension: their shared conviction that the theory and practice of storytelling and the philosophy of history are inextricably linked. Their melancholy fixation on the past and its material remnants is methodical, because it seeks to know what is lost in order to understand what is present. To recount the unrecounted means, as Sebald programmatically explained his poetology in his last public speech, to undertake 'an attempt at restitution' (CSe 215/ CSg 248).

Notes

1. B Hutchinson, *W.G. Sebald: Die dialektische Imagination* (Berlin/Boston: De Gruyter, 2009), p. 57.
2. J Ryan, Fulgurations: Sebald and Surrealism, in: *The Germanic Review* 82:3 (2007), pp. 227–249 (231).
3. N Preuschoff, *Mit Walter Benjamin: Melancholie, Geschichte und Erzählen bei W.G. Sebald* (Heidelberg: Winter, 2015); L Banki, *Post-Katastrophische Poetik: Zu W.G. Sebald und Walter Benjamin* (Paderborn: Fink, 2016); E Riedl, *Raumbegehren: Zum Flaneur bei W.G. Sebald und Walter Benjamin* (Lang: Frankfurt, 2017). Notable earlier analyses include E Santner, *On Creaturely Life: Rilke, Benjamin, Sebald* (Chicago: Chicago University Press, 2006); A Lemke, Figurationen der Melancholie: Spuren Walter Benjamins in W.G. Sebalds ›Die Ringe des Saturn‹, in: *Zeitschrift für deutsche Philologie* 127:2 (2008), pp. 239–267.
4. Sebald's editions of Benjamin's works are listed in SM 377–441, 382–383; for a reconstruction and analysis of the archival traces of Sebald's Benjamin reception cf. L Banki, *Post-Katastrophische Poetik: Zu W.G. Sebald und Walter Benjamin* (Paderborn: Fink, 2016), pp. 16–20.
5. P Schmucker, *Grenzübertretungen: Intertextualität im Werk von W.G. Sebald* (Berlin/Boston: De Gruyter, 2012), p. 229.

6. Santner, *On Creaturely Life*.
7. W Benjamin, *The Origin of German Tragic Drama* (London: Verso, 1998), pp. 177–178.
8. Ibid., p. 177.
9. Ibid., p. 139.
10. Sebald's copy of W Benjamin, *Ursprung des deutschen Trauerspiels* (Frankfurt Suhrkamp, 1963), p. 150 (DLA).
11. Benjamin, *The Origin of German Tragic Drama*, p. 193.
12. Ibid., p. 140.
13. Ibid., p. 157.
14. Ibid.
15. I Wohlfahrt, Anachronie: Interferenzen zwischen Walter Benjamin und W. G. Sebald, in: *Internationales Archiv für Sozialgeschichte der deutschen Literatur* 33:2 (2008), pp. 184–242.
16. Santner, *On Creaturely Life*, p. 62.
17. W Benjamin, *The Arcades Project* (New York: Belknap, 2002), pp. 388–389 (K 1,2).
18. W Benjamin, Theses on the Philosophy of History, in: *Illuminations* (New York: Schocken, 1969), pp. 431–447 (432, II).
19. U Schütte, *Interventionen: Literaturkritik als Widerspruch bei W.G. Sebald* (Munich: Ed. Text + Kritik, 2014), p. 31.
20. Benjamin, The Rigorous Study of Art, in: *Selected Writings*, vol 2: *1927–1934* (Cambridge, MA: Belknap, 1999), pp. 666–670 (668).
21. Benjamin, Theses on the Philosophy of History, pp. 431–447 (437, IX).
22. Ibid., p. 435 (VII).

CHAPTER 22

Philosophical Models

Paul Thompson

This essay examines philosophical influences upon W.G. Sebald's writing. Sebald, as holder of a chair in European Literature and a writer concerned with (the loss of) memory and the decay of cultures and civilizations, whose 'scholarly and critical writings [. . .] drew on the same sources and centre as his imaginative works',[1] could scarcely have functioned without a mind turned towards philosophical thought, writing and models. While he largely kept his distance from literary theory, it is not an overstatement to say that Sebald was 'deeply interested in philosophy'.[2]

Even a quick glance at the bibliography of his working library (SM 377–441) reveals that Sebald took a wide-ranging interest in philosophical writings, both canonical and unorthodox. However, the philosophical works of Immanuel Kant (1724–1804), Georg Wilhelm Friedrich Hegel (1770–1831) and Arthur Schopenhauer (1788–1860), to name only these three giants of German idealist philosophy, remain conspicuously absent, while he owned multiple works by wayward twentieth-century thinkers such as Ludwig Wittgenstein (1889–1951). Equally unsurprising is that Critical Theorists such as Walter Benjamin (1892–1940), Theodor W. Adorno (1903–1969), Ernst Bloch (1885–1977) and Max Horkheimer (1895–1973) are well represented in his working library.

The post-structuralist theorists who dominated the academic discourse of the 1980s and 1990s represent another noticeable gap. Though JJ Long attempted to trace Michel Foucault's (1926–1984) influence on Sebald's writings, the library contains only a copy of *Folie et déraison* (*Madness and Civilization*, 1961), and not a single book of post-structuralist figureheads such as Jean Baudrillard (1929–2007), Jacques Derrida (1930–2004) and Jacques Lacan (1901–1981). The only exception to Sebald's general rule of ignoring "frog fog", as this branch of French thought is also sarcastically known in England, is a copy of *Kafka: Toward a Minor Literature* by Deleuze/Guattari, tellingly more literary criticism than philosophy.

Philosophical texts and ideas undeniably exerted a major influence on Sebald's thinking and writing, but they were not those of the "usual suspects" amongst academics. This essay will show that many thinkers and areas of thought, sometimes from schools considered outré or marginalized, were of importance to him. For example, take Elias Canetti (1905–1994). Sebald deemed his *Masse und Macht* (*Crowds and Power*, 1960) to be an intellectual treasure trove. In it, Canetti's often idiosyncratic treatment of obscure cultural and anthropological behaviours led to surprising insights and conclusions, which were usually dismissed by ethnologists in academia. Nevertheless, or precisely for this reason, the influence of Canetti pervades Sebald's critical and literary writings.

Sebald notoriously cared little for academic niceties such as accurate footnotes. Nevertheless, the endnotes to his early academic monographs and critical essays identify many unorthodox, forgotten, or ignored thinkers who exerted a considerable influence – names that normally pass under the radar of literary scholars who believe, wrongly, that he was only interested in the standard theoretical works that influenced his generation and peers (see chapter 18 in this volume).

Since exploring all important influences on Sebald would be beyond the scope of this essay, I shall present only two obvious inspirations – Ludwig Wittgenstein (1889–1951) and Claude Lévi-Strauss (1908–2009) – and then move on to the less obvious influence of phenomenology. Finally, I shall look at Sebald's interest in (heretical) religious traditions and sundry other overlooked influences.

Wittgenstein: A Biographical Model

Sebald's working library contains seven works by Ludwig Wittgenstein (SM 423–424). His first serious literary attempts were experimental scripts, starting in the early 1980s with an unpublished film script on the final days in the life of Immanuel Kant, written for German television but never broadcast.[3] He then drafted a script on Wittgenstein in the mid-1980s, which again was never realized but was published on 22 April 1989, on the occasion of the philosopher's centenary, in the *Frankfurter Rundschau* (SM 324–333).[4] Though drama was a medium Sebald abandoned, his scripts show his early interest in the 'crossover between biography, fiction, and documentary' (SM 9), an interest that would eventually emerge in his well-known books (see chapter 9 in this volume).

As Sebald makes the reader of *Austerlitz* aware early on, the eponymous protagonist is a *Doppelgänger* of Wittgenstein. When the narrator compares the eyes of nocturnal animals to 'the fixed, inquiring gaze found in certain painters and philosophers who seek to penetrate the darkness which surrounds us purely by means of looking and thinking' (Ae 3/Ag 11), the fourth pair of eyes that look at us from the page are those of Wittgenstein, cropped from a 1947 photograph.

The phenomenological significance of Austerlitz's rucksack (Ag 63/Ae 55),[5] which I will come to later in this chapter, is heightened by, and heightens, the physical similarity Sebald creates between the protagonist and the philosopher. Whenever the narrator sees a photograph of Wittgenstein, he feels as though Austerlitz were gazing out at him, and whenever he sees Austerlitz he sees the 'disconsolate philosopher' (Ae 56/Ag 64), who also toted a rucksack. This establishes a kind of spiritual kinship between the two.

While Sebald does repeatedly introduce unacknowledged quotations from and allusions to Wittgenstein's writings into his own, the philosopher serves primarily as a biographical model. His biography was as fascinating as his writings were impenetrable, Sebald admitted in an interview (G 229). Martin Klebes correctly concludes, therefore, that Sebald has 'nothing to say about Wittgenstein, in a certain sense'.[6] However, he took the *émigré* philosopher to be the epitome of the extraterritorial intellectual.

Even more than in the case of Austerlitz, there are biographical similarities between Wittgenstein and Paul Bereyter in *Die Ausgewanderten* (*The Emigrants*). Bereyter's career in and attitude towards teaching mirrors that of Wittgenstein, who taught for six years at three different elementary schools in remote mountain villages in Lower Austria where, for example, he would whistle and play the clarinet (AW 61/E 41), or bite down on his handkerchief, angered by the 'wilful stupidity' of his pupils (AW 52/E 35).[7] However, as regards relating Wittgenstein to Austerlitz or to Bereyter, Klebes warns that seeing one as the other 'does not unlock an essence in either of the two relata'.[8]

The opposite applied to Sebald. He recognized a sort of predecessor and kindred spirit in the eccentric Wittgenstein, a fellow German-speaking outsider in British academia. To Sebald, therefore, it must have seemed a meaningful coincidence that his three initials match those of the three syllables of Wittgenstein's last name.

Lévi-Strauss: Writing as *Bricolage*

Our experience of reading Sebald can be like looking at an assemblage of images, clippings and personal recollections. As reading him reminds us of our own scrapbooks, we become immersed in Sebald's mental reconstruction of the past, from pieces genuine and imagined, in effect Bachelardian resonances and repercussions: 'It's one way of making obvious that you don't begin with a white page [. . .] You do have sources, you do have materials.'[9] Sebald claimed a randomness in his research methodology – 'like a dog running through a field' after fresh scents[10] – but nevertheless an integrated whole emerges, a complete literary work.

Sebald makes a direct claim to work according to Lévi-Strauss's 'system of bricolage', which he explains as 'a kind of untamed way of working, of pre-rational thought, where one rummages around amongst chance finds, until somehow they assemble themselves'.[11] It is not surprising that Sebald had such a rapport with the schizophrenic poet Ernst Herbeck, whose poetics seem to rely on following false trails to arrive somewhere near a true insight (BU 135), a methodology that strikes a sympathetic string with Lévi-Strauss's concept of untamed, prerational *pensée sauvage* ("wild" thinking).

However, Sebald's assemblages are not necessarily to be trusted, according to Barbara Hui, as he is more interested in composing a cogent work of art than in exhaustively researching the bases of his descriptions for factual accuracy.[12] Family photo-albums, flea market discoveries and such may have been 'a treasure-trove of information'[13] for him, but the photos he reproduces, whether of people, places, or objects, often seem to have lost their definition as he photocopied them several times to blur and render them richly ambiguous.[14] Their intentionally multivalent connection with the text increases interpretive possibilities and has nothing to do with orthodox in-text illustrations.

Sometimes, Sebald's chance finds even attain central status as in the case of a postcard bought at a Manchester jumble sale. It features a boy in a page costume which he later claimed was the fictional character Austerlitz as a child, a fiction Sebald extended beyond his text by (falsely) claiming in interviews (G 198) that it showed the colleague whose story was told in the novel.[15] Such strategies of authorial self-staging can be understood as a form of extra-textual *bricolage*, an extension of his intertextual poetics based on assembling textual references, allusions and quotations, as well as the documentary, the adapted fact and the freely invented.[16]

Phenomenology: Merleau-Ponty, Heidegger

Moving on to less obvious yet important influences, we need to consider phenomenology. In its basic form, phenomenology is the study of the major part perception plays in human experience. This approach was well within Sebald's ken. His awareness of its basis was expressed, in passing, in his 1973 PhD thesis on Alfred Döblin, where he speaks of that author's rejection of any attempt at an analytical representation of reality: 'What [Döblin] therefore demanded was a merely phenomenological description. The artist simply had to reiterate, to quote, what he perceived.'[17]

Sebald retained this basic appreciation throughout his career, remarking in 2001 that 'a walker's approach to viewing nature is a phenomenological one' (EM 81), in which instant-to-instant sensory changes evoke resonances and repercussions in our consciousness.[18] Where his work pierces the loss of memory and reveals a vivid mental image, such as when he has Luisa Lanzberg describe the living room of her childhood home (AW 287–288/E 195) or Austerlitz see himself as a little boy in Liverpool Street Station (Ag 201/Ae 193), the result is somehow cinematic, imaginative, what Gaston Bachelard calls 'the theatre of the past'.[19]

The Liverpool Street memory depends greatly on Austerlitz's rucksack functioning as a catalyst for recovering his lost memory; its *presence* evokes a *past* event, as Maurice Merleau-Ponty says, 'because I carry this particular significance within myself'.[20] Sebald uses Merleau-Ponty's concept of the 'pre-human gaze' of objects, in his essay on the super-realist paintings of his friend Jan Peter Tripp:

> In Tripp's work, more clearly than ever before, the *nature morte* represents the paradigmatic expression of what we leave behind. Looking at it, we become aware of what Maurice Merleau-Ponty, in *L'Oeil et l'esprit*, has called '*le regard pré-humain*', for in such painting the role of the observer and the observed object are reversed. (PC 159/LH 174)

Sebald also picked up on this figure of thought in his important essay on Gerhard Roth's novel *Landläufiger Tod* (*Common Death*, 1986), where he reminds the reader: 'Our metaphysical (over)view springs from a profound fascination in which our relationship to the world is temporarily reversed. In looking, we sense how things look at us, understand that we are not there to penetrate the universe but to be penetrated by it' (UH 158).

If we are to consider phenomenology in Sebald's mid-twentieth-century Germany, it would be impossible to omit Martin Heidegger. And indeed, Sebald owned a copy of Heidegger's *Einführung in die Metaphysik* (*An Introduction to Metaphysics*, 1935) in which he made emphatic underlinings and annotations.[21] His relationship to Heidegger, though, was not unproblematic. Sebald joined Freiburg University in autumn 1963 to study German and English literature, some thirty years after Heidegger assumed the rectorate of the university in May 1933. In his rectoral speech, *Die Selbstbehauptung der deutschen Universität* (*The Self-Assertion of the German*

University, 1934), Heidegger pledged his allegiance to the new Nazi regime.[22] Though Heidegger resigned shortly afterwards, Sebald considered the 'Freiburg Rector with the Hitler moustache' (SM 344), the epitome of a politically compromised academic and repeatedly attacked his writings on Hölderlin and Hebel as 'Heideggerian fog' (PC 8/LL 12).

Sebald nevertheless shared a decided interest in metaphysics and a sense of the destitute nature of the world with Heidegger,[23] and he agreed with the philosopher's definition of *lethe* (as 'concealment, forgetting, and destruction'[24]) and its opposite, *aletheia*, in the *Parmenides* lectures. The latter correspond to moments of revelation in Sebald such as those from *The Emigrants* and *Austerlitz* mentioned above, or Austerlitz's sudden recovery of the Czech language from his lost childhood (Ae 219/Ag 227). Sebald considered Heidegger's reinstatement to academia in 1950 as emblematic of all he detested about deliberate amnesia in post-war Germany. If Heidegger had any influence on Sebald, it was to fuel Sebald's determination to stimulate the collective memory.

Metaphysics: Gnosticism, Zoroastrianism and Superstition

'Various antique belief systems, like Zoroastrianism, Gnosticism, Manichaeism and more recent forms of cultural pessimism, cannot be rated as definite influences on [Sebald], not least because none of them match his radicalism', according to Burns and Will.[25] However, close inspection of Sebald's early poetry and his critical essays from the 1970s, as undertaken by Peter Schmucker, reveals the reverse.

Schmucker detects a marked 'modern Gnosticism'[26] that bears the influence of the writings of sixteenth-century mystic Jakob Böhme and the nineteenth-century theologian Franz von Baader. References to the Gnosis – an heretic strand of Christianity, claiming access to spiritual knowledge about the divine nature of man – can be detected in Sebald's essays on Adalbert Stifter (BU 173) and Peter Handke (BU 177). In the essay on Thomas Bernhard, Sebald highlights the 'gradual darkening of the world' (BU 107) as a key element of Gnostic metaphysics pervading Bernhard's novels *Verstörung* (*Gargoyles*, 1967) and *Frost* (1963).

Allusions and references to the Persian religion of Zoroastrianism are also to be found in Sebald's early poetry. For instance, 'Poesie für ein Album' ('Poetry for an Album') refers to the Zoroastrian deities 'Ormuzd and Ariman' (LWe 82/LWg 52), which represent the polar opposites good and evil and make the religion structurally similar to Gnosticism. In the early 1970s, Sebald wrote the poem 'Mithräisch' ('Mithraic'), whose title

refers to the ancient Persian deity Mithra, who watched over the obser-
vance of contracts and was later also worshipped as the sun god. The
subject of the cryptic poem is the Zoroastrian god of creation Zarwan, who
looks disappointedly on the failed work of his 'offspring', whose negligent
actions leave behind a destroyed, miserable creation, which is why he
scowls and departs on a 'sea-goat' (LWe 65/LWg 41).

What may have attracted Sebald to the dualistic worldview of
Zoroastrianism is its Manichean orientation, which he could relate to his
own pessimism. Growing up in a Catholic environment, with a staunchly
Catholic mother, Sebald's interest in other religions and heretic branches
of Christianity, as well as Judaism, may have been a way to explore spiritual
matters beyond the strictures of Catholicism.

In fact, Sebald's poetry of the 1970s and 1980s serves as a repository of
premodern popular beliefs such as esotericism, superstition, alchemy and
astrology.[27] There are numerous references and allusions to the practice of
astrology in his work, which is not surprising given that the speaker in
Nach der Natur (After Nature, 1988) believed that 'the cold planet Saturn
ruled the hour's / constellation' (AN 86/NN 76).[28] Sebald wasn't a firm
believer in astrology – but he did not want to discard it as totally irrelevant,
either. 'And if one thing interests me, it is metaphysics', he told an
interviewer, 'I am not seeking an answer, [...] I just want to say, This is
very odd indeed' (EM 165).

Conclusion: Overlooked Influences

This essay only touches on the manifold influences idiosyncratic thinkers,
outdated schools of thought and philosophical traditions had on Sebald's
world view and writings. Many others could be named. For example, the
works of Paracelsus[29] and the cultural anthropological tradition of
shamanism[30] provide a hidden yet constitutive layer of reference in After
Nature. The speaker explicitly recalls reading 'the works of Paracelsus [...]
in the basement of the university library' (NN 85/AN 97): Sebald's considerable interest in shamanism is less obvious, though he does mention
Mircea Eliade's study Shamanism: Archaic Techniques of Ecstasy (1951) in
the bibliography of his PhD thesis (RM 300).

As Uwe Schütte has shown, the writings of Stanisław Lem (1921–2006),[31]
Rudolf Bilz (1896–1976)[32] and Pierre Bertaux (1907–1986)[33] also had considerable influence on Sebald's essayistic and literary work from the very
start. Long passages from Lem and Bertaux, although not acknowledged,
are quoted verbatim in the Kant television script. The Polish futurologist

also looms large in Sebald's critical essays from the early 1980s. Ideas culled from Lem's *GOLEM XIV* (1973) particularly the notion of 'negative evolution', exerted an influence on the 'natural history of destruction', Sebald's negative philosophy of history (see chapter 13 in this volume).

Bertaux's speculative essay *La mutation humaine* (*The Mutation of Mankind*, 1964), meanwhile, is a point of (hidden) reference in critical essays, for instance on Herbert Achternbusch (1938–2022) and Franz Kafka (1883–1924), as well as in the Corsica Project. The influence of Bilz's paleoanthropological writings runs through Sebald's critical corpus, leaving discernible traces in *Die Ringe des Saturn* (*The Rings of Saturn*) and the Corsica Project as well. Finally, Sven Meyer has shown – picking up a trail down laid by Sebald in an interview (EM 81) – that the heretic theories of outsider scientist Rupert Sheldrake (b. 1942) played a role in Sebald's renegade thinking and writing.[34]

In conclusion, Sebald's deep interest in metaphysics, a discipline of thought cast aside in the course of reason's victory march during the last two hundred years, is key for a full understanding of his writings, both critical and literary.

Notes

1. M Hamburger, Translator's note, in: Sebald, *JP Tripp, Unrecounted* (London: Hamish Hamilton, 2004), pp. 5–6.
2. R Burns, W Will, The Calamitous Perspective of Modernity: Sebald's Negative Ontology, in: *Journal of European Studies* 41:3–4 (2011), pp. 341–358 (345).
3. U Schütte, Durch die Hintertür: Zu W.G. Sebalds unveröffentlichter Szenenreihe über das Leben und Sterben des Immanuel Kant, in: Schütte (ed.), *Über W.G. Sebald. Beiträge zu einem anderen Bild des Autors* (Berlin/Boston: De Gruyter, 2017), pp. 65–98.
4. M Hutchins, ›Der Gedanke kommt ihm wie eine Erlösung‹: Restitution and False Redemption in Dramatic Texts by W.G. Sebald, in: Schütte (ed.), *Über W.G. Sebald. Beiträge zu einem anderen Bild des Autors* (Berlin/Boston: De Gruyter, 2017), pp. 51–64.
5. The rucksack depicted in *Austerlitz* belonged to a friend of Sebald, the poet Stephen Watts (SM 302–303).
6. M Klebes, *Wittgenstein's Novels* (London: Routledge, 2006), p. 5.
7. E Ingebrigtsen, *Bisse ins Sacktuch: Zur mehrfachkodierten Intertextualität bei W. G. Sebald* (Bielefeld: Aisthesis, 2016), pp. 129–140.
8. Klebes, *Wittgenstein's Novels*, p. 117.
9. A Lubow, Preoccupied with Death, but Still Funny, in: *New York Times*, 11 December 2001.

10. U Schütte, Out of the Shadows, in: *Times Higher Education*, 22 September 2011, pp. 44–47 (47).

11. S Löffler, Wildes Denken: Gespräch mit W.G. Sebald, in: F Loquai (ed.), *Porträt: W.G. Sebald* (Eggingen: Isele, 1997), pp. 135–137 (132).

12. B Hui, Mapping Historical Networks in ›Die Ringe des Saturn‹, in: M Zisselberger (ed.), *Undiscover'd Country: W.G. Sebald and the Poetics of Travel* (Rochester: Camden House, 2010), pp. 277–298 (284).

13. Löffler, Wildes Denken, p. 132.

14. S Ward, Ruins and Poetics in the Works of W.G. Sebald, in: JJ Long, A Whitehead (eds.), *W.G. Sebald: A Critical Companion* (Edinburgh: Edinburgh University Press, 2004), pp. 58–71 (60).

15. J Wood, Sent East, in: *London Review of Books* 19 (2011), pp. 15–18.

16. S Seitz, Bricolage, in: M Niehaus, C Öhlschläger (eds.), *W.G. Sebald-Handbuch: Leben – Werk – Wirkung* (Stuttgart: Metzler, 2017), pp. 150–155.

17. Sebald, *The Revival of Myth: A Study of Alfred Döblin's Novels* (PhD thesis: UEA, 1973), p. 108.

18. G Bachelard, *The Poetics of Space* (London: Penguin, 2014), p. 7.

19. Ibid., p. 30.

20. M Merleau-Ponty, *The Phenomenology of Perception* (London: Routledge & Kegan Paul, 1962), p. 413.

21. Burns, Will, Calamitous perspective of modernity, p. 345.

22. M Heidegger et al., The Self-Assertion of the German University: Address, Delivered on the Solemn Assumption of the Rectorate of the University Freiburg the Rectorate 1933/34: Facts and Thoughts, in: *The Review of Metaphysics* 38:3 (1985), pp. 467–502.

23. P Arnds, While the Hidden Horrors of History are Briefly Illuminated: The Poetics of Wandering in ›Austerlitz‹ and ›Die Ringe des Saturn‹, in: M Zisselsberger (ed.), *The Undiscover'd Country* (Rochester: Camden House, 2010) pp. 322–334 (330).

24. Ibid., p. 328.

25. Burns, Will, Calamitous perspective of modernity, p. 345.

26. P Schmucker, *Grenzübertretungen: Intertextualität im Werk von W.G. Sebald* (Berlin/Boston: De Gruyter, 2012), p. 21.

27. These are expertly uncovered and elucidated by Iain Galbraith in the Notes to his edition of the poems (LWe 171–213).

28. U Schütte, *Figurationen: Zum lyrischen Werk von W.G. Sebald* (Eggingen: Isele, 2014), pp. 37–42.

29. T Hoorn, Auch eine Dialektik der Aufklärung: Wie W.G. Sebald Georg W. Steller zwischen Kabbala und magischer Medizin verortet, in: *Zeitschrift für Germanistik* 19:1 (2009), pp. 108–120.

30. L Kunze, *Der Schamane mit der Feder. Ökologie und Mitleidenschaft in W.G. Sebalds ›Nach der Natur‹* (Göttingen: Wallstein, 2022).

31. U Schütte, Negative Evolution. Zur Rezeption von Stanisław Lem bei W.G. Sebald, in: *Prace Literaturoznawcze* 10 (2022), pp. 23–48.

32. U Schütte, *Interventionen: Literaturkritik als Widerspruch bei W.G. Sebald* (Munich: Ed Text & Kritik, 2014), pp. 302–307.

33. U Schütte, Europäische Peripherien: Sebald, Tübingen, Bertaux, in: *Weimarer Beiträge* 2 (2022), pp. 300–311.

34. S Meyer, Keine Kausallogik: Zum Zusammenhang in W.G. Sebalds Schreiben, in: Schütte (ed.), *Über W.G. Sebald: Beiträge zu einem anderen Bild des Autors* (Berlin/Boston: De Gruyter, 2017), pp. 19–28.

CHAPTER 23

History

Lynn L Wolff

Literature has long been seen as a way to gain knowledge of the past, and W.G. Sebald's works demonstrate the power of the literary discourse to explore, preserve and provide an understanding of history. Dealing primarily with events of twentieth-century European history in general and the Holocaust in particular, he also weaves in strands of eighteenth- and nineteenth-century history, exploring the Napoleonic wars, the silk trade and colonialism, as well as their after-effects. While a sense of the historical pervades his prose, Sebald insists on the legitimacy of the literary discourse, never making it the mere servant of history.

That is, Sebald's works go beyond transporting historical knowledge, showing instead how literature can be considered a form of knowledge in itself. Sebald's attention to history, in particular how historical events are recorded and recounted, and his attention to literature, in particular how literary texts are constituted and their relationship to truth and reality, are concerns voiced consistently throughout his works – poetry and prose, literary criticism and essays – and these concerns both inform his judgments of other literary works and influence the creation of his own fictional prose form.

Sebald's Hybrid Poetics: Literature as Historiography

Distinct from traditions of documentary literature on the one hand and the historical novel on the other, Sebald's works can be seen as a new hybrid discourse of literature as historiography. By blurring the boundaries between these separate and at times disparate discourses, Sebald's texts combine the possibility and potentiality of fiction with direct references to an extra-textual reality, as lived by individuals, recounted in documents, or evidenced in artefacts. It is not his main purpose to create a fiction that is historically substantiated through documentation, but rather to write a new form of historiography that is consciously literary and that problematizes the writing process and the standards by which we judge authenticity, documentary status, historical truth and even truth in general. With this concept of literature *as* historiography or "literary historiography", I would like to emphasize how these two distinct discourses are brought into contact in such a way that preserves the dialectical potential of their relationship, while the new form that emerges is more than the sum of its parts.

This discursive tension in Sebald's innovative form of fiction, as well as the way he brings various fields into dialogue and draws on a variety of sources from different disciplines, is also why his works elude traditional genre distinctions. In integrating images in his works, photographs in particular, Sebald points to multiple levels of reference within one and the same text. This intermedial strategy, while not unique to Sebald, further contributes to the hybridity of his prose form.[1] Sebald's complex use of images does not follow one consistent strategy, and the relationship between text and image is not static, but rather it shifts and changes as we read. Furthermore, the visual material points to both the constructedness of the text and the process behind its construction.

In this way, Sebald challenges the idea of art as imitation: the literary work is not a re-presentation of something ontologically prior to the text but a presentation of something that comes into being only with the text. While incorporating images in a complex manner and simultaneously reflecting on this within the literary discourse, Sebald thematizes the acts of seeing, remembering and knowing, while also raising fundamental questions of literature's relationship to "truth" and "reality", questions of realism, authenticity, the documentation of history and subsequently the writing of history – that is, historiography.

That history can be told objectively or "realistically", is never taken for granted in Sebald's works, but, rather, doubt and suspicion are continually cast upon purported verisimilitude in the representation of history. An illustration of this problem can be found in *Die Ringe des Saturn* (*The Rings of Saturn*). While visiting the historical memorial site of the Battle of Waterloo, and after viewing a large panorama in particular, the narrator formulates the following critique: 'This then, I thought, as I looked round about me, is the representation of history. It requires a falsification of perspective. We, the survivors, see everything from above, see everything at once, and still we do not know how it was' (RSe 125/RSg 151–152).

This perspective is 'falsified' in the sense that it obscures access to the past, and more precisely, for the way it deceives the viewer into thinking that they can see and, by extension, know everything. The illusion at the heart of this impossible perspective impedes knowledge of the past, which further occludes any possibility of understanding the past. Literature, by contrast, becomes a privileged site for gaining access, in particular emotional access, to the past, precisely because it can focus on individual experience.

Literary Historiography as an 'Attempt at Restitution'

Sebald's innovative form of fiction presents both a critique of and an alternative to official modes of historical representation, offering a rewriting of history that incorporates unconsidered or underestimated sources and privileges the literary discourse as a means of approaching, translating and ultimately representing past experiences and events. It is a search for meaning and for a truth that lies beyond facts that drives Sebald to challenge discursive and disciplinary borders in his approach to writing, which he describes as follows:

> That temptation to work with very fragmentary pieces of evidence, to fill in the gaps and blank spaces and create out of this a meaning which is greater than that which you can prove, led me to work in a way which wasn't determined by any discipline. It wasn't history, it wasn't literary criticism, it wasn't sociology, but it was all of these things together.[2]

By connecting aesthetic concerns – the fundamental problem of art's relationship to reality – to the particular case of the Germany's recent past, for example, Sebald's works explore the ethical dimension of literature, and of post-war literature in German specifically. He explicitly addressed these concerns in his lectures on poetics, given in Zurich in 1997 and published as *Luftkrieg und Literatur* (*On the Natural History of Destruction*),[3] and he returned to these ideas and to the role of literature in a lecture given just a few weeks before his death in 2001. In this lecture, given at the opening of the Literaturhaus in Stuttgart, Sebald posed the question, so central to any author: '*A quoi bon la littérature?*' (What is literature good for?) (CSe 204/CSg 247); to which he offered the following answer: 'Perhaps only to help us to remember, and teach us to understand that some strange connections cannot be explained by causal logic [. . .]' (CSe 204/CSg 247).

Sebald reveals such 'strange connections' by way of his narrators who traverse varied landscapes across countless countries, speak multiple languages and often merge with their subjects. They explore and observe artefacts that range from massive architectural structures to delicate photographs, found by chance between the pages of a well-worn book. Be they official representations of history presented in museum dioramas, classical paintings of famous battles, or personal accounts of the past, like a journal or a drawing, all of these traces are considered and contemplated by Sebald's narrators and characters. But it is often the most incidental detail that captures one's attention, while the historical artefacts, traditionally accepted as "authentic", are sceptically questioned.

Sebald's narratives reconceptualize boundaries of time, space and memory though not necessarily according to a rationally explicable system. His narratives are ones of conjecture, attempts at explanation are prefaced with a provisional 'perhaps', a tentative 'it seems to me', or a suggestive 'it might be'. Through what appear to be coincidences and sudden inexplicable insights, as opposed to explanations of 'causal logic', connections are established between individual experience and a greater historical framework. Moreover, it is through literature, in particular in the form of nonlinear narratives, that such non-rational insights and flashes of recognition are possible.

Sebald asserts the value of literature, in response to the question – 'What is literature good for?', by stating, 'There are many forms of writing; only in literature, however, can there be an attempt at restitution over and above the mere recital of facts, and over and above scholarship' (CSe 205/CSg 248). This can be connected to two major aims of Sebald's literary historiographical project. First, Sebald is working towards an understanding of the past on an individual level, as opposed to a master narrative or a purported objective account of history. Second, through the rehabilitation of an individual's story and through the exploration of the emotional and mental experience of rediscovering one's own past, Sebald sees the possibility of restitution.

At the basis of this attempt at restitution – through literature that goes beyond the 'mere recital of facts' – is an ethical imperative, one that demands the responsibility of the author towards his subjects as well as the engagement of its readers. The text–image relationship that is characteristic of Sebald's works is also constitutive of his poetics of engagement for the way in which it activates the reader on various levels, with the literary text itself and beyond with broader questions of history and memory.

Against Historical Erasure: Unearthing the Past through Individual Memory

To elucidate the idea of restitution, let us look at a key passage from *Austerlitz*, the last major work to be published during Sebald's lifetime. In contrast to the multiple stories and narrative strands that characterize his earlier works *Schwindel. Gefühle.* (*Vertigo*), *Die Ausgewanderten* (*The Emigrants*) and *The Rings of Saturn, Austerlitz* centres on the eponymous character's search for his origin and identity.

In this work, a nameless first-person narrator makes the acquaintance of the protagonist, Jacques Austerlitz, in 1967, and the two continue to meet coincidentally over the next thirty years. This is a mediated, multi-layered and a-chronological narrative that spans close to sixty years and ranges geographically from Belgium to England, Czechoslovakia, Germany and France, but we never lose sight of the protagonist Austerlitz. An architectural historian and avid amateur photographer who lives in London, Austerlitz discovers late in life that he has long repressed his own past: that he was born in Prague and rescued from the Nazi occupation on a so-called Kindertransport, a children's transport, thus escaping the fate that millions of Jews did not. In Austerlitz's search for his past – specifically for traces that lead to the fate of his mother – and in the efforts to reconstruct his own experiences and to recover repressed memories, Sebald situates this individual story within a greater political and collective past. That is, the writing of *Austerlitz* is at the same time an indirect approach to representing the Holocaust.

A key scene in *Austerlitz* illustrates Sebald's idea of 'restitution' in a tangible way – he presents a harsh critique of the architectural erasure of history while showing the power of the literary discourse to reveal multiple layers of time and space simultaneously. The construction of the new Bibliothèque nationale in Paris has covered up, literally paved over, a part of history, and one that is very close to Austerlitz's own past.[4] It is not through archaeological digging that this history is revealed, but rather through individual memory. In his discussions with a librarian acquaintance named Henri Lemoine, Austerlitz learns that the site on which the new national library was built served as a collection point for the confiscated possessions of the deported Jews of Paris.

While looking out from one of the four towers of the new library, Lemoine recounts this little known history to Austerlitz, enumerating in particular all who took part in the emptying of some 40,000 apartments – 'an army of no fewer than fifteen hundred removal men' were involved in the 'highly organized programme of expropriation and reutilization', such as 'the financial and fiscal authorities, the residents' and property registries, the banks and insurance agencies, the police, the transport firms, the landlords and caretakers of the apartment buildings' (Ae 401/Ag 407) – and highlighting that those who appraised the possessions – 'over five hundred art historians, antique dealers, restorers, joiners, clockmakers, furriers, and couturiers' – were 'guarded by a contingent of Indochinese soldiers' (Ae 402/Ag 408).

This extensive array of involved parties calls into question the oft-stated claim that "no one knew". Though this is not explicitly stated here, Lemoine nevertheless voices the bitter reproach that they 'must undoubtedly have known' (Ae 401/Ag 407). The reference to 'a contingent of Indochinese soldiers' points to the entanglement of colonialism and National Socialism that warrants further exploration and could open further opportunities for restitution. This scene demonstrates how individual memory can counter institutional or state-sanctioned memorialization projects that in fact cover up the past. Without individual memory and without narration, the history of the site on which the Bibliothèque nationale was built would remain literally buried.

In this climactic passage in *Austerlitz*, there is also a sense of vertigo, evoked through the contrast between the elevated locus of narration – from the eighteenth floor of the library's southeast tower that offers a sprawling view of Paris – and the depth of the invisible history in the area surrounding the library. A further sense of vertigo – between intratextual and extratextual reality, between story and history – is created through the insertion of a photograph (Ae 388/Ag 394), apparently taken from inside one of the library's four towers, presumably from the eighteenth floor, where Austerlitz and Lemoine stand. The photograph, as a two-dimensional image, calls to mind the surface of "reality" – here the architectural cityscape that reveals nothing of the past – and recalls other moments in the book, when the characters are frustrated time and again in their search for both historical truth or personal memory as they study photographs, film footage, or other forms of documentation.

Illustration 16 – Bibliothèque nationale, Paris, photographed by Sebald (not used in *Austerlitz*)

The photograph of the new Bibliothèque nationale within *Austerlitz* encapsulates the problem of representation: inserted into the text *before* Lemoine's narration, the photograph both parallels and foreshadows how the cityscape reveals nothing of the past. It is Lemoine's narration that reveals what lies underneath the surface of the city and what lies in the past. The history that architecture has covered up would remain invisible without personal memory, and through literature, this individual memory has the potential to become part of collective knowledge.[5]

Conclusion: Engagement through Intermediality

As mentioned above, the text–image relationship is central to Sebald's poetics of engagement. In one sense, the photograph of the Bibliothèque nationale functions self-reflexively, and in another sense, it mirrors the invisibility of the past, and taken together, this passage in *Austerlitz* captures an important principle in Sebald's use of images and in his writing more broadly: namely, it conveys an understanding of photographs as signs that refer to reality while preserving the awareness of their ontological status as signs and not as that reality to which they refer.

As we see across Sebald's œuvre, photographs possess an inherent power to activate memory and to enable the process of remembering, but, most importantly, we see the necessity of a human voice to make the photographs both legible and meaningful. Sebald's works illustrate that the process of representation – the translation of history or personal experience into arbitrary signs – is by no means a natural or fluid one. The use of images, in this scene in *Austerlitz* in particular, reminds us of the need for narration and the power and potential of literature as a form of restitution.

W.G. Sebald's works are concerned with coming to terms with Germany's National Socialist past, but not only that. They are marked by a more universal concern – shared by literature and history alike – of finding appropriate ways to represent the past in order to better understand it. What makes Sebald's work stand out among other authors writing in the second half of the twentieth century, is how they do not fit the mould of traditional historical novels, nor are they an example of historical writing that employs literary flourishes. While seeming to embody the past, his texts critically question historical representation, and just as efforts are made to unearth and reconstruct the past, the processual nature of such attempts are laid bare.

In creating a new hybrid form that fuses the work of both the historiographer and the poet, to draw on the fundamental distinction Aristotle makes in his *Poetics*, Sebald's literary historiography illuminates the unique potential of literature to perform the interdiscursive transfer from experience to representation, from event to narrative and from history to story, but, most importantly, Sebald's works reveal the power of literature to create a space where readers can emotionally and empathetically engage with the past.

Notes

1. For a detailed contextualization of Sebald's works in relation to other twentieth-century authors using intermedial strategies, cf. T Steinaecker, *Literarische Foto-Texte: Zur Funktion der Fotografien in den Texten Rolf Dieter Brinkmanns, Alexander Kluges und W.G. Sebalds* (Bielefeld: Transcript, 2007).
2. C Bigsby, *Writers in Conversation with Christopher Bigsby*, vol. 2 (Norwich: EAS, 2001), p. 153.
3. For an illuminating reading of Sebald's lectures on poetics, cf. TS Presner, What a Synoptic and Artificial View Reveals: Extreme History and the Modernism of W.G. Sebald's Realism, in: *Criticism* 46:3 (2004), pp. 341–360. For connections between *Luftkrieg und Literatur* and Sebald's fictional prose, cf. G Jackman, 'Gebranntes Kind?' W.G. Sebald's 'Metaphysik der Geschichte', in: *German Life and Letters* 57:4 (2004), pp. 456–471.
4. For an intricate analysis of this passage, cf. J Cowan, Sebald's ›Austerlitz‹and the Great Library. A Documentary Study, in: G Fischer (ed.), *W.G. Sebald: Schreiben ex patria/Expatriate Writing* (Amsterdam: Rodopi, 2009), pp. 193–212, and J Cowan, Sebald's ›Austerlitz‹ and the Great Library. History, Fiction, Memory. Parts I and II, in: *Monatshefte* 102:1 (2010), pp. 51–81 and 102:2 (2010), pp. 192–207.
5. Similar to Cowan's detailed investigation of the sources for the Bibliothèque nationale passage, Marcel Atze has convincingly shown the significance of H. G. Adler's *Theresienstadt* book for later scenes in *Austerlitz*, cf. M Atze, W.G. Sebald und H.G. Adler: Eine Begegnung in Texten, in: R Vogel-Klein (ed.), *W.G. Sebald: Mémoire, Transferts, Images / Erinnerung, Übertragungen, Bilder. Recherches germaniques* Hors série 2 (2005), pp. 87–97 (90).

CHAPTER 24

Polemics

Uwe Schütte

W.G. Sebald made a remarkable entry into academia. The first critical monograph he contributed to German Studies in his home country, a study on the Wilhelmine playwright Carl Sternheim (1878–1942), published in 1969, opens with nothing short of a declaration of war against *Germanistik*: 'The aim of the present study is to revise the image of Sternheim as propounded by German studies', the 25-year-old scholar boldly proclaimed, 'and it goes without saying that this revision will predominantly take the form of a dismantling' (SH 7).

Which indeed it did: Sebald did not just attempt to destroy the reputation of Sternheim himself, whose works had enjoyed a notable renaissance in post-war Germany, but he also viciously attacked leading professorial figures in *Germanistik* for their failings as he perceived them. Sebald retained this inclination towards confrontation and polemics to the end. His final work of literary criticism, the contentious *Luftkrieg und Literatur* (*On the Natural History of Destruction*), set waves of debate rippling across Germany and abroad. In his last German interview, conducted with the journalist Uwe Pralle, published posthumously, Sebald even took on the first commandment of political discourse in Germany by challenging the singularity of the Holocaust: 'I by no means consider the disaster wrought by the Germans, as horrendous as it was, as a unique event – it developed, with a certain consequentiality, from within European history.'[1]

As this last in a long line of examples shows, Sebald was regularly at odds with received wisdom. Waywardly opinionated, recalcitrant, sometimes cantankerous, he challenged prescribed thinking in matters political, academic and historical and chafed at political correctness. The unconditionally pessimistic outlook of his 'natural history of destruction' (see chapter 13 in this volume) was a provocation not just to the academic community. The striking absence of female authors in his literary criticism, too, feels remarkable from a contemporary perspective.

This essay will investigate the broad spectrum of polemical writing in Sebald's œuvre to explore what may have informed the persistently antagonistic and at times aggressively confrontational stance of his writing and person.

An Angry Young Man: Dissertations and Academic Reviews of the 1970s

Sebald wrote only two monographs: the book on Sternheim, published in 1969, which was based on his multiply-revised master's thesis, and the book of his extensively reworked English PhD thesis from 1973 on Alfred Döblin (1878–1957),[2] which came out in 1980.[3] Neither study would have qualified him for a degree today. They are acerbic polemics which Sebald used to position himself as an academic punk rebel against the establishment of post-war German literary studies.

However, Sebald was fortunate: generous advisors and examiners approved both studies despite them being rife with examples of academic malpractice, relying on quotations taken out of context and on indefensible generalizations and aggressive statements to make a point, and suppressing contradictory evidence.

His external PhD examiners expressed serious reservations owing to the dissertation's lack of 'respect for the interpretative techniques of traditional literary criticism, which the candidate too easily dismisses'.[4] Nevertheless, they passed the thesis, with one examiner, an Oxford don, stating: 'The candidate's general approach is bold and provocative, a quality which I value in a doctoral thesis.'[5]

Thus, Sebald's early academic work tells us more about the author himself than it does about Sternheim and Döblin, two German-Jewish writers whom he, absurdly, accuses of having been proto-Nazis. His monographs read as expressions of protest against a *Germanistik* he would later characterize as 'stricken with almost premeditated blindness' (CSe 216/CSg 249), founded by conservative senior academics now intent on blocking out their Nazi past.

Or as Sebald puts it through the mouthpiece of Austerlitz: 'When I began my own studies in Germany I had learnt almost nothing from the scholars then lecturing in the humanities there, most of them academics who had built their careers in the 1930s and 1940s and still nurtured delusions of power' (Ae 43/Ag 51). Sebald's view that 'all my teachers had gotten jobs during the Brownshirt years and were therefore compromised' (EM 290) may have been exaggerated, but his general point remains.

The actual target of Sebald's proxy attacks on authors such as Sternheim and Döblin were the leading representatives of *Germanistik*, including Wilhelm Emrich, the renowned editor of Sternheim's collected works. Sebald repeatedly condemns Emrich as indicative of a tendency among German post-war literary scholars 'to rehabilitate authors discredited by the Hitler regime out of an underlying fear that their own rehabilitation may be far from complete'.[6] It turns out that, in Emrich's case, Sebald had got it right: as emerged in 1996, Emrich had been an erstwhile convinced (and later, in post-war Germany, convicted) National Socialist who had spent the rest of his life concealing his involvement.

Even more than his academic research, it was the reviews Sebald published between 1971 and 1975 in the *Journal of European Studies*, the house journal of the University of East Anglia, that served as the perfect outlet for his resentment of German studies. Most of the around fifteen English-language reviews from this period are scathing, full of invective, malice and arrogance. Many of them are *ad hominem* attacks, questioning the reviewed academics' ability to deal with literary works in an appropriate manner. At times, Sebald even sarcastically denigrates the potential reader, stating, for example, 'that only a bureaucratic mind will derive any pleasure from reading'[7] the work reviewed. Again and again, Sebald seeks to unmask the scholars he targets as reactionaries, observing of one work that, in it, 'any truly progressive German criticism is pushed under the mat'.[8]

Another of Sebald's targets was that perennial favourite of, especially, German academics: literary theory. He repeatedly railed against a use of theoretical jargon 'which can only be described as self-parody'[9] and observed about *Germanistik*: 'It appears we are currently witnessing [. . .] the gradual transformation of a form of literary criticism neglectful of criticism to one neglectful of literature.'[10]

In many respects, the stance informing Sebald's literary criticism of the period 1969–1975 is typical of its generation, of the rancorous protest of the generation of 1968 against authority in general and the academic establishment in particular. Yet while his German compatriots of the same generation marched in protest and threw Molotov cocktails, Sebald conducted a one-man guerrilla war against *Germanistik* from his desk in East Anglia, with his reviews as missiles.

Love or Hate: Polemics and Provocation in the Critical Essays of the 1980s

The Kant Project, on which Sebald embarked c. 1980/81 (see chapter 9 in this volume), turned him into a writer and set him off on the parallel tracks of literature and literary criticism. During this decade, he produced a further thirty-five critical essays, mostly on Austrian literature, that came under one of two categories: acerbic polemics in the vein of his earlier criticism, but also deeply empathetic essays in which Sebald writes with great affection about authors with whom he feels a special affinity. The latter category includes figures such as Ernst Herbeck (1920–1991), Herbert Achternbusch (1938–2022), Jean Améry (1912–1978) or Peter Weiss (1916–1982), whom Sebald approached less as a literary critic and more as kindred spirits, emphatically taking their side. He seemed not to know the middle ground of objective, balanced literary analysis that ordinarily distinguishes academic scholarship. In his engagement with it, literature was ruthlessly divided into friends or foes.

Accordingly, the publication of his Döblin monograph in March of 1980, a full seven years after submitting his thesis, afforded him the opportunity of attending two colloquia on Döblin, in New York in December 1981, and in Freiburg in June 1983, and giving provocative papers on the author in front of his assembled colleagues. Accusations levelled at Döblin included his alleged homosexual tendencies and a purported penchant for necrophilia, claims Sebald supported – as he did in his thesis – by taking passages of Döblin's work out of context and simplistically applying them to the author himself.

Sebald also drew audacious and scurrilous parallels between the Jewish exile and democrat Döblin and a number of authors on the far right by alleging that Döblin had written rape scenes in a similar style to them. Rather than scholarly contributions to research on Döblin, such talks are opportunities for performative self-staging where Sebald gets to present himself to his colleagues as an academic nonconformist.

Even essays intended to lavish praise, such as Sebald's paean to the novel *Die Wiederholung* (*Repetition*, 1986) by Peter Handke (b. 1942), invariably include acerbic barbs against *Germanistik*. In Sebald's reading, the novel embodies the transcendental power of true literature 'to render visible a more perfect world by force of language alone' (UH 163), and he laments indignantly that 'the parasitic species [...] that feeds on literature for a living' (UH 164) would fail to recognize the poetic agenda of such a work and prosaically dismiss it as esotericism.

Germanistik, in Sebald's view, simply lacks the proper sensibility to appreciate

> the metaphysics developed in Handke's books, through which he aspires to transform what he experiences and perceives into language. As a discipline, it clearly no longer has any scope for granting discursive space to metaphysics. And yet, wherever and whenever art comes into being, it does so in intimate proximity with metaphysics. (UH 163–164)

Sebald's obdurate adherence to practices or sciences deemed irrational, superstitious or outdated, such as metaphysics, was a further aspect of his dissident attitude both in his literary and in his critical work. Siding with the underdog and the marginalized, with minority positions and lost causes (see chapter 18 in this volume) was another form of provocation through which he sought to confront his discipline and colleagues.

Another aspect, finally, was his calculated violations of academic taboos on language and thought offensive or disadvantageous to minority groups. This concerns in particular Sebald's use of the offensive word 'Neger' (negro) in his prose literature (see chapter 32 in this volume). A further example is the provocative analogy he draws between abattoirs and concentration camps. Even in his dissertation, Sebald had already identified a structural approximation between the industrial raising and slaughter of livestock and the industrially organized genocide of European Jews (RM 68).

Later, in an essay on Achternbusch, he wrote: 'The common denominator between Auschwitz and the animal concentration camps is the extreme exploitation of nature.' It is time for us, argues Sebald, to understand as a human species that 'the fate of the pigs in the death factory is in fact our own'.[11] This is Sebald writing not for the sake of cheap provocation, or to play the scholar-rebel, but in righteous melancholy anger and concern at humankind's ruthless exploitation of our fellow animals and the natural environment.

What he says about the resistance fighter Jean Améry could easily be applied to Sebald himself here: with the writerly means at his disposal, he, too, combats what he takes to be wrongdoing or injustice 'out of a principle of solidarity with victims and as a deliberate affront to those who simply let the stream of history sweep them along' (NHD 159/CSg 159). Sebald as a fervent champion of challenging causes – that picture of him emerged from the critical essays that he wrote in the 1980s. In no way did he ever shy away from resorting to polemics if he felt it necessary to grab the attention of his readers.

Sebald the Iconoclast: Toppling Jurek Becker and Alfred Andersch in the 1990s

If Sebald's polemical side had receded somewhat in the 1980s, it came emphatically to the fore again at the beginning of the 1990s, the decade that saw him achieve his international breakthrough as a bestselling literary author. For one thing, he was now in a position to confront *Germanistik* with the full force of his newly-won acclaim. In response, he was lambasted for having 'delusions of grandeur'.[12]

Even more crucially, Sebald now felt in a position to show the representatives of *Germanistik*, and of German post-war literature, "how to do it right". He especially enjoyed schooling the latter, for he considered these his 'teachers *ex negativo*'.[13] Döblin, for example, is reproached by Sebald for the 'cruelty' of his 'bloody phantasmagorias' and for invoking 'every imaginable atrocity in a perverse "aestheticization" of reality' (RM 265–266).

Rather than sensitize and alienate their readers, Sebald believed that such brutal depictions of violence had a deadening effect – and so paved the way aesthetically for the very real brutality of National Socialism. Sebald himself was always very careful to avoid direct representations of atrocity, especially where the Holocaust was concerned, for fear that these might 'paralyze, as it were, our moral capacity', as he put it: 'The only way in which one can approach these things, in my view, is obliquely, tangentially, by reference rather than by direct confrontation' (EM 80).

The 1990s witnessed two major polemics, both informed by a similar desire on Sebald's part to distance himself from his literary predecessors: against Jurek Becker (1937–1997) and against Alfred Andersch (1914–1980). The former piece, from 1991, a comprehensive reckoning with Polish-born German-Jewish author and Holocaust survivor Jurek Becker, was so vehemently polemic it could only be published posthumously in 2010. In the essay, titled, 'Ich möchte zu ihnen hinabsteigen und finde den Weg nicht' ('I Would Descend to Them But Cannot Find the Way'), Sebald criticizes the 'false realism'[14] of Becker's literature and 'the author's emotional absence'.[15] He rejects Becker's novel *Jakob der Lügner* (*Jakob the Liar*, 1969), which has been the subject of several screen adaptations, as a failure, disparaging Becker for his use of humour and the grotesque in his treatment of his childhood in the ghetto of Łódz (Litzmannstadt) on the grounds that this makes it seem 'like the setting to some musical'[16] or a scene from 'a melodramatic popular novel'.[17]

The main flaw Sebald identified in Becker's literature was his 'mnemonic embargo' ('Erinnerungsembargo'),[18] which supposedly made it impossible for Sebald 'to cite even a single passage in his prose that bore any linguistic trace of memory'.[19] In stark contrast to other Holocaust survivor authors whom Sebald discusses sympathetically, such as Primo Levi (1919–1987) or Jean Améry, Becker fails to meet Sebald's criteria as a literary witness to National Socialist persecution, and Sebald condemns him harshly for it.

However, while Sebald may consider him a 'teacher *ex negativo*', Becker has informed his writing in more than one respect. Becker's inability to recall his childhood provides an important motif for the figure of Austerlitz and, like Becker, Austerlitz loses his mother tongue. Austerlitz is tortured, as Becker himself was all his life, by the fact that, as Becker says in an essay on pictures taken of the Litzmannstadt ghetto by National Socialist photographer Walter Genewein (1891–1974), of those who remained in the camps: 'I would descend to them, but I cannot find the way.'[20]

Though the photographs depict the world of the camps in which Becker grew up, they are unable to rouse any recollection of the horrors of his childhood in him. The photos remain "dead". In the 'Max Ferber' chapter of *Die Ausgewanderten* (*The Emigrants*), Sebald effectively takes over as an

Illustration 17 – Walter Genewein, Litzmannstadt weavers

author where he feels Becker has fallen short. In its much-praised final passage (AW 349–350/E 236–237), Sebald uses one of the Genewein photographs – depicting three Jewish women weaving in the ghetto's textile workshop – and transforms the historical document of the past into an allegorical vision of the mythological Fates, which draws the narrator into the Jewish women's frame.

Alfred Andersch, meanwhile, the target of Sebald's second main polemic of the 1990s, was the first non-Jewish writer – after Sternheim, Döblin and Becker – to become the object of Sebald's wrath. After (supposedly) having been interned in Dachau for three months as a young communist, he was placed on a pedestal by the German post-war literary scene. Andersch stoked the adulation by presenting himself as a fearless antifascist who (so he claimed) had risked life and limb by deserting before the end of the war, as a result of which his writing carried significant moral authority in post-war Germany.

In reality, Andersch had behaved a great deal less courageously and rather more opportunistically during the Third Reich than his post-war self-image could accommodate. These political and moral shortcomings were uncovered in a biography that came out in 1990 and laid bare his political and moral shortcomings, even as it sought to excuse these,[21] prompting Sebald's fierce attack on Andersch's person and work in which he reviles the author for his duplicity and hypocrisy.

The Andersch essay, which was published in 1993, illustrates perfectly the approach at work in all of Sebald's polemics: he makes morality the touchstone of literature, positing a close, if not to say causal, correlation between ethics and aesthetics, undeterred in his conviction that 'when it comes down to it, aesthetics are always a question of ethics' (UH 115). Where Sebald was concerned, someone who had morally invalidated themselves as an individual was not in a position to produce aesthetically valid literature as an author. The artist's work reflects his biography; and vice versa.

Accordingly, and supporting his case with evidence drawn from the recent biography, Sebald systematically set about painting Andersch as an unprincipled opportunist. Among his key charges was that Andersch was quick to leave his Jewish wife in 1943 to expedite his membership of the National Socialist *Reichsschrifttumskammer* (the writers' subdivision of the *Reichskulturkammer* or Reich Chamber of Culture) and went on to marry a painter with excellent contacts to high-ranking National Socialists. Yet he consistently denied having been published at all during the Third Reich in an effort to present himself as a victim of fascist persecution and a resistance fighter and opponent of Hitler's regime.

Against this biographical backdrop, Sebald reads Andersch's entire body of work as a large-scale fictional repainting of his life in a heroic light. As an attempted conversion of moral shortcomings into literature, Andersch's books reveal a character 'plagued by ambition, egotism, resentment, and rancour', making them, in Sebald's eyes, a literary failure also: 'His literary work is the cloak in which those qualities wrap themselves, but its lining [. . .] keeps showing through' (NHD 144–145/LL 146–147).

By daring to launch such a vigorous attack on a sacrosanct author, Sebald also gave other Germanists licence to probe more deeply into Andersch's biography during the war. Further evidence of biographical distortions and attempted self-exoneration came to light and lastingly damaged the author's previously untouchable reputation. By questionable means, it would seem that Sebald had, once again, achieved an unimpeachable outcome.

Literature and the Air War: Germans as Victims?

In 1982, Sebald had already criticized German post-war literature in an academic essay for failing to pay sufficient literary tribute and accord a proper space in cultural memory to the horrifying impact of the Allied bombing campaigns on German civilians. In the autumn of 1997, he returned to his provocative claim in the context of three public poetics lectures at the University of Zurich and took advantage of this more prominent forum to accuse post-war authors of having comprehensively failed to engage with the topic at all. His condemnation caused a serious media stir, triggering enduring heated debates in both Germany and internationally on how the German past ought to be commemorated.

Ten years after German reunification, Sebald had questioned a cornerstone of the political left, the unassailable taboo against publicly discussing German civilian suffering during the war. However, the object of his critique went beyond the moral or literary failings of German post-war literature. The air-war essay that emerged from his Zurich lectures is closely entwined with his fictional prose writing of the same period, the stories of *The Emigrants* and his novel *Austerlitz*: in both, Sebald aims to bring to the surface the suppressed traumas of the twentieth century and give voice to the unspoken suffering of its victims.

It is in this sense that the Allied firestorms unleashed on German cities appear as a counterpoint in his writing to the crematoria burning in the concentration camps. Sebald's intention was not to draw simplistic juxta-positions or relativize German guilt; his aim was a more broadly provoca-tive one: in the context of his negative history of philosophy, he viewed both historical catastrophes, yoked together under the sign of fire, as devastating stations in a natural history of destruction.[22]

This profoundly pessimistic *Weltanschauung* disputed both the Enlightenment myth of teleological progress and religious promises of salvation. In their stead, Sebald viewed all religious, political and economic systems as tending towards inescapable, all-encompassing catastrophic destruction, towards an entropy humankind is powerless to oppose, since we are ourselves a part of it (see chapter 13 in this volume).

Against this backdrop, a narrative prose work such as *Austerlitz* emerges more clearly not as a comforting tale of miraculous deliverance, but as an episode of transient happiness at best. Towards the end of his life, literature for Sebald could at most aspire to find glimpses of fleeting hope within overwhelming hopelessness and mark moments of futile resistance against the all-consuming force of the natural history of destruction.

Conclusion: A Polemical Mind?

What was the origin of Sebald's irresistible lifelong impulse to polemicize? There seems to be no easy answer. Coming of age during the anti-authoritarian era of 1968 undoubtedly played a part. But in this he resem-bled many of his contemporaries who, like him, embarked on "the long march through the institutions" only to lose their radical views and become good conformist citizens as soon as they themselves had climbed to positions of power. Sebald, by contrast, kept his rebellious nature and his polemical instincts firmly alive.

Social mobility may hold the key here. Not unlike many Austrian authors of the 1970s with provincial, lower-class backgrounds like his own, Sebald understood literature and academia as a vehicle for social emancipation. They had advanced him, the village schoolboy, to a professorship in England and to international literary fame. However, as sociological research has shown, social advancement through the educa-tional route may, paradoxically, be accompanied by a significant fear of failure and experience of loss and uncertainty.

Social climbers in academia may feel as if they do not belong or experience imposter syndrome or a sense of having betrayed their origins.[23] Perhaps unavoidably, this will give rise to frustration and aggression, which may be directed against oneself or, may have been the case for Sebald, against others.

A sense of inadequacy, informed by self-consciousness about his background and transmuted into polemics, seems to speak especially loudly from Sebald's academic dissertations and reviews of the 1970s. In the 1980s, the inspiration for his uncompromising intransigence became increasingly visible: in his savage, and often unjustified, condemnation of other authors and academics, he was modelling his accusatory language on Thomas Bernhard (1931–1989) and his judgmental tone on Karl Kraus (1874–1936).

A further factor was Sebald's (self-imposed) outsider status in many areas of his life. Leaving behind *Germanistik* for a post in England marginalized him in relation to German academia. Moreover, his publications of the 1980s were often deliberately designed to antagonize the representatives of *Germanistik* and so further alienate him from them.

The 1990s witnessed a peak stage of escalation when Sebald switched over to literary production himself and became increasingly successful. Finally, he was able to sever all ties to his colleagues across the channel. Sebald's combativeness reached its pinnacle in his moral condemnation of Becker and Andersch. In keeping with his conviction that the core moral truth of any work of literature derives from the 'complex question of the relationship between ethics and aesthetics' (NHD 45/LL 52), Sebald was merciless in his verdicts, not just about the texts themselves but also about their authors.

As Ruth Klüger reminds us, in his literary criticism, 'Sebald broke the taboo against the biographist approach we Germanists have been taught to disdain as naïve'.[24] Yet his biographism is merely the obverse of his literary writing, for this, too, is invariably rooted in the biographies of the figures informing it. Not least for this reason, the narrative mode and the critical mode are inseparable for Sebald.

Indeed, it may be that his implacably critical rejection of German postwar literature is what it took for Sebald to feel authorized as a writer of aesthetically and morally valid literature himself. And even as his work reveals problematic blind spots of his own and displays a deep-seated and at times querulous disregard for conventions and rules, it is hard to dispute that this is what he became.

Notes

1. U Pralle, Mit einem kleinen Strandspaten Abschied von Deutschland nehmen [interview], in: *Süddeutsche Zeitung*, 22 December 2001.
2. R Sheppard, W.G. Sebald's Reception of Alfred Döblin, in: S Davies, E Schonfield (eds.), *Alfred Döblin: Paradigms of Modernism* (Berlin/New York: De Gruyter, 2009), pp. 350–376.

3. U Schütte, *Interventionen: Literaturkritik als Widerspruch bei W.G. Sebald* (Munich: Ed. Text+Kritik, 2014), pp. 67–104, 115–156.
4. Qtd. in: Sheppard, Sebald's Reception of Döblin, p. 356.
5. Ibid.
6. Sebald, *Carl Sternheim: Kritiker und Opfer der Wilhelminischen Ära* (Stuttgart: Kohlhammer, 1969), p. 129.
7. Sebald: review of J Schulte-Sasse, Literarische Wertung, in: *Journal of European Studies* 1:3 (1971), p. 273.
8. Ibid.
9. Sebald, review of L Giesz, Phänomenologie des Kitsches, in: ibid., p. 274.
10. Sebald, review of H Glaser et al., Literaturwissenschaft und Sozialwissenschaften: Grundlagen und Modellanalysen, in: *Journal of European Studies* 2:1 (1972), p. 76.
11. Sebald, The Art of Transformation: Herbert Achternbusch's Theatrical Mission, in: *A Radical Stage: Theatre in Germany in the 1970s, and 1980s* (Oxford: Berg, 1990), pp. 174–184 (184).
12. M Durzak, Sebald – der unduldsame Kritiker: Zu seinen literarischen Polemiken gegen Sternheim und Andersch, in: G Fischer (ed.), *W.G. Sebald: Schreiben ex patria/Expatriate Writing* (Amsterdam: Rodopi, 2009), pp. 435–445 (444).
13. T Hoffmann, Polemik, in: M Niehaus, C Öhlschläger (eds.), *W.G. Sebald-Handbuch: Leben – Werk – Wirkung* (Stuttgart: Metzler, 2017), pp. 155–158 (157).
14. Sebald, Ich möchte zu ihnen hinabsteigen und finde den Weg nicht: Zu den Romanen Jurek Beckers, in: *Sinn und Form* 2 (2010), pp. 226–241 (226).
15. Ibid., pp. 227–228.
16. Ibid., p. 231.
17. Ibid.
18. Ibid., p. 234.
19. Ibid.
20. Becker, Die unsichtbare Stadt, in: I Heidelberger-Leonard (ed.), *Jurek Becker* (Frankfurt: Suhrkamp, 1992) pp. 25–27 (25).
21. S Reinhardt, *Alfred Andersch: Eine Biographie* (Zurich: Diogenes, 1990).
22. Cf. the essay on Feuer in Schütte, *Annäherungen: Sieben Essays zu W.G. Sebald* (Cologne: Böhlau, 2019), pp. 179–218.
23. J Reuter et al. (eds.), *Vom Arbeiterkind zur Professur: Sozialer Aufstieg in der Wissenschaft* (Bielefeld: Transcript, 2020).
24. R Klüger, Wanderer zwischen falschen Leben: Über W.G. Sebald, in: *Text+Kritik* 158 (2003), pp. 95–102 (99).

CHAPTER 25

Holocaust

Jakob Hessing

Although German authors now rarely live and work abroad permanently, as W G. Sebald did, shortly before he was born a whole generation, many of them Jewish, left Nazi Germany and continued their literary work in exile. Objectively, Sebald could not regard his emigration to England in the 1960s as an exile since he went there voluntarily. However, this essay is less about his biography than the worlds he created in his imagination.

Sebald created three fictional characters – Henry Selwyn, Max Ferber and Jacques Austerlitz – who, like himself, left continental Europe for England. All three were of Jewish origin, and two of them – Max Ferber and Jacques Austerlitz – were escaping annihilation under the Nazi regime. Sebald, born in 1944, was not a victim of the Third Reich, but, in his literary texts, he has his narrator meet and record the stories of others who were.

Not surprisingly, some therefore consider Sebald to be a 'Holocaust writer',[1] but theirs is an external perspective since they read Sebald in a context independent of his œuvre. I am, however, not interested in the pre-established framework "Holocaust literature" but rather a different set of questions. Whom did Sebald choose to write about? What determined his choice and what stories do his characters tell? The two examples I shall examine are the painter Max Ferber and the architectural historian Jacques Austerlitz.

Life and Art

Sebald was almost fifty when he published *Die Ausgewanderten* (*The Emigrants*), four long stories that – when they appeared in English translation in 1996 – established his international fame. Only two of them discuss Nazi Germany, 'Dr. Henry Selwyn' and 'Max Ferber', and only the latter addresses the Holocaust directly. The narrator of 'Max Ferber' begins by telling us of his arrival in the city of Manchester, where, like Sebald, he spent his early years in England. In the nineteenth century, its artificial port had been the centre of the global industrial revolution but had since fallen into decay. Amid its ruins, he meets Max Ferber in his studio:

> He drew with vigorous abandon, frequently going through half a dozen of his willow-wood charcoal sticks in the shortest of time [...]. The concomitant business of constantly erasing what he had drawn with a woollen rag already heavy with charcoal, really amounted to nothing but a steady production of dust [...]. Time and again, at the end of a working day, I marvelled to see that Ferber, with a few lines and shadows that had escaped annihilation, had created a portrait of great vividness. (E 161–162/AW 236–237)

Although he has many conversations with the painter, when the narrator leaves Manchester in 1969 he still knows little of Ferber's past. Only twenty years later, at the end of 1989, he comes across one of his paintings in a gallery. Soon thereafter, he learns in an article that Ferber, who had grown up Jewish in Munich, had been sent to England in 1939, at the age of fifteen, whereas his parents were deported to the East in November 1941, where they were murdered by the Nazis.

The narrator then returns to Ferber's studio after his long absence, and the painter finally tells him of the pain behind his ceaseless labour at the easel. During his first two years in England, he had received letters from his parents but found it difficult to answer them. Once they stopped, Ferber initially felt relieved and only later, gradually, did he come to realize why their communication had broken off.

After the war, Ferber decided to cut himself loose from his past and stay in England. He went to Manchester to study art, but the city held a fateful surprise for him. He found that 'the German and Jewish influence was stronger in Manchester than in any other European city; and so, although I had intended to move in the opposite direction, when I arrived in Manchester I had come home, in a sense' (E 192/AW 283).

It is a crucial moment in Sebald's œuvre when Ferber's past catches up with him. Labouring under the shock of a separation he cannot overcome, he tries desperately to recover images of his past but only achieves 'a steady production of dust' (E 162/AW 236). Is his art a performative act? Is the dust the objective correlative of his mourning for his dead parents? Does it provide insight into Sebald's poetics?

A German Dilemma

Sebald was born and raised in the Allgäu, a remote area in rural Bavaria where, according to Sebald, nobody cared to remember Germany's recent history. He was in his late teens when, for the first time, he was shown documentary footage of the Holocaust at school, with no explanation or context.[2]

After the war, the most notable way young Germans attempted to come to terms with the silence of their parents was the students' revolt of 1968. Many of the rebels adhered to Critical Theory as practised by the Frankfurt School, an analytical approach to social philosophy that challenges power structures. They defined themselves as a New Left, believed that Hitler's "Third Reich" was the disastrous result of capitalism, and never mentioned the background of their teachers.

They did not seem to realize that all of them – Theodor W. Adorno (1903–1969), Walter Benjamin (1892–1940), Max Horkheimer (1895–1973), Herbert Marcuse (1898–1979) and Erich Fromm (1900–1980) – were German Jews who fled into exile when Hitler came to power. Their Marxism did not allow them to accept the Nazis' deadly hatred of the Jews as an objective force in history and thus prevented them from confronting the Holocaust.

Sebald also belonged to this "Generation of 68". Like other young German intellectuals, he avidly read some proponents of Critical Theory but was no ideologue. More importantly, in 1968 he no longer lived in Germany and took no part in the students' revolt. Thus, no ideological blinders prevented him from addressing German crimes and yet, when dealing with his difficult heritage, he still faced obstacles that were virtually insurmountable for a German writer of his generation.

In preparation for the Holocaust, the Nazis attempted to erase Jews from the German consciousness. They were systematically removed from Germany's public sphere. They had to "sell" their businesses to "Aryans" and could no longer exercise their professions. Their books were burned and Jewish artists could not perform for German audiences. Jews had to be "forgotten" before the *Endlösung* (final solution) could be implemented.

After the war, many Germans kept up this sham and Sebald thus grew up in a world of oblivion. When he began to wonder what had happened, he had no context and, the historical void in which he had been raised left its mark on everything "Jewish" in both his academic publications and his literary work.

A Tale of Two Voices

Throughout his academic career, Sebald was interested in German writers of Jewish origin. Before he came to England, he wrote a thesis on Carl Sternheim (1878–1942) at the University of Fribourg in Switzerland. During the twilight of the German Empire Sternheim had been a successful playwright, but after World War One he suffered from mental illness and his writing deteriorated. Sebald criticized his later texts and blamed his mental problems on his assimilation with and kowtowing to a German society on the verge of collective insanity (SH 48, 61–62). Sebald does not offer much empirical evidence to support his argument and his thesis is not convincing as academic research (see chapter 24 in this volume).

However, it was a step down his long road to becoming a writer, an early example of his interest in the type of ambiguous Jewish characters he would later create in his literary œuvre. For Sebald, the modern era was the age of alienation. The industrial revolution brought irreversible change, breaking up lives everywhere. Since Jews played a major, suffering role in the eventual industrialization of genocide, Manchester holds a special place in Sebald's intellectual biography. Here he met German-Jewish emigrants for the first time, including his 'Mancunian landlord', Peter Jordan (1923–2020),[3] who became one of Sebald's models for Max Ferber in *The Emigrants*.

Manchester plays an important role in 'Max Ferber'. Ferber speaks of 'the German and Jewish influence' in the city, and of his feeling that, by moving there, he 'had come home, in a sense' (E 192/AW 283). However, it was Sebald who discovered the city's German-Jewish history when he moved to Manchester in 1966 (G 105–106) and it was he who transferred this experience to Ferber.

Sebald's protagonists never speak for themselves but rather only through his narrator, who mediates between them and the reader. Sebald referred to this narration-within-a-narration as a 'periscopic' technique he learned from Thomas Bernhard (1931–1989), and he used it to remain at one remove from his Jewish protagonists. Nevertheless, in one interview, Sebald stated that his 'biography had overlapped' with those of the Jewish protagonists in *The Emigrants* (G 81).

He is in fact accused by some critics of usurping the lives of Jews, by others of lending them his voice. Both readings, however, fail to acknowledge that his narrator and his protagonist are fictional characters created by Sebald himself. What, then, do they converse about, and who supplies the subject matter?

As stated, Max Ferber's thoughts about Manchester mirror Sebald's personal experience, and, as will be shown, Jacques Austerlitz's ideas are very similar to those of Sebald himself. Before turning to *Austerlitz* (2001), however, let us take one more look at 'Max Ferber'.

Artist and Scholar

After the narrator's reunion with Ferber, during which he learns of his tragedy, when he is on the point of leaving, Ferber hands him a parcel. It contains a memoir his mother wrote shortly before her death. She had grown up in a small village, but her family moved to a larger town when she was nearly sixteen. These are her reflections on the eve of her deportation by the Nazis:

> If I think back nowadays to our childhood in Steinach [. . .], it often seems
> [. . .] as if it were still going on, right into these lines I am now writing. But
> in reality, as I know only too well, childhood ended in January 1905 when
> [. . .] we moved into a three-storey house in Kissingen. (E 207–208/AW
> 306–307)

For her, this was 'the first step on a path that grew narrower day by day and led inevitably to the point I have now arrived at' (E 208/AW 308). This account was allegedly written by Ferber's mother, but the language is that of the narrator, or rather, the author – the unmistakable "Sebald sound" characteristic of his entire œuvre. The music of his sentences is that of an elegy to accompany the 'attitude of mourning' (G 115) he once stated was appropriate in the face of destruction and loss.

This statement came in an interview conducted shortly after publication of *Die Ringe des Saturn* (*The Rings of Saturn*), a book central to Sebald's understanding of the Holocaust. In it, he walks through East Anglia as if the English countryside were a global theatre and reads past events connected with the dreary landscape as a universal history of calamity.

A profoundly pessimistic historiosophy informs Sebald's writing: he sees human "progress" as inextricably bound with a penchant for self-destruction. When 'Max Ferber' opens, Manchester, once 'the industrial Jerusalem' (E 165/AW 242), is presented in a state of decay; towards its close, Ferber's mother believes the social rise of her family has led 'inevitably' to her impending death (E 208/AW 308). Sebald's *Weltanschauung* is deterministic, and in *The Rings of Saturn* it is expounded most elaborately.

The Rings of Saturn also serves as a link between *The Emigrants* and *Austerlitz*, where Sebald comes closer to the Holocaust than anywhere else in his œuvre. Both Ferber and Jacques Austerlitz were sent to England on Kindertransports before the Nazis could murder them, and both are in search of lost parents. Comparing them will help us to determine what guided Sebald in creating his protagonists.

At the outset of 'Max Ferber', while watching Ferber at his easel, the narrator observes that he is 'constantly erasing what he had drawn'. At its close, the narrator says of his own attempt to tell Ferber's story: 'I had covered hundreds of pages with my scribble, in pencil and ballpoint. By far the greater part had been crossed out, discarded, or obliterated by additions' (E 230/AW 345). Does the narrator imitate Ferber, who cannot recover the memory of what he wishes to draw, or does Sebald project his own struggle with his painful subject onto Ferber? This difficult question arises due to Sebald's complex narrative structure and is as relevant to Austerlitz as to Ferber.

If Ferber is the counterpart of the artist within Sebald, the architectural historian Jacques Austerlitz reflects his intellectual interests. Sebald has his narrator first meet both Ferber and Austerlitz in 1967, and time is a central theme in *Austerlitz*. At Antwerp's main railway station, Austerlitz points out the position of the clock high on the wall of the entrance hall: 'just where the image of the emperor stood in the Pantheon [...] as governor of a new omnipotence [...] In fact, Austerlitz said [...] not until [the railway timetables] were all standardized around the middle of the nineteenth century did time really reign supreme' (Ae 13–14/Ag 21–22). One would expect an argument like this in a cultural study. Thus: Who is speaking here – the fictional protagonist, or Sebald himself, whose previous book was a cultural study about an English landscape?

The Sound of Mourning

None of Sebald's characters have a language of their own. They all sound like their author, including Austerlitz: 'A clock has always struck me as something ridiculous, a thoroughly mendacious object, perhaps I have always resisted the power of time [...] in the hope, as I now think, [...] that time will not pass away, [...] that I can turn back and go behind it' (Ae 143–144/Ag 151–152).

These words are spoken nearly thirty years after Austerlitz and the narrator first met, while walking through the Royal Observatory at Greenwich – and they express the poetics of Sebald, who, in his writing, hoped to reverse the irreversible passage of time. He hopes against hope, of course. Neither Ferber at his easel nor Austerlitz on his journey into the past will ever resurrect their dead parents. In his last public appearance in Germany, a month before he died, Sebald defined literature as an 'Attempt at Restitution' (CSe 206–215/CSg 240–248), but the attempt must fail. Thus, the mourning reverberating in his œuvre is ultimately not an attitude but rather an authentic sentiment that underlies his life and art.

How are we to define the relationship between the narrator and Sebald's protagonists? Despite being based on real people, the latter are wholly fictional characters. The narrator in turn is a fictionalized version of Sebald himself. And Sebald has given not only the narrator aspects of his personal biography but also Ferber and Austerlitz.

The memoir ostensibly composed by Ferber's mother was based on a manuscript written by Thea Gebhardt, the aunt of Sebald's former landlord, Peter Jordan.[4] Jordan provided it to him in 1987 and Sebald rewrote its language, added and omitted details, changed the name of the aunt, and, finally, he changed the name of his protagonist as well.

A feature common to both 'Max Ferber' and *Austerlitz* is a period of approximately twenty years during which the narrator and the respective protagonists have no contact with each other. This time gap corresponds to Sebald's biography. Both he and the narrator last see Ferber/Jordan in 1969 and then do not meet them again until the late 1980s, early 1990s, respectively. In *Austerlitz*, the gap runs from 1975, when Sebald went back to Germany for a short time, and ends in December 1996. The latter date is significant since it was precisely then that Sebald abandoned his Corsica Project in favour of *Austerlitz*.

During their reunion in the early 1990s, Ferber finally chooses to tell the narrator about his childhood and youth in Germany – although he could have done so already in the 1960s. Austerlitz too tells the narrator about his past during their reunions in the mid-1990s, but he could not have done so previously since he knew nothing of his past until later in life and the slow return of his memory was a painful process of recovery. For many years it was disguised as an intellectual endeavour, but in a famous scene at London's Liverpool Street Station his defences break down and their psychological roots are revealed.

Austerlitz, like 'Max Ferber', is a text about dislocation. In the former, however, Sebald uses a different strategy. Unlike Ferber, Austerlitz does not merely talk to the narrator but also takes two practical steps of great importance. At a critical moment, he loses faith in his architectural studies and abandons them and, shortly thereafter, he travels to Prague, where he was born.

Austerlitz's search for his past corresponds to Sebald's own drive to research the past. As Austerlitz gave up his architectural studies, Sebald transitioned from academic essays to literary texts in order to give his life a new direction and in his prose seek out traumatic events long hidden from consciousness. It is no accident that the narrator accompanies Austerlitz and Ferber and reports on their search for their childhoods. This 'periscopic' technique' (EM 80) of narration-within-a-narration mirrors Sebald's own attempt to understand his early years in Germany.

However, Sebald was not able to overcome all the difficulties he faced on that journey. He could not focus solely on the Holocaust as a catastrophic German-Jewish encounter and instead spoke of a 'history of calamities' encompassing all of mankind and the entire planet. The reason why the tragedy he mourns is not specifically German or Jewish but universal is that, in the part of Germany where he grew up, there was no memory of the Jews and, so, the Jewish characters he later invented had hazy, all-but-forgotten Jewish origins and could know no more about themselves than Sebald knew about them.

Sebald was aware of this, of course. The period in which his narrator was separated from Ferber and Austerlitz were years of learning for Sebald himself. Where he touched upon the horrors of the Holocaust, he was honest enough to let Jewish survivors speak for themselves, as paradigmatically illustrated by his use of

H.G. Adler's massive study of Theresienstadt in connection with *Austerlitz*. Sebald also did not hide inherent ironies. When he put his own criticism of modern civilization into the mouth of Austerlitz, he had him demonstrate the destructive power of time via the invention of trains, the means by which Jewish victims of the Holocaust were transported to their death.[5]

Like Austerlitz, Sebald too wanted to return to his roots in the end. He was planning a book about his parents' generation, his childhood, and the Germany he left behind as a young man (see chapter 15 in this volume). However, he turned to prose fiction too late in life, and his death came too early.

Notes

1. B Prager, The Good German as Narrator: On W.G. Sebald and the Risks of Holocaust Writing, in: *New German Critique* 96 (2005), pp. 75–102.
2. M Jaggi, The Last Word, in: *The Guardian*, 21 December 2001.
3. Ibid.

4. K Gasseleder, Erkundungen zum Prätext der Luisa-Lanzberg-Geschichte, in: M Atze, F Loquai (eds.), *Sebald. Lektüren.* (Eggingen: Isele, 2005), pp. 157–175.
5. For a thorough reading of *Austerlitz* from a Judaistic point of view, cf. V Lenzen, Spinne im Schädel, in: J Hessing, V Lenzen, *Sebalds Blick* (Göttingen: Wallstein, 2015), pp. 101–264.

CHAPTER 26

Photography

Nick Warr

Photography in the work of W.G. Sebald is an inconstant element, both in terms of material and process. From his first experimental text and image assemblages for the journals *Manuskripte* and *Proposition*, through to the unfinished World War Project (see chapter 15 in this volume), Sebald engaged with many different orders and modes of photography. In addition to the snapshots and studio portraits that 'act like barriers and weirs' to 'stem the flow' of the text (EM 42) there are prints from microfilm, photocopies, 16 mm motion picture film enlargements, colour slide transparencies and numerous other forms of found photographic material.

Photography is also not the only type of image making evident in his published work. Alongside the amateur and professional photographic prints, Sebald includes drawings, paintings, engravings, lithographs, plus a wide variety of other printed matter. In this respect, like the pattern books of the Norwich weavers in *Die Ringe des Saturn* (*The Rings of Saturn*), Sebald's books are catalogues for the image in the age of its technological reproducibility. However, though multifarious in appearance, all Sebald's images share a common essence, a fundamentally uncanny nature. For Sebald, photography is performative, it is an act of doubling, of creating or revealing 'a secondary form of existence'.[1]

Though descriptions of photographs abound throughout his œuvre, sustained accounts of the photographic act or process are curiously absent from Sebald's prose fiction. When they do occur, for example: with the honeymooning 'young Erlanger' (V 127/SG 142) in front of the Pizzeria Verona in *Schwindel. Gefühle.* (*Vertigo*); on New Jersey's 'edge of darkness' (E 88/AW 129) with Uncle Kasimir in *Die Ausgewanderten* (*The Emigrants*); and in the 'little cubbyhole behind the chemistry lab' (Ae 107–108/Ag 115–116) at Stower Grange school in *Austerlitz*, it is always by proxy.

A similar distance from the photographic act is rehearsed by Sebald in various interviews. In these inquiries into his method, he makes a point of expressing a deliberate indifference to acquiring or demonstrating any technical proficiency in relation to cameras, preferring instead 'cheap', fully automatic models manufactured for convenience over quality.[2] Through such statements the mechanics of image making are ceded to the apparatus. When the narrator of Sebald's literary work does encounter a professional photographer, they are portrayed as eldritch characters, the 'savage' 'deaf mute' of the Via Roma (V 125/SG 141) and the silver poisoned lab assistant whose 'face and hands turned blue in strong light' (E 165/AW 241). They are creatures of dark rooms, like the noctambulist *acciatori* of Corsica, 'beings who are somehow blurred and out of place' (CSe 33/CSg 35) who inhabit the realm of the living but are 'in a way in the service of death' (CSe 32/CS 34).

Photography, 'in essence', surmises Sebald in *Campo Santo*, is 'after all [. . .] nothing but a way of making ghostly apparitions materialize by means of a very dubious magical art' (CSe 26/CSg 28).

The Pictorial Turn

The reality of Sebald's experience of photography's 'shadow realm' (CSe 32/CSg 34) is far less phantasmagorical than it is a consequence of the interdisciplinary nature of the University of East Anglia (UEA), Norwich. The university accepted its first students in 1963 and by 1965 had set up a Photographic Department as part of its School of Fine Art (later the School of Art History). In 1970, Sebald joined the University as both an Assistant Lecturer and as a post-graduate research student. An early documented interaction between Sebald and the Photographic Department occurred on the 21 March 1985, when Sebald notes 'Grünewald slides' in his appointment diary (SM 631) as a reminder to cross the university campus to pick up some 35 mm film transparencies (now in the UEA Archive) from Michael Brandon-Jones.

Brandon-Jones had joined the UEA as a Photographic Technician in 1966 and by the time of his first encounter with Sebald oversaw a busy professional dark room in the Sainsbury Centre for Visual Arts, the university's art gallery. Alongside documenting the gallery's activities, Brandon-Jones' principal duties were to produce the visual materials required for Art History teaching and research. It was in this capacity that Sebald contacted him to make some photographic reproductions from Wolf Lücking's art historical study *Mathis: Nachforschungen über Grünewald*.[3] This was not an unusual request as it was common practice for faculty from other Schools to approach Brandon-Jones if they required images for a lecture or publication (images were often provided to publishers as 35 mm slides).

Illustration 18 – Grünewald slide, Michael Brandon-Jones, b/w reversal positive,
21 March 1985

The timing of Sebald's request suggests that he was either considering incorporating images with the publication of his poem 'Wie der Schnee auf den Alpen' ('As the Snow on the Alps') in *Manuskripte*[4] or using the slides to accompany the reading of the poem at the Literarisches Colloquium Berlin in September 1985 (SM 632). As Iain Galbraith notes, by November 1985, Sebald had a completed typescript of the tripartite narrative poem *Nach der Natur* (*After Nature*) ready to send to publishers. This moment, proposes Galbraith, suggests a 'narrative turn' in Sebald's literary ambitions, as the fragments of earlier unpublished lyrical poems were revised and reconstituted into an 'epic' form that prefigures and rehearses the concerns of his later prose fiction (LWe xiv).

However, when understood in relation to a burgeoning creative partnership with Brandon-Jones, this shift from the lyric should also be considered as part of a more elemental creative reorientation, a 'pictorial turn' in Sebald's work.

Fugitive Images

Except for the six monochrome landscapes by Thomas Becker included by the publisher Franz Greno as endpapers to the first edition of *After Nature* in 1988, Sebald's poetry is consistently considered a creative enterprise discrete from photography. Nevertheless, the troubling presence of the photograph as a point of peculiar friction and discomfort within the text persists throughout his poetry subsequent to *After Nature*.

'Am 9. Juni 1904' and 'Neunzig Jahre später', published in the Swiss magazine *Die Weltwoche* (June 1996), includes a reproduction of a postcard from Badenweiler written by Anton Chekhov (1860–1904), as well as images of the playwright's and General Fyodor Keller's (1850–1904) simultaneous funeral processions from Nikolayevsky railway station, Moscow. Two photographs are also included with the poems published in Franz Loquai's *W. G. Sebald, Porträt 7* (1997), the first collection of critical material on Sebald. A family photograph of Georg, Rosa and Anna Sebald visiting Hain Park in 1943 (DLA) accompanies the poem 'In Bamberg', and Jan Peter Tripp's painting *Das Land des Lächelns* (*The Land of Smiles*, 1990) for the poem 'Ein Walzertraum' ('A Waltz Dream').[5]

Though 'Wie der Schnee auf den Alpen' appears in *Manuskripte* without any images there is evidence (in the form of short strip of 35 mm film negative) that Sebald asked Brandon-Jones to prepare a reproduction of a family photograph for 'Die dunckle Nacht fahrt aus' ('Dark Night Sallies Forth'), the final section of *After Nature* published in the March 1987 issue of *Manuskripte*. The photograph, a cabinet card printed in Lagerlechfeld, Bavaria and dated 1905, depicts the marriage of Sebald's maternal grandparents, Theresia Harzenetter and Josef Egelhofer, whose betrothal he evokes at the beginning of the poem.

In a subsequent Dutch translation of 'As the Snow on the Alps' (1986) and 'Dark Night Sallies Forth' (1987) by Huub Beurskens for the journal *Het Moment*, images are interlaced throughout both texts.[6] In the latter, a full-page reproduction of *Alexanderschlacht* (*The Battle of Alexander at Issus*) by Albrecht Altdorfer splits the final section of the poem, whilst in the earlier publication eight details from paintings by Grünewald punctuate all but one of the poem's eight sections (section five has two images). Considering the publication of the first translation of Sebald's work in *Het Moment* in winter 1986, it seems likely that the images provided to the editors of the Amsterdam based journal were produced by Brandon-Jones the previous year (reproductions were available from published sources held by the UEA library) and that what is exhibited in 'As the Snow on the Alps' is an experimental manifestation of the montage technique that was to find its acme in *The Rings of Saturn*.

For example, the image of the 'misshapen princess Artemia' (AN 8/ NN 9) evoked in section one appears in section five (a detail from Grünewald's Heller Altarpiece) after Sebald describes the 'panic-stricken

Illustration 19 – Wedding portrait Josef & Theresia Egelhofer, 1905

kink in the neck to be seen in all of Grünewald's subjects' (AN 27/NN 24). A similar displacement between description and illustration, ekphrasis and photographic facsimile occurs with the image of the cudgel wielding 'stilt-legged bird-like beast [...] with human arms' (AN 26/NN 23). The description of this inhuman tormentor of St Anthony occurs in section five but the reader is already familiar with its grotesque form, as this specific detail from the Isenheim Altarpiece bisects the first section of the poem at the mention of art historian Wilhelm Fraenger (1890–1964) 'whose books were burned by the fascists' (AN 6/NN 8).

Untethered from their illustrative duty, these 'fugitive images' (CSe 160/CSg 197) may at first appear ornamental until the reader encounters their written counterparts. At this instance, a play of peculiar resonances between the textual and the pictorial, the reader, and their double (the viewer) is initiated. As subliminal stimuli the images enact on a personal scale the mnemonic correspondences that the poem performs on a macro scale across the centuries. 'Remembrance', concludes Sebald, 'in essence is nothing other than a quotation. And quotation incorporated into a text (or painting) by montage compels us [...] to probe our knowledge of other texts and pictures and our knowledge of the world' (Ue 90/LH 184).

By the time this version of the poem was published, Sebald had been teaching courses on silent film for six years (SM 130) and was no doubt well versed in the cinematic mechanisms of montage and the Kuleshov Effect. Meaning, according to such filmic strategies, cannot not be gleaned from the discrete contemplation of individual images but exists only as an epiphenomenon, an effect derived from interaction of sequential components.

Though Sebald attributed no definitive collective name to the prose pieces and research he commenced after completing the typescript of *After Nature* in 1985 (work that would eventually become chapters in *Vertigo* and *The Emigrants*), the fact that he referred to it as 'Prosaarbeit mit Bildern' ('prose work with images') in a 1987 funding application (see chapter 10 in this volume) to the Deutscher Literaturfonds (German Literature Fonds) articulates a confidence in his ability to realize such a technically demanding project.[7] However, the proposed visual complexity of this project appears less speculative and untested when it is considered in relation to the his essay on the work of Peter Weiss (written between autumn 1985 and early 1986), 'Die Zerknirschung des Herzens' ('The Remorse of the Heart').

Though Sebald's Weiss essay appeared in the Danish academic journal *Orbis Litterarum* without images, material in the UEA archives shows that it was conceived as an illustrated essay.[8] Brandon-Jones produced over twenty colour and black and white 35 mm slide reproductions of Weiss's artworks from various sources as well as paintings by Rembrandt (1606–1669) and Théodore Géricault (1791–1824).[9] When the essay was later reprinted in the *Frankfurter Rundschau* (15 December 1990), three Brandon-Jones reproductions were included.[10]

Wild Working

This Weiss text, notes Uwe Schütte, constituted part of an unrealized 'Projekt zur Nachkriegsliteratur' ('Project on [German] Post-War Literature') that by 1987 had the working title *Die Rekonstruktion der Erinnerung* (*The Reconstruction of Memory*).[11] In the UEA archives of Brandon-Jones's work there are approximately thirty 35 mm slides labelled 'Post War' (in English) by Sebald. Predominately reproductions of photographs from publications by Victor Gollancz (1893–1967), Hans Erich Nossack (1901–1977) and Alexander Kluge (b. 1932), they were most likely made in association with Sebald's 1982 essay on the literary reflection of Allied bombing campaigns, 'Zwischen Geschichte und Naturgeschichte' ('Between History and Natural History').[12] Though none of the images were published in 1982, Brandon-Jones rephotographed the sources again for Sebald in 1998 for *Luftkrieg und Literatur* (*On the Natural History of Destruction*). If the slides were prepared for the 1982 article (and the film type and mount are consistent with that date), then these would constitute the first Sebald/Brandon Jones photographs.

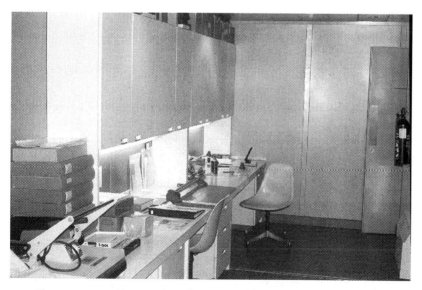

Illustration 20 – Photography Office in the Sainsbury Centre, UEA. Michael Brandon-Jones, c. 1985

Other slides prepared by Brandon-Jones in this period include numerous reproductions of works by self-taught and institutionalized artists with mental health problems such as Adolf Wölfli (1864–1930), Teresa Ottalo (1800–1870), Aloïse Corbaz (1886–1964), Clarence Schmidt (1898–1978) and Emile Ratier (1894–1984), from sources such as Michel Thévoz's *Art Brut* (1976) and Leo Navratil's *Die Künstler aus Gugging* (*The Gugging Artists*,1983), most likely relate to material compiled by Sebald for an unrealized outsider artist essay.[13]

It is in this collection of photographs, labelled 'Art Brut' by Sebald, that the Weiss slides are filed, alongside the Grünewald images and a dozen reproductions of artworks by Tripp, including portraits of patients at the Weissenau psychiatric clinic dating from the 1970s. One such portrait, *Ein leiser Sprung* (*A Quiet Jump*, 1974) was to feature in Sebald's 1993 essay on Tripp (Ue 82/LH 176). Another portrait by Tripp of the institutionalized judge and writer, Daniel Paul Schreber, gifted to Sebald by Tripp in 1976, was to prove a catalyst for Sebald to find something else to do 'besides giving lectures and holding seminars. Much of what I have written later derives from this engraving', Sebald concluded in 2001, 'even in my method of procedure' (CSe 210/CSg 243).

Art Brut (raw art) was a term coined by artist Jean Dubuffet shortly after World War Two to describe art that existed autonomously from any convention or tradition and often associated with the artwork of institutionalized individuals such as Tripp's Weissenau subjects. Art Brut is antithetical to the culture that marginalizes it makers. Often constituted from detritus it is private act of transmogrification. It is a fundamentally 'closed-circuit' whose essence 'lies in its illegibility, its incommunicability, and its indecipherability.'[14]

For Sebald, Art Brut represented an alternative way of working that exists in parallel to rather than as part of Europe's tainted cultural legacy. If, as Walter Benjamin declares, there is 'no document of culture which is not at the same time a document of barbarism',[15] then in the opaque images of 'Art Brut' Sebald saw an improvised methodology that could stem the transmission of civilisation's brutish scheme.

The Sebald/Brandon-Jones 'Art Brut' (photographs, made between 1982 and 1988) (the date of the most recent painting by Tripp reproduced, *Nature morte* (1988) (LH 180/PC 166)) demonstrate not just Sebald's decided interest in marginalized art (see chapter 18 in this volume) but more importantly so his intent to incorporate images into his work prior to the publication of *After Nature*. They also, through their subject matter, document the constituent elements of a critical pictorial procedure that

Sebald tentatively explored with his poetry and later more explicitly through his prose. In this respect they constitute an unintended family album of Sebald's photographic method. In an interview with Sigrid Löffler in 1993 (SM 639), Sebald is asked if 'the visual material' he incorporates into his work should be considered on 'an equal footing with the text'? 'I work according to the system of bricolage' Sebald responds, 'a form of wild working, of pre-rational thinking, where you rummage around in randomly accumulated found objects until they somehow fit together'[16] (see chapter 22 in this volume).

The idea of bricolage, developed by Claude Lévi-Strauss (1908–2009) in his 1963 text, *La Pensée sauvage* (*The Savage Mind*, 1973), conceptualizes the way in which societies combine and recombine different symbols and cultural elements into characteristically recurring patterns.[17] For Lévi-Strauss, the work of bricolage finds a parallel in the 'tinkering' of a handyman, who improvises solutions to problems with discarded items that they have amassed according to an undefined potential usefulness. The idea of bricolage, theorized by Thévoz as 'the aesthetics of tinkering' is a central tenet of his history of Art Brut (and is represented visually in Thévoz's text by the work of French farmer and psychiatric patient Auguste Forestier (1887–1958)). Forestier's 'Figure with Wolf's Ears Riding a Cow' (1935–1949), argues Thévoz, must not be considered as a sculpture but as an assemblage of 'pre-constituted elements' whose 'maker wished to preserve the disparate, equivocal character of the parts and so took care to avoid integrating them into an organic whole'.[18]

If, as Schütte claims, *After Nature* represents the emergence of Sebald the writer 'fully-formed', then the Sebald's 'Art Brut' (collection constitutes the residue of the pupa stage of his mature visual imagination.[19] (A phase in which the structure of an antecedent form is dissolved so essential elements can reconfigured, see chapter 18 in this volume). In his 1981 *Manuskripte* essay on outsider poet Ernst Herbeck (1920–1991), Sebald writes that the work of the *bricoleur* 'is composed of scraps and fragments [...] it is an operative object which, assigned to a merely heuristic purpose, already carries the next destruction within itself' (BU 138–139).

The Sebald/Brandon-Jones collection of 35 mm film slides should be considered, like Forestier's enigmatic figure (a colour reproduction of which it contains), not as just in terms of its components but also in its entirety as an operative object. A heuristic entity, the destruction and repurposing of which provided not just the material for Sebald's subsequent work in *Manuskripte* (and in turn his book length projects), but also a template for his collaboration with Brandon-Jones. After their work on the 'Art Brut' project, how Sebald and Brandon-Jones worked together remained consistent until their work on *Austerlitz* was completed in September 2000. As the back matter states in the 1993 German hardcover edition of *Die Ausgewanderten*, the 'visual material' was 'compiled by the author' and the 'photographic work' was by 'Michael Brandon-Jones, Norwich'.

Notes

1. C Scholz, But the Written Word is Not a True Document: A Conversation with W.G Sebald on Literature and Photography, in: L Patt, C Dillbohner (eds.), *Searching for Sebald: Photography after W.G. Sebald* (Los Angeles: ICI Press, 2007), pp. 104–109 (105).
2. Ibid., p. 106.
3. W Lücking, *Mathis: Nachforschungen über Grünewald* (Berlin: Frölich & Kaufmann, 1983).
4. Sebald, Wie der Schnee auf den Alpen, in: *Manuskripte* 26:92 (1986), pp. 26–31.
5. For details of Becker's images, cf. L Patt, Searching for Sebald: What I Know for Sure, in: L Patt, C Dillbohner (eds.), *Searching for Sebald*, pp. 16–97 (21–22); 'Ein Walzertraum' was previously published with the Tripp painting in: *Neue Zürcher Zeitung*, March 1993. The poem and the reproduction had originally appeared in, JP Tripp, *Die Aufzählung der Schwierigkeiten: Arbeiten von 1985–92* (Offenburg: Reiff, 1993), p. 119.
6. Sebald, Als de sneeuw op de Alpen, in: *Het moment* 3 (1986), pp. 120–143 and Sebald, de donkere nacht zet, in: *Het moment* 6 (1987), pp. 129–148.
7. The 1987 application includes some photocopied photographs, cf. U Schütte, *W.G. Sebald: Leben und literarisches Werk* (Berlin/Boston: De Gruyter, 2020), p. 44.
8. Sebald, Die Zerknirschung des Herzens: Über Erinnerung und Grausamkeit im Werk von Peter Weiss, in: *Orbis Litterarum* 41:3 (1986), pp. 265–278.
9. Several colour reproductions of Weiss's paintings were copied from the UEA's Library copy of P Weiss, I Bartsch, P Spielmann, *Der Maler Peter Weiss: Bilder, Zeichnungen, Collagen, Filme* (Berlin: Frölich & Kaufmann, 1982).
10. Sebald, Die Zerknirschung des Herzens: Über Erinnerung und Grausamkeit im Werk von Peter Weiss, in: *Frankfurter Rundschau*, 15 December 1990; reprinted in: CSg 128–148/NHD 173–195.
11. U Schütte, *Interventionen: Literaturkritik als Widerspruch bei W.G. Sebald* (Munich: Ed. Text+Kritik, 2014), pp. 367–368.
12. Sebald, Zwischen Geschichte und Naturgeschichte: Versuch über die literarische Beschreibung totaler Zerstörung mit Anmerkungen zu Kasack, Nossack und Kluge, in: *Orbis Litterarum* 37:4 (1982), pp. 345–366; reprinted in: CSg 69–100/CSe 68–101.

13. M Etzler, *Writing from the Periphery: W.G. Sebald and Outsider Art* (PhD thesis: Berkeley, 2014), pp. xix–xx.

14. K Minturn, Lévi-Strauss, and the Idea of Art Brut, in: *RES: Anthropology and Aesthetics* 47 (2004), pp. 247–258 (258).

15. W Benjamin, On the Concept of History, in: E Jephcott et al. (eds.), *Walter Benjamin: Selected Writings. Vol. 4, 1938–1940* (Cambridge, MA: Harvard University Press, 2003), p. 392.

16. S Löffler, Wildes Denken, in: F Loquai (ed.), *W.G. Sebald* (Eggingen: Ed. Isele, 1997), pp. 135–137 (136).

17. JJ Long, In the Contact Zone: W.G. Sebald and the Ethnographic Imagination, in: *Journal of European Studies* 41:3–4 (2011), pp. 413–430.

18. M Thévoz, *Art Brut* (London: Academy Editions, 1976), p. 69.

19. U Schütte, *W.G. Sebald* (Liverpool: Liverpool University Press, 2018), p. 31.

CHAPTER 27

Paintings and Ekphrasis

Leonida Kovač

In his essay 'Wie Tag und Nacht: Über die Bilder Jan Peter Tripps' ('As Day and Night, Chalk and Cheese: On the Pictures of Jan Peter Tripp'), Sebald remarked: 'Remembrance, after all, is in the end nothing other than a quotation. And the quotation interpolated into a text or an image forces us [. . .] to revisit what we know of other texts and images, and reconsider our knowledge of the world' (PC 169/LH 184). Just prior to this, he wrote: 'And what is the business of painting in any case but a kind of pathological investigation in the face of the blackness death and white light of eternity?' (PC 167/LH 182).

In what follows I will undertake an associative stroll through Sebald's œuvre along the hidden paths suggested by his writings, associatively linking various themes in Sebald's writings connected with paintings and ekphrasis.

The Falsified Perspective

Sebald was inspired to write his poem 'Ein Walzertraum' ('A Waltz Dream', 1993) by *Das Land des Lächelns* (*The Land of Smiles*, 1990), a painting by his friend Jan Peter Tripp (b. 1945), and poem and painting are usually published together. Tripp's uncanny picture shows a dressed yet barefoot man lying stretched out on wooden table. Does he rest uncomfortably? Is he laid out on a catafalque? Three suitcases are visible under the table, and there is a hat on the one in the middle, under the man's relaxed palm.

The opening lines of Sebald's accompanying poem are: 'The traveller / has finally arrived / at the border post // A customs official / has untied his laces / removed his shoes' (LWe 108–110/LWg 74–75). This lyrical commentary on his close friend's painting exemplifies a key mode of Sebald's writing: ekphrasis as a means of uniting word and image. It is also characteristic that Sebald's ekphrastic discussion of Tripp's work alludes to yet another painting, Rembrandt's *The Anatomy Lesson of Dr Nicolaes Tulp* (1632): 'Dr. Tulp will soon be here / in his black hat, prosectorial / instruments in hand' (LWe 109/LWg 75).

In *Die Ringe des Saturn* (*The Rings of Saturn*), Sebald connected his reflections on this work by Rembrandt with the extraordinary person and work of Thomas Browne (1605–1682), a physician, polymath and writer whose skull, prior to being buried for the second time, was exhibited at the Norwich Hospital Museum in the East Anglian town where Sebald had worked for thirty years. The narrator of *The Rings of Saturn* speculates that, in January 1632, Browne attended the public dissection of the body of the executed thief Adrian Adriaanzoon, or Aris Kindt, which later became the subject of Rembrandt's painting.

Reproductions of this painting are interpolated into Sebald's text twice: first the entire image is spread across a double page of the book, and then an excerpt focusing on Kindt's body is shown at the bottom of a page (RSg 24–26/RSe 14–16). The narrator concludes that the 'unshapely [left] hand' on which Tulp begins his work – rather than, as was usual, the abdomen – is a sign of violence done to Kindt, and that Rembrandt identified with the victim rather than with his client, the Guild (RSg 27/RSe 17). The narrator claims, namely, that Rembrandt purposefully portrayed the left hand in anatomically incorrect fashion as a gesture of protest against the Guild. The matter, however, is more complicated than Sebald, or indeed most of his commentators, want to make us believe.[1]

In the course of his description of an unpleasant journey to The Hague to see *The Anatomy Lesson* at the Mauritshuis Museum, the narrator tells us that the museum is located in a palace Governor Maurits built in May 1644, exactly three hundred years before the narrator's birth, with wealth he had acquired by participating in the colonial plundering and exploitation of Brazil. This history of one of Europe's most prominent museums is another example of Sebald's discursive practice: he links art – as he elsewhere does twentieth-century genocidal policies – to European colonialism – that is, to political and military power and mass murder.

The digression on the Mauritshuis is connected to the narrator's reflection on the Battle of Sole Bay, fought in 1672 between the English and Dutch fleets. This passage beings with an ekphrastic description of the narrator's vision of the battle during his walk through Southwold, and continues with a general critique of pictorial representations of naval battles: 'While most of the accounts of the battles fought on the so-called fields of honour have from time immemorial been unreliable, the pictorial representations of great naval engagements are without exception figments of the imagination' (RSe 76/RSg 95). Sebald refers here to the works of Dutch painters Abraham Storck (1644–1708), Willem van der Velde (1633–1707) and Philip James de Loutherbourg (1740–1812), concluding that, despite their realistic intentions, they failed to convey any impression of what actually happened on the ships.

Sebald is hence implying that history painting – and by extension historiography – is that we complete our limited knowledge of history with our fantasy. It is for this reason that, upon viewing the Panorama of the Battle of Waterloo in the rotunda that now stands on that battlefield in Belgium, Sebald has his narrator conclude that 'the enormous mural, one hundred and ten yards by twelve, painted in 1912 by the French marine artist Louis Dumontin [recte Dumoulin]', is based, as are indeed all artistic representations of history, on 'a falsification of perspective' (RSe 124–125/ RSg 151–152).

Melancholia

In his ninth thesis in 'Über den Begriff der Geschichte' ('On the Concept of History', 1940), Walter Benjamin (1892–1940) employs Paul Klee's monoprint *Angelus Novus* (1920) to depict history as an unbroken sequence of catastrophes. It serves as a foil to Sebald's description in *The Rings of Saturn* of the 1992 storm passing through Rendlesham Forest near Orford, whose trees had previously been devasted by a hurricane in 1987. A defence fortress was built at Orford in 1165, and, between 1913 and 1983, the British Ministry of Defence used the Orford Ness peninsula as a military base, where, among other things, weapons of mass destruction were tested (RSg 272–278/RSe 228–233). Sebald knows no distinction between natural and man-made disasters, both being part of his pessimistic view of history as a 'natural history of destruction' (see chapter 13 in this volume).

In the autobiographical third section of Sebald's first published literary work, *Nach der Natur* (*After Nature*), the narrator portrays himself as melancholic, born under the sign of Saturn (NN 76/AN 86). This links *After Nature* with *The Rings of Saturn*, where he writes of the omnipresence of disasters of all kinds. The original title of the latter book, 'Unter dem Hundestern' ('Under the Dog Star'), also reminds us of Albrecht Dürer's engraving *Melencholia I* (1514), where a skinny dog lies curled up at the feet of a sitting, frowning, winged female figure holding a compass in her hand.

In a critical essay on the Germans' inability to mourn – that is, on the inadequate response of German post-war literature to the horrors of the Holocaust and the firestorms in which Allied air forces destroyed German cities between 1942 and 1945 – entitled 'Konstruktionen der Trauer: Günter Grass und Wolfgang Hildesheimer' ('Constructs of Mourning: GG and WH'), Sebald noted that discovering the truth was 'the business of the dog described by Benjamin as the emblematic beast of melancholy' (CSe 113/CSg 112). In the same essay, Sebald assigned Dürer's *Melencholia I* political connotations:

> If the political activity in which, as Grass constantly emphasizes, he sees something more real than the construction of utopian plans, thus succeeds in warding off a despair that is moving in itself, then Dürer's Melancholia has made her way into his travelling bag as fellow traveller and angel of his guilty conscience. (CSe 119/CSg 117)

In *The Rings of Saturn*, Dürer's engraving is incorporated into an ekphrastic description of the narrator's prematurely deceased colleague Janine Dakyns, without whose help he could not have traced the wanderings of Thomas Browne's skull:

> Once when I remarked that sitting there amidst her papers, she resembled the angel in Dürer's *Melancholia*, steadfast among the instruments of destruction, her response was that the apparent chaos surrounding her represented in reality a perfect kind of order, or an order which at least tended towards perfection. (RSe 9/RSg 18–19)

The dog, being 'the emblematic beast of melancholy' (CSe 113/CSg 112), is also present in a micro-poem by Sebald that is paired with Tripp's drawing of Rembrandt's eyes in their collaborative work *Unerzählt* (*Unrecounted*): 'Like a dog / Cézanne says / that's how a painter / must see, the eye / fixed & almost / averted' (Ue 51 US /Ug 45). In his quotation of Cézanne, Sebald accurately and succinctly describes his own method of perception. For Sebald, the negative gradient of history ultimately cannot be halted, and gazing at it directly would be as paralysing as staring directly into Medusa's eyes. However, his indirect melancholic gaze and ekphrastic descriptions suspend and render it not only bearable but beautiful, a brief sunset before the inevitable, everlasting night.

Walser, Painting, Writing, Ash

Sebald expressed his philosophy that everything was connected most eloquently in his essay 'Le promeneur solitaire' on the Swiss writer Robert Walser (1878–1956). In that essay, he also compared Walser's writing to the painting process: 'The playful – and sometimes obsessive – working with a fine brush of the most abstruse details is one of the most striking characteristics of Walser's idiom' (PC 131/LH 142). Sebald himself employs abstruse details in his ekphrastic descriptions. Ekphrasis is a key thread in Sebald's textual fabric, and inspiration for it can be found not only in Walser but also in Sebald's fascination and identification with the life and work of Jean-Jacques Rousseau (1712–1778).

In his essay on Rousseau, 'J'aurais voulu que ce lac eût été l'Océan … ', Sebald paid particular attention to the philosopher's herbarium, quoting from *Les rêveries du Promeneur Solitaire* (*The Reveries of the Solitary Walker*, 1782) in which Rousseau wrote of his commitment to describing plants in great detail. In addition, via a quotation from Jan Starobinski (1920–2019), who studied the theme of transparency in Rousseau's work, Sebald mentions Rousseau's fascination with the process of vitrification, whose opposite is 'pulveriza-tion, which kills the light and reduces human society to a dark, indistinguishable and impenetrable mass' (PC 58/LH 66).

The theme of pulverization – reducing to dust – is explicitly articulated in 'Max Ferber', the final story in *Die Ausgewanderten* (*The Emigrants*). Ferber, whom the narrator visits in his Manchester studio, was modelled on London-based painter Frank Auerbach (b. 1931) and, so, shares his characteristic painterly procedure. By saying 'I am here, as they used to say, to serve under the chimney' (E 192/AW 283), Ferber refers not only to the smokestacks of nineteenth- and early twentieth-century industrial Manchester, under which an exploited proletariat worked, but also to those of the incinerators under whose rain of ash the victims of the Holocaust were made to serve. According to the narrator, Ferber 'felt closer to dust [. . .] than to light, air or water' (E 161/236). This suggests that the painter's 'prime concern was to increase the dust' which is why his painterly work 'really amounted to nothing but a steady production of dust, which never ceased except at night' (E 162/AW 236).

The theme of pulverization in 'Max Ferber' leads rhizomatically back to Walser. In his essay on Walser, Sebald argues that nothing in twentieth-century German literature comes close to the intense pathos of Walser's vignette *Asche, Nadel, Bleistift, und Zündhölzchen* (*Ash, Needle, Pencil and Match*, 1915), which resonates as a subtext in Sebald's literary work. "Poor" materials such as dust and ash are correspondingly ennobled by Sebald and made into metaphors of artistic endeavours. Painting and writing are ekphrasticly combined so as to direct the reader's attention to that which is normally ignored, belittled and rejected.

Historical Transversals

Sebald has Ferber arrive in Manchester in 1943 and – significantly – leave that town only once: to go to Colmar to study the Isenheim Altarpiece (1512–1516), the masterpiece by Mathias Grünewald (1470–1528). Sebald's long poem *After Nature* portrays the German Renaissance painters Mathias Grünewald and Albrecht Altdorfer (1480–1538) as exemplary artists but also as representatives of opposite attitudes towards Jews.

Sebald provides an example of the "falsified perspective" of historiography by pointing out in the first section of *After Nature* that Grünewald's marriage to the Jewess Enchin does not feature in the Grünewald study that art historian Walther Karl Zülch 'produced in ancient Schwabach type / in the year 1938 for Hitler's birthday' (AN 13–14/NN 13). Then, in the final, autobiographical section of *After Nature*, Sebald links his conception to his mother's vision of Nuremberg aflame under Allied bombardment.

His description of his mother's experience then segues into a description of the Altdorfer painting *Lot und seine Töchter* (*Lot and his Daughters*, 1537) in Vienna's Kunsthistorisches Museum, which shows a city in flames in its background. Altdorfer's reference is to Sodom and Gomorrah, and only a month before Sebald's mother saw Nuremberg ablaze, Hamburg had been ravaged by firestorms in Operation Gomorrah, the consequences of which Sebald described in harrowing detail in *Luftkrieg und Literatur* (*On the Natural History of Destruction*). Altdorfer's painting is thus linked with war across space and time and is made a symbol of the 'natural history of destruction' under which – Sebald implies – all of us were conceived.

Sebald concludes *After Nature* with an ekphrastic description of a dream in which the narrator undertakes a shamanistic flight from Norwich to Munich to see Altdorfer's famous painting *Alexanderschlacht* (*The Battle of Alexander at Issus*, 1529). His route is exactly that taken by Allied bombers from East Anglian airfields to German cities (NN 96–97/AN 109–110). Sebald does not mention it, but Altdorfer, whom, as stated, he twice linked with Allied firestorms, took part in the persecution of Jews and the destruction of a synagogue in 1519 as a city councillor of Regensburg. The 'marks of pain' (Ae 16/Ag 24) that run throughout history have left their traces in art as well.

Conclusion

In his last speech, 'Ein Versuch der Restitution' ('An Attempt at Restitution'), Sebald recalls a gift he received in 1976 from his life-long friend Jan Peter Tripp: an engraving the artist had made of the mentally ill senatorial president Daniel Paul Schreber with a lobster in his skull.[2] As Sebald concedes: 'much of what I have written later derives from this engraving, even in my method of procedure: in adhering to an exact historical perspective, in patiently engraving and linking together the apparently disparate things in the manner of a still life' (CSe 210/CSg 243–244).

This method is analogous to that applied by Aby Warburg (1866–1929) when compiling his project *Bilderatlas Mnemosyne: On Photography, Archives, and the Afterlife of Images* from 1925 until his death in 1929. Although Warburg is never referenced by Sebald, the work of that 'founder of an anthropology of images and of the iconology of their intervals'[3] informs Sebald's œuvre. By contemplating the history of images as a history of tragedy,[4] as Sebald did constantly, Warburg inaugurated a new epistemology of knowledge.

In Sebald's writing, ekphrasis is used to deconstruct paintings and trace the connections in them across space and time. Sebald's concept of non-chronological time via 'remembrance [that] is nothing other than a quotation' (PC 169/LH 184) is analogous to Warburg's concept of the 'afterlife of images'. Such afterlife is inseparable from the theme of 'spectral materialism'[5] that permeates Sebald's œuvre.

Notes

1. Rembrandt appears to have portrayed the left hand being dissected as a second right hand, but, as Adrian Nathan West has pointed out, it is in fact shown in anatomically correct fashion except for the *abductor digiti minimi*, cf. AN West, Nostalgia for Probity in the Era of the Selfie: W.G. Sebald's American Imitators, in: Schütte (ed.): *Über W.G. Sebald: Beiträge zu einem anderen Bild des Autors* (Berlin/Boston: De Gruyter, 2017), pp. 283–295 (292–294).
2. Sebald, falsely or purposely, claims the animal to be a spider, cf. M Krüger, Zerstreute Reminiszenzen, in: S Stegmann, T Hoffmann (eds.), *Verschachtelte Räume: Sebald Reminiszenzen* (Leonberg: Keicher, 2022), pp. 22–29 (23). Tripp's etching is replicated on p. 24.
3. G Didi-Huberman, *Atlas or the Anxious Gay Science* (Chicago: Chicago University Press, 2018), p. 158.
4. Ibid.
5. On spectral presence, cf. E Santner, *On Creaturely Life: Rilke, Benjamin, Sebald*, pp. 52–58.

CHAPTER 28

Media Theory

Florian Leitner

'I well recall one of those flickering short films that teachers could borrow from local film and slide libraries in the Fifties' (RSe 53/ RSg 70). This passage from *Die Ringe des Saturn* (*The Rings of Saturn*), which refers to a documentary about industrial fishing, is also emblematic of W.G. Sebald's approach to media technology. Unfortunately, this only becomes entirely clear in the German original, where the author speaks of 'schwarzes Gestrichel' to describe the 'black dashes' that 'durchzittern' or 'tremble all over' the screen when the old, scratched film copy is projected.

The memory of the materiality of the medium precedes the memory of the signifiers: even before addressing what the images showed, the narrator directs our attention to the technical disturbances that left their mark on them. The dance of black dashes is a good example of what media theory calls "noise": an interference that masks or distorts the actual message the medium is supposed to relay. In electronics, one typical source of noise is interfering radio signals, in cinematographic media, scratches on a film reel or dust particles on a lens or in a projector beam.

By focusing on this noise, Sebald establishes an arresting perspective: that of media theory. It is based on a shift of focus away from incorporeal concepts such as thoughts and ideas, and onto the physical objects, or "media", involved in conveying them. The shift implies these media are not just instruments that store and transmit information, not just material hardware that processes immaterial software, but that they *are* the information. As Friedrich Kittler (1943–2011) claimed, 'there is no software',[1] it is just a notion that dissimulates what is actually going on in the materiality of the hardware, and 'the truth can only reside in the medium itself, not in its messages'[2] – another version of Marshall McLuhan's (1911–1980) famous catchphrase, 'the medium is the message'.

As the following essay will argue, this perspective can be observed repeatedly in portrayals of visual apparatuses – as found in painting, photography, film and video – across Sebald's œuvre.

Sebald and Kittler

While McLuhan's work forms the basis of media theory in general, Kittler is often considered the founding father of what is known in the English-speaking world as German Media Theory.[3] Kittler, like Sebald, was admired by a dedicated crowd of disciples, and his status as a legendary figure is not the only similarity he shares with Sebald. Both were German intellectual exports who have recently enjoyed significant success in the anglophone world, shaping the global understanding of German thought while influencing English-language academia and literature, and both achieved international fame in English translations that inevitably flattened their highly distinctive writing styles. This can be observed, for example, in the English version of the aforementioned passage from *The Rings of Saturn*: the word 'Gestrichel', a nonstandard instance of wordplay that establishes a focus on media technology and noise, is omitted and the uncommon verb 'durchzittern' is simply translated as 'flickering' (RSe 53/RSg 70).

Sebald and Kittler also shared a number of biographical details. Born less than a year apart at the end of World War Two, both men attended high school at the southern edge of the Federal Republic and enrolled as students at the prestigious University of Freiburg. Both eventually became literature professors and had a life-long animosity towards mainstream German philology. And, although their life projects were rather different, some of their interests were related. Kittler's insistence on the entanglement of military and media history[4] and Sebald's fascination with aerial warfare and fortress architecture might have been inspired by similar cultural influences.

The same could be said of their practical engagement with media technology, which formed part of the myths surrounding them. Many anecdotes about Kittler mention the electronic circuit boards and the soldering iron on his desk at Berlin's Humboldt University, and no account of Sebald's writing practice is complete without evoking 'the copy room at the University of East Anglia', where Sebald used copiers 'to degrade, deplete, and scumble [...] presumably crisp(er) photographs down to blocks of indiscriminate "leaden grays"'[5] that he then incorporated into his texts.

Sebald's use of images in his creative process is thus reminiscent of Kittler's interest in disturbances and distortions – noise – as a necessary component of any medium.[6] In the language of media theory: Sebald used photocopiers as a source of visual noise to partly erase information originally contained in photos.

Dust and Visual Media

The shift that media theory is occupied with – from immaterial information to the materiality of communication technologies – can be observed
not only in Sebald's use of the copy machine but also in the way he writes
about visual media. An example can be found in 'Dr. K.s Badereise nach
Riva' ('Dr. K. Takes the Waters at Riva') from *Schwindel. Gefühle.*
(*Vertigo*).

The story contains the earliest reference to cinema in Sebald's prose: on
his journey through northern Italy in September 1913, Franz Kafka (1883–
1924) had gone to the movies and Sebald's narrator wonders which film he
might have seen (see chapter 34 in this volume). The text refers to a letter
from Kafka to his fiancée Felice Bauer, which mentions that he had cried in
a cinema in Verona.[7] Kafka provided no further details about the experience, but Sebald imagines that 'he sat in the surrounding darkness, observing the transformation into pictures of the minute particles of dust glinting
in the beam of the projector' (V 150/SG 166).

By inventing this scene – and falsely attributing it to Kafka – Sebald
shifts the attention away from the film images (the message), and from
their psychological effect (Kafka's tears), to the materiality of cinema which
manifests itself as a beam of light in a dark room (the medium). The fact
that the beam is rendered visible only by the presence of dust particles
illustrates a crucial insight of media theory: the medium can only be
observed in moments of disturbance, such as when a source of noise – in
this case the dust – makes itself known. Dust here comes to represent the
materiality of the medium – and this is characteristic of the way Sebald
perceives visual media in his prose.

Projectors and film reels are solid objects; light beams and their reflections on screens are not. The medium of cinema might therefore appear to
be partly immaterial – erroneously, however, since photons are part of the
material world. In Sebald, dust is not only a form of noise but also
a metaphor for this fallacy: a manifestation of matter that is nearly intangible to human senses and therefore appears almost immaterial. This
becomes evident in 'Il ritorno in patria' in *Vertigo* when the narrator
inspects an old, cluttered attic in his home village and describes the dust
he sees 'swirl' in the air as 'glinting particles of matter dissolving into
weightlessness' (V 227/SG 248).

The scene is reminiscent of Sebald's description of the cinema in
Verona, not only because of the presence of dust in the air but also because
of the observation of 'the blade of light that slanted through the attic

window' and 'cut through the darkness' (V 227/SG 247–248). The light illuminates the dust like a beam emanating from a projection cabin in a dimmed theatre. It also eventually reveals a fantastic character, 'the grey chasseur' (V 222/SG 243) – really a decommissioned tailor's dummy, wearing the uniform of a huntsman. The figure turns out to be almost as insubstantial as an image on a film screen: upon being touched by the narrator, the uniform 'crumbled into dust' (V 227/ SG 248). Dust not only appears as a kind of noise that forms part of the medium of cinema but also as a metaphor for the intangible materiality of cinematic images.

The most important appearance dust makes in Sebald's prose, however, occurs in the 'Max Ferber' section of *The Emigrants*. Ferber's workplace is dimly lit, reminiscent of the cinema in 'Dr. K. Takes the Waters at Riva' and the attic in 'Il ritorno in patria'. And, as in those cases, it is dust that catches the narrator's attention: 'Since he applied the paint thickly, and then repeatedly scratched it off the canvas as his work proceeded, the floor was covered with a largely hardened and encrusted deposit of droppings, mixed with coal dust' (E 161/AW 235). Although he is a painter, Ferber is not interested in the graphic shapes he creates on canvas but rather in the interminable process that dissolves those visual signifiers into an entropic mass. His work, the narrator notes, 'really amounted to nothing but a steady production of dust' (E 162/AW 236).

Ferber is modelled after the painter Frank Auerbach (b. 1931), but he also resembles the old master Frenhofer from Honoré de Balzac's (1799–1850) short story *Le Chef-d'œuvre inconnu* (*The Unknown Masterpiece*, 1831). Much like Ferber, Frenhofer added layer upon layer to a female portrait that was to be his masterpiece but, in the end, he cluttered the canvas with so many visual forms that nothing could be seen. Frenhofer was thus still focused on the visual signifiers, even though they eventually cancelled each other out. Ferber, by contrast, concentrates on the medium itself, the substance the signifiers are made of, the crusts of paint and the black dust. Despite their similarities, it is Ferber, not Frenhofer, who performs the media-theoretical shift of perspective.

The substance of the medium – in this case, coal dust – leaves the canvas and occupies the extra-medial space, mixing with the coal dust that was generally present in the air of Manchester. In doing so, not only does it invade Ferber's studio but also the artist's body. 'Especially on days when Ferber had been working in charcoal', the narrator notes, 'the fine powdery dust had given his skin a metallic sheen' (E 164/AW 240). This process of media technology crossing its boundaries is underlined by Ferber when he draws a parallel between 'the darkening of his skin' and 'silver poisoning, the symptoms of which were not uncommon among professional photographers' (E 164/AW 241). Ferber reports that 'there was a photographic lab assistant in Manchester whose body had absorbed so much silver [...] that he had become a kind of photographic plate' (E 165/AW 241). Although it slides into the absurd, the anecdote illustrates another central postulate by McLuhan: media are not only tools that extend human bodies, but they penetrate these bodies and turn them into functions of themselves.

Sebald's treatment of dust in his prose echoes his practice of repeatedly photocopying images in order to degrade their quality. In an interview, he stated that he did this because the photos 'must not stand out; they must be of the same leaden grain' as the text.[8] As Lise Patt puts it in relation to *The Rings of Saturn*, he 'employs the dust and light of the Xerox machine' to reduce visual icons 'to mere piles of dust' that are 'stripped of all but the most minimally discernible content'.[9] When Sebald turns his photos into leaden grain, he operates like Ferber: he produces black dust.

Memory and Noise

Memory is one of the central topics in Sebald, and his descriptions of visual media are not least interested in how they are intertwined with practices of memory and how medial noise interferes with these practices. In *Campo Santo*, among others, noise serves as a parable for fading memories: according to traditional Corsican belief, we are told, the faces of the ghosts of the deceased 'blurred and flickered at the edges, just like the faces of actors in an old movie' (CSe 31/CSg 34).

In *The Emigrants*, however, the medial noise that interferes with memory is not a metaphorical one. When Dr. Selwyn and his friend Edward Ellis present photographic slides, the last image catches the narrator's attention – it is shattered in the projector so that 'a dark crack fissured across the screen' (E 17/AW 28–29). As Klaus Bonn suggests, it is 'by virtue of the margin of that tear, perhaps, which has left a furrow in the memory' that the narrator remembers the slide years later.[10] The medial noise in this case is not a disturbance but an aid to memory.

Sebald's most detailed description of the precarious relation between image technology and memory can be found in *Austerlitz*. The title character watches the Nazi propaganda film *Theresienstadt*, shot in the concentration camp of the same name. He only has an incomplete video copy and slows it down in the hope of finding an image of his mother, who was interned in the camp and killed. The passage may have been inspired by the connections Roland Barthes (1915–1980) drew between photography and death,[11] but we are also reminded of the video artist Douglas Gordon and his ground-breaking installation *24 Hour Psycho* (1993). Gordon slowed down a video copy of Alfred Hitchcock's (1899–1980) *Psycho* and made it last for 24 hours – allowing, among other things, for a more analytical look at the gruesome crime at the centre of the movie and the voyeuristic presentation of its female victim.

However, this kind of optical insight remains unavailable to Austerlitz: the scope of the Holocaust defies visualization, and despite slowing down *Theresienstadt* he is unable to correctly identify an image of his mother – also because visual noise interferes with the video images: 'The many damaged sections of the tape, which I had hardly noticed before, now melted the image from its centre or from the edges, blotting it out and instead making patterns of bright white sprinkled with black' (Ae 348/ Ag 353).

Noise and the Natural History of Destruction

Sebald has a particular interest in documentaries and newsreels. When he mentions them in his writings, as Bonn has pointed out, 'almost all films of this kind revolve around one of the central themes that subcutaneously aligns all of Sebald's texts: the process of civilisation as a natural history of destruction'.[12] *Theresienstadt* in *Austerlitz* and the educational film about industrial fishing in *The Rings of Saturn* are typical examples of this. Bonn argues that the bodies Austerlitz describes as blurred in slow motion are a visual allegory of the actual destruction of the same bodies in the genocide.[13] However, it is crucial that these films do not simply *portray* episodes of a natural history of destruction – as technical objects with their scratches and blurry images, they are themselves deteriorating, and therefore *are part* of this history. In Sebald, dust and other forms of noise direct our attention to the transitory materiality of media in general.

Not least because of their deterioration, media are always-already entangled with extra-medial realities – in a way that exceeds and even undermines the immaterial ideas they were originally designed to transmit. Media thus constitute a stubborn materiality that, like dust, spreads everywhere but refuses to convey universal meaning – just as the VHS tape of *Theresienstadt* refuses to reveal information about Austerlitz's mother or Sebald's emigrant characters are dispersed all over the world but fail to find definite meaning in their scattering. Throughout Sebald's work, characters encounter material residua of information which have been disseminated in the most unlikely places, and which resist providing ultimate sense. Human bodies and media matter are therefore intertwined in an interminable quest for signification. There is no fixed meaning to be found, however – except that there are humans, and there is matter, and they are both on the move.

Notes

1. F Kittler, There Is No Software, in: *The Truth of the Technological World: Essays on the Genealogy of Presence* (Stanford: Stanford University Press, 2014), pp. 219–229.
2. F Kittler, Rock Music: A Misuse of Military Equipment, in: *The Truth of the Technological World*, pp. 152–164 (159).
3. An important step for establishing 'German Media Theory' as a label was G Lovink, Whereabouts of German Media Theory, in: *Zero Comment: Blogging and Critical Internet Culture* (New York: Routledge, 2008), pp. 83–98. For an analysis of the American adaptation of the label cf. G Winthrop-Young, The Kittler Effect, in: *New German Critique* 44:3 (2017), pp. 205–224.
4. Cf. Kittler, Rock Music: A Misuse of Military Equipment.
5. L Patt, Intermezzo Vertigo, in: *Searching for Sebald: Photography After W.G. Sebald* (Los Angeles: Institute of Cultural Inquiry, 2007), pp. 44–103 (49).
6. F Kittler, Signal-to-Noise Ratio, in: *The Truth of the Technological World*, pp. 165–177.
7. F Kafka, *Briefe 1913–März 1914*, ed. H-G Koch (Frankfurt: Fischer, 1999), pp. 295. Kafka did not post the letter at first and only sent it off together with a later message to Felice on 6 November.
8. D Sornig, Picturing the Story: Image and Narrative in Brian Castro and W.G. Sebald, in: *TEXT: The Journal of the Australian Association of Writing Programs* 8:1 (2004), p. 155, qtd. in: Patt, Intermezzo Vertigo, p. 49.
9. Patt, Intermezzo Vertigo, pp. 49–50.
10. K Bonn, W.G. Sebalds laufende Bilder: Der Film und die Worte, in: *Arcadia* 42:1 (2007), pp. 166–184 (176).
11. R Barthes, *Camera Lucida* (New York: Hill & Wang, 1981).
12. Bonn, Sebalds laufende Bilder, p. 179.
13. Ibid., pp. 183–184.

CHAPTER 29

Travel Writing

David Anderson

For all the formal and generic ambiguity of Sebald's work, it is productive to consider it through the frame of "travel writing". This essay outlines how this might be attempted, before contextualizing the work in relation to relevant trends in human geography. Finally, it sketches Sebald's reception by contemporary travel writers, particularly in Britain, where he lived for most of his life, where many of the places he described are located and where many of the journeys he narrated either begin or end.

Travel is omnipresent in Sebald's work. *Nach der Natur* (*After Nature*) recounts the peregrinations of the late-medieval painter Matthias Grünewald and the eighteenth-century botanist Georg Wilhelm Steller, before reproducing the emigration from the Allgäu to Manchester that Markus Zisselsberger has called Sebald's 'original journey'.[1] *Schwindel. Gefühle.* (*Vertigo*) narrates the travels of Stendhal, Kafka, and again Sebald himself in Italy, and to his birthplace, Wertach im Allgäu. The four stories of *Die Ausgewanderten* (*The Emigrants*) trace migrations within and beyond Europe, one of them ('Max Ferber') restaging Sebald's 'original journey' while tangling it with those of the troubled artist Ferber himself, who visits Grünewald's Isenheim Altarpiece on one of the few occasions he leaves Manchester, thus doubly revisiting *After Nature*.

Die Ringe des Saturn (*The Rings of Saturn*) is structured as a walking tour through the English counties of Norfolk and Suffolk, prompting meditative digressions on everything from the history of artificial illumination to the horrors of imperial conquest. Its German subtitle, 'eine englische Wallfahrt' (an English Pilgrimage), is absent from the English version yet remains legible in the text's numerous 'pilgrimages'.

Austerlitz's initial meetings between the narrator and Jacques Austerlitz occur during a series of visits to Belgium; haunting accounts of nineteenth-century architecture in Brussels and Antwerp feed into parallel descriptions of the City of London, Prague and Paris later on (Ae 1/Ag 9). The text's vision of Europe is one scored by unhappy excursions, this time centring

Illustration 21 – Sebald embarking on a walk, Norfolk, c. 1995

on Austerlitz's own 'original journey' from Prague to London as a Jewish refugee from Nazi Europe. Finally, the fragmentary expositions of the unfinished Corsica Project use visits to sites on the island, such as Ajaccio's Maison Bonaparte, as prompts to melancholic reflections on history and nature.

Sebald's work often alludes to texts where travel has been a key motif, even if they are not considered travel writing as such. The narrator's Italian journey in 'All'estero' (*Vertigo*'s second part) plays on the heritage of Italian journeys in German literature, particularly Thomas Mann's novella *Tod in Venedig* (*Death in Venice*, 1912). Elsewhere, the invocation not only of travel as a theme but also of travel writing as a genre distinctive for its 'heterogeneity and hybridity'[2] seems key.

In *The Rings of Saturn* and the Corsica Project, movement through space creates a narrative structure on which to hang other material. These texts also seem agonisingly aware of the associations of travel writing with the European imperial projects, when such literature was a crucial means of dispersing information and dramatizing derring-do, yet the fact that today 'travel writing is generally perceived as not being at the cutting edge in terms of the factual information that it provides',[3] as Thompson observes, is of a piece with the narrator's self-fashioning as an outmoded figure and a pervasive atmospherics of *lateness*.

"Travel" as Genre

As Jonathan Raban pointed out in *The New Granta Book of Travel* in 2011, works termed "travel writing" can be so varied that they often 'have little in common beyond their shared use of the first-person pronoun'.[4] Yet the presence of this "I" as a device to authorize the written material as "true" is vital. Thompson stresses that 'generally speaking, travel writers do *not* have the same licence as novelists to simply make things up; to do so is to risk one's narrative being classed as fiction, or worse, as fraudulent'.[5] The associations help us make sense of Sebald's borrowing of travel writing motifs, which can be understood as ways of confronting anxiety about any perceived "fraudulence" emerging from the ethical dilemmas of representing real traumatic histories in fiction.

A consistent first-person narrator who seems to resemble Sebald himself; the inclusion of photographs and other documentary material gathered on visits; a special attentiveness to place and environment: by adopting the devices and manners of travel writing, in which the presence of the traveller as an "authorizing" figure is indispensable, Sebald partially resuscitates the "author" only to problematize him anew. Yet this too has precedents in travel writing: in a 2000 essay, Sebald discussed the 'promiscuity' of Bruce Chatwin's writing as 'a later flowering of those early travellers' tales going back to Marco Polo where reality is constantly entering the realm of the metaphysical and the miraculous' (CSe 180/CSg 216). "Travel writing" is figured here as an indeterminate space where the authentic and the imagined are subtly interwoven.

The connection between travel and a problematized relationship to the idea of authenticity helps to make sense of the seemingly contradictory categorisation of a work like *The Rings of Saturn* as 'East Anglia (England) – History – Fiction; East Anglia (England) – Description and travel – Fiction', as it is logged by the British Library. It might even illuminate the apparently tautologous description of a work like *Campo Santo* by its English publishers as 'Sebaldian', which perhaps inheres in precisely this conjunction.

Similarly, "travel writing" also helps make sense of Sebald's later blurring of academic and non-academic writing. The late pieces published in *Logis in einem Landhaus* (*A Place in the Country*) fuse the creative and critical via special attentiveness to place. In the essay concerning Jean-Jacques Rousseau's stay on the Île Saint-Pierre in Switzerland, for example, Sebald's sense of affinity with Rousseau, then working on his own "Corsica project" (a new constitution for the island), is conveyed in terms of mutual identification with the same surroundings.

Such an approach clearly resonated with Sebald from an early stage, given his impatience with academic conventions. In a letter to his friend Reinbert Tabbert dated 7 April 1970, Sebald states that, during a holiday he planned to take in France prior to assuming his position at the University of East Anglia, he would visit the house in Bordeaux where Hölderlin had been a tutor in 1802. Sebald wrote, in English, that it would 'probably tell me more about him to look at the façade of this place than to read the latest news from the intellectual stock-exchange'.[6] The acerbic reflection helps us comprehend his attraction to travel writing as a way of synthesizing scholarly and creative.

Space, Place and Tourism

Sebald's work bears a timely link with the spatial turn in the humanities. Associated with thinkers such as geographer Edward Soja, this turn can be understood in relation to key changes in the experience of space, place and travel in the late twentieth century: the sense of the world 'getting smaller' and more connected, and of authentic 'places' being replaced by the disenchanted 'spaces' of 'circulation, consumption and communication', as the French sociologist Marc Augé put it in his pithy 1992 study *Non-Places: Introduction to an Anthropology of Supermodernity*.[7]

Augé's later comments on the French term 'mondialisation', literally 'globalisation', are instructive. The word points to both 'the extension over the whole surface of the planet of the so-called free market and the technological networks of communication and information', as well as 'to what we might call planetary awareness or consciousness' – an agonized sense of the earth as 'a single planet, a fragile, threatened body' accompanied by a 'social awareness' of the widening gap between rich and poor.[8]

Sebald's writing must be understood in this context. Emphasizing the immediate bodily experience of places, and often rendering place in strikingly bodily terms (Dunwich Heath in *The Rings of Saturn* or Liverpool Street Station in *Austerlitz*, for example), it nevertheless sustainedly reflects on the disconnections suggested and produced by the 'non-place' and the contemporary experience of travel. The views of Norwich from the hospital window at the opening of *The Rings of Saturn*, for example, could be productively read alongside anthropologist Michel de Certeau's reflections on the view from the World Trade Center in *The Practice of Everyday Life* (1980), with its meditations on how technology might be said to have transformed the world into a map of itself, blurring tactile reality with disembodied representation.[9]

In Sebald's writing, this 'spectator' of modernity, present within and yet irreparably detached from the world, is fused with the older figure of the saturnine melancholic (the invocation of the heavenly bodies bearing its own relation to travel and navigation). The uncanny effect of "vertigo" produced by this fusion is, in Sebald's writing, closely connected to a sheer fascination with the atmospherics of place or *genius loci*. Certain sites are invested with an overwhelming gravity relating to the narrator's own past, to wider historical episodes, or both, and it is striking how often Sebald's narrator and characters return to places they have already been, or have read about.

This is the case in 'All'estero', for example, which not only recounts two separate visits by the narrator to the same locations in Vienna and Northern Italy, but also points to longstanding familiarity and is in turn underwritten by the narrator's realization – 'to my amazement, and indeed to my considerable alarm' (V 59/*Schwindel. Gefühle.* 71) – that one of these visits falls on the anniversary of Casanova's escape from the Doge's Palace, about which he has been reading.

Though himself often seemingly on holiday, Sebald's narrator has a horror of the touristic. In *Vertigo*, he is kept awake by 'the confused blathering' of a group of holidaymakers, 'most of whom, as I realised with some dismay, were compatriots of mine' (V 93/*Schwindel. Gefühle.* 106–107). The elevated register and depiction of these figures as "the walking dead" are enough to betray the narrator's stylized outmodedness here, but it might nevertheless surprise readers that a text like *The Rings of Saturn* had its origins in an article written for the weekly newspaper *Zeit* in 1974, 'Die hölzernen Engel von East Anglia: Eine individuelle Bummeltour durch Norfolk und Suffolk' ('The Carved Wooden Angels of East Anglia: A Leisurely Tour Through Norfolk and Suffolk', SM 319–323). Listing good hotels and outings, this piece recommends the region to readers seeking a novel travel experience (see chapter 4 in this volume).

Yet, just as it sets into relief the stylization of *The Rings of Saturn*, so it also suggests another way of reading the amplified melancholy of the literary text, whose vision of 'combustion as the hidden principle behind every artefact we create' might itself be seen as anticipating a new mode of

Illustration 22 – Orford Ness, photographed by Sebald, March 1994

tourism apt to the concerns of the "Anthropocene" and attuned to the reason suggested by Jonathan Raban for the success of *The Rings of Saturn* – his sense that 'we are all exiles now" (RSe 170/RSg 202).[10] If modern tourism has its roots in the "grand tour" of the eighteenth century and cultivation of a refined aesthetic sensibility, then the mournful digressions of *The Rings of Saturn* might be considered a similar model for our own historical moment, aimed at cultivation of an appropriately saturnine state of mind.

English Journeys

In his 2013 study of Sebald, VS Naipaul and Bruce Chatwin, which focuses on the axiomatic tension between 'wonder' and 'disenchantment' in the contemporary period, Simon Cooke stated that translation, obviously a significant feature of Sebald's work for anglophone readers, in fact inheres in the original German writing, 'which comes into being, in part, through acts of translation', often dwelling on the 'talismanic resonance' of particular English terms.[11] Translation, as Cooke observes, is 'part of the experience of travel and language', and Sebald's writing, with its often pre-translated quality (large stretches of *Austerlitz*'s dialogue, for example, are said to have taken place in French) 'is concerned with its own translatability or untranslatability from the first'.[12]

The fact that Sebald intervened heavily in his English translations, and had a hand in his French and Italian translations as well to some degree, only amplifies the way that, for readers of these languages, "travel" inhabits not only the subject but the very substance of the text. This links up with the fact that the narrator in *Vertigo* is repeatedly mistaken for an English rather than a German tourist. On visiting Wertach im Allgäu, he actually states himself to be an English foreign correspondent. These incidents might be taken as a clue for the way that Sebald drew on examples of English travel writing, as well as pointing to the way that his work has been taken up by English-language writers whose interest in space and place has been bracketed under the term psychogeography.

Carole Angier refers to a tale told by Sebald during his Manchester years that he had been commissioned by a German newspaper to travel around the north of England, 'to check menus for any trace of continental cuisine' as a way of gauging Britain's readiness to join the Common Market. 'His answer was always the same: there wasn't any'.[13] Angier is inclined to believe this anecdote, though it quite obviously was simply a joke. It also refers us to a submerged point about Sebald's performance of a certain mode of 'Englishness': Sebald's own copy of JB Priestley's *English Journey* (1934) contains numerous pencil markings alongside Priestley's variously barbed descriptions of bad dinners and poor hospitality.

Incidents like that at the Albion Hotel in Lowestoft in *The Rings of Saturn*, when the narrator is presented with 'a fish that had doubtless lain entombed in the deep-freeze for years' (Rse 43/RSg 58), echo this self-fashioning. The narrator's consistent negative attitude towards modernist architecture is of a piece with this performance – his criticisms of the Bibliothèque nationale in Paris (in *Austerlitz*), for example, resonate with the-then Prince of Wales's acid reflections on the British Library in 1989's *A Vision of Britain* and the sense of modernism as irreparably un-English. Similarly, Sebald's depictions of country houses in *The Rings of Saturn* and *Austerlitz* were shaped by his reading of the self-described 'country house snooper' and arch conservative John Harris.

The significance of East Anglia in terms of a British national imaginary should be drawn out somewhat here. On the one hand, criticisms (like Cooke's) of Sebald's depiction of this region's remoteness as pure stylization are misplaced, tending to overlook the actual marginality of Suffolk, a county whose underdevelopment well into the twentieth century is key to its representation in works like Ronald Blythe's *Akenfield* (1969). On the other, the significance of Blythe's book and Peter Hall's 1974 film of the same name is also, clearly, the centrality of Suffolk to a certain anti-urban national imaginary. The attraction of touristic interest to the county prompted by *The Rings of Saturn* plays into the hands of this version of Englishness.

East Anglia also prompts a connection with contemporary British trends in travel writing. Sebald's papers at the Deutsches Literaturarchiv (German Literary Archive) contain examples of hand-drawn walking maps of East Anglia produced by a local cartographer named 'Wilfrid George' – a near homonym of Sebald's initialized 'Winfried Georg'. One of Sebald's own copies of these maps features a playful 'S' added in pen after Wilfrid George's initials. For a writer preoccupied by coincidence and unexpected affinities between strangers, the discovery of these maps must have been an odd experience. And the impression generated by this coincidence, of travel imagined not so much an encounter between self and other as an extended "journey" into the self, is apt to the British trend of psychogeography that has been roughly contemporaneous with Sebald's writing.

The British psychogeographers have sometimes taken Sebald to task for the version of Englishness his works seem to buy into: Stuart Home and Phil Smith, for example, have castigated his depiction of Lowestoft's decline in *The Rings of Saturn*. Other responses, like those of Raban and Robert Macfarlane, have been more convivial, recognizing the striking similarities between his work and their own preoccupations, where life-writing and an interest in the atmospherics of space and place are fused in what Christopher Gregory-Guilder has termed 'autobiogeography'.[14]

On some occasions, Sebald's depiction of places as haunted by history are strikingly in key with contemporary British trends. Iain Sinclair, perhaps the most prominent psychogeographer, produced a 2013 pamphlet entitled 'Austerlitz and After: Tracking Sebald' (republished with light alterations in 2017's *The Last London: True Fictions from an Unreal City*). Sinclair refers to the writer suspiciously as 'Professor Sebald', accepting the similarity of their activities and their crossed paths through the 1980s and 1990s as a curiosity, at least. Yet if there is friction here, it only demonstrates the energy created by Sebald's presence within the field of "travel writing" as it has most recently been conceived.

This should be taken as a measure of the fact that, just as the tradition and tropes of "travel writing" offer useful ways of understanding Sebald's work, so its contemporary manifestations can no longer be fully grasped without his contribution.

Notes

1. M Zisselsberger, *The Undiscover'd Country: W.G. Sebald and the Poetics of Travel* (Rochester: Camden House, 2010), p. 6.
2. C Thompson, *Travel Writing* (Abingdon: Routledge, 2011), p. 12
3. Thompson, *Travel Writing*, p. 29.
4. J Raban, Introduction, in *The New Granta Book of Travel* (London: Granta, 2012), p. vii.
5. Thompson, *Travel Writing*, p. 16.
6. R Tabbert, Max in Manchester, in *Akzente* 50:1 (2003), p. 29.
7. M Augé, *Non-Places: An Introduction to Supermodernity* (London: Verso, 2008), p. 63.
8. Augé, *Non-Places*, p. x.
9. M De Certeau, *The Practice of Everyday Life* (Berkeley: California University Press, 1984), p. 92.
10. Raban, *New Granta Book of Travel*, p. xv.
11. S Cooke, *Travellers' Tales of Wonder: Chatwin, Naipaul, Sebald* (Edinburgh: Edinburgh University Press, 2013), p. 163.
12. Ibid., p. 169.
13. C Angier, *Speak, Silence: In Search of W.G. Sebald* (London: Bloomsbury, 2021), p. 241.
14. C Gregory-Guilder, *Autobiogeography and the Art of Peripatetic Memorialization in Works by W.G. Sebald, Patrick Modiano, Iain Sinclair, Jonathan Raban and William Least Heat-Moon* (PhD thesis: Sussex, 2005).

CHAPTER 30

Ecocriticism and Animal Studies

Lisa Kunze

'Ecopoetics' is a theoretical designation that springs to mind when reading
Sebald's texts because the term 'nature' was already included in the title of his
literary debut: *Nach der Natur* (*After Nature*). Man's relationship with
nature, how we perceive and react to the natural environment, always
plays a key role in Sebald's work. Whether this is strikingly obvious, as in
After Nature, or later in *Die Ringe des Saturn* (*The Rings of Saturn*) and in his
fragmentary Corsica Project, or almost incidentally such as in his other
literary works, or indeed in reflections about his fellow writers in his literary
critical essays, Sebald consistently dealt with ecological matters. He perceives
nature as a dynamic network in which all elements – landscapes, people,
animals, plants, things – are mutually interconnected. The advancing degradation of our natural environment is at the epicentre of this ecological view
of the stability of the natural eco-system.

Sebald's Ambivalent Concept of Nature

Sebald's work must first be situated in the literary or social context of
Germany in the 1980s. From the founding of the Green Party in 1980 to
concern over "acid rain" causing severe forest dieback, and the Chernobyl
nuclear disaster in April 1986, many German writers had good reasons to
review the impact of man-made environmental destruction. Axel
Goodbody puts *After Nature* and *The Rings of Saturn* in a series with
Hans Magnus Enzensberger's *Der Untergang der Titanic* (*The Sinking of
the Titanic*, 1978), Max Frisch's *Der Mensch erscheint im Holozän* (*Man in
the Holocene*, 1979), Günter Grass's *Die Rättin* (*The Rat*, 1986) and Christa
Wolf's *Störfall* (*Accident: A Day's News*, 1987).[1] The coincidental emergence
of ecocriticism as a concept in literary criticism as well as the subfield of
Animal Studies prove to be a rich source of interpretative approaches to
Sebald's texts.[2]

However, Sebald's concept of nature is also at odds with itself because he treats nature both as a self-destructive force and as a precious good that it is vital to preserve. On the one hand, nature undergoes constant self-decomposition, which is one aspect of Sebald's concept of a natural history of destruction (see chapter 13 in this volume). On the other hand, nature is found to be worthy of protection, being eroded and degraded by human actions. Man's role in this is equally ambivalent: at times, we appear to be the helpless victims of the ferocity of nature and its indiscriminate acts that leave us defiant and at her mercy; at other times, nature is the victim of man-made destruction.

Sebald hence follows a dialectical pattern of thought in that man is not exclusively nature's opponent but rather an integral part of the natural world; at the same time, however, he is the product of nature and thus complicit in nature's self-destruction:

> Humankind's endeavours end in melancholy, barren emptiness and death, because humankind is just one further experiment undertaken by nature on its inexorable path to self-destruction. It is not primarily that we destroy nature, but that nature, using us as one of its agents, destroys itself.[3]

As part of nature, we contribute to a non-human tendency for self-decomposition. Our involvement in this is particularly drastic, since our technical know-how makes our influence potentially longer-lasting, while the destructive possibilities are enhanced and perfected.

Environmental Destruction

Sebald's literary texts always point to environmental destruction as a variety of human and non-human agents acting in concert. In *The Rings of Saturn*, on his way across Suffolk the narrator observes the destructive influences of specific aspects of his environment, and he realizes as he follows up the 'traces of destruction' (Rse 3/RSg 11) that, on careful inspection, rather than being in remote spots they are much more closely interconnected parts of an ecological network. The process of erosion becomes a paradigm for this perception of nature's destruction, for which the Dunwich episode is a perfect example. The local inhabitants of this area are responsible for the 'steady and advancing destruction [. . .] of the dense forests' (Rse 169/RSg 201).

This sets up the erosion of stretches of coastline, so the sea washes away the land and engulfs man's habitable living environment. Sebald envisages the disappearance of Dunwich as humans acting in concert with the forces of nature. This clarifies Sebald's ambivalent portrayal of man's relationship with nature, since in the lengthy account of the storm tides near Dunwich people appear as the helpless victims in a desperate battle against nature's overpowering force (RSg 191/Rse 158). However, the inhabitants' actions further reinforce the erosion process, so they become another cog in the wheel of self-destruction by nature.

This cycle is illustrated even more clearly by the example of the 'natural history of the herring' (Rse 54–59/RSg 70–77). The narrator highlights not only man's terrible treatment of animals but also the ecological circumstances which this approach to nature brings about. The agricultural use of fertilizers and pesticides causes the pollution of rivers and waterways and – in addition to overfishing – the decline of fish stocks, in turn, impacting the fisheries industry and ultimately leading to the socio-economic decline of coastal towns, like Lowestoft. Besides, the effect of the toxic substances doesn't just stop with the fish: the fishermen's catch is processed into fishmeal; the toxins re-enter the human food chain because of animal feed in livestock farming. After a while, marine pollution again takes a toll on humans.

The Corsica Project sheds light on another facet of man and nature acting in concert together. Here, Sebald is particularly interested in how landscapes affect people, that is, how landscapes influence us and how they further affect the way in which we react to nature. Richard Gray therefore refers to the Corsica Project as 'fundamentally eco-psychologic':

> Corsica thus represents for him a locale in which transformations of the natural environment and the mentality of its human occupants are intimately intertwined. These investigations seek to highlight the imbrications between ecology of the island and the psychology of the human beings who live there.[4]

As he wanders through the 'endless undulations of vegetation' and the 'solitude' of the Corsican forests, the narrator acknowledges that the residents who live here 'on such a godforsaken island' must feel as though they are 'condemned to life-long captivity' and can only experience 'feelings of oppression' and even fear towards the surrounding flora and fauna (KP 141). The way in which the people treat nature is a result of such fear. The narrator speculates that 'the much-lauded Corsican will for freedom, the blind rage with which they defended their property & honour against the slightest violation' is to be understood as 'a pathological reaction to the fear that they could be ousted from the place where they were until now, by a neighbour, by the constant looming threat of nature' (KP 142).

The influence of the surrounding landscape on the temperaments of the Corsican inhabitants becomes the reason why their mountain villages resemble fortresses where they shelter from nature that they spend their lives being afraid of. The feeling of an ever-looming threat explains the blind rage of their approach to nature – when they go hunting or destroying the forests. The people's aggressive urge proves to be a building block of the natural history of destruction.

Nature as an Ensemble of Actors

This perception of natural destruction as an ensemble of different elements has one consequence in Sebald's texts that is noticeable as an exceptional case in its historical literary context. He never just sees humans as actors whose deeds have knock-on effects for the eco-system. Rather, humans as well as non-human individuals, their acts and creations are agents within a comprehensive network. The inspiration for this is the concept of the actor-network theory that the sociologist Bruno Latour developed in his book *Politiques de la nature* (*Politics of Nature*, 1999).

In Sebald's work this culminates in the anthropomorphizing of animals, things, natural phenomena and landscapes. In this sense, Dominic O'Key calls Sebald's writing style both 'ecopoetic' and 'zoopoetic': 'Sebald's texts destabilize the human's claims to narrative superiority, and thus propose what David Herman has recently theorized as a "narratology beyond the human"'.[5] According to the ambivalent relationship of nature as both a self-destructive force and a resource that is worth preserving, there are different purposes for this writing strategy. Sometimes, the aim is to demonstrate nature's ferocity and overwhelming force over humans. At other times, however, it is to highlight the fragility of the natural eco-system.

The sequence in the first part of *After Nature* emerges as the epitome of anthropomorphized, self-destructive nature in Sebald's work, in which the description begins of the 'Temptation of Saint Anthony' on Grünewald's Isenheim Altarpiece: 'the absence of balance in nature / which blindly makes one experience after another / and like a senseless botcher / undoes the thing it has only just achieved' (AN 27/NN 24). Human qualities are ascribed to nature; it is presented as the 'crazy / senseless botcher' and random experimenter. This image is continued in 'And if I Remained by the Outermost See': 'nature / in a process of dissolution, in a state / of pure dementia' (AN 63/NN 56).

In *The Rings of Saturn* the image is again evoked in the description of the 'grotesqueries with which nature, with an inventiveness scarcely less diseased, fills every vacant space in her atlas' (Rse 21/RSg 32–33), and the never-ending mutations, which 'go far beyond any rational limit' (Rse 34/RSg 34). Its deliberate action is suggested with verbs like 'undo' and 'fill'; words like 'senseless', 'pathological', 'rational' and 'dementia' transfer human categories to nature. Thus, nature appears as an autonomous agent whose impact is always directed against herself, and humans are part of the collateral experiment and unable to act.

Identification and Becoming-Animal

In direct contrast, Sebald also uses nature anthropomorphism to visualize man's inconsiderate treatment of the environment and its disastrous consequences. In particular, emphasis is given to nature's vulnerability and suffering. This is generally the case when the spotlight is on the relationship between humans and animals that is characterized by people's 'domination and violence': 'Sebald's texts repeatedly return to this issue of our attitude towards animals which underlines man's deeply disturbed relationship with nature.'[6] The narrator repeatedly assumes a special role: thanks to the change in focus from the external to the internal, he sort of seems to slip into the animals' skin, to merge with them and to suffer with them.

In *The Rings of Saturn* there are several examples of such convergence between the narrator and an animal. The anthropological difference is therefore called into question due to the narrator 'becoming-animal' and the animal's anthropomorphism. O'Key calls these scenes 'moments of cross-species interaction'.[7] A particularly impressive example is the meeting with the hare at Orford Ness: through the eyes of the hare, which he frightened off and now escapes him, the narrator looks back at himself as a source of the animal's fear: 'and in its eyes, turning to look back as it fled and almost popping out of its head with fright, I see myself, becoming one with it' (Rse 235/RSg 280).

A similar incident occurs with the Chinese quail at Somerleyton Hall park estate. In its captivity, the quail has fallen into a 'state of dementia' and is 'running to and fro along the edge of its cage and shaking its head every time it was about to turn, as if it could not comprehend how it had gotten into this fix' (Rse 36/RSg 50). The narrator adopts the perspective of the quail inside the cage and imagines it has human feelings, a sensation of being cornered, and the attempt to understand this situation. Such scenes of 'cross-species interaction' show how, for Sebald, animals are not only

Illustration 23 – Sebald with Labrador puppy Maurice

'regarded as props on the historical stage [. . .], but as individuals with the capacity to steer their actions',[8] as creatures that act and feel independently. Emily Jones writes on this point:

> Sebald's narrators rebel against anthropocentrism: rather than seeing them as passive objects, the narrators' attention to animals' material presence belies a concern not only for human history and the narrators' individual experiences, but also for the present-day environment on its own terms.[9]

The Secret Life of Things

It is noteworthy that Sebald's adoption of such 'cross-species interaction' doesn't just stop with animals. He uses the same strategy, for example, in *After Nature* to observe an inanimate object. The Bering Expedition yacht was battered by gales and driven by the waves against the rocks: 'Jammed there it lies, groans / for a while amid boulders, / as though in its last extremity / it might yet reach dry land' (AN 64–65/NN 57). Just as animals are assumed to have control over situations, here a sailing yacht supposedly has sensations similar to human ones.

However, individual objects are not only transformed in this sense as agents. In 'Dark Night Sallies Forth', the entire landscape has been stricken and scarred by industry. When the narrator glances down at the Rhine in his dream flight, he notices 'the murmur / of the millionfold proliferating molluscs, / woodlice and leaches, the cold putrefaction, / the groans in the rocky ribs' (AN 110/NN 96–97). In 'And if I Remained by the Outermost Sea', polluted nature is described alongside the disease-ridden ship's crew who are 'rotting away', while the 'millionfold proliferating molluscs' are a reminder of the 'festering ulcers' (AN 64/NN 57). The image of the 'rocky ribs' completes the association with an ailing body from which only a final 'groaning' sound is audible. Humans already seem almost to have driven nature to the point of extinction.

This description of a stricken landscape is repeatedly used in Sebald's work. For example, the image of the 'rocky ribs' re-emerges in the Corsica Project when 'the bare skeleton of the craggy rock' (KP 207) emerges from the remnants of the dying shrubland. This anthropomorphizing description of the landscape makes this intangible entity an organism that is suffering from man-made degradation.

Sebald's narrators not only perceive that but suffer with the stricken landscape. The lyrical voice in the poem 'Schaurige Wirkung des Höllentälers auf meine Nerven' ('Eerie Effects of the Hell Valley Wind on My Nerves') feels 'diffuse pain reaching into / the upturned leaves on the trees' (Lwe 83/LWg 54). In *Schwindel. Gefühle.* (*Vertigo*) the narrator falls into a kind of shock-induced paralysis during his train journey through Germany – it makes him worry about 'something like an eclipse of my mental faculties' – as he looks at the countryside, which is described as 'straightened out and tidied up [. . .] to the last square inch and corner, [. . .] thoroughly parcelled up and segmented'. Nature, which has been suppressed by being clipped and cultivated, appears to him as 'appeased and numbed in some sinister way' – his own state of shocked paralysis is an empathetic merging with this numbed landscape (V 253–254/Schwindel. Gefühle. 276–277).

The same dynamic, which lets the narrator feel the consequences of the degradation of the natural environment on his own body, also emerges in *The Rings of Saturn*. After his hiking excursion across Suffolk he is 'taken into hospital in Norwich in a state of almost total immobility' and his illness is explained by the memory of 'the paralysing horror that had come over [him] when confronted with the traces of destruction, reaching far back into the past, that were evident even in that remote place' (Rse 3/RSg 11). Similarly, in *The Emigrants* Henry Selwyn suffers with nature: he senses on his own body how it 'was groaning and collapsing beneath the burden we placed upon it' (E 7/ AW 13).

Suffering as a Universal Experience

At the sight of dead moths in his apartment, Austerlitz asks, 'I wonder what kind of fear and pain they feel while they are lost' (Ae 133/Ag 141). This question can be read as a reference to Jeremy Bentham (1748–1832), in his *Introduction to the Principles of Morals and Legislation* (1789), where he expressed the proposition about the ability of animals to suffer: 'The question is not, Can they *reason*? Nor, Can they *talk*? But, Can they *suffer*?'[10] For Austerlitz, the answer to the concluding question is clear: all living creatures, including moths, can undergo suffering. This basic assumption underlies his speculation about what kind of fear and pain they endure (Ae 133/Ag 141). However, Sebald further elaborates on this question in his texts not only by ascribing this capacity for suffering to man and animals but also to plants, landscapes – and all nature.

In summary, we can conclude that nature and culture are no longer an opposing duo in Sebald's texts but rather they are intrinsically attuned to each other. Besides humans, he also perceives non-human nature – plants and animals, the marine eco-system or soil conditions – as well as human creations and inanimate artefacts as actors in a system that appears as a continually changing, dynamic network. Moreover, Sebald is convinced that all the elements of this network resemble each other in their capacity to endure suffering.

Notes

1. A Goodbody, Life Writing and Nature Writing in W.G. Sebald's Rings of Saturn, in: A Hornung, Z Baisheng (eds.), *Ecology and Life Writing* (Heidelberg: Winter, 2013), pp. 335–351 (346).
2. H Detering, Was heißt ›Ecocriticism‹? Theoretische Fragen und deutsche Debatten, in: *Gegenwartsliteratur: Ein germanistisches Jahrbuch* 19 (2020), pp. 23–46.
3. G Bond, On the Misery of Nature and the Nature of Misery: W.G. Sebald's Landscapes, in: JJ Long, A Whitehead (eds.), *W.G. Sebald: A Critical Companion* (Seattle: University of Washington Press, 2004), pp. 31–44 (34).
4. R Gray, *Ghostwriting: W.G. Sebald's Poetics of History* (London: Bloomsbury, 2017), p. 365.
5. D O'Key, W.G. Sebald's Zoopoetics: Writing after Nature, in: R Borgards et al. (eds.), *Texts, Animals, Environments: Zoopoetics and Ecopoetics* (Freiburg: Rombach, 2019), pp. 217–227 (225).
6. H Schmidt-Hannisa, Aberration of a Species: On the Relationship between Man and Beast in W.G. Sebald's Work, in: A Fuchs, JJ Long (eds.), *W.G.*

Sebald and the Writing of History (Würzburg: Königshausen & Neumann, 2007), pp. 31–43 (36).

7. O'Key, Sebald's Zoopoetics, p. 224.
8. K Kończal, Auf den Spuren eines ‚verkehrten Miniaturuniversums': Tiere im Werk von W.G. Sebald, in: *Comparatio* 8:1 (2016), pp. 143–170 (148).
9. E Jones, Animal Encounters and Ecological Anxiety in W.G. Sebald, in: P Barton et al. (eds.), *Of Rocks, Mushrooms and Animals: Material Ecocriticism in German-speaking Cultures* (Dunedin: University of Otago, 2017), pp. 97–129 (100).
10. J Bentham, *An Introduction to the Principles of Morals and Legislation* (Oxford: Clarendon, 1907), p. 311.

PART IV

Reception and Legacy

CHAPTER 31

Sebald Scholarship

Lynn L. Wolff

Reading W.G Sebald is not a matter of light entertainment since the detailed accounts and complex webs of connections challenge even the most attentive reader. One must actively engage with the text and consider the multiple questions that arise from the blend of fact and fiction, the tension between word and image, and the status of the auto-fictional first-person narrator within a prose form that defies easy classification. His works demand that we reflect on our own position in relation to the events and experiences depicted, and they demand that we reflect on the various forms of representation possible within literary discourse.

With an eye to the importance of literary scholarship in contributing to a better understanding of Sebald's œuvre and the specific literary achievements of his individual works, this essay will provide a brief overview of developments, outline the themes and trends, and highlight possibilities for future research.

Overview and Developments

Sebald wrote poetry as a high school student and was working on a novel while at university, but his literary production began in earnest in the 1980s and 1990s. As an academic, he taught courses for over thirty years at the University of East Anglia in Norwich and published essays on nineteenth- and twentieth-century German-language literature. As of his death in 2001, he left behind a body of published work that includes two volumes of poetry, four major works of prose fiction and four volumes of essays, plus two academic monographs (and an unpublished English version of his PhD thesis). Posthumous publications, some drawn from his archive held by the Deutsches Literaturarchiv (German Literature Archive), include two further books of poetry, a volume that includes short essays and the prose fragments of his unfinished Corsica Project and an important collection of interviews.

In contrast to this relatively modest body of work, one of the characteristics of Sebald scholarship is the sheer number of publications produced
within a relatively short period of time. A 'Porträt' of Sebald – including
some of his poems, interviews and essays by scholars and critics – was
edited by Franz Loquai and appeared during Sebald's lifetime[1] and, in
2003, Sebald was featured in the *Text+Kritik* series which aims to bridge
the gap between academia and a broader public.[2]

The first monograph on Sebald, written by Mark R. McCulloh and also
published in 2003, provides an introduction to the author by focusing on
his fictional prose with some considerations of his 'elemental poem' *Nach
der Natur* (*After Nature*) and the published version of his lectures on
poetics, *Luftkrieg und Literatur* (*On the Natural History of Destruction*).[3]
McCulloh's monograph includes an annotated bibliography that lists
primarily reviews of Sebald's works, plus eight scholarly articles and the
aforementioned volume edited by Loquai.

Now, twenty years later, there are hundreds of articles on Sebald, close
to forty monographs, and almost as many edited volumes or special issues
of journals, all with a strict focus on Sebald.[4] A further dimension of
scholarship considers Sebald from various comparative perspectives.[5]
There is also a meta-level of scholarship, consisting of research overviews
that take stock of existing research. Viewed together, such review essays
and bibliographic surveys chart the development of Sebald scholarship over
the last twenty years.[6]

Initially, Sebald was more quickly and more positively received in the
Anglo-American world, while within the German-speaking scholarly context there was a sense of scepticism, rooted in a superficial assessment of
Sebald as an 'academic turned author', and, further, as a scholar who had
produced unorthodox literary essays within *Auslandsgermanistik* (a label
often used with an air of condescension for German studies research done
outside of Germany).

Despite this early imbalance in reception, Sebald scholarship can be
considered not only international but also transnational. Three significant
edited volumes, all based on international conferences, appeared on both
sides of the Atlantic at approximately the same time and treated similar
concerns.[7] The number of publications beyond the borders of North
America, the UK and Western Europe is growing, demonstrating both
the reach of interest in Sebald and the important engagement of translators
in making his works accessible to non-German speakers.[8] In terms of
translation and circulation, Sebald's works can certainly be described as
belonging to "world literature".

In the early phase of reception and research, many publications appeared simultaneously, leading to a great deal of thematic overlap. In his 2007 bibliographic survey of over one hundred individual works of scholarship, JJ Long aptly identified that 'there has been a marked tendency for recent criticism to become predictable and repetitive'.[9] Long's further observation of an epigonal trend – 'It is as though the digressive and leisurely nature of Sebald's texts generates an equally meandering mode of critical writing'[10] – is less the case in scholarly publications of the last ten years, but this continues to apply to journalistic articles and essays published in magazines. Indeed, Sebald's style and tone invite imitation, at times out of admiration, at times in sly playfulness.

The greatest attention has been paid to Sebald's fictional prose, as opposed to his poetry or essays, many of which still await translation into English. Specifically, *Die Ausgewanderten* (*The Emigrants*) and, even more so, *Austerlitz* have garnered the most significant scholarly interest. Due to the prominent thematic role of the Holocaust in these two works, a picture of Sebald as a 'Holocaust author' has emerged.[11] While these works deal with Germany's National Socialist past, this is not Sebald's only subject, and several scholars have highlighted his broader understanding of history, often through an examination of his aesthetic strategies.[12]

An important development in Sebald scholarship is the attention paid to his own critical engagement with literary works and how he challenged traditional forms and conventions of scholarly writing. Early contributions that shed light on this area include Martin Klebes's analysis of Sebald's studies of Carl Sternheim and Alfred Döblin, Sven Meyer's investigation of the particular prose form of both Sebald's essays and stories and Ulrich Simon's examination of Sebald's concept of literature as well as his self-presentation as an author and provocative stance as literary scholar.[13]

Further in this vein, Peter Schmucker focuses on Sebald's use of intertextuality to provide valuable insights into the connection between the author's literature and literary scholarship,[14] and Uwe Schütte argues that Sebald's own form of literary criticism – 'a subjective combination of philological analysis and personal reportage' – helped pave the way for his work as an author.[15] Another development in scholarship is the more critical stance towards Sebald's self-stylization and his ethics as an author, which serves to balance out the overwhelming positive reception of his works.[16]

Trends and Themes

With the publication of the first biography of W.G. Sebald, twenty years after his death, one might expect a new era of scholarship to begin. While it is still too early to tell whether this will indeed be the case, the biography as well as its reception have already rekindled old accusations against the author and made clear that the differences between literary criticism and literary scholarship are not to be underestimated.

Carole Angier asserts of her book *Speak, Silence: In Search of W.G. Sebald*: 'This is a biography, not a work of literary criticism.'[17] In fact, Angier is quite frank about the opinions and conjectures that guide her approach. Beyond her personal assessment: 'W.G. Sebald is the most exquisite writer I know', Angier stakes this claim in the broadest possible terms as well: 'Today W.G. Sebald is the most revered twentieth-century German writer in the world'.[18]

Despite such laudatory, albeit unsubstantiated, statements, Angier is driven to track down the sources and models for Sebald's characters and stories, and attempts to determine what is "true" and "real" in his works as opposed to what can be deemed stolen or an outright lie.[19] It is quite perplexing then, when Angier defends Sebald against claims that his work is 'exploitative' or 'an appropriation of suffering that is not his' by stating: 'The unique empathy of his work was genuine.'[20] Rather than delving any further into the inherent tension (contradiction even) in Angier's biography, it is more important to reiterate what risks getting lost in discussions that are (overly and overtly) invested in a biographical dimension, namely: a differentiated understanding of fiction and an appreciation for the way literary discourse generates multiple meanings.

The tension between fact and fiction is indeed central to Sebald's works and certainly one reason why they fascinate and engage his readers. Although he draws from extratextual reality and explicitly points to this through his use of photographs, his literary works cannot be simply reduced to their source material. Studies that approach the interrelation of fact and fiction in Sebald's works from both a thematic and formal point of view have illuminated the ethical and aesthetic dimensions at stake. These discussions have gained in complexity and nuance as more scholars consider both his intellectual influences and reading practices, traces of which can be found in the markings and marginalia of his working library.

Two exemplary studies in this respect are monographs by Ben Hutchinson and Paul Whitehead. Hutchinson meticulously shows how Sebald's literary style, narrative structure, and citation practice are manifestations of his underlying concern with the philosophy of history.[21] Whitehead's study not only theorizes the aesthetic dimension of the marginal for Sebald's understanding of history and historical representation but also provides a practical overview of Sebald's marginalia in key works of his personal library.[22]

For anyone interested in the biographical and autobiographical dimensions of Sebald's texts, as well as the connections across his life, work, reception and influence, the following publications are essential references: the English and German Sebald handbooks and the introductions to Sebald by Uwe Schütte,[23] and two films by Thomas Honickel from 2007 (*W.G. Sebald: Der Ausgewanderte* and *Sebald. Orte.*), along with the volume *Curriculum Vitae*, which presents the full versions of the interviews Honickel conducted for his films.[24] These works effectively draw on Sebald's background as a way to contextualize his body of work, without pursuing a strictly biographical interpretation of his texts.

In addition, Frank Schwamborn's monograph should be highlighted since it serves as both an introduction and a scholarly study. In detailed close readings of Sebald's major fictional works, he engages extensively with research from both sides of the Atlantic, as well as with interviews and reviews. Schwamborn proceeds chronologically through each work in an essayistic fashion – neither wed to a singular theory nor insistent on a particular thesis – thus guiding readers through the intricacies of Sebald's fiction, pointing out recurring themes, motifs and stylistic tendencies.[25]

The most consistent themes in Sebald scholarship, as represented in monographs, edited volumes and individual articles, include the following: history, exile and trauma, specifically the representation of the Holocaust; memory, mourning and melancholia; photography and intertextuality; nature and travel. Further thematic aspects, like gender, sexuality and religion have been considered by some scholars, but there is room for further studies. Approaches informed by psychoanalysis, ecocriticism and queer theory have been particularly illuminating of aspects within Sebald's works that intersect with the main concerns of history, memory and trauma.[26]

Already in 2005, Ruth Vogel-Klein emphasized the importance of 'synergy' in approaching Sebald's works, especially considering the variety of themes in his œuvre, and this still holds true today.[27] That is to say, the broad thematic scope of Sebald's works, which encompasses both local and global concerns, as well as concerns for all living beings, his strategies of intermediality and intertextuality and the ways in which his texts defy traditional genre categories, invite a plurality of methodological approaches and theoretical perspectives.

Future Directions

A starting point for any study of Sebald remains the English-language Sebald handbook *Saturn's Moons* with its six-part bibliographic survey. In addition to primary and secondary bibliographies, the survey includes a bibliography of reviews, an audio-visual bibliography, a list of interviews and a detailed chronology of Sebald's life that highlights the autobiographical aspects of his fictional works.[28] The handbook also includes a catalogue of Sebald's working library and a contextualizing essay, both by Jo Catling, that provide an excellent overview for anyone planning to work with author's library at the Deutsches Literaturarchiv (German Literature Archive, DLA) in Marbach.

Sebald's *Nachlass* (literary estate), housed by the DLA since 2004, is a rich source that can provide further insights and impulses for future research. The archive contains manuscripts and letters, as well as the aforementioned working library with Sebald's colourful marginalia. A further collection of Sebald's photographs was added to the literary estate in 2021 and offers further possibilities for understanding the visual dimension of his works and his approach to writing. His unfinished World War Project, as well as his correspondence, which often requires permission to access, are yet to be explored in detail by scholars. Paving the way in highlighting unpublished materials from the archive is an essay collection that also strives to portray a more diverse picture of Sebald, as its subtitle indicates: 'Contributions to a Different Image of the Author'.[29]

Yet another direction for future scholarship would be an engagement with Sebald's works by digital means. The complex networks Sebald creates through direct references and surreptitious citation, as well as the spatial and visual dimensions of his works, all lend themselves to digital approaches. One example is Barbara Hui's LITMAP project, which offered readers an interactive, geo-spatial orientation in Sebald's *Die Ringe des Saturn* (*The Rings of Saturn*), allowing them to zoom in on individual localities and zoom out to gain a better understanding of the greater networks across the text.[30]

Underscoring the collaborative and iterative nature of digital humanities projects like LITMAP, David Kim and Mark Phillips undertake a network analysis of *The Emigrants* that invites future scholars to work in the same vein while also demonstrating the ways close and distant reading can inform each other.[31] Such approaches promise to shed new light on the archaeological structure and intertextual networks within Sebald's fictional prose form. However, one must keep in mind the technical limits, especially if these modes of scholarly inquiry only exist in a digital form online.

While Sebald's texts are very rich in themselves – for example, the text–image relationship, the intertextual references and the thematic connections across his œuvre – perhaps the best thing that could happen for Sebald scholarship would be a broader contextualization. There are many insightful discussions of Sebald in comparison with other post-war and contemporary authors and artists,[32] but there is room to expand with regard to a contextualization of Sebald – for example, beyond the twentieth century and beyond European borders.[33]

Furthermore, there is room for contextualization of both his poetics and his worldview by comparing them to those of other authors working at the intersection of literature, history and philosophy, as well as authors using intermedial strategies.[34] Moving beyond the question of Sebald's influence on other authors and building on discussions of Sebald within the context of world literature, scholarship bringing Sebald's works into dialogue with authors from around the world would greatly enrich our understanding of the specificities of literary discourse and the role of literature today.[35]

Notes

1. F Loquai (ed.), *W.G. Sebald* (Eggingen: Ed. Isele, 1997).
2. HL Arnold (ed.), *W.G. Sebald. Text+Kritik* 158 (2003), [2](2012).
3. M McCulloh, *Understanding W.G. Sebald* (Columbia: University of South Carolina Press, 2003).
4. The majority of monographs on Sebald have been written in German, but the publications counted here also include those in Dutch, English, French and Italian. From a qualitative standpoint, several of these studies (often published PhD theses) could have benefitted from closer consideration of one of the many research overviews that exist.
5. This selection of comparative studies illustrates the range of themes and approaches: L Campos, *Fictions de l'après: Coetzee, Kertész, Sebald. Temps et contretemps de la conscience historique* (Paris: Classiques Garnier, 2012); M Läubli, *Subjekt mit Körper: Die Erschreibung des Selbst bei Jean-Jacques Rousseau, Karl Philipp Moritz und W.G. Sebald* (Bielefeld: Transcript, 2014); T Hoorn, *Naturgeschichte in der ästhetischen Moderne: Max Ernst, Ernst Jünger, Ror Wolf, W.G. Sebald* (Göttingen: Wallstein, 2016); H Finch, L Wolff (eds.), *Witnessing, Memory, Poetics: H.G. Adler and W.G. Sebald* (Rochester: Camden House, 2014).
6. For example R Sheppard, Dexter – Sinister: Some Observations on Decrypting the Mors Code in the Works of W.G. Sebald, in: *Journal of European Studies* 35:4 (2005), pp. 419–463 and Sheppard, Woods, Trees, and the Spaces In-

Between: A Report on Work Published on W.G. Sebald 2005–2008, in: *Journal of European Studies* 39:1 (2009), pp. 79–128; JJ Long, W.G. Sebald: A Bibliographical Essay on Current Research, in: A Fuchs, JJ Long (eds.), *W. G. Sebald and the Writing of History* (Würzburg: Königshausen & Neumann, 2007), pp. 11–29, L Wolff, Das metaphysische Unterfutter der Realität: Recent Publications and Trends in W.G. Sebald Research, in: *Monatshefte* 99:1 (2007), pp. 78–101, Wolff, Zur Sebald-Forschung, in: M Niehaus, C Öhlschläger (eds.), *W.G. Sebald-Handbuch: Leben – Werk – Wirkung* (Stuttgart: Metzler, 2017), pp. 312–317; M Zisselsberger, A Persistent Fascination: Recent Publications on the Works of W.G. Sebald, in: *Monatshefte* 101:1 (2009), pp. 88–105 and U Schütte, Neues aus der Sebald-Industrie: Eine polemische Perspektive, in: *Weimarer Beiträge* 64:4 (2018), pp. 617–627.

7. Cf. R Vogel-Klein (ed.), *W.G. Sebald: Mémoire, Transferts, Images / Erinnerung, Übertragungen, Bilder. Recherches germaniques.* Hors série 2 (2005); S Denham, M McCulloh (eds.), *W.G. Sebald: History – Memory – Trauma* (Berlin/New York: De Gruyter, 2006); M Niehaus, C Öhlschläger (eds.), *W.G. Sebald: Politische Archäologie und melancholische Bastelei* (Berlin: Schmidt, 2006).

8. A 2014 issue of the Polish quarterly *Konteksty* (*Contexts*) features Sebald with a focus on 'anthropology, literature, and photography' and includes a selection of Sebald's texts and previously published articles, translated into Polish, as well as essays written originally in Polish. A special issue of the fortnightly Czech publication *A2* was published in 2021 (#25–26) on the topic of 'W.G. Sebald and the Wreckage', including excerpts from *On the Natural History of Destruction*, translated into Czech. An issue of the Portuguese language journal *Philia*, which focuses on philosophy, literature and art, featured several articles on Sebald on the twentieth anniversary of his death: *Philia* 3:2 (2021).

9. JJ Long, W.G. Sebald: A Bibliographical Essay on Current Research, in: A Fuchs, JJ Long (eds.), *W.G. Sebald and the Writing of History* (Würzburg: Königshausen & Neumann, 2007), pp. 11–29 (28).

10. Ibid., p. 23

11. Required reading on the topic of history, memory and trauma, without pigeonholing Sebald as a 'Holocaust author', is A Fuchs, *Die Schmerzensspuren der Geschichte: Zur Poetik der Erinnerung in W.G. Sebalds Prosa* (Cologne: Böhlau, 2004).

12. B Mosbach, *Figurationen der Katastrophe. Ästhetische Verfahren in W.G. Sebalds ›Die Ringe des Saturn‹ und ›Austerlitz‹* (Bielefeld: Aisthesis, 2008); C Hünsche, *Textereignisse und Schlachtenbilder: Eine sebaldsche Poetik des Ereignisses* (Bielefeld: Aisthesis, 2012); L Wolff, *W.G. Sebald's Hybrid Poetics: Literature as Historiography* (Berlin/Boston: De Gruyter, 2014).

13. M Klebes, Sebald's Pathographies, in: S Denham, M McCulloh (eds.), *W.G. Sebald: History – Memory – Trauma* (Berlin/New York: De Gruyter, 2006), pp. 65–75; S Meyer, Im Medium der Prosa: Essay und Erzählung bei W.G. Sebald, in: R Vogel-Klein (ed.), *W.G. Sebald: Mémoire, Transferts, Images /*

Erinnerung, Übertragungen, Bilder. Recherches germaniques. Hors série 2 (2005), pp. 173–185; U Simon, Der Provokateur als Literaturhistoriker: Anmerkungen zu Literaturbegriff und Argumentationsverfahren in W.G. Sebalds essayistischen Schriften, in: M Atze/ F Loquai (eds.), *Sebald. Lektüren.* (Eggingen: Ed. Isele, 2005), pp. 78–104.

14. P Schmucker, *Grenzüberschreitungen: Intertextualität im Werk von W.G. Sebald* (Berlin/Boston: De Gruyter, 2012). A further important contribution to discussions of Sebald and intertextuality that also draws valuable insights from Sebald's working library in the German Literature Archive is E Ingebrigtsen, *Bisse ins Sacktuch: Zur mehrfachkodierten Intertextualität bei W.G. Sebald* (Bielefeld: Aisthesis, 2016).

15. U Schütte, *Interventionen: Literaturkritik als Widerspruch bei W.G. Sebald* (Munich: Ed. Text+Kritik, 2014), pp. 23, 52.

16. F Schley, *Kataloge der Wahrheit: Zur Inszenierung von Autorschaft bei W.G. Sebald* (Göttingen: Wallstein, 2012); M Gotterbarm, *Die Gewalt des Moralisten: Zum Verhältnis von Ethik und Ästhetik bei W.G. Sebald* (Paderborn: Fink, 2016).

17. C Angier, *Speak, Silence: In Search of W.G. Sebald* (London: Bloomsbury, 2021), p. 397.

18. Ibid., pp. viii, 427.

19. Angier uses a broad range of terms to designate Sebald's "lies", among others: 'fib' (p. 262), 'whopper' and 'trick' (p. 420), 'slip' (p. 423).

20. Ibid., p. 435.

21. B Hutchinson, *W.G. Sebald: Die dialektische Imagination* (Berlin/New York: De Gruyter, 2009).

22. P Whitehead, *Im Abseits: W.G. Sebalds Ästhetik des Marginalen* (Bielefeld: Aisthesis, 2019).

23. U Schütte, *W.G. Sebald: Einführung in Leben und Werk* (Stuttgart: UTB, 2011); extended and updated version: *W.G. Sebald: Leben und literarisches Werk* (Berlin/Boston: De Gruyter, 2020); Schütte, *W.G. Sebald* (Liverpool: Liverpool University Press, 2018).

24. T Honickel, *Curriculum Vitae: Die W.G. Sebald-Interviews*, ed. U Schütte, K Wolfinger (Würzburg: Königshausen & Neumann, 2021).

25. F Schwamborn, *W.G. Sebald: Moralismus und Prosodie* (Munich: Iudicium, 2017).

26. For example E Santner, *On Creaturely Life: Rilke, Benjamin, Sebald* (Chicago: Chicago University Press, 2006); J Groves, Writing After Nature: A Sebaldian Ecopoetics, in: C Schaumann, H Sullivan (eds.), *German Ecocriticism in the Anthropocene* (New York: Palgrave Macmillan, 2017), pp. 267–292; H Finch, *Sebald's Bachelors: Queer Resistance and the Unconforming Life* (Oxford: Legenda, 2013).

27. R Vogel-Klein, Avant Propos, in: Vogel-Klein (ed.), *W.G. Sebald: Mémoire, Transferts, Images / Erinnerung, Übertragungen, Bilder. Recherches germaniques.* Hors série 2 (2005), pp. 1–2.

28. See the section A Bibliographic Survey, in: J Catling, R Hibbitt (eds.), *Saturn's Moons: W.G. Sebald – A Handbook* (London: Legenda, 2011), pp. 446–658.

29. U Schütte (ed.), *Über W.G. Sebald: Beiträge zu einem anderen Bild des Autors* (Berlin/Boston: De Gruyter, 2017).

30. While the project no longer appears to be active, it is nevertheless worth mentioning as a model for future attempts to engage with Sebald's work in a digital way. The frame of the original project is available here: https://bar barahui.net/litmap/. For an overview of the project, cf. https://barbarahui.net /about-litmap.html and B Hui, Mapping Historical Networks in *Die Ringe des Saturn*, in: M Zisselsberger (ed.), *The Undiscover'd Country: W.G. Sebald and the Poetics of Travel* (Rochester: Camden House, 2010), pp. 277–298.

31. D Kim, M Phillips, Project Two: Patterns of the Anthemion: Discovering Networks of Coincidence in W.G. Sebald's ›Die Ausgewanderten‹, in: *Transit* 10:1 (2015): https://transit.berkeley.edu/2015/kim_phillips/.

32. D Osborne, *Traces of Trauma in W.G. Sebald and Christoph Ransmayr* (Oxford: Legenda, 2013); D McGonagill, *Crisis and Collection: German Visual Memory Archives of the Twentieth Century* (Würzburg: Königshausen & Neumann, 2015).

33. Exemplary in this regard is A Itkin, *Underworlds of Memory: W.G. Sebald's Epic Journeys through the Past* (Evanston: Northwestern University Press, 2017).

34. Sebald holds a prominent place in Silke Horstkotte's study *Nachbilder: Fotografie und Gedächtnis in der deutschen Gegenwartsliteratur* (Cologne: Böhlau, 2009) and the volume as a whole is particularly valuable for the array of contemporary authors considered (among others Ulla Hahn, Monika Maron and Uwe Timm).

35. A step in this direction is the special edition of *Boundary 2* 47:3 (2020), edited by Sina Rahmani and devoted to the theme of *W.G. Sebald and the Global Valences of the Critical*.

CHAPTER 32

Sebald in Translation

Martin Schauss

'Does one begin to translate elegies at the age of fifteen or sixteen because one has been exiled from one's homeland?' (Rse 182/RSg 217). This question is attributed to Michael Hamburger (1929–2007), the German-British poet and translator of Paul Celan (1920–1970) and Friedrich Hölderlin (1770–1843), who appears in *Die Ringe des Saturn* (*The Rings of Saturn*) and who would also go on to translate the poetry of his friend, W.G. Sebald. Sebald was no writer-in-exile, despite often being depicted as such, but his thematic concerns and idiosyncratic manipulation of the German language are tied to his life in England and distance from his native country and culture. The narrator of *The Rings of Saturn* thus feels an affinity with Hamburger and other such exiled, exophonic writers. He's preoccupied by the question, 'where does the urge to translate come from?' and claims that Edward FitzGerald (1809–1883) described translating Omar Khayyám (1048–1131) as 'a colloquy with the dead man' (Rse 200/RSg 238).

Sebald's translations of others were limited to a small number of poems and academic texts. However, his position as a German-language writer in England means his own work is by nature one of cultural translation. From this perspective, translation figures everywhere in Sebald's literature and raises ethical questions regarding dominant historical narratives. This understanding shapes the present essay, which gives special attention to his English translations, not only because he was heavily involved in them, but also because his *émigré* life is inextricable from his status in the anglosphere as the pre-eminent German writer of the late twentieth century.

Sebald as "Holocaust Author"?

Sebald's position as an author of world literature is reflected by translations of his prose, poetry and essays into over thirty languages. His success in the dominant anglophone market helped establish him in other countries and substantially influenced the tenor and themes of his international reception. One catalyst was Susan Sontag's celebration of *Die Ausgewanderten* (*The Emigrants*) as a 'sublime' 'masterpiece'.[1] Indeed, Sebald's remarkable success in the anglosphere from 1996 onward easily outshines the cautiously positive reception in his home nation; within months the English translation of *The Emigrants* had outsold all his German books.[2]

In France, Sebald's star rose instantaneously with publication of *Les Émigrants* in 1999 and his translator Patrick Charbonneau won the Laure Bataillon translation prize. By comparison, in Spain, *Los emigrados* (1996) initially flopped. Its translation and cover design were heavily criticized and a new edition with a revised translation was published. It was only with the Spanish version of *The Rings of Saturn* in 2000, and a change of translator, that Sebald became a household name. There were even more curious paths to fame, for example in Russia, where, fourteen years after his death, a translation of his polemic essay *Luftkrieg und Literatur* (*On the Natural History of Destruction*) and an influential essay by Maria Stepanova eventually amplified his reputation.

Despite a varied international history of interpretation (especially in recent years), focusing for example on his environmental concerns or playful repurposing of sources, Sebald has been predominantly categorized (and marketed) as a Holocaust author. There are multiple reasons for this, among them the publication to huge acclaim of *Austerlitz*, which in the anglosphere, unlike in Germany, was immediately proclaimed to be his *chef-d'oeuvre*. After his death, Sebald received the National Book Critics Circle Award for *Austerlitz*, as well as, tellingly, the Koret Jewish Book Award for his contribution to literature.[3] The American critic Richard Eder placed Sebald alongside Primo Levi as 'the prime speaker of the Holocaust',[4] one of many such awkward associations that overlooked the fact that Sebald was neither Jewish nor a survivor of the concentration camps.

Sebald's reception was also shaped by the sequence of translation, which often differed from the original order of publication. In English and many other languages, *The Emigrants* was translated first, often long before the earlier works *Nach der Natur* (*After Nature*) and *Schwindel. Gefühle.* (*Vertigo*). As Mark McCulloh notes, the elegiac tone of *The Emigrants*, its memorialization of Jewish (or partly Jewish) lives, its glum ruminations on urban decay and its mythical atmosphere of destruction 'set the tone for the future reception of his works'.[5] Indeed, although his humour has recently found more recognition in the anglosphere, Sebald's playful allusions and puns, the wry smile that accompanies the matter-of-fact tone of his originals, proved difficult to render in English, adding to the serious tone of its reception.

The Task of the English translator

Michael Hulse began work on *The Emigrants* in 1994 and the translation appeared in 1996. He then went on to translate *The Rings of Saturn* (1998) and *Vertigo* (2000). The professional relationship between the two men was difficult; Hulse's account of it can be found in *Saturn's Moons* (SM 195–208), and Sebald's version can be found in his interviews and correspondence (G 120, SM 360–361).[6]

Anthea Bell was therefore chosen to translate *Austerlitz* (2001) and *On the Natural History of Destruction* (2003), and also translated the posthumous collection, *Campo Santo* (2005). Sebald had asked Michael Hamburger to translate his first published work, *Nach der Natur* (*After Nature*, 2002), and Hamburger would also translate the collaboration with Jan Peter Tripp, *Unerzählt* (*Unrecounted*, 2004). *Über das Land und das Wasser: Ausgewählte Gedichte 1964–2001* was translated by Iain Galbraith as *Across the Land and the Water: Selected Poems, 1964–2001* (2011), while Jo Catling translated the essay volume, *Logis in einem Landhaus* (*A Place in the Country*, 2013). The two volumes on Austrian literature, *Die Beschreibung des Unglücks* and *Unheimliche Heimat* – essential in providing a fuller picture of Sebald's literary convictions – have been translated into Spanish (abridged), Portuguese and French, but are not yet available in English, apart from two essays published in academic journals.

During his lifetime, Sebald took an active part in translating the English (and, to a much lesser extent, the French) versions. He would return draft translations with countless corrections and queries, sometimes rewriting entire passages (SM 202–203). He reviewed these drafts together with his friend and departmental secretary, Beryl Ranwell, who had, he said, a 'good English ear' (SM 359). However, 'corrections' might not be quite right, as Sebald regularly overruled perfectly sound translations and changed the original meaning. As writers like Samuel Beckett (1906–1989), who translated themselves had done, Sebald sacrificed faithfulness to the original to iron out what he perceived as stylistic shortcomings of the German, or to intensify the mood or sonority of a passage.[7]

Hulse was a diligent, careful translator and paradoxically this didn't always make for an easy collaboration.[8] He remained baffled, for instance, at Sebald's treatment of non-German source materials. In *The Rings of Saturn*, Sebald had mis-rendered Joseph Conrad's English in German and changed details to suit his narrative. When Hulse queried this, Sebald admitted:

> I often change [quotations] quite deliberately. The long quote, for instance, in which Apollo describes Vologda was substantially rewritten by me. [. . .] I therefore now changed your version, which goes back to the proper source, so that it follows more closely my own (partly fabricated) rendering of the passage. There is a great deal in the text that is simply made up. (SM 200)

Refusing to go back to the original source text, Sebald in fact translated his own mistranslation once over. Playing fast and loose with "faithful" renditions is in keeping with his roguish interweaving of literary and historical materials, but it put Hulse in a tricky spot.

In Anthea Bell, Sebald found someone who more closely matched his ideal image of the translator. He had no problem complaining to Bell about her predecessor's shortcomings, about the drafts he had to send back and what he felt to be Hulse's helplessness when it came to matters botanical and entomological (at which Bell excelled).[9] Sebald felt an affinity with Bell – who was already well-known for her translations of *Asterix* – and took pleasure in the back and forth on translation puzzles like the vernacular names of butterflies (SM 212–213).

Sebald's complicated relationship with translation was bound up with his emigrant language status and what he felt to be the lack of interest in "foreign" languages and responsible translation practices in his adopted country. In 1989, Sebald set up the British Centre for Literary Translation at UEA and, throughout his academic career, taught German literature, in time adding other European literatures, reluctantly doing so in translation when required (see chapter 6 in this volume).

He intervened in theoretical conversations about translation in lectures and interviews, and his interest in how literature crossed borders, and how the hegemonic anglosphere received foreign-language writers, influenced the way he modified translations of his work. Referring to German translations of English literature, Sebald commented that nothing is more irritating than seeing the original language shine through in the target language, arguing that translators who let themselves continually be 'infected' by the original dabble in bastardized forms (G 129).

It is thus inaccurate to conclude that Sebald 'furiously re-Germanised' Hulse's translations to 'convey the original as closely as possible'.[10] His sense of a faithful and responsible translation was much more complicated than that. Above all else, he believed the English version needed to sound right and, in its own way, be as rhythmic as his original German.

Obstacles of Sebald's '*Kunstsprache*'

A more grammatically complex language such as German automatically poses problems for the English translator, and Sebald added to them with his long sentences, regionalisms (sprinklings of his native Allgäu dialect), neologisms, unacknowledged citations and archaic prose style modelled on nineteenth-century writers such as Johann Peter Hebel (1760–1826) and Gottfried Keller (1819–1890). In translation, Sebald said in an interview, 'you tend to lose some of the finer grain, particularly as regards shadings of earlier forms of German' (SM 359). He is aware of the difficulties his 'Kunstsprache' ('art(ificial) language') (G 254) causes the translator: 'the hypotactical structures of German, let alone in the form which I give them, are very difficult to render in English'.[11]

Indeed, Sebald's syntax – with its typical delay of subject and main verb in the long sentence, or the prolonged syntactical separation of corresponding elements – is a struggle for the translator seeking to recreate the rhythmic effects and vertiginous deferral of the original. What is more, English has no means to adequately represent the special subjunctive that, in German, adds 'a strong sense of the tentative, the uncertain'[12] to the reported tales of other characters while avoiding repetition of the name of the person whose speech is being reported.

Sebald's foible for antiquated terms is another puzzle. How can one convey the historical horror of a term like 'Dreiviertelarier' used to describe Paul Bereyter in *The Emigrants*? The English solution, 'three quarters an Aryan' (E 50/AW 74), is only a clinical definition. This brings up the general issue of German compounds in which each part of the word conveys meaning in addition to the whole. Consider the following simple sentence which, in the original, appears highly symptomatic not just of the speaker, Max Ferber, but of Sebald's endeavour in general: 'Die bruchstückhaften Erinnerungsbilder, von denen ich heimgesucht werde, haben den Charakter von Zwangsvorstellungen' (AW 266). Compare the English: 'The fragmentary scenes that haunt my memories are obsessive in character' (E 181). The translation softens the psychoanalytic overtones and changes the object of the 'haunting' from Ferber to Ferber's memories.

The translation loses meaning by rendering 'Erinnerungsbilder' (literally 'memory images', with an overtone of 'souvenir') as 'scenes',

'heimsuchen' (with its proximity to 'unheimlich' or 'uncanny') as 'haunt',
and 'Zwangsvorstellungen' (images that force themselves on the mind) as
'obsessive'. Even the Latin-based 'fragmentary' doesn't carry the same
notes as 'bruchstückhaft' (literally, 'like a broken piece'), which registers
more resolutely the connection between memory and *bricolage*.

We find in *Austerlitz* a passage of astonishing lexical similarity. On his train
journey through Germany, Austerlitz identifies 'das Original der so viele Jahre
hindurch mich heimsuchenden Bilder' – 'the original of the images that had
haunted me for so many years' (Ag 324/Ae 316). The English has no chance of
recreating the syntax of deferral and repression expressed in the German. In the
sentence that follows, Austerlitz experiences 'eine zweite Zwangsvorstellung,
die ich lange gehabt hatte' (Ag 316) – 'another idea which had obsessed me over
a long period' (Ae 324). The image, of a lost twin brother, is tied in the original
not only to the compulsive, involuntary (Proustian) nature of Austerlitz's
memory, but also to the emblematic passage in 'Max Ferber' cited above.
While the English versions are consistent, even lyrical, they cannot quite keep
up with the 'ghosts of repetition' (RSe 187/RSg 223) that inhabit the German
texts, an indication that the internal references that crisscross Sebald's original
œuvre can only be conveyed in part.

Another obstacle facing the translator is Sebald's inclusion of trouble-
some vocabulary such as Nazi jargon and the word 'Neger' ('negro'). It
would be easy to get swept away by his extended sentences and consistently
melancholy tone were it not for numerous discomforting linguistic
moments that interrupt our stupor. Bell comments on the difficulty of
translating the nine-page sentence containing Austerlitz's account of
Theresienstadt. It was crucial not to break up that sentence, she notes,
because its length, rhythm and gradient reflect 'the terrible, pointless,
bureaucratic industry of the Nazis'.[13]

Scattered throughout the sentence are snippets of Nazi jargon:
Heimeinkaufsverträge; *Rückkehr nicht erwünscht*; *Verschönerungsaktion* (Ae
335–339/Ag 343–347). Although these terms are defined in paraphrase, their
inclusion in German forces the English reader to consider the euphemistic
perversity of Nazi bureaucracy. The following list of extremely complicated
Nazi jargon, which occurs just prior to the long sentence, was purposely left
untranslated, in the hope that something of its ideological nature and
juxtaposition of empty rhetoric and horrific significance would nevertheless
shine through: 'I had finally discovered the meaning of such terms and
concepts as *Barackenbestandteillager, Zusatzkostenberechnungsschein, Baga-
tellreparaturwerkstätte, Menagetransportkolonnen, Küchenbeschwerdeorgane*
[. . .]' (Ae 330/Ag 338).

Sebald's use of 'Neger' in *Vertigo* and *The Emigrants* but also in his poetry and critical essays is a complicated case that cannot comprehensively addressed here. Differences in cultural context render such a racist term untranslatable, as defined by Emily Apter.[14] When the narrator is clearly ventriloquizing an antiquated, provincial viewpoint, Hulse opts for 'negro', for example when African-American GIs are described in rural Bavaria: 'as for those negroes, no one knew what to make of them' (E 70/ AW 102). One also notes the sexist term 'Weiber' (translated as 'women-folk') in the same passage. It is, however, less evident why the narrator should catch sight of a 'Negerfamilie' ('negro family') in Upstate New York (E 105/AW 154). Here and elsewhere, the translation attempts to neutralize the offending term by substituting 'black'. If, as Uwe Schütte has argued, Sebald probably intended them as intentional 'stumbling blocks' combining preservation of outdated vernacular with 'a calculated provocation that aims not to offend but to irritate the reader',[15] then the translation suggests that, in this case, Sebald's provocation might have been misguided.

Sebald was often asked why, given his excellent command of the language, he didn't write his books in English. He usually replied that he didn't feel at home in the language, and that he would be loath to abandon his native German. However, his responses were occasionally more ambiguous: 'I think that it either happens or it doesn't' (SM 363). In the end, it did happen. *For Years Now* (2001), the last book published in his lifetime, was a collection of miniature poems written in English paired with screen prints by Tess Jaray.

When Michael Hamburger embarked on the translation of *Unrecounted*, he found overlap between those German poems and the English ones in *For Years Now*, and understood that Sebald had reimagined his own poems, rendering them no more faithfully than he had his "translations" of sources incorporated into his prose. It was thus that 'only under / a dark sky' could become 'only / in brightest daylight' (Ue 3).

Notes

1. S Sontag, W.G. Sebald: The Emigrants, in: *Times Literary Supplement*, 29 November 1996.
2. U Schütte, *W.G. Sebald* (Liverpool: Liverpool University Press, 2018), p. 25.
3. On these prize awards cf. U Schütte, Gratulationen: W.G. Sebald und seine Literaturpreise, in: C Jürgensen, A Weixler (eds.), *Literaturpreise: Geschichte und Kontexte* (Stuttgart: Metzler, 2021), pp. 367–390.
4. R Eder, Excavating a Life, in: *New York Times Book Review*, 28 October 2001.

5. M McCulloh, Two Languages, Two Audiences: The Tandem Literary
   Œuvres of W.G. Sebald, in: S Denham, M McCulloh (eds.), *W.G. Sebald:
   History – Memory – Trauma* (Berlin/New York: De Gruyter, 2006), pp.
   7–20 (8).
6. Cf. also correspondence between Sebald, Hulse and Bill Swainson (DLA).
7. L Wolff, *W.G. Sebald's Hybrid Poetics: Literature as Historiography* (Berlin/
   Boston: De Gruyter, 2014), p. 225.
8. For a speculative account of their 'conflict', cf. C Angier, *Speak, Silence: In
   Search of W.G. Sebald* (London: Bloomsbury, 2021), p. 348.
9. Letters to Anthea Bell, 17 Dec [Nov?] 2000, 28 Dec [Nov?] 2000, in:
   Austerlitz Übersetzungen (Mappe 1–4) (DLA).
10. Angier, *Speak, Silence*, pp. 348–349.
11. St. Jerome Lecture 2001: W.G. Sebald in conversation with Maya Jaggi &
    Anthea Bell, in: *In Other Words: The Journal for Literary Translators* 21 (2003),
    pp. 5–18 (10).
12. McCulloh, Two Languages, p. 16.
13. A Bell, On Translating W.G. Sebald, in: R Görner (ed.), *The Anatomist of
    Melancholy: Essays in Memory of W.G. Sebald* (Munich: Iudicium, 2003), pp.
    11–18 (13).
14. E Apter, *Against World Literature: On the Politics of Untranslatability*
    (London: Verso, 2003).
15. U Schütte, Troubling Signs: Sebald, Ambivalence, and the Function of the
    Critic, in: *Boundary 2* 47:3 (2020), pp. 21–59 (53).

CHAPTER 33

The Sebaldian

Adrian Nathan West

No author has cast so long a shadow over prose writing of the past twenty years as W.G. Sebald. Indeed, he and Thomas Bernhard – whose own style is refracted, particularly in certain dialogic stretches, in Sebald's work, and whose trademark fulmination is pastiched in *Austerlitz*, in which Sebald admitted he had finally wished to pay explicit homage to the Austrian prodigy – may well be the only German-language authors of the twentieth and twenty-first centuries to have bequeathed a canon of readily identifiable verbal and syntactical peculiarities to fiction writers in a range of other languages (EM 77–86). We cannot speak of followers of Günter Grass, Ingeborg Bachmann or Heinrich Böll in English or French, and the adjective "Kafkaesque" has become as denatured as its English counterpart, "Orwellian," denoting a vulgar middle ground between bureaucratic, oppressive and weird.

But already, twenty years after Sebald's untimely death, the term "Sebaldian" calls to mind a specific set of features common to dozens of prose texts across a variety of languages. In an earlier essay, I looked specifically at Sebaldian aspects of the novels of two contemporary American authors, Ben Lerner and Teju Cole.[1] Here, I would like to offer a tentative description of the Sebaldian in the light of Sebald's broader influence on world literature. To do so, I will select intuitively a number of distinguishing marks of the Sebaldian; I say *intuitively* keeping in mind that the Sebaldian describes not that which is characteristic of Sebald's texts per se, but rather the features of a vaguely defined and still-evolving corpus of texts that imitate, incorporate, or bear the imprint of a reading of Sebald by their authors, but that also, perhaps more importantly, react and contribute to the immense prestige Sebald's writing has accumulated in the years since his death.

Embedded Photography

A hallmark of the Sebaldian text is the black-and-white photograph, generally uncaptioned. To say this is polemical, as more than a few writers have noted that such images appeared in any number of texts before the publication of Sebald's *Die Ausgewanderten* (*The Emigrants*), at times attempting in this way to gainsay his apparent influence. Javier Marías (1951–2022) and Geoff Dyer (b. 1958) have both remarked that their use of such photographs precedes Sebald's; Sebald himself attributed the idea of including images in his text in part to the influence of Alexander Kluge (b. 1932) and Klaus Theweleit (b. 1942) (G 84).

But who creates and who popularizes an artistic technique are two different questions, and the assertion of antecedents or a more or less obscure tradition behind Sebald's placement of imagery in his texts doesn't diminish his centrality in the diffusion of this practice over the past twenty years, particularly as numerous authors who have used this technique have readily acknowledged his importance to them (among them virtually all those examined in the present essay).

Terry Pitts, whose blog, *Vertigo*, has become an essential resource for Sebald scholars, maintains a comprehensive list of imagery-embedded literature. He cites as a first example of the genre Georges Rodenbach's extraordinary symbolist text *Bruges-la-Morte* (1892) and lists forty-odd imaginative works that might be conceived as predecessors; but in their failure to generate imitators, they must be thought of alternately as preliminary stages or, in the case of the many that faded into obscurity, as evolutionary dead-ends. Both Franco Moretti (b. 1950) and Colin Martindale (1943–2008) have examined artistic change in a Darwinian light, drawing on the supposition that a more or less constant rate of random variation presents evolutionary possibilities which either proliferate or perish in the artistic field, depending on whether they represent an evolutionary advantage vis-à-vis their predecessors.

A glance at the volumes on Pitts's list prior to the publication of *The Emigrants* reveals two main trends: illustrated poetry volumes and collage works emerging from or influenced by French surrealism. Apart from these, there is a smattering of works of difficult classification and occasional fictions or hybrid texts with didactic or memorialistic valences (a separate but interesting tradition is the use of collage in Black American satire among writers like Ishmael Reed (b. 1938) and Darius James, b. 1954). My sense is that the overwhelmingly avant-garde tendency of such works proved too inefficacious, in aesthetic terms, to establish embedded imagery as a literary technique of first resort for writers intent on wider readership, and that Sebald's primary innovation was the marrying of embedded imagery to the use of fiction as an instrument or signifier of moral awareness.

It is for this reason that strong moralistic tendencies appear in so much contemporary image-embedded fiction written in his wake, with a particular focus on the use of photography as testimony of forgotten or neglected crimes or tragedies, as in the work of Daša Drndić (1946–2018) or in Mathias Énard's (b. 1972) moving account of two brothers from the French Sudan conscripted to fight in World War One, then transported to a POW camp in Zossen, Germany, where the Central Powers hoped to convince them to wage jihad against the Allies.[2]

Similar developments allowed Theresa Hak Kyung Cha's *Dictée* –a difficult-to-classify work that first appeared in 1982 and that anticipates Sebald in its use of photographs and other realia to explore themes of exile and linguistic disconnection – to emerge from obscurity decades after its publication. While the #ReadWomen Twitter campaign and its knock-on effects in the press helped reconfigure the private act of reading as a public act with moral implications, increased awareness of sexual violence in the wake of the #MeToo movement shed additional light on Cha's murder, giving rise to a number of memorials, most prominently an obituary for her in *The New York Times* of 7 January 2022, part of its "Overlooked" series of significant figures whose deaths went unreported in the paper.[3]

Spurious Biography

Biography seems to have interested Sebald in the main as a focal point for affective visions and moral intuitions. This is even true in his critical writings, which present highly tendentious portraits of Peter Weiss (1916–1982), Alfred Döblin (1878–1957), Robert Walser (1878–1956) and others, to such a degree that his scholarly work is perhaps best viewed as a series of preliminary exercises for his fictions, if not as of a piece with them. The controversies surrounding the distortions or lack of acknowledgment of sources in *The Emigrants* and *Austerlitz* clearly bespeak Sebald's uninterest in biographical fidelity as such. His creative approach to the genre bears a closer resemblance to such texts as Thomas De Quincey's 'The Last Days of Immanuel Kant' (1827) or Georg Büchner's *Lenz* (1839) than to twentieth-century models.

This hybrid approach to protagonists, which makes use of but owes nothing to established fact, is now a mainstay of such contemporary novels as Kate Zambreno's *Drifts* (2020) and Agustín Fernández Mallo's *Trilogía de guerra* (*The Things We've Seen*, 2021). For Zambreno, Rainer Maria Rilke's search for a 'quiet space inside himself in which to work'[4] becomes a cipher for her own search for mental peace during pregnancy in a moment of economic precarity, thus extending a life-writing project with feminist overtones that now stretches across several books.

In *The Things We've Seen*, the monologue by Kurt, the supposed fourth astronaut on the Apollo moon mission and former soldier in Vietnam, is part and parcel of the shift in Fernández Mallo's work from a fragmentary, anecdotic aesthetics reminiscent of William S. Burroughs to a conspicuous engagement with the Sebaldian themes of war and loss as reflected in private testimony, in memory and in landscape and architecture (a change that has, moreover, paid off, with *War Trilogy* winning one of Spain's most prestigious literary prizes, the Premio Biblioteca Breve, in 2018).

An air of novelty, which Colin Martindale considers the driver for aesthetic innovation, seems to cling to the pseudo-biographical method even twenty-one years after Sebald's death. Sebald's fiction may be well known, but such examples as the International Booker judges' description of Maria Stepanova's *Pamyat', Pamyat'* (*In Memory of Memory*, 2017) as unclassifiable or Mark Haddon's assertion that Benjamín Labatut invented 'an entirely new genre' with his *Un verdor terrible* (*When We Cease to Understand the World*, 2020) reveal the extent to which the imagination of the anglophone critical establishment has yet to fully digest Sebald's influence – and the situation is little different in Europe and South America.

Archive

The archive, like the photograph, serves a legitimating effect in Sebald's texts with regard both to the events the narrator describes and the fidelity of his account of them. And an enthusiasm for the archival, even for the trappings of the archival – onomastics, sourcing, precise dating and the like – is a salient trait of recent novels in the Sebaldian mould. If above, I have referred to a range of writers of different nationalities to give some sense of the geographical extent of Sebald's influence, here I will focus on a single text, *Colonel Lágrimas* (*Colonel Lágrimas*, 2014) by Costa Rican author Carlos Fonseca (b. 1987), as exemplary of the use of archive in the post-Sebald novel.

Fonseca's subject is a Mexican mathematician residing in solitude in the Pyrenees, where he composes tales based on a succession of historical figures. The child of Russian Jewish emigrants – almost immediately, the key figure is revealed to be a classic Sebaldian loner, his birth and background bearing the scars of one of the great disasters of the twentieth century, which he takes refuge from in precise but unnecessary digressions – he witnesses war in Spain in 1936, in Paris in 1940, in Vietnam at the end of the 1960s. His thoughts on these events, rather than following a straight line from memorialization to denunciation, meander through a series of capsule biographies of the painter Mary Gartside and the trapeze artist Maria Spelterini, ruminations on alchemy, an etymology of the word *Hasid* and an account of the Tlatelolco massacre.

Fonseca's novel is in part a fictionalized account of the later years of the mathematician Alexander Grothendieck, who abandoned and repudiated his theoretical work in favour of a monastic life as a vegetarian and pacifist and wrote an extraordinary religious memoir in which he described God as the author of human dreams; as Fonseca fictionalizes Grothendieck through the character of his colonel, he strives to add verisimilitude to the colonel's surroundings by alternating between purely imagined passages, pastiches of Grothendieck's writings and the kind of ominous antiquarian trivia that abounds in Sebald's novels.

Elsewhere, referring to the role of the archive in Sebald's work, Fonseca has written 'we find in [his pages] the Janus face of our computerized society, in which everything finishes up in the archive, obsolete amid thousands of obsolete, and yet in which we feel a growing nostalgia for History in the old sense of the term.'[5] This nostalgia is borne out in the Sebaldian novel through deliberate concealment of the merely fictional whereby, just as factual elements may be freely integrated into a fictional narrative, the fictional demands redemption through archival trappings that are thought to endow it with a moral import that transcends, to quote Sebald, the 'authorial writing, where the narrator sets himself up as stagehand and director and judge and executor in a text', which he himself claimed to find 'unacceptable'.[6]

From Trait Cluster to Genre

In a review of Ben Lerner's *Leaving the Atocha Station* (2011), Hari Kunzru writes of 'an emerging genre, the novel after Sebald, its 19th-century furniture of plot and character dissolved into a series of passages, held together by occasional photographs and a subjectivity that hovers close to (but is never quite identical with) the subjectivity of the writer.'[7] I have elsewhere described this genre as the 'belletristic selfie'.[8] It is noteworthy that the Sebaldian novel emerged not during Sebald's lifetime or even immediately after his death, but closer to the 2010s, when Wikipedia and assorted social media sites began to approach peak usage. With Wikipedia, as British critic Simon Ings has noted, 'There's nothing aristocratic about erudition now. It is neither a sign of privilege, nor (and this is more disconcerting) is it necessarily a sign of industry. Erudition has become a register, like irony, like sarcasm, like melancholy.'[9]

If, in principle, Sebald's *flâneurs* are meant to be provoked into erudite or haunting recollections by their experiences and the coincidences they come across, Wikipedia and Internet resources in general have made it possible to fill in the blank spaces of more or less vague imaginative premises with research performed on the fly. At the same time, the migration of self-representations online has encouraged the rise of virtue-signalling and censorious behaviours that exert significant pressure on the publishing industry (the term virtue-signalling now has something slanderous about it, but this says nothing against the concept's utility, and there is no doubt that publishers are scrambling to offer an image of probity to their audiences and that this extends to the types of books they prefer to publish).

If Joe Moran is right that representations of the personality of the author – interviews, photographs, biographical sketches and social media artefacts – are 'primarily a means of product differentiation',[10] then the Sebaldian has come to encompass a category of authors who, not only in their prose, but also through these self-representations, adopt a fatidic solemnity with regard to various subsets of moral and aesthetic concerns already present in Sebald's work: World War Two, colonialism, the baleful and unknowable consequences of scientific progress, the voices of the suppressed and silenced and so on.

The evolutionary fitness of Sebaldian novels and their authors are evinced in their persistence over at least the past decade, and the apparent reluctance of the reading public to dismiss them as merely derivative; this in turn can likely be explained by the integration of readers into networks of self-representation in some ways analogous to those of authors, but with their identities determined by the cultural products they consume rather than those they produce. Doubters would be encouraged to visit websites like Goodreads, LibraryThing, Reddit or Twitter, or to do a Google image search for Sebald quotes. They would find an endless array of Facebook-ready selections of the author's words in wretched italic fonts splashed across stock images of seashores, mountains and cloudy skies.

Future Directions for Research

Sebald studies would benefit from a large-scale quantitative analysis of the stylistic features of his texts to the end of isolating the conceptual, lexical and syntactical peculiarities that embody the Sebaldian; such work would ideally be performed not only with the originals, but with their translations. This would allow the study of Sebald's influence to go beyond the impressionistic and would also eliminate certain traits that may at first appear Sebaldian but are in fact present in many authors' work. Sebald's long sentences are often remarked upon, but this superficial observation ignores the relative commonality of hypotaxis in literary German prose as well as alternative examples in languages into which he has been translated (in Spanish, for example, where complex sentences are the norm even in non-literary prose, a relative succinctness and an absence of modifiers is what stands out in the writing of Sebald epigones like Ricardo Menéndez Salmón, b. 1971).

Quantitative analysis would surely highlight the contrast between the salience of reported speech and the infrequency of the German Subjunctive I in which such speech is typically portrayed, a feature necessarily obscured in translation; the frequency and function of the lexeme *tatsächlich*, which generally appears in the English versions as *indeed* (part of a broader tendency towards the elevation and antiquation of Sebald's register in English) but the functions of which are distributed across a range of adverbial phrases in French and Spanish (*en fait, de fait, effectivement* and *de hecho* and *efectivamente*, respectively); the theme of scarce presences evinced by the frequent use of the word *kaum* (scarcely or hardly) across Sebald's texts; or coincidences of affective and topographical or architectural terms. Such a data-driven approach would liberate scholars from a merely impressionistic approach to Sebald's heirs through fine-grained textual comparison, while also providing a basis to observe the modulations of Sebald's influence in the coming years.

Notes

1. AN West, Nostalgia for Probity in the Era of the Selfie: W.G. Sebald's American Imitators, in: U Schütte (ed.), *Über W.G. Sebald: Beiträge zu einem anderen Bild des Autors* (Berlin/Boston: De Gruyter, 2017), pp. 283–295.
2. M Énard, *Compass* (London: Fitzcarraldo, 2017), pp. 285–295.
3. D Saltzstein, Overlooked No More, in: *New York Times*, 7 January 2022.
4. K Zambreno, *Drifts* (New York: Riverhead, 2020), p. 82.

5. C Fonseca, Marta Aponte Alsina [review], in: *Revista otra parte*, www .revistaotraparte.com/literatura-iberoamericana/pr-3-aguirre/.

6. J Wood, An Interview with W.G. Sebald, in: *Brick Magazine* 59, https://bri ckmag.com/an-interview-with-w-g-sebald/.

7. H Kunzru, Impossible Mirrors, in: *The New York Times Book Review*, 7 September 2014.

8. West, Nostalgia for Probity, p. 285.

9. S Ings, Things Mankind Was Not Supposed to Know: The Dark Side of Science, in: *Spectator*, 14 November 2020.

10. J Moran, *Star Authors: Literary Celebrity in America* (London: Pluto, 2000), p. 32.

CHAPTER 34

Film

Andrew J. Webber

Sebald's 'Kafka im Kino' ('Kafka Goes to the Movies'), a response to the volume *Kafka geht ins Kino* (*Kafka Goes to the Cinema*) by actor and author Hanns Zischler, is an established starting point for discussions of Sebald and cinema, and so too here. There is the "going to the cinema" of Zischler's title and the "being at or in the cinema" of Sebald's original German modulation. To be in the cinema can also extend to being "in cinema", whereby the writer works from within a framework conditioned by film as cultural technology – including producing texts that are ready for filming.

By considering a set of points at which Sebald's work intersects with cinema, this chapter will extend the terrain of "cinema in Sebald" to take stock of whether a limited series of textual encounters with film, some fleeting and oblique, can indeed situate the writer within the logics of the medium. To elaborate on a cue provided by Mattias Frey, cinema might be a form of echo-chamber around Sebald's writing,[1] or – given the particular visual bearing of the medium – a hall of mirrors. For, if there is a key determining feature of cinema for the purposes of Sebald's writing, it is as an apparatus that (re)produces the sorts of echoes and mirrorings that preoccupy the narrative worlds he creates.

Cinematic Histories

In 'Kafka Goes to the Movies', Sebald undertakes an essayistic experiment in being with Kafka "in the cinema", one that involves a broader scoping of the history of the medium and its place in a genealogy of visual cultural technologies. He initially invokes a trenchant experience from his own filmgoing history: a viewing of Wim Wenders' German road movie, *Im Lauf der Zeit* (*Kings of the Road*, 1976), in which Zischler played one of the protagonists.

A film about the history of cinema as an institution travelling through time, *Im Lauf der Zeit* (literally, 'in the course of time') is also intensely self-reflexive, a film-about-film. Sebald – or his essayistic persona – recalls a particular scene from it as the establishing sequence for his essay, the sort of memory that persists from a medium he sees as particularly prone to evanescence. The scene inaugurates the male friendship of this road movie, as two men are brought together in cinema. Bruno, who is 'shaving in the open air', witnesses the second man driving his Volkswagen Beetle into a river: 'For an eternal moment the Beetle sails through the air as if it had learned to fly' (CSe 157/CSg 194).

The spectacular moment of viewing is cast by memory into the suspension of an eternal present. It is captured in terms that Goethe famously applied in 1827 to the novella genre, as the film unfolds after 'this extraordinary event ('unerhörte Begebenheit'), presented by Wenders without much ado' (CSe 157/CSg 194), but in a version that, *pace* Goethe, has not happened. Firstly, Bruno is in fact shaving inside his van, and this matters, given that the vehicle, its movement, its (wind)screen and its mirrors, are so bound up with Wenders' exploration of the ontology of cinema as a travelling medium.[2] In 'Via Schweiz ins Bordell: Zu den Reisetagebüchern Kafkas' ('To the Brothel by Way of Switzerland: on Kafka's Travel Diaries'), Sebald registers the nexus of automated travel and the cinema in a reminiscence of Kafka travelling through Munich with Max Brod, with the sound of the car tyres evoking a cinematograph releasing film-like 'memory-strips' (CSe 141/CSg 180). These cinematically inflected travels with Max constitute another kind of road movie and also form the basis of the fellow-travelling across time of Sebald's narrator (as Max) and Dr. K. in *Schwindel. Gefühle. (Vertigo)*.

A similar logic of time travel is at work in the Wenders sequence. Bruno's reaction as viewer to the extraordinary event is accordingly enacted, mute and with exaggerated mimicry, as a kind of silent film sequence viewed through the windscreen – part of the film's play with the history of the medium. And the event itself is not as spectacular as Sebald apparently remembers. The 'Beetle' does not fly but ploughs straight into the water. Along with the modified echo of Goethe, it is tempting to read 'ohne viel Aufhebens' as a pun ('without much uplifting') that registers the false, or falsified, cinematic memory of lift-off. And if we can do this, we are presented here with 'being in cinema' as a particular condition of illusionism, with a constitutional bearing on Sebald's broader concern with the unreliability of things 'im Laufe der Zeit' (this, a recurrent formulation in his writings).

The misremembered sequence stands instead as a mock version of the kind of deathly experience that Sebald, joining 'Kafka in (the) cinema', sees at the affective core of the ambivalent relational proximity of cinema: the pain of 'identification' as bound up with 'estrangement' (CSe 160/CSg 197). Film viewers see themselves extinguished, again and again, through the extreme experience of the other on screen. This iterative model for film is also embedded in an intermedial network. The essay at once connects the viewing conditions of the contemporary subject, flooded by image stimulation, with those of Kafka's time, and with the more general media-archaeological constitution of cinema.

This form of being 'in (the) cinema' involves association with the logic of still photography (through the frames that make up film) and with such proto-cinematic technologies of visual spectacle as the camera obscura and the Kaiser-Panorama, and thereby with the uncanny predicaments of automatism and spectrality that Sebald, with Kafka, sees at work in such medial avatars. To echo Laura Mulvey, film emerges as a medium inflicting death twenty-four times a second.[3] It is not by chance that, both here and in *Vertigo*, Sebald imagines Kafka as an identificatory viewer of the 1913 *Doppelgänger* film, *Der Student von Prag* (*The Student of Prague*, 1913), where a parapsychological drama of suicidal self-estrangement is projected through the smoke and mirrors of the early cinematic apparatus (SG 173–174/V 151–152). This foundational cinematic spectacle serves to frame the structures of duplication, seriality and mutation that are seen to characterize Kafka's writing, and that situate Sebald and his practice alongside him. This is the logic of stereoscopy, of forms of double vision, as driven by repetition compulsion.

This also accounts for how, at the essay's end, the deceased Kafka is placed once more in the cinema for a phantom viewing of Leni Riefenstahl's *Triumph des Willens* (*Triumph of the Will*, 1935). The projected viewing, in the dark time after Kafka's death and before Sebald's birth, takes up the features of duplication and seriality from the earlier cinematic encounters in the essay and ramifies them into the sort of mass behaviour that is the particular domain of the mass medium of film, rendering it particularly susceptible to political manipulation. The focus on the encampment and the figures emerging from it in order to form the throng congregating around the *Führer*, is part of a leitmotif in Sebald's attention to cinema as an identificatory medium of gathered viewing.

It will return as such in the recalling of Austerlitz's father's viewing of the 'spectacular' Riefenstahl film (Ag 243–244/Ae 239) and seeing the camp-followers of National Socialism streaming into the march of history. It also

connects with those who are subject to the violence of that march and
a preoccupation with nomadic, extraterritorial states of being that is
particularly attuned to the itinerant and time-based workings of cinema.

Displaced Persons

Cinematic nomadism plays a particular role in *Die Ausgewanderten* (*The
Emigrants*), as in the scene from the 'Ambros Adelwarth' narrative where
Cosmo over-identifies with the 'mirror reversals' (E 97/AW 141) of cinematic spectacle in a psychotic encounter with Fritz Lang's *Dr. Mabuse, der
Spieler* (*Dr. Mabuse, the Gambler*, 1922). As noted by Carol Jacobs, the
desert caravan that is seen by Cosmo to emerge from the screen and bear
him away in Lang's fantasy drama of hypnotic illusion also resonates with
the final dream sequence from another classic of New German Cinema and
filmic intertext for *The Emigrants*: Werner Herzog's *Jeder für sich und Gott
gegen alle* (*The Enigma of Kaspar Hauser*, 1974).[4] A viewing of this film of
a displaced person is recalled by Sebald's narrator in the 'Dr. Henry
Selwyn' narrative, and here too the memory of being in (the) cinema is
embedded in a composite apparatus of image projection, integral to
Sebald's broader preoccupation with optics.

The scene is set by a viewing of a slide-show, with the images projected
onto a screen in a wooden frame. As Jacobs notes, the German term
'Leinwand' ('screen') (AW 26/E 17) does service as both canvas and
(metonymically) cinema screen,[5] with painting and film bound together
through the mediation of photographic slides. The screen is placed in front
of a mirror, in a way that both resonates with the specularity of images
(how they mirror things but also offer themselves as mirrors for viewers)
and – through the blocking by the canvas – with the blind mirrors that run
through Sebald's work. The pictures tremble on the screen, as if caught
between the conditions of still and moving image. The crypto-cinematic
viewing scene is also characterized by the spectacle of dust in the cone of
light from the projector, described as a 'prelude to the pictures themselves'
(E 17/AW 26). As in the cinematic experience recalled by Dr K. in *Vertigo*,
where film images are seen to develop out of the dust particles in the cone
of light (SG 172/V 150), the apparatus becomes involved in what is
projected (see chapter 28 in this volume).

When one of the images – a Cretan landscape, flooded by light, with
a mountain appearing as a 'mirage' (E 18/AW 28) behind – is held too long,
the glass of the slide cracks, and the logic of projection (the specular casting
of an image onto another surface) means that the damage is experienced as

a tear transferred to the screen. It is this image, cracked in glass and apparently torn on canvas, that provokes the narrator's memory of seeing a similar scene in the Herzog film at a London cinema. The narrator describes the scene where Kaspar introduces his dream of the Caucasus, which – unlike the dream of the desert caravan earlier in the film – is projected without voice-over narration.

Dream and dreaming subject are collapsed in the grammar of the formulations that introduce the mind-screen sequence, culminating in Bruno S.'s (grammatically inaccurate) phrase in Berlin dialect: 'mich hat vom Kaukasus geträumt' ('the Caucasus dreamt me'). Sebald's narrator describes the camera tracking from right to left over a panoramic landscape, though without noting that there is also a break here, as the continuity of the tracking sequence is interrupted and restarted from a different point. If this is a 'panoramic view' (E 18/AW 29), then it should also be understood in a media-archaeological sense, as we are presented with a canvas, a still image, in which the only motion is that of camera's uneven, jittery scan, punctuated by the break in its transmission.

Cinema after Sebald

Such scenes from (the) cinema, remembered and misremembered, with their self-reflexive character in relation to the production and reception of images through film, and what is given, held and lost in that process, have a bearing also on the question of Sebald as represented in cinema. Sebald's writing, punctuated by photographic images, with its exploratory attention to the visual evidence of things, might seem to lend itself to film, in the mode of slow cinema and with a particular affinity to the essay genre.

Grant Gee, who made the film *Patience: After Sebald* (2012) as a tribute through re-enactment of the narrative odyssey in *Die Ringe des Saturn* (*The Rings of Saturn*), describes that appeal not least as an effect of the particular texture and quality of the imagery in Sebald's writing.[6] This also accounts for the aesthetic bearing of Tacita Dean's 2007 essay film, *Michael Hamburger*, which takes its cue from Sebald's encounter with the émigré poet and translator in one of the episodes of *The Rings of Saturn*. Dean's film watches attentively, from a perspective that is constantly framed and measured, where the possibility of coming together with its human subject is deferred and displaced by exquisite attention to images from his environment.[7]

And the same sort of logic of displacement applies to the implicit cinematographic treatment of Sebald's narrator's reading of the iconography of Rembrandt's *Anatomy Lesson of Dr Nicolaes Tulp* (1632) in Christian Petzold's *Barbara* (2012). The articulated viewing afforded by the 'anatomical' camerawork serves to highlight the condition of absence that haunts the text's rendering of the painting and its visual evidence, and the distance from the human subject on the dissection slab at its centre.[8]

The 2014 film *Austerlitz* by Stan Neumann also explores the tension between the potential for identification (of or with self and of or with others) and the estrangement to which it is subject in Sebald's novel *Austerlitz* (2001) and in his work at large. Neumann's *Austerlitz* melds the essay form, in an account of his own identificatory experience with the text, and a fictional (re-)enactment of key scenes from it, with Austerlitz played by Denis Lavant. The balding Lavant, with his gnarled physiognomy, is established as a figure of identification for Sebald's Austerlitz, notwithstanding the comparison of the ever-youthful protagonist with Fritz Lang's Siegfried (Ag 10/Ae 6). In its representation of Austerlitz's practice of photographic bricolage, drawing on images in Sebald's archive and mapping their scrutiny via exploration of key sites from the narrative, the film ramifies the text's effects of visual displacement and blocking, what Dora Osborne calls its blind-spots.[9]

Neumann's Austerlitz, as cinematic double, thus engages in a reconstruction of the reconstructions recorded in Sebald's text, with scenes from the narrative at once proffered for the time-based viewing that film can afford and recurrently subject to the distancing intervention of the apparatus. The frame of the viewfinder of Austerlitz's camera, scanning architectural features – not least, blind windows – and other scenes, combines the logic of still and motion images, as though it were a movie camera producing films within the film.

Neumann also incorporates sequences from both the Nazis' propaganda film of the Theresienstadt ghetto, re-enacting the slow-motion scrutiny described in Sebald's text (Ag 352/Ae 345), and the more obliquely referenced cinematic exploration of the vicissitudes of memory, *Last Year in Marienbad* (1961), directed by Alain Resnais (Ag 293/Ae 289). The two works – the falsified documentary and the riddling fiction film – and the proliferating still photographs alike are accordingly interrogated for their testimonial reliability, for the account they can give of lives lived in particular places and times.

Sebald's 'archival subjects', to recall JJ Long's characterization of Austerlitz,[10] derive in part from film archives, ranging from *The Student of Prague*, caught between the cinema of attractions and narrative film, through the 'doppelgangers and shadow figures' (CSe 148/CSg 186) of

Weimar cinema, via Nazi documentaries, wartime newsreels, mid-century education films, and the French and German new waves. Resnais' essay film, *Toute la mémoire du monde* (*All the World's Memory*, 1956), positing the Bibliothèque nationale in Paris as global archive, is accordingly an apt filmic reference near the end of *Austerlitz*.

Indeed, another film could be added to the archive, encoded in the reference to Austerlitz's mother playing Olympia from Offenbach's *Hoffmanns Erzählungen* in 1938 (Ag 230/Ae 226), the year in which Riefenstahl released her encomium to the Berlin games, entitled *Olympia*. Behind those archives lie the pre-cinematic cultural technologies of the camera obscura, the diorama, the panorama and still photography as an avatar persisting alongside cinema.

Documentary Afterlives

In the films that have been inspired by Sebald's narratives, the archival subjects – protagonists and narrators – are subject in turn to forms of re-production or post-production, as the cross-medial holdings continue to accrue. A paradigmatic case for this approach is presented by the Ukrainian film maker Sergei Loznitsa. His film *On the Natural History of Destruction* (2022) borrows the title (of the English version) of Sebald's book *Luftkrieg und Literatur* and is inspired by, though not based on, his essayistic collection. Rather, Loznitsa's film draws on archive footage of the aerial bombing of German cities underlaid with historic audio material and quotations from Sebald's book.

By contrast, Loznitsa intentionally avoided referring to Sebald's text in his documentary film *Austerlitz* (2016). This critique of 'dark tourism' shows masses of summer-time tourists at former concentration camps such as Sachsenhausen and Auschwitz, limits itself to the perspective of a silent observer who records behaviour with his camera. The film took the title of Sebald's book in order to emphasize diametrically opposed approaches to the Holocaust: commercially exploited tourist attractions versus the twentieth-century heart of darkness, which Sebald believes literature can and should only approach tangentially. With cinematic means, Loznitsa – implicitly but provocatively – poses a central question about the role of sites imbued with the horror of the Holocaust in today's culture of memory.

Sebald himself has also been the subject of documentary filmwork by German director Thomas Honickel, who examined Sebald's work and life from a dual perspective. Starting in 2006, borrowing the biographical approach Sebald preferred, he undertook a pioneering filmic quest for the traces the author had left behind. The result was the film portrait *W.G. Sebald: Der Ausgewanderte* (*W.G. Sebald. The Emigrant*, 2007), in which he asked relatives, school friends, companions and colleagues for their memories of Sebald.[11] In a parallel endeavour, Honickel created the film essay *Sebald. Orte.* (*Sebald. Places.*, 2007), which features buildings, cities and landscapes with significance for Sebald's life and playing a central role in his work.

Honickel's two films provide us with a complementary dual perspective on Sebald by cinematically emulating his poetics. He translates the Sebaldian iconotext into filmic images, questions witnesses about the subject of his biographical interest, and – with excerpts from texts and voice-over commentaries – inserts mute buildings and places into an intermedial dialogue that translates Sebald's literary methodology into another form of afterlife in the language of documentary film.

Notes

1. M Frey, Theorizing Cinema in Sebald and Sebald with Cinema, in: L Patt (ed.), *Searching for Sebald: Photography after W.G. Sebald* (Los Angeles: Institute of Cultural Inquiry, 2007), pp. 226–241 (229).
2. A Webber, Narcissism and Alienation: Mirror-images in the New German Cinema, in: M Brady, H Hughes (eds.), *Deutschland im Spiegel seiner Filme* (London: CILT, 2000), pp. 118–137.
3. L Mulvey, *Death 24x a Second: Stillness and the Moving Image* (London: Reaktion, 2005).
4. C Jacobs, *Sebald's Vision* (New York: Columbia University Press, 2015), pp. 33–34.
5. Ibid., p. 193 (n. 32).
6. G Gee in interview, https://celluloidwickerman.com/2017/09/11/interview-grant-gee-james-leyland-kirby-the-caretaker-on-w-g-sebald-hauntology/.
7. A Webber, Visiting Michael Hamburger on Film, in: J Crick et al. (eds.), *From Charlottenburg to Middleton: Michael Hamburger (1924–2007): Poet, Translator* (Munich: Iudicium, 2010), pp. 98–112.
8. A Webber, Good Work: Speed, Slowness and Taking Care in Christian Petzold's ›Barbara‹, in: A Fuchs, JJ Long (eds.), *Time in German Literature and Culture, 1900–2000: Between Acceleration and Slowness* (Basingstoke: Palgrave, 2015), pp. 173–188.
9. D Osborne, Blind Spots: Viewing Trauma in W.G. Sebald's ›Austerlitz‹, in: *Seminar* 43:4 (2007), pp. 517–533.

10. JJ Long, *W.G. Sebald: Image, Archive, Modernity* (Edinburgh: Edinburgh University Press, 2007), p. 162.

11. Transcriptions of the close to thirty interviews conducted in Britain and Germany can be found in T Honickel, *Curriculum Vitae: Die W.G. Sebald-Interviews*, ed. U Schütte, K Wolfinger (Würzburg: Königshausen & Neumann, 2021).

CHAPTER 35

Pop Music

Hendrik Otremba

W.G. Sebald lived in England from 1966 until his death in 2001. During this period, the country became a hotbed of pop culture, which had a significant impact on countries across the western world. In terms of the development of pop music, this boom stretches from the Beatles' experimental turn of the late 1960s to the prog rock of the early 1970s and to punk towards the end of the decade. The multiple experimental facets of post punk then marked another artistic apex at the beginning of the 1980s, leading eventually to the emergence of rave music, resonating in the success story of the Brit Pop of the 1990s, whose influence on major bands is still felt today.

Both British and German contemporary literature were influenced by this boom in pop music. The literary scene of the 1990s, the decade in which Sebald published most of his literary works, was shaped by references to, and intermedial interactions between, pop culture and literature, as exemplified in the novels of Nick Hornby and Irvine Welsh. Germany saw the arrival of the genre of "pop-literature" in the second half of the 1990s, as epitomized by novels such as Christian Kracht's *Faserland* (*Fatherland*, 1995) or Benjamin von Stuckrad-Barres' *Soloalbum* (1998).

Sebald's writings, however, were not in the least affected by the developments in pop music and pop culture in his chosen country, and he also remained detached from trends in the German literary scene. With the exception of a distinctive passage in *Die Ausgewanderten* (*The Emigrants*), neither his works nor his interviews indicate that his literary and critical works were influenced by popular music. There seems, then, to be a gaping gulf between Sebald and pop music – it simply did not concern him.

Classical and Amateur Music: Sebald's Passions

Sebald was instead interested in classical music, particularly that of the Romantic era. However, his literary works contain no distinctive clues that would point towards an intensive reception of classical music. At best,

these traces are found in his essays, such as when he writes of Gustav
Mahler (1860–1911) that 'the passages of his music I like best are those
where you can still hear the Jewish village musicians playing in the distance'
(CSe 143/CSg 182). The most detailed references to classical music can
instead be found in interviews, such as the radio interviews in which Sebald
discusses Johann Sebastian Bach (1685–1750) and Vincenzo Bellini (1891–
1936).

Two composers fascinated Sebald in particular: Franz Schubert (1797–1828)
and Robert Schumann (1810–1856). In an interview, he remarked that
Schubert was 'for me, the most unfathomable of all. In his works there is an
odd chromaticism that reminds me of something I cannot think back to,
that's how far behind me it is' (G 153). As well as being mentioned in the
Corsica Project (KP 187), Sebald comes to speak of Schubert in his essay on
the poet Mörike, where he pays tribute to the 'masterful strokes of genius [. . .]
readily to be found in the hidden shifts of his chamber music' (PC 79/LH 88).

Of all composers, however, it was Schumann that had the most
profound impact on Sebald. The composer from Düsseldorf appears
repeatedly in Sebald's poetry of the early 1980s.[1] In 1985 Sebald even
seriously considered writing a film script about Schumann's life,
likely motivated by his tragic end: Schumann famously attempted
to take his own life by jumping into the Rhine in 1854, leading to
his subsequent admission to a psychiatric institution. Though Sebald
abandoned his plans for the film script, the composer remained
lodged in his memory, as is evidenced by Austerlitz and Marie's
brief discussion of 'poor Schumann' (Ae 301/Ag 309).

Just as significant as his passion for classical music – potentially even
more so – was Sebald's interest in forms of popular music which can
heuristically be classified as "amateur music". This affinity for music
beyond the conservatoire and the charts can in turn be traced back to
Sebald's predilection for the self-taught, hobbyists and dilettantes of all
kinds (see chapter 18 in this volume.) Worth mentioning here is the
amateur ensemble of circus musicians who appear in both the Corsica
Project (KP 185–187) and *Austerlitz*, playing a 'transverse flute, a rather
battered tuba, a drum, a bandoneon, and a fiddle' (Ae 382/Ag 388), but
also the

> Lithuanian buskers in the pedestrian zone of a north German town [. . .]
> One had an accordion, another a battered tuba, the third a double bass. As
> I listened, hardly able to tear myself away, I understood why Wiesengrund
> once wrote of Mahler that his music was the cardiogram of a breaking heart.
> (CSe 143/CSg 182)

Music by such travelling amateur musicians is celebrated by the narrator in the most emphatic, glorifying terms It is the very unprofessionalism of these musicians that allows them to create stunning music, the likes of which the narrator has never heard before:

> From the first piece onwards, it felt as if I were listening to something that had long faded away yet with which I was deeply acquainted, a kind of village music that is produced when none of the musicians can read music, and the instruments are a little out of tune and falling apart. (KP 187)

Now, given Sebald's broad lack of interest in pop music, his influence on an array of important figures in the world of pop music is even more striking. Some of today's globally most significant musicians either declare themselves to be keen readers of his works, name his books as a defining influence, or produce art that makes concrete reference to his writings. At the same time, connections inspired by Sebald can be observed in the transmedial threshold between music and literature, especially when musicians start to work as authors too, or they are already active in both artistic disciplines. His writings, as can be clearly demonstrated, have also inspired representatives of contemporary experimental music, and influenced them down to the formal aspects of their work.

Pop Music and (Failed) Memory

In Sebald's works, pop music appears only in accidental flashes – as unexpectedly as a reproduction of Grünewald's Isenheim Altarpiece in the stairwell of a Northern Irish farmhouse in the film *Cal* (1984). Mark Knopfler produced the soundtrack to this film, and Sebald once requested the instrumental piece 'The Long Road' whilst participating in a German radio programme (G 135). While this borderline kitschy Knopfler composition exemplifies the branch of pop music based on guitars, Sebald dismisses the electronic branch of pop music in an essay on Austrian literature as 'ghastly'.[2]

Given how detached Sebald was from pop music, it is all the more salient that a quotation from the Rolling Stones song 'As Tears Go By' (1965) is woven into *The Emigrants*: 'The songs they played dated from the Sixties, songs I heard countless times in the Union bar in Manchester. It is the evening of the day. The vocalist, a blonde girl with a voice still distinctly child-like, breathed passionately into the microphone, which she held up close to her lips with both hands. She was singing in English, though with a pronounced French accent. *It is the evening of the day, I sit and watch the children play*' (E 121/AW 178–179). The Stones' piece, though, is not identified as the source of the quote. Another reference to pop music is found soon afterwards, where the narrator names only the performer and the corresponding song title. The original German text says: 'Procul Harum. *A whiter shade of pale.* Die reine Rührseligkeit. [Pure sentimentality.]' (AW 178).[3]

The text thus implies that the Stones lyrics quoted above are taken from a song by Procul Harum. This unreliable attribution leads us to suspect that Sebald intended to reflect on his central theme – failing or unreliable memory – by means of pop music. Tellingly, the French singer of the amateur band covering 'A Whiter Shade of Pale' is described as follows: 'At times, when she could not remember the proper words, her singing would become an ethereal hum' (E 121/AW 178). Whatever cannot be remembered via words, can only be hummed. The unaccompanied melody testifies to the failure of memory, and yet the result can indeed be wonderful.

Sebald and the Musical Avantgarde (Caretaker, Fratti, Heemann)

The album perhaps most known for its connection to Sebald is *Patience (After Sebald)* (2012), the soundtrack to Grant Gee's essay film of the same name, created by the British avant-garde musician The Caretaker (Leyland James Kirby). The album contains more than one parallel with Sebald's literary techniques and themes. Music is used as a source to turn towards the past, and simultaneously to thematize the occasional failure of attempts to remember. The source material for the soundtrack was a gramophone record, marked with heavy signs of wear and tear, of Schubert's song cycle *Winterreise* (*Winter Journey*, 1827).[4]

Kirby created his music via the distortion of sound material – a method typical of his Caretaker project – and by emphasizing the inadequacies of the original source material, which in extreme cases manipulated the old recording beyond recognition. Kirby's music undertakes acoustically what the poetics of Sebald's texts seeks to achieve: the pieces of his soundtrack associate motifs such as loneliness, memory and disappearance by only allowing limited acoustic access to its source (*Winter Journey*), by virtue of the old, worn shellac record's medial shortcomings (see chapter 28 in this volume).

Kirby's musical works thus far are arguably the clearest example of the hauntological, following Jacques Derrida and Mark Fisher.[5] In this case he turns to the supernatural, which haunts Sebald's writing via its confrontation with the ghosts of the past. The connection to Sebald becomes even more distinct when we consider the titles of the twelve pieces of which the soundtrack consists, as they refer to significant passages from *Die Ringe des Saturn* (*The Rings of Saturn*). The tracks can be viewed as hauntological meditations, whose intoxicating, peaceful sound evokes an effect similar to that produced by a concentrated reading of Sebald's texts.

The Guatemalan musician Mabe Fratti's second album, *Será que ahora podremos entendernos* (*Will We Now Be Able to Understand Each Other?*, 2021), is indebted to a musical engagement with Sebald, as too is her debut album *Pies Sobre La Tierra* (*Feet on the Ground*, 2019). Fratti explicitly 'cited the ambulatory, multi-layered narrative of W.G. Sebald's *The Rings of Saturn* as a source of inspiration.'[6]

Vocally, Fratti certainly represents a more conventional form of pop music, although her experiments are grounded in a style of cello playing that is similar to Arthur Russell's. Though lyrics in Fratti's works are limited and prone to repetition, her method of constructing music allows for a comparison with Sebald: 'Like the narrator of Sebald's novel, Fratti wanders through *Será que ahora podremos entendernos* building each song from improvisations between fixed start and end points.'[7] As is the case in Sebald's *The Rings of Saturn*, Fratti's music progresses by association and spur of the moment, that is to say: it is governed by Sebaldian principles such as detour, wandering off the beaten track, getting lost, and pausing for melancholic reflection.

In 2012, the German experimental musician Christoph Heemann published, in an overt reference to Sebald, an instrumental album called *The Rings of Saturn*, which consists of barely intelligible voice recordings, field recordings, minimalistic sound fragments and the stripped-back playing of electronic instruments. Over a period of ten years Heemann read Sebald's prose work repeatedly so as to devote himself to it on a tonal level.

Consequently, Heemann's work can be described as a musical rendition of his reading experience. The album embarks upon an acoustic search which, thanks to its long gestation, translates Heemann's extensive intellectual interaction with the text into a web of sound. It is in this way that seven of the untitled songs develop images, the concreteness of which varies. These images, each of differing accessibility, bear a resemblance to the excursions of Sebald's English pilgrimage. Oscillating between clarity and abstraction, they leave the reader with a dense, demanding listening experience.

Sebald was influential in the development of each of the three examples from the domain of avant-garde music examined above. Through these examples, it becomes evident that Sebald's influence makes itself felt more clearly in their formal language than in their lyrics, which are in any case largely absent as the songs are primarily instrumental pieces. The process of (here tonal) wandering can be considered a principle learnt from Sebald.

Sebald, Pop and Writing Musicians

Sebald is often named as a favourite author, especially amongst artists who work as both musicians and writers. This affinity for Sebald is typically stronger than the mere naming of names. *The Rings of Saturn* occupies a special place in Sebald's corpus of works, and Nick Cave, for example, includes it in his list of the twelve novels that were most significant for him (alongside works by Melville, Nabokov, Faulkner et al.).[8] Cave's album *Skeleton Tree* (2016) contains a piece named 'Rings of Saturn', which reflects on the failure to communicate with a woman due to emotional paralysis. The rings of Saturn constitute the final motif of the lyrics: 'And then [she] reaches high and dangles herself like a child's dream from the rings of Saturn.'

Cave's highly melancholy œuvre often finds itself in Sebald-style atmospheres of loss and suffering, evoked by the performance of music in a fragile, sorrowful voice. What is striking about 'Rings of Saturn' is the immense density of the song's lyrics. Such lyrical density is typical of Cave as it is, but here it reaches an ephemeral climax, thus bringing together the song writing and prose writing of an artist who has seen considerable success with his numerous albums and two novels.[9]

Patti Smith also names Sebald's works in her list of recommended reads.[10] She gave a concert entitled *Max: A Tribute* as part of the 2011 festival *After Sebald: Place and Re-Enchantment*, held at Snape Maltings, Suffolk. Here, Smith recited a previously unpublished poem dedicated to Sebald, alongside passages from *Nach der Natur (After Nature)*.[11]

In her prose volume *M Train* (2015), Smith dedicates three pages to Sebald, and describes *After Nature* as a drug that opened paths into countless new worlds. She also pays an extremely poetic homage to the writer:

> He squats on the damp earth and examines a curved stick. An old man's staff or a humble branch turned with the saliva of a faithful dog? He sees, not with eyes, and yet he sees. He recognizes voices within silence, history within negative space. He conjures ancestors who are not ancestors, with such precision that the gilded threads of an embroidered sleeve are as familiar as his own dusty trousers.[12]

Illustration 24 – Patti Smith, Snape Maltings, January 2011

The inspiration Smith drew from Sebald can clearly be seen in her literary writings, in which she borrows his motifs and adapts his techniques. Sebald's perspective of the wandering first-person narrator, who converses with the ghosts of history, is similarly employed in her prose work *The Year of the Monkey* (2019). The book describes an aimless pilgrimage, which she relates aesthetically to Sebald's works by means of photographs inserted into the text.

Smith, who launched her career first as a poet in the early 1970s and later entered the world of punk rock through the scene around the New York Punk club CBGB, has always been a prominent admirer of poets such as Charles Baudelaire (1821–1867) or William Blake (1757–1827), whom she honours via readings combined with memorial concerts. Traces of their writing are also present in Smith's extensive lyrical works, whilst in her prose writing no influence is formally as striking as Sebald's.

The Scottish musician David Byrne, a founding member of New York band Talking Heads, takes *The Rings of Saturn* as the starting point of his *Bicycle Diaries* (2009) in order to shed light on the present by reflecting on the past, discussing his bicycle journeys through some of the world's largest metropoles in the style of a pilgrimage. His experiences on two wheels enable him to ruminate on various themes of civilization: prompted by what he sees, Byrne reflects on architecture, memory, history, art, philosophy and knowledge, thus programmatically following the example of his literary role model. Byrne here consciously applies to his cycle ventures Sebald's approach of using walking as an opportunity to bring together anecdotes and excurses in a narrative style, and he nods to his idol through this respectful adaptation.

In Germany, where Sebald enjoys notably less fame as a writer, overt references to him by musicians are also few and far between. Dirk von Lowtzow, though, names him not just as an important author in a biographical sense,[13] but also pays homage to Sebald in the lyrics to 'Sirius', which are based on facets of the Sebaldian cosmos. The songwriter, singer, and guitarist of "discourse rockers" Tocotronic, which was founded in 1993 and has since enjoyed sustained popularity in Germany, is known for his lyrics' rich array of references and allusions.

The title song of the EP *Sirius* (2022) begins with a clear nod to *The Rings of Saturn*: 'Die letzten Tage im August / Stehe ich unter dem Sirius' ('When August draws to an end, / I stand under the sign of the Dog Star', cf. RSg 11/RSe 3). In the lyrics of the song, which itself is marked by reverberating vocals and gentle guitar chords, the astrological influence of the dog sign Sirius is related to the melancholy present in Sebald's book, whose original title was *Unter dem Hundestern* ('Under the Dog Star').

Like Sebald, Lowtzow portrays literary writing and artistic work as an obsession, an unhealthy habit, or a craving for recognition, whereby he understands artistic creation as a complex compulsion that does not necessarily honour its promise of salvation. In the direct address to Sirius there emerges a closeness that recounts a humble submission to writing, just as the writing of *The Rings of Saturn* may have signified for Sebald.

Conclusion: Why *The Rings of Saturn*?

By this point, I have stated often enough that combing through Sebald's works for references to pop music does not at all yield a great many results. Rather, a passion for classical music shines through in interviews with Sebald, as well as in the autobiographical memoir 'Moments musicaux'. In this essay, Sebald acknowledges his aversion to, or even rejection of, Bavarian folk music, which he described as having 'taken on in retrospect the character of something terrible which I know will pursue me to my grave' (CSe 183/CSg 224–225). In this regard, not only is Adorno's damning verdict of the musical products of the culture industry responsible for Sebald never developing an interest in forms of popular music, but so too are Sebald's encounters with the popular musical style of the foothills of the Alps.

Yet, Sebald's influence on renowned representatives of the sphere of pop music remains remarkable. It is striking that these musicians almost unanimously name *The Rings of Saturn* as a source of inspiration. The reason for this is seemingly that the mode of narration of the prose work is comparable to a specific musical principle: as is the case on an album or in a song, the listener/reader experiences the passing of time via a wandering journey (i.e., by listening to music), which is sustained by a melancholy emotional state. Excursions, in the form of songs, are undertaken in this basic mood. These excursions are based on a fundamental interest in knowledge, and they ruthlessly recapitulate the horrifying crimes of civilization.

Not only does the narrative process of *Rings of Saturn* make possible a convergence of literature and pop music by means of its formal distinctiveness, but so too does the melancholy foundation of the narrated content. Furthermore, Sebald's influence on the literary works of some of the artists named above is a further indication of their intellectual proximity. Sebald's wandering, melancholic, historicizing gaze can be identified as a point of reference in songs, album concepts, formal approaches, conscious transmedial translations and literary works.

It is for this reason that his book on the narrator's walk through East Anglia proves itself to be Sebald's true *opus magnum*, thanks to the success of its seamless, discursive method of montage. It is nothing less than a treasure trove of tools, from which popular culture has drawn, and from which it will continue to draw in the future.

Notes

1. U Schütte, *Figurationen: Zum lyrischen Werk von W. G. Sebald* (Eggingen: Isele, 2014), pp. 122–127.
2. Sebald, Damals vor Graz: Randbemerkungen zum Thema Literatur & Heimat, in: K Bartsch, G Melzer (eds.), *Trans-Garde: Die Literatur der 'Grazer Gruppe'* (Graz: Droschl, 1990), pp. 141–153 (152).
3. It is noteworthy that the translation omits both the band name and the slightly derogatory qualification of the song by the narrator, only stating its title: 'A whiter shade of pale' (E 121).
4. F Schwabel, Intermediale Formen der Sebald-Rezeption in der populären Musik, in: P Ferstl (ed.), *Dialogues Between Media* (Berlin/Boston: De Gruyter, 2021), pp. 251–261 (254).

5. M Fisher, *Ghosts of My Life: Writings on Depression, Hauntology and Lost Futures* (Winchester: Zero, 2014).

6. https://pitchfork.com/reviews/albums/mabe-fratti-sera-que-ahora-podremos-entendernos/.

7. Ibid.

8. www.theredhandfiles.com/recommend-your-favourite-texts/.

9. N Cave, *And the Ass Saw the Angel* (London, Black Spring Press, 1989), *The Death of Bunny Monroe* (London, Canongate, 2009).

10. www.themarginalian.org/2015/11/02/patti-smith-favorite-books-m-train/.

11. U Schütte, *Annäherungen: Sieben Essays zu W.G. Sebald* (Cologne: Böhlau, 2019), pp. 254–255, Schwabel, Intermediale Formen, pp. 252–253.

12. P Smith, *M Train* (London: Bloomsbury, 2015), p. 67.

13. www.welt.de/print/die_welt/literatur/article191438803/Biografie-in-Buechern-Dirk-von-Lowtzow-Musiker.html.

CHAPTER 36

Literary Prizes

Uwe Schütte

'Car crash kills author tipped for Nobel Prize'[1] is how Sebald's death was announced in the right-wing newspaper *The Telegraph*. Robert McCrum's obituary for the *Guardian* referred to him 'being spoken of as a likely Nobel laureate'.[2] While speculative at the time of his death in December 2001, the prediction that Sebald was destined for the highest literary acclaim was not implausible given how celebrated *Austerlitz* has been in the anglophone world, with its author at the height of his international fame when he died.[3]

Obituaries in Sebald's native country, by contrast, mostly registered their surprise at the estimation of his literary calibre overseas. Writing for *Frankfurter Rundschau*, Thomas Medicus, for instance, marvelled with reference to Mel Gussow's tribute in *The New York Times*: 'Sebald a contender for the Nobel Prize? The literary elite gathered in *The New York Times*, who've appropriated him as one of their own, as a "writer's writer", clearly seem to think so.'[4]

One reviewer of Sebald's collected essays on Alemannic literature, *A Place in the Country*, even conjures up a vision of hand-wringing despair in the Royal Swedish Academy at the news of the author's unexpected passing:

> One pictures the Swedish Academy, who had considered Sebald a contender for its high prize, folding its hands in grief at the sad news, and looking out their stately drawing room windows in hopes of finding some other worthy Nobel laureate in the palm of the desperate continent.[5]

Yet the solidifying of rumours and speculation over Sebald's tragically missed Nobel accolades into hard certainties in the first decade after his death was in fact due to a consequential misapprehension: in an interview with the Swedish popular magazine *Vi* in 2007, Horace Engdahl, a member of the Nobel Committee for Literature, was asked if there were any recently deceased authors who could, in his opinion, have received the award. Engdahl's strictly personal assessment, in which he mentions Sebald alongside Ryszard Kapuściński (1932–2007) and Jacques Derrida (1930–2004),[6] taken in conjunction with already circulating rumours regarding Sebald's Nobel contention, then hardened into the misleading claim that he had actually featured on a shortlist of prospective laureates.[7]

Sebald's Literary Standing in Germany

There is no mention anywhere in the German press of surprise or regret at the fact that Sebald never received Germany's most prestigious literary award, the Büchner Prize, which is awarded annually by the Deutsche Akademie für Sprache und Dichtung (German Academy for Language and Literature), the country's most renowned literary society. Sebald was made a corresponding member of the society in October 1996, in at least partial tribute to the quality of the four literary works he had published by this point: from *Nach der Natur* (*After Nature*) in 1988 to *Die Ringe des Saturn* (*The Rings of Saturn*) in 1995.

However, membership in the Academy is neither a prerequisite for, nor a guarantee of, receiving the Büchner Prize. Sebald did appear on a long list in 1997 and even made it onto the short list for the prize, but he didn't receive it. He continued to be long-listed every year between 1998 and 2001,[8] but opposition from jury members whom he had offended with his often highly polemical literary-critical attacks from the early stages of his academic career on respected authors such as Carl Sternheim (1878–1942), Alfred Döblin (1878–1957) and, later, Alfred Andersch (1914–1980) meant that he consistently failed to attract enough votes for the award itself.

His indiscriminate denunciation of German post-war literature in his Zurich lectures on the air-war in German literature (1998/99) *On the Natural History of Destruction* played a further significant role in this and contributed to his status as something of a *persona non grata* in German culture and academia (see chapter 24 in this volume). By contrast, Sebald's critical polemicizing had no effect on the wealth of awards he received internationally, where he was recognized on the merit of his literary achievements alone.

Early Success

Even if he was denied the ultimate national and international honours, Sebald did achieve quite considerable critical acclaim early on in his literary career in Germany. Though his literary debut, the book-length prose poem

After Nature from 1988, went largely unnoticed when it first came out, it was awarded the Fedor Malchow Prize for nature poetry three years later, which also made up for the fact that Sebald had failed to win the 1990 Ingeborg Bachmann Prize at the Festival of German-Language Literature in Klagenfurt, Austria, where he had read from an early version of the 'Paul Bereyter' story from *Die Ausgewanderten* (*The Emigrants*).

In 1994, Sebald went on to receive a full three awards: the Johannes Bobrowski Medal, which was presented to him at the same time as the Berlin Literature Prize, and the LiteraTour Nord Prize. The latter, in November 1993, required Sebald to travel to the four Northern German cities of Oldenburg, Bremen, Hamburg and Hanover and give a reading in each. On this occasion, *The Emigrants* came through for him, and Sebald triumphed against his four competitors. Yet he loathed reading tours of any sort, and the journey gave rise to a number of poems that reflect the strain and sense of alienation he was clearly experiencing, mostly vividly in 'An einem Herbstsonntag 94' ('One Sunday in Autumn 94', LWg 90–91/LWe 145–146).

The earlier literary recognitions of 1994 took Sebald to Berlin. Together with six other authors, he had already been awarded the Berlin Literature Prize in February of that year. In June 1994, at the awards ceremony for the prize at the Literarisches Colloquium Berlin, the six laureates, as is customary, competed for the Johannes Bobrowski Medal by reading from unpublished works. Sebald received an award, alongside the Swiss writer Erica Pedretti (1930–1922), for his reading of a passage from *The Rings of Saturn*, where the narrator walks through Dunwich Heath to visit Michael Hamburger in Middleton.

But the accolade carried a sting in its tail. Commentators on the competition agreed that the 1994 medal winners were not outstandingly deserving but merely 'solidly average'.[9] The jury spokesman, prominent literary critic Reinhard Baumgart (1929–2003), practically apologized for the selection of Pedretti and Sebald by explaining that it had not necessarily been 'the jury's intention to reward only the best authors'.[10] As Sebald learnt the hard way, in the world of literary prize-giving, recognition and humiliation often go hand in hand.

Perhaps this was the reason – in addition to the medal's weight of almost four kilogrammes and its 'indescribably hideous' (SM 121) appearance – that prompted Sebald to relieve himself of the trophy by launching it into the lake waters of the Lesser Wannsee in Berlin, not far from the grave of writer Heinrich von Kleist (1777–1811), before catching a flight back to England.[11]

Growing Recognition

With *The Rings of Saturn* from 1995, Sebald published a work of prose narrative that still stands out today for its wide-ranging thematic digressions and its formal diversity somewhere between associative travelogue, literary essay and biographical vignette. His receipt of two important literary awards in 1997 can thus be understood as a recognition of his growing aesthetic complexity and innovative troubling of genre boundaries.

In April 1997, the award of the Mörike Prize meant that Sebald had to give a speech on his relationship to the author in whose honour the prize is named, the poet Eduard Mörike (1804–1875). Sebald's honorary address was published under the title 'Was ich traure weiß ich nicht: Kleines Andenken an Mörike' ('Why I Grieve I Do Not Know: A Memento of Mörike') in the 1998 essay collection *Logis in einem Landhaus* (*A Place in The Country*). Especially in comparison with the other Alemannic author portraits Sebald included in the collection (on Johann Peter Hebel (1760-1826), Gottfried Keller (1819-1890) and Robert Walser (1878–1956) among others) it becomes clear that writing about Mörike was largely a compulsory exercise for him. Sebald spends more time discussing Mörike's biography than his poetry, he embarks on extended tangents on the music of Franz Schubert (1797–1828), and he depicts the author as a victim of his time and personal circumstances.[12]

Being awarded the prestigious Heinrich Böll Prize in November 1997 also required Sebald to give an acceptance speech. Titled 'Feuer und Rauch: Über eine Abwesenheit in der deutschen Literatur' ('Fire and Smoke: On an Absence in German Post-war Literature', SM 338–342), the speech was a literary hybrid of autobiography, fiction and essay writing. It was based on preliminary work drawn up for the Corsica Project (see chapter 13 in the volume) Sebald had recently abandoned, so on work that would later come to inform *Austerlitz*, but it also incorporated material from the three poetics lectures Sebald had given around the same time in Zurich on the literary response to the Allied bombing campaign against German civilians.

The author who had lent his name to the prize, Heinrich Böll (1917–1985), was closely associated with Cologne, and Sebald addressed the aerial destruction of the city head-on in his speech: 'Cologne in flames – it took me a long time to come even close to imagining what it looked like here and elsewhere in Germany at the end of the war' (SM 340). This sets up a segue to his controversial thesis from *Luftkrieg und Literatur* (*On the*

Natural History of Destruction), according to which German post-war authors had failed to capture for posterity precise and detailed images of the destruction and atrocity caused by the air war.

Against this backdrop, Sebald invokes Böll's novel *Der Engel schwieg* (*The Angel Was Silent*). Though written around 1949/50, the book only came out posthumously in 1992, as Böll had worried its explicit wartime themes would be poorly received by contemporary readers. Sebald takes this as confirmation of his thesis and praises the suppressed work for:

> conveying an approximation of the horror that threatened to overcome anyone who really sought to look around the antechamber of death. [...] Böll's posthumous novel marks a blind spot in our historical atlas. Never has what happened then been allowed to enter public consciousness, let alone the school curriculum. (SM 341)

With its striking amalgamation of different forms of discourse, *Fire and Smoke* clearly signposts Sebald's evolution as an author during the last four years of his life. It belongs among the hybrid texts he wrote towards the end of the 1990s in that, like these, it dissolves the demarcation lines between essay writing and literature: in their fusion of polemical literary criticism, semi-fictional autobiography, literary narrative and philosophical meditation, they opened up a new perspective in Sebald's writing, which was truncated by his premature death.

Early Recognition Abroad

Publication of *The Emigrants* by Harvill Press in London in the spring of 1996, to wide-spread critical acclaim, led to a swift literary breakthrough for Sebald in the English-speaking world. His use of illustrations, a technique inspired by German authors such as Rolf Dieter Brinkmann (1940–1975) or Alexander Kluge (b. 1932) and uncommon in anglophone literature, caused a particular stir. The combination of images and text soon became his trademark in the anglosphere and garnered him critical attention but also recognition as an artist, which in turn was reflected in the accolades he received.

Sebald gained his first international literary award in England, in 1997, when he won the Jewish Quarterly/Wingate Literary Prize, which is awarded by the journal and funded by philanthropist Harold Hyam Wingate. Exceptionally, the prize that year was shared between Sebald, for *The Emigrants*, and Clive Sinclair (1948–2018) for his story collection *The Lady with the Laptop*, as both were considered equally deserving.[13]

Sebald's next international prize came from the USA, in the form of the Los Angeles Times Book Prize for Fiction, awarded for *The Rings of Saturn* in 1998.

One year later, Sebald repeated the unusual achievement of receiving two awards in a single year for his first two works to appear in translation, but this time in France: in 1999 Sebald won the Prix Laure-Bataillon for *Les Émigrants* (translated by Patrick Charbonneau) and the Prix du Meilleur livre étranger for *Les Anneaux de Saturne* (translated by Bernard Kreiss). The former was a dual award that recognized both the author and his translator. The latter was awarded to Sebald in the category 'Essay', shedding an interesting light on the work's French reception.

Both texts had come out with Actes Sud, in January and September of 1999 respectively, meaning that, as he had in the anglosphere, Sebald made his literary debut in the francophone world with *Les Émigrants*. Again as it had there, this determined his reception and earnt him a reputation, virtually overnight, as an author in exile and chronicler of German-Jewish lives.[14]

Breakthrough in Germany

In 2000, Sebald reached the height of his public recognition in Germany with the award of two prestigious literary prizes: the Joseph Breitbach Prize and the Heinrich Heine Prize. It is worth noting that the dual distinction came in the immediate wake of the country's caustic debate over Sebald's provocative air war lectures in Zurich. It should therefore be seen as a reflection of his increased notoriety in Germany, as well as belated recognition of the literary quality of his books, which, not least because of his residence abroad, had initially received less attention on the German literary scene.

The jury of the Joseph Breitbach Prize, which at €50,000 (then DM 85,000) carries the largest endowment of any German literary award, explicitly acknowledges Sebald's international success in its reasoning for the recognition: 'Sebald's works, published in numerous translations, are the foundation of his global success and have generated an ongoing debate on post-war literature. Susan Sontag regards him as one of the greatest representatives of contemporary literature.'[15] The outsider Sebald had become a 'an international author from Germany', whom they would now readily claim as one of their own. As the *Frankfurter Rundschau* ventured: 'For the first time, everyone can get behind the Breitbach

Prize, and it seems as if the Breitbach Prize might even give the Büchner Prize a run for its money where the renown of its authors is concerned.'[16]

Only a few months later, Sebald went on to receive the Heinrich Heine Prize of the city of Düsseldorf, another of the country's most significant literary prizes. Again, the recognition came with an obligation to give a speech on the award's eponymous author, Heinrich Heine (1797–1856). This time, Sebald side-stepped the commitment by reading 'Die Alpen im Meer' ('The Alps in the Sea', CSg 39–50/CSe 36–48), a fragment from the abandoned Corsica Project.

He justified his breach of the implied contract between awarding body and recipient with an excuse as polite as it was disingenuous: 'Rather than weary my audience with tedious digressions on Heine's biography and works, I shall read you an account of a journey which, though rather un-Heinean, still has several points of contact with his life.'[17] The awards ceremony in December 2000 was the last of Sebald's lifetime. His acceptance speech on the forests of Corsica is a highly complex text. It combines allegorical, philosophical, essayistic and literary-critical modes of writing,[18] and it offers a tantalizing glimpse of what the Corsica Project could have become, had Sebald not moved on from it.

Posthumous Postscript: Prizes for *Austerlitz*

In quantitative terms, *Austerlitz* is the most successful of Sebald's narrative prose works. It garnered him five posthumous awards, four of them in English-speaking countries. In the United Kingdom, he was awarded the Jewish Quarterly/Wingate Literary Prize again in 2002, as well as *The Independent*'s Foreign Fiction Prize.

Writer Marina Warner (b. 1946) delivered the ceremonial address for the latter and honoured *Austerlitz* as a 'masterpiece, in temper so elegiac, grave and solitary, an eloquent epitaph for its author'.[19] Warner is following the dominant tendency in anglophone Sebald reception here of reading *Austerlitz* as the author's literary legacy. Yet her speech is also astutely perceptive in the way in which it reads the novel against the established Holocaust-centric grain of English-language criticism, observing that Sebald 'found a sensitive, oblique way of honouring the dead of the Shoah. But *Austerlitz* is also a memorial to unbelonging and forgetting, dispossession and homelessness, the continuing predicament of many political casualties today from Rwanda to Palestine'.[20]

In the USA, Sebald was posthumously awarded the 2001 National Book Critics Circle Award and the 2002 Koret Jewish Book Award – Special

Award for Literature. The latter was created for the specific purpose of being able to honour *Austerlitz* after the fact.[21] By contrast, Sebald received only one posthumous award in Germany, the 2002 Bremen Literature Prize, which was accepted in his name by his German publisher Michael Krüger (Hanser), at the award ceremony in the Bremen State Theatre in January 2002.

Attempt at a Conclusion

In the course of his relatively brief writing career of barely a decade-and-a-half, Sebald was recognized with a total of seventeen literary awards. This is indisputably testament to the considerable esteem in which his work was held. And yet, of those seventeen awards, a full eight are prizes he received outside of Germany, among them four posthumously for *Austerlitz*. The significant popularity Sebald and his final novel enjoyed especially in anglophone and francophone countries thus rather puts in perspective the late recognition he finally achieved in Germany.

The two aspects of Sebald – as a belligerent and sometimes churlishly aggressive academic on the one hand and a sensitive author revered for his empathy on the other – go some way towards explaining why reservations about him persisted on the German literary scene and in literary studies, reservations that also informed the decisions of award-giving bodies. This was an open secret in his native Germany, or as one well-known critic put it: 'With W.G. Sebald, the Breitbach Prize is being awarded to an author who year after year has been missing out on the Büchner Prize. For once, Breitbach has pipped Büchner to the post.'[22]

The recalcitrant side of Sebald is easily missed from an anglophone perspective. In an insightful essay, based on the Sebald Lecture he gave in London in 2010, Will Self points out that literary awards bestowed by cultural functionaries tend to be aimed at affirming the functionaries themselves, which curtails the oppositional autonomy of a recipient's work. This is a fate Self would like to see Sebald spared: 'I am interested in saving Sebald from the ossification of this kind of critical regard which is the preserve of arts functionaries and their selective lists.' Alluding to the British obsession with dog competitions, Self poignantly adds: 'It's pets that win prizes, and I don't believe that Sebald was anyone's pet.'[23]

Notes

1. N Reynolds, Car crash kills author tipped for Nobel Prize, in: *Telegraph*, 17 December 2001.
2. R McCrum, WG Sebald's quietly potent legacy, in: *Guardian*, 13 May 2013.
3. M Gussow, W.G. Sebald, Elegiac German Novelist, Is Dead at 57, in: *New York Times*, 15 December 2001.
4. T Medicus, Leichtfüßiger Schwerarbeiter der Erinnerung, in: *Frankfurter Rundschau*, 17 December 2001.
5. A Wilcox, Why Sebald Matters, in: *Brooklyn Rail*, 6 May 2014.
6. Ö Abrahamson, Ständigt denna Horace, in: *Tidningen Vi* 2 (2007).
7. Email Anders Olsson, 28 June 2022. My sincerest thanks to Olsson for clarifying the misinformation that has so far been uncritically perpetuated in Sebald research, including publications of my own.
8. Email Anke Leonhardt, 24 January 2019.
9. J Plath, Medaillen ans Mittelfeld, in: *Tageszeitung*, 21 June 1994.
10. T Rietzschel, Verschenkt, in: *Frankfurter Allgemeine Zeitung*, 20 June 1994.
11. Personal communication by Sebald to me, upon his return.
12. U Schütte, *Interventionen: Literaturkritik als Widerspruch bei W.G. Sebald* (Munich: Ed. Text +Kritik, 2014), pp. 573–585.
13. El Hombre Valeroso: An Interview with Clive Sinclair, https://contrappassomag .wordpress.com/2017/07/25/el-hombre-valeroso-an-interview-with-clive-sinclair/.
14. On the French reception cf. R Vogel-Klein, Frankreich, in: M Niehaus, C Öhlschläger (eds.), *W.G. Sebald-Handbuch* (Stuttgart: Metzler, 2017) pp. 309–312.
15. Press release, Akademie der Wissenschaften und der Literatur (Joseph-Breitbach-Preis, 2000).
16. H Böttiger, Zuvorgekommen, in: *Frankfurter Rundschau*, 21 July 2000.
17. J Kruse (ed.), *Heine Jahrbuch* 40 (2001) (Stuttgart: Metzler, 2001), p. 174.
18. C Albes, Nature Writing: Zur Brauchbarkeit eines neuen Gattungsbegriffs für das Verständnis von Sebalds Prosa am Beispiel des Essays ›Die Alpen im Meer‹, in: G Dürbeck, C Kanz (eds.), *Deutschsprachiges Nature Writing von Goethe bis zur Gegenwart: Kontroversen, Positionen, Perspektiven* (Stuttgart: Metzler, 2020), pp. 265–280.
19. Manuscript of laudatory speech, made available to me by Marina Warner.
20. Ibid.
21. Email Steven. J. Zipperstein, 12 December 2019.
22. Böttiger, Zuvorgekommen.
23. W Self, Absent Jews and Invisible Executioners, in: J Cook (ed.), *After Sebald: Essays and Illuminations* (Woodbridge: Full Circle, 2014), pp. 95–114 (100).

CHAPTER 37

Visual Arts and Exhibitions

Terry Pitts

Visual artists have been inspired by W.G. Sebald perhaps more than any other writer in the past century. This may in part be due to the fact that he himself thought of writing in visual terms. He claimed to 'work like a painter' (SM 352) and, among other things, so admired visual art's ability to suspend time that he strove to achieve the same effect in his work (SM 353). Fittingly, his work was strongly influenced by numerous painters from the pages of art history. In his books he included extended segments and reproductions of well-known paintings by famous artists such as Pisanello (1395–1455), Grünewald (1470–1528), Rembrandt (1606–1669), Turner (1775–1851) and Auerbach (b. 1931), to name but a few (see chapter 27 in this volume).

Above all, Sebald himself emboldened such a vibrant response from contemporary visual artists with his imaginative use of photographs and other images, some of which he found, and some of which he took himself, as an integral part of his own writing. He then went a step further and collaborated with living artists in the making of two books of his poetry late in his life.

These were his final publication, *For Years Now: Poems by W.G. Sebald, Images by Tess Jaray* (2001), and his first posthumous publication, *Unerzählt: 33 Texte und 33 Radierungen* (*Unrecounted: 33 Texts and 33 Etchings*, 2003), a collaboration with his long-time friend, the hyperrealist artist Jan Peter Tripp. 'Much of what I have written', Sebald confessed, referring to a present gifted by Tripp, 'derives from this engraving, even in my method of procedure: in adhering to an exact historical perspective, in patiently engraving and linking together apparently disparate things in the manner of a still life' (CSe 210/CSg 243–244).

East Anglian Landscapes

From as early as 2000, visual artists began making artworks that dealt specifically with Sebald's books, especially related to the places that he

331

wrote about. Due to its focus on the landscape and ecology of East Anglia, *Die Ringe des Saturn* (*The Rings of Saturn*) was the book that first served as the inspirational magnet for artists. It has also continued to attract more artistic interest than any of Sebald's other books, in part because it contains an easily identifiable itinerary which artists (and readers) could follow (see chapter 35 in this volume).

Its geographic turf is where Sebald made his home for roughly three decades – East Anglia, an area that has been described as 'a richly evocative terrain that is unusually flooded with both water and memory, and the accumulated flotsam of history.'[1] However, even when Sebald seemed to be simply describing a landscape in one of his books, it inevitably led him elsewhere – into memory, into history, into a kind of eco-melancholy (see chapter 4 in this volume). It is this richness of meaning, this multiplicity of possibilities that artists have responded to in his work.

Take the example of the British artist Marcus Coates (b. 1968), whose artwork *Britain's Bitterns* consisted of eleven dead bittern specimens displayed in a vitrine. Coates's work asked the viewer to simultaneously admire the beauty of the bird, grasp a sense of the failing ecology of East Anglia, and imagine the bittern's Old Testament role as a messenger of doom.

One of the aspects of Sebald's work that has inspired artists has been the often-idiosyncratic way he addressed themes which we might describe as personal or individual in nature, such as exile, memory, trauma and death. The artistic challenge here is to find a way to transfer such themes into a visual vocabulary. One innovative example is that of the German artist Karen Stuke (b. 1970), whose large and elaborate installation *Wandelhalle: Stuke after Sebald's ›Austerlitz‹* employed numerous colour and black-and-white photographs that are slightly out of focus, evoking a sense of distant, indistinct memories. Her photographs, which often look as if they had been double- or even multiple-exposed, were created with a handmade pinhole camera that had no lens, creating an eerie, ghostly effect.

In another example, an entire exhibition, *L'Image Papillon*, was held at the Musée d'Art Moderne Grand-Duc Jean, Luxembourg in 2013 specifically to bring together the works of the sixteen artists inspired by the way Sebald addresses 'the complex relations that link image and memory'.[2]

Artists have also connected with more global themes in Sebald's books, such as capitalism, colonialism, history and war. One such example is the project *W.G. Sebald* (2003), by the British artist Tacita Dean (b. 1965). By closely reading the Roger Casement section of *The Rings of Saturn*, she discovered to her amazement that a distant relative of hers was the judge

Illustration 25 – Karen Stuke, installation view of *Stuke after Sebald's ›Austerlitz‹*, 2013

who condemned Casement to death after his conviction for high treason in 1916. Her project addresses how her family's past intersected with British politics, the Irish question, the Marconi Scandal, the Titanic and several other key historical episodes.[3]

Other artists have been inspired by Sebald's work with one of the most important and resonating themes of the twentieth century, the archive, to address topics such as research, knowledge systems and bureaucracy in a Sebaldian manner. An excellent example is *Terezín*, a project by the Portuguese photographer Daniel Blaufuks (b. 1963), who was inspired by a photograph of Theresienstadt in *Austerlitz*. In his exhibition and 2010 book about this ghetto and concentration camp, Blaufuks includes new photographs of historical photographs, archival documents and original journals, as well as his images of the camp as it appears today.

Still other artists have been more impressed by Sebald's voice than by his content. They have either been affected by the melancholy that imbues his writing or by his tendency to effortlessly digress from topic to topic. One artist who took the subject of Sebald's "voice" quite literally is the British artist, Jane Benson (b. 1972). She demonstrated how an artist can make a radically different type of artwork based on Sebald's writing in her project

Song for Sebald (2017), which combines visual media and an original music composition by the American composer Matthew Schickele.

Benson took *The Rings of Saturn* and removed every part of the text except the syllables that comprise the musical scale – do, re, mi, fa, so, la, ti. The result was a piece of 'potential music', she said. 'Sebald's prose reflects its author's experience of radical dislocation; his narrators often seem to stand apart from their physical and textual surroundings, the stories they tell – at once personal and impersonal – reflect the creative potential of estrangement and disorientation'.[4]

Tess Jaray

Tess Jaray (b. 1937) is the first of three artists I have selected who have created a large work project based on Sebald's works. The Austrian-born, British artist made the earliest notable response by a visual artist to Sebald's work in 2000, with her limited-edition series of large screen prints based upon *The Rings of Saturn*. These were actually pairings of screen prints, with the left print being an intensely coloured, monochrome image of patterned dots that suggest geometric forms and the right print containing a quotation from either *The Rings of Saturn* or *Schwindel. Gefühle. (Vertigo)*.

Jaray said she was drawn to 'his distortion of and evocation of space, and strange ability to focus both on distance and nearness simultaneously, to make space and memory appear to be the *same thing*, giving a sense of spinning between past and future'.[5] Even though her work is utterly abstract, it is, in some ways, a fascinating match for Sebald's writing. The scale of her pieces can be seen as celestial or microscopic at the same time and the pairing between her patterns and the quotations from Sebald demands that the viewer actively participate in unravelling any possible relationship.

This project then led to a collaboration between Jaray and Sebald on the artist's book *For Years Now*, which was published in December 2001, just a few days before Sebald's death. The book consists of twenty-three of Jaray's colourful images paired with Sebald's haiku-like "micro-poems". These are all very short pieces, none longer than ten lines and most lines containing fewer than four words. Sebald wrote the English texts and this was the only time he published a literary text directly in English.[6]

Tacita Dean and Post-Medium Art

Over the years, Sebald has attracted the attention of more than his share of post-medium artists, namely, artists who feel free to create art in multiple mediums. Because Sebald was a rare writer who wrote both in the academic world and in the spheres of prose fiction and poetry, and also used photographs and images creatively within his writing, we might think of him as the literary equivalent of a post-medium artist.

When the critic Rosalind Krauss introduced the term 'post-medium condition', she also suggested that post-medium artists tend to borrow from and reinvent outmoded artistic mediums. This is exactly what Sebald did when he derived his own innovative version of writing, which feels as if it were adapted more or less directly from past literature.

The writer Geoff Dyer (b. 1958) opined:

> The first thing to be said about W.G. Sebald's books is that they always had a posthumous quality to them. He wrote – as was often remarked – like a ghost. He was one of the most innovative writers of the late twentieth century, and yet part of this originality derived from the way his prose felt exhumed from the nineteenth.[7]

The most notable post-medium artist to use Sebald as a jumping off point for her work has been the internationally renowned British artist Tacita Dean, who has referenced Sebald in a film, an artist's book, and a series of images, each tangentially or directly related to Sebald. Typical of Dean's sideways approach to Sebald is her film *Michael Hamburger* (2007). Hamburger, a poet and translator, was another German ex-pat living in England. He was one of Sebald's closest friends and translated some of his poetry. A visit to his house forms a significant episode in *The Rings of Saturn*. By making a film about Hamburger, Dean was, in essence, filming Sebald in absentia.[8]

In an earlier work called *The Russian Ending* (2001), Dean made a series of photogravures based on flea market postcards depicting explosions, shipwrecks, funerals, ruined landscapes and other events suggesting death. (The title refers to a one-time Danish cinema tradition of needing to create a special tragic ending to movies especially for Russian audiences.) On the surface of each postcard, Dean had scrawled notations that resembled a cinematographer's directions. Because of its pessimistic image of world history and its use of the imagery of disasters, this series has been closely associated with Sebald.

More directly, Dean created an artist's book in the form of an exhibition catalogue for the Musée d'Art Moderne de la Ville de Paris called *W.G.*

Sebald (2003), an elusive illustrated text about how she originally became fascinated with Sebald's writing. Dean's art, like Sebald's, often works elliptically, without directly referencing its primary subject.

Elina Brotherus

Because Sebald's books tend to include specific locales and identifiable itineraries, artists have paid homage to him by literally following in his footsteps and depicting or responding to what they find in the locations he wrote about. One intriguing artist has explored a text and a geographic area from Sebald's writing that has been ignored until now – his unfinished piece 'Campo Santo', which was based on two visits to Corsica in the mid-1990s.[9]

In 2019, the Finnish photographer Elina Brotherus (b. 1972) created the project *Sebaldiana: Memento Mori*, which led her to the very locations in Corsica that Sebald refers to in his writings. In thirty-six stunning, large colour landscape photographs, the photographer posed herself contemplating the same views that Sebald must have seen himself nearly twenty-five years earlier.

> Sebald became my guide to Corsica. I went to places he mentions: the forest of Aïtone and the massif of Bavella, the hotel, the beach and the cemetery in Piana and its backcountry with sculptural rock formations. I was remembering my dead. I looked for places so beautiful that I would like to bury them there, were I Corsican.[10]

By placing herself within the photograph, both as a photographer making a self-portrait and as a person contemplating the landscape, Brotherus stands in for Sebald, who is the writer of and, in the form of his eponymous fictional narrator, a character in his prose fictions. The figure of Brotherus contemplating the landscape also reminds us of an iconic painting by the German Romantic painter, Casper David Friedrich, *Der Wanderer über dem Nebelmeer* (*Wanderer Above the Sea of Fog*, 1818). A second part of Brotherus's project involves fifty-seven cyanotypes called *Herbarium Pianense*. These are simple blue silhouettes of the same weeds that Sebald admired growing up around the gravestones in Piana.

Exhibitions

As Sebald's writings began influencing more and more visual artists, museum curators also started to pay attention. By 2007, the first of several major museum exhibitions based on his work appeared. Called *Waterlog*, it was held at both the Norwich Castle Museum and Art Gallery and the Sainsbury Centre for the Visual Arts and was a response to *The Rings of Saturn*. Nearly every piece in *Waterlog* was created specifically for this exhibition, amongst them Dean's film on Hamburger and Coates' *Britain's Bitterns*. Simon Bode, one of the co-curators of the exhibition explained that the 'unifying sensibility' he believed the nine visual artists in *Waterlog* shared with Sebald was 'elegiac, enquiring, understated, almost hesitant'.[11]

After *Waterlog*, most succeeding group exhibitions, like *After Nature* (2008), *Altermodern* (2009) and *Melancholia* (2017), even though claiming inspiration based on Sebald's work, have given the definition of Sebaldian an elasticity that allowed them to include art that referenced practically anything he mentioned or even vaguely hinted at in one of his books, plus subjects he never directly mentioned like immigration or government surveillance. And, unlike *Waterlog*, few, if any, of the artworks in these succeeding exhibitions were made specifically in response to Sebald's works but were instead already existing artworks deemed by the curators to share philosophical traits with Sebald's writings. Nevertheless, these exhibitions demonstrate that Sebald's influence had, for a time at least, reached the highest echelons of the art world.

After Nature, held at New York City's influential New Museum, was focused on (and took its title from) Sebald's book of poetry *Nach der Natur* (*After Nature*). The website for the exhibition described it as 'a requiem for a dying planet', thus announcing its dire ecological themes and continuing somewhat the themes begun in *Waterlog*. However, it wasn't just the subject matter of Sebald's books that attracted the exhibition's curators and artists. Like Sebald, the more than two dozen artists in *After Nature* all 'share an interest in archaic traditions and a fascination for personal cosmologies and visionary languages. It is a peculiar form of magic[al] realism that emerges from the works on view, coupled with a renewed belief in art as a tool for mythmaking.'[12]

The exhibition *Melancholia*, held at King's College, London, responded to the abiding sense left by all of Sebald's books that he suffered from a kind of melancholy, a deep, incurable sadness with no single, easily-identifiable cause. The exhibition's website asked if Sebald's melancholy was 'Freud's formulation, an indulgent, unproductive form of mourning?' or was it 'a form of sadness that is ultimately uplifting because it enables loss to bring with it a consciousness of life and its more startling possibilities?'[13]

The exhibition *Altermodern*, held at London's Tate Britain was based on 'the idea of the archipelago' and, purportedly, 'the writings of a German émigré to the UK, Winfred [sic] Georg Sebald', but it had tenuous connections to Sebald's books at best. Curator Nicolas Bourriaud called the contemporary artist a 'cultural nomad' and said: 'There are no longer roots to sustain forms, no exact cultural base to serve as a benchmark for variations, no nucleus, no boundaries for artistic language.'[14] One suspects that Sebald would have argued otherwise.

In 2019, the Norwich Castle Museum and Art Gallery and the Sainsbury Centre for the Visual Arts at UEA once again collaborated, this time creating a pair of exhibitions in honour of Sebald's seventy-fifth birthday. While the former, titled *Lines of Sight*, focused on the local connections to Sebald's *The Rings of Saturn*, the Sainsbury Centre exhibition, called *W. G. Sebald: Far away – but from where?*, was devoted to the photographs Sebald took for his own books but also exhibited Tess Jaray's prints, Tacita Dean's film of Michael Hamburger and a very large multi-panel work by Julie Mehretu (b. 1970), all of which, the curator Nick Warr suggested, spoke to themes of architecture and erasure.

Conclusion

It is evident that, two decades after Sebald's death, his work continues to be relevant to visual artists, as inspiration and source material for new artworks in a variety of media. It is interesting to note that nearly all of these artists are from the British Isles or the United States, and rarely from Europe. Karen Stuke is one of very few German artists who have developed work based upon Sebald's œuvre. Sadly, visual artists only began to turn their attention to the work of Sebald when he had less than two years left to live, and most of what has been done has occurred after his death. We are left to wonder how he might have responded to this outpouring of artworks responding to his books had he lived beyond the age of fifty-seven.

Notes

1. S Bode, Foreword, in: *Waterlog: Journeys Around an Exhibition* (London: Film and Video Umbrella, 2007), p. 6.
2. www.mudam.com/exhibitions/l-image-papillon.
3. T Dean, W.G. Sebald, in: *Seven Books (Selected Writings)* (Göttingen, Paris: Steidl, ARC/Musée d'Art Moderne, 2003).

4. https://janebenson.net/2017-songs/.

5. T Jaray, *The Rings of Saturn and Vertigo, Tess Jaray W.G. Sebald* (London: Purdy Hicks, 2001), n. p.

6. A Englund, W.G. Sebald's Late Lyrics Between Words, Images and Languages, in: *Interlitteraria* 20:2 (2015) pp. 123–141; U Schütte, *Figurationen: Zum lyrischen Werk von W.G. Sebald* (Eggingen: Ed. Isele, 2014), pp. 111–152.

7. G Dyer, W.G. Sebald, Bombing, and Thomas Bernhard, in: *Otherwise Known as the Human Condition: Selected Essays and Reviews* (Minneapolis: Graywolf, 2011), p. 205.

8. There is also a German television documentary on Hamburger by Frank Wierke: *Michael Hamburger: Ein englischer Dichter aus Deutschland* (*MH: An English Poet from Germany*, 2007).

9. The two drafts of the abandoned Corsica project in the Nachlass in were published in the catalogue of the 2008/09 Sebald exhibition at the Deutsches Literaturarchiv in Marbach (WS 129–209).

10. www.elinabrotherus.com/photography#/sebaldiana-memento-mori-2019/.

11. Bode, Foreword, p. 6.

12. https://archive.newmuseum.org/exhibitions/928. For a more critical assessment of the exhibition cf. Schütte, *Annäherungen. Sieben Essays zu W.G. Sebald* (Cologne: Böhlau, 2019), pp. 240–242.

13. www.kcl.ac.uk/Cultural/-/Projects/Melancholia-%E2%80%93-a-Sebald-variation.

14. www.theguardian.com/artanddesign/2009/feb/02/altermodern-tate-triennial.

CHAPTER 38

The Cult of Sebald

Ian Ellison

In a literary landscape that can seem increasingly watered-down, hollowed-out and flattened, the contemporary need for authorial greatness is ever more seductive. Readers and critics must look abroad if great writers like those of yesteryear are not to be found closer to home. This is one possible explanation for the extraordinarily possessive way in which Anglo-American readers have hurled themselves upon the life and work of W.G. Sebald. Despite the deplorably low number of translated books published in English, he is one of the very few writers of the late twentieth century to have earned his own adjective (see chapter 3 in this volume). In the foreword to one of the earliest essay anthologies on Sebald's work back in 2006, his reception in the anglophone sphere was described as nothing short of a literary phenomenon.[1] So it remains.

A cult develops once adoration for a writer transcends the realm of the purely literary. Entering into other areas, such as popular music (see chapter 35 in this volume) or the visual arts (see chapter 37 in this volume), writers become transmuted into stars or idols. That is to say, a persona is constructed which is disconnected from the real individual writer. Authors become like a blank surface onto which certain fans – and not necessarily serious readers – project their own (mis)conceptions.

The cult of Sebald was already coming into being during the final few years of his life, which Sebald himself realized as his refusal to be labelled as a Holocaust writer reveals. Since his death in December 2001, the growth of his cult has steadily increased, often verging on the hagiographic. The suddenness both of Sebald's rise from the obscurity of a provincial Allgäu village to international stardom late in his life and of his unexpected demise just half a decade later are key to his cult status. Almost unavoidably, this ascribed a messianic quality to his profile as an author.

Paradoxically, it was his general reticence to grant interviews when still alive that undoubtedly amplified his posthumous apotheosis. Sebald professed a wariness of the promotional circus in which writers are often required to join, rarely featuring in the media. His dislike of appearing in public meant that he was often unwilling to travel to London to partake in literary events. In Germany, Sebald was virtually absent from the media, except for his 1980 televised attendance at the contest for the Ingeborg Bachmann Prize in Klagenfurt, Austria.

As in the case of the American novelist Thomas Pynchon, famous for withholding almost all details of his private life from public scrutiny, reclusive authors are ripe for cultification. The scarcity of their appearances in public life seems only to heighten readers' curiosity, whetting the appetite for any new nuggets of biographical information and even encouraging the impulse not only to follow in the footsteps of autofictional narrators but also to stalk the authors themselves.

Anglophone Adoration

The trajectory of Sebald's ascension to the status of a cult author can be swiftly and conveniently charted between two key moments whose long-lasting influence still permeates perceptions of his literary output decades later. First, his initial meteoric entry into the anglophone literary scene (a convenient shorthand for New York publishing if ever there was one), predominantly thanks to the hyperbolic influence of the philosopher and critic Susan Sontag, whom Sebald would eventually join on stage at 92nd Street Y, New York's pre-eminent cultural and community centre on the Upper East Side of Manhattan in New York City in what would become his final recorded appearance.

Writing in the *Times Literary Supplement* five years earlier, Sontag had enthused that

> W.G. Sebald's *The Emigrants* (Harvill) is the most extraordinary, thrilling new book I've read this year ... indeed for several years. [...]. It is an unclassifiable book, at once autobiography and fiction and historical chronicle. A *roman d'essai*? Even that label does not do justice to the non-existent genre to which Sebald's masterpiece belongs. A book of excruciating sobriety and warmth and a magical concreteness of observation, it relates the narrator's quest to discover the truth about four lives – four people who left Germany at different times in this century. I know of no book which conveys more about that complex fate, being a European at the end of European civilization. I know of few books written in our time but this is one which attains the sublime.[2]

There is much mythologizing to unpack in this endorsement, later used as a jacket blurb for the novel's paperback release. It anticipates in numerous ways how Sebald would be subsequently received by vast swathes of his Anglo-American readership: the assumption that his books might well have been originally composed in English; the construction of lines of literary inheritance and influence; the contrivance of a romantically dark Germanic aura of exalted mystique around both the author and his work.

The second defining moment of Sebaldian consecration came just months prior to his death. A mere five years after Sontag's introductory encomium, the ultimate canonization of Sebald's œuvre was assured by Richard Eder's review of *Austerlitz* in the pages of the *New York Times*. Selectively misquoting Theodor W. Adorno, Eder trumpeted that 'Sebald stands with Primo Levi as the prime speaker of the Holocaust and, with him, the prime contradiction of Adorno's dictum that after it, there can be no art'.[3] Despite his having treated the Holocaust with great sensitivity in his prose fictions, this joint honour with Levi was hardly a status actively sought by Sebald as a writer.

Nevertheless, comparisons with Kafka, Nabokov, Proust, Calvino and Borges in many reviews by notable mainstream critics including James Wood, Christopher Hitchens and Cynthia Ozick served to ensure that Sebald would be immortalized as a German writer whom Anglo-American readers in particular could adore. It was, moreover, the perception of Sebald as a so-called 'Holocaust writer', despite his objections to the term, which secured his lasting public veneration in the anglosphere. Yet paramount focus on the ravages and aftermath of the Holocaust is apt at best to understate and at worst to ignore significant facets of Sebald's work that exceed the events of modern European totalitarianism.

Looking back at the long twentieth century from the age of Auschwitz in this way may, moreover, risk a form of teleological distortion that casts his literary output as an ultimate expression of mourning and a culmination of artistic response to the worst atrocities of the National Socialist regime. In fact, Sebald was keen to stress in an interview with the *Jewish Quarterly* that he was not an unabashed philo-Semite (EM 167). Placing stones on his gravestone according to Jewish custom, as some pilgrims to the churchyard of St. Andrew's in Framingham Earl, Norfolk have done, illustrates the wishful thinking that, despite any evidence, Sebald was of hidden Jewish ancestry.[4]

Indeed, readers and critics excessively keen to associate Sebald with the Jewish diaspora may baulk at his assertion in a 1993 interview that migration constituted the defining catastrophe at that time in Germany (G 87–95) or his denial of the singularity of the Holocaust in his final German interview (G 252–263). Nevertheless, the myth-making that emerged in the wake of his

Illustration 26 – St Andrew's churchyard, Framingham Earl, Norfolk

astronomical rise to success and acclaim, followed by his sudden demise, has proved tenacious.

Cult Cornerstones

Despite the fact that *For Years Now*, a book of epigrammatic poems composed by Sebald interspersed with monochrome – but, crucially, colourful – patterns designed by the British visual artist Tess Jaray (b. 1937), was published merely a few days prior to Sebald's death on 14 December 2001, the perception persists that *Austerlitz* was the last of his works to be published while he yet lived. This is a crucial element of the cult of Sebald: this bestselling novel with grainy photographs and a clear principal narrative of

lost memories and childhood trauma, rather than the more accurate yet
potentially disorienting diversion towards a side-line in collaborative work,
seems to appeal more to readers and to critics as a fitting capstone to Sebald's
literary career.

Adoration for *Austerlitz* is one of the substantial cornerstones of the cult
of Sebald, not only given its subject matter, but also since its author died
almost immediately after publication, and prematurely. This added into
the mix the pinch of tragedy so often necessary for acquiring posthumous
cult status, which almost inevitably ensues when pop stars die suddenly at
a relatively young age. Though hardly a member of the ghoulishly named
cult phenomenon of the "27 Club" (Jimi Hendrix, Janis Joplin, Kurt
Cobain, Amy Winehouse et al.), Sebald's premature death at the age of
57 has more often than not in the anglophone world led him to be clad in
the messianic garb of a redeemer figure.

Obituaries across the media of the day allowed for an opportunistic
reconstitution of Sebald as a sentimental artefact, a palliative literary
object that could be smuggled posthumously into the already crowded
room of the Anglo-American world's bad conscience. A notable recurring
feature of these obituaries was the fretful observation that Sebald's
sudden death had denied him the literary world's highest accolade, the
Nobel Prize (see chapter 36 in this volume), even though he was never
considered for it.

In his Sebald Lecture given in London in 2010, Will Self highlighted
the self-congratulatory manner in which Sebald had been claimed by the
cultural establishment in the United Kingdom in particular. Beyond
the subjective matter of artistic merit, Self diagnosed a deeper reason
for the way in which scholars and artists of all stripes from across the
Anglo-American cultural landscape had chosen to cast Sebald as a kind of
literary demigod.

Not only was he placed on a pedestal as an idealized iteration of the
figure of the Good German; by dint of his having lived and written in
England, both the man and the work were also ripe for misappropriation in
the name of national self-aggrandizement.

'In England', Self wrote,

> Sebald's one-time presence among us – even if we would never be so crass as
> to think this, let alone articulate it – is registered as further confirmation that
> we won, and won because of our righteousness, our liberality, our inclusive-
> ness and our tolerance. Where else could the Good German have sprouted
> so readily?[5]

Here, Self pinpoints a mechanism that is quite easy to understand from a socio-psychological point of view, and which also applies to many German-speaking countries: a substantial slice of the left-liberal cultural elite, suffering from rising nationalistic tendencies at home and a populist dumbing down of their own societies, tries to break away. In attempting to cleanse themselves, they profess an allegiance to "foreign" writers, whom they may co-opt into their own cultural sphere as a shining example of their own idealized self-perception.

The cult of Sebald is inescapably anglophone and there exists nothing like the posthumous adoration of his work in the Germanosphere. Nevertheless, unlike certain writers he admired, drew on for inspiration, and is often associated with, such as Joseph Conrad and Vladimir Nabokov, Sebald was reluctant to adopt the English language in his written work. Unwilling to make the sacrifice, as he saw it, of relinquishing his mother tongue, he professed an attachment to the German in which his prose remains sharper, richer and more profound than in translation, despite his long-held reservations regarding the country's history and society (EM 51).

For Sebald, any sense of *Heimat* – that distinctly Germanic affiliation to geographical roots inflected with a spiritual sense of belonging (see chapter 1 in this volume) – was clearly more linguistic and aesthetic than merely geographical. Even so, this has not prevented him from being co-opted in the anglophone world into the fold of nature writing that has enjoyed a renaissance in recent decades. While such writing can present the natural world as a disturbed, uncanny and socially contested space, it can also evince a tendency towards constructing an ideal of "natural" space as empty of human history and social conflict. This threatens to occlude the spectres of latently fascistic ways of valuing and relating to the natural world that all too often haunt modern nature writing (the threat to the land; simplistic heuristics of urban versus rural, social versus natural; a fear of change and of the outcomes of human action).

Nevertheless, nature writing's popular appeal is undeniable. Alongside rambling routes through East Anglia that recreate passages from *Die Ringe des Saturn* (*The Rings of Saturn*) and walking tours of London tracing the haunts of Jacques Austerlitz, there is now the Sebald Footpath in the Allgäu. This successful tourist attraction traces the route taken by the narrator in *Schwindel. Gefühle.* (*Vertigo*) from the Oberjoch Pass in Austria down to his hometown of Wertach. Sebaldian nature writing has also gone virtual. Robert Macfarlane, whose own travelogues as well as his recent collaborative prose poem *Ness* (2019), illustrated by Stanley Donwood, include grainy monochrome images in self-conscious homages to Sebald's work, set up a global Sebald reading group on Twitter. Using the hashtag #TheReadingsOfSaturn to pose questions or reflections about *The Rings of Saturn* every day or so between 9 July and 31 August 2018, Macfarlane was joined by many hundreds of users from all around the world.[6]

This remarkable reception of a particular curated version of Sebald's œuvre within the English-speaking world acted, moreover, as a catalyst for his reception and establishment in much smaller book markets, such as those of Japan, South Korea, or Slovenia, where publishers were ready and willing to commission translations which subsequently propelled Sebald far beyond the borders of Europe. Ultimately, Sebald's dubious (mis) appropriation in anglophone literary and popular culture proved a prerequisite for a German writer from provincial Allgäu to be posthumously beatified globally as an institution of world literature.

Literary Knighthood

Numerous other artists and writers have consistently sought association with Sebald, even while simultaneously distinguishing themselves (see chapter 33 in this volume). One notable international contribution to the cult of Sebald comes in the form of Javier Marías (1951–2022). Undoubtedly one of the most critically acclaimed and commercially successful of contemporary Spanish novelists and translators, Marías both played a formative role in the establishment of the cult of Sebald and was irrevocably shaped by it.

In a piece written shortly after Sebald's death, Marías professed bitter outrage at having recently spied in an auction catalogue a first edition of *Austerlitz* on sale for £550, remarking correctly that, if Sebald were still around, the book would have been worth much less. The bitterness of this was made decidedly acute, Marías confesses, given that he had corresponded with Sebald, who had – however briefly – 'become someone real to me, who could have ended up being a friend, [. . .] no longer just an author I admired'.[7] There is surely no greater indication of an author's pop cultural canonization than the public's willingness to spend extortionate amounts of money on rare editions of their works which become held up as hallowed relics.

Marías also twice published his Spanish translations of Sir Thomas Browne's *Hydriotaphia, Urn Burial* (1658), a crucial Sebaldian intertext in *The Rings of Saturn*, although the only discernible distinction between the two editions beyond the images of the island in the later version, is the inclusion of a new dedication. Translated into English by Eric Southworth, Marías's 'Translator's Note' reads:

> This fifth volume in the Kingdom of Redonda series is dedicated *in memoriam* to W.G. Sebald (1944–2001), Duke of Vertigo and invisible friend, who wrote some extraordinary pages about Sir Thomas Browne and died unexpectedly on a Norfolk Road, not far from the interred and disinterred urns.[8]

Ascribing a melancholy mystique to Sebald's death, Marías's dedication suggests an almost perverse symmetry or suitability to Sebald's demise, however unexpected the event may have been. He also alludes to his own contribution to the idolization of Sebald on the world literary stage in having bequeathed him a duchy on the half-jokingly contested and uninhabited territory of the Caribbean island of Redonda, whose fictional kingship Marías assumed in the late 1990s.

Their association appears to have been mutually beneficial and inspirational. In a rare endorsement written for the English translation of Marías's *Negra espalda del tiempo*, Sebald had confessed himself to have been 'greatly impressed by the quality of Marías's writing, especially by its clinical elegance'.[9] Sebald's private library at the Deutsches Literaturarchiv (German Literary Archive) in Marbach am Neckar holds four letters, comprising six pages in total, which were sent by Marías to Sebald between 2000 and 2001. Many reviewers of Marías's remarkable novels have drawn comparisons between his and Sebald's writing. In *The Guardian*, Marina Warner (b. 1946) professed that he 'has something of W.G. Sebald's consciousness in flux' and Sarah Emily Miano (b. 1974) cited the purported fact that 'W.G. Sebald spoke of him [Marías] as 'a "twin writer"', though the sole source for this appears to be Marías himself.

Blind Spots

It is one thing, then, to acknowledge literary significance, but it is something else entirely to claim Sebald's work as unique, as it is to subsequently instrumentalize that asserted originality in order to claim one's own original originality *a posteriori*. Nevertheless, it is clear that in needing to assert one's distance from Sebald, his genre-defining and genre-crossing centrality is assured. The cult status of any artist requires genre boundaries to be traversed, and in Sebald's case his appropriation in the world of visual art and media is, perhaps, even more striking than in the literary realm (see chapter 37 in this volume). Few writers in any language have, moreover, reached the cult status of being parodied in *Private Eye* as the 'Sebald sound' was by Craig Brown in 1998.[10] Fairly or unfairly, for better or for worse, Sebald sets the terms of the debate.

In Sebald's work, failure and loss are rewarding. Yet in the Anglo-American cult of Sebald an entire gamut of Germanophone writers and their works go unappreciated as influential, such as Klaus Theweleit's illustrated volumes of cultural criticism, Hans Magnus Enzensberger's *Der Untergang der Titanic* (*The Sinking of the Titanic*, 1978), or the work of Alexander Kluge. Perhaps, however, this is merely the obverse of Sebald's own iconoclasm *vis-à-vis* German-Jewish writers such as Jurek Becker, Carl Sternheim and Alfred Döblin, as well as his striking omission of Ingeborg Bachmann (to take just one obvious female absence) from his two essay collections on Austrian literature.

Whereas Sebald was once instrumentalized as a posthumous spokesperson for a German generation confronting the ruins of the twentieth century, with distance the limitations of this approach are clear. The cult of Sebald serves as a cautionary reminder of the inherent dangers of overstating the melancholia of modernity, of complacently revering aesthetic modes of representing this and of sanctifying a writer's life and work as something both more and less than the sum of their parts.

Notes

1. S Denham, Foreword: The Sebald Phenomenon, in: S Denham, M McCulloh (eds.), *W.G. Sebald: History – Memory – Trauma* (Berlin/New York: De Gruyter, 2006) pp. 1–6.
2. S Sontag, in: *Times Literary Supplement* 4887 (1996), p. 15.
3. R Eder, Excavating a Life, in: *New York Times*, 28 October 2011, p. 10.
4. www.newyorker.com/books/page-turner/always-returning.
5. W Self, Absent Jews and Invisible Executioners, in: J Cook (ed.), *After Sebald: Essays and Illuminations* (Ipswich: Full Circle), pp. 95–114 (106).
6. https://twitter.com/RobGMacfarlane/status/1015180699786203136.
7. J Marías, El amargo valor de algunos muertos, in: *Harán de mí un criminal* (Madrid: Alfaguara, 2003), pp. 196–198.
8. T Browne, *La religión de un médico y El enterramiento en urnas*, transl. J Marías (Barcelona: Reino de Redonda, 2002), p. 5.
9. J Marías, *Dark Back Of Time*, transl. E Allen (London: Chatto & Windus, 2003). Promotional material.
10. *Private Eye* 958 (1998).

Further Reading

1 Allgäu

C Angier, *Speak, Silence: In Search of W.G. Sebald* (London: Bloomsbury, 2021), pp. 27–56, 87–173.

C Duttlinger, A Wrong Turn of the Wheel: Sebald's Journeys of (In)Attention, in: M Zisselsberger (ed.), *The Undiscover'd Country: W.G. Sebald and the Poetics of Travel* (Rochester: Camden House, 2010), pp. 92–115.

R Görner, Im Allgäu. Grafschaft Norfolk: Über W.G. Sebald in England, in: *Text +Kritik* 4:2003, pp. 23–29.

T Honickel: *Curriculum Vitae: Die W.G. Sebald-Interviews* (Würzburg: Königshausen & Neumann, 2021), pp. 27–53.

M Klebes, No Exile: Crossing the Border with Sebald and Améry, in: G Fischer (ed.), *W.G. Sebald: Schreiben ex patria/Expatriate Writing* (Amsterdam/ New York: Rodopi 2009), pp. 73–90.

U Schütte, Immer anderwärts: Zur mehrfachen Ambivalenz der Heimat bei W.G. Sebald, in: K Wolfinger (ed.), *Die literarische Provinz: Das Allgäu und die Literatur* (Berlin: Lang, 2021), pp. 139–160.

K Wolfinger, (Un)Heimliches Allgäu: W.G. Sebald und seine ‚Heimat‘, in: U Schütte (ed.), *Über W.G. Sebald: Beiträge zu einem anderen Bild des Autors* (Berlin/Boston: De Gruyter, 2017), pp. 157–176.

2 Grandfather

M Anderson, A Childhood in the Allgäu: Wertach, 1944–52, in: SM 16–37.

U Schütte, *Annäherungen: Sieben Essays zu W.G. Sebald* (Cologne: Böhlau, 2019), pp. 41–75.

U Schütte, *W.G. Sebald: Leben und literarisches Werk* (Berlin/Boston: De Gruyter, 2020), pp. 9–12.

U Schütte, *W.G. Sebald* (Liverpool: Liverpool University Press, 2018), pp. 5–9.

C Steker, Tauchen im Laubmeer: W.G. Sebald und die Sprache der Pflanzen, in: U Schütte (ed.), *Über W.G. Sebald: Beiträge zu einem anderen Bild des Autors* (Berlin/Boston: De Gruyter, 2017), pp. 177–193.

3 Manchester

A Englund, Bleston Babel: Migration, Multilingualism and Intertextuality in W.G. Sebald's ›Mancunian Cantical‹, in: A Englund (ed.), *Languages of Exile: Migration and Multilingualism in Twentieth-Century Literature* (Berne: Lang, 2013), pp. 261–280.

T Honickel, *Curriculum Vitae: Die W.G. Sebald-Interviews*, ed. U Schütte, K Wolfinger (Würzburg: Königshausen & Neumann, 2021).

JB Howitt, Michel Butor and Manchester, in: *Nottingham French Studies* 12:2 (1973), pp. 74–85.

J Ryan, Sebald's Encounters with French Narrative, in: S Wilke (ed.), *From Kafka to Sebald: Modernism and Narrative Form* (New York: Continuum, 2012), pp. 123–142.

R Tabbert, Max in Manchester, in: *Akzente* 50:1 (2003), pp. 21–30.

4 East Anglia

C Albes, Die Erkundung der Leere: Anmerkungen zu W.G. Sebalds ‚englischer Wallfahrt' ›Die Ringe des Saturn‹, in: *Jahrbuch der deutschen Schillergesellschaft* 46 (2002), pp. 279–305.

J Beck, Reading Room: Erosion and Sedimentation in Sebald's Suffolk, in: JJ Long, A Whitehead (eds.), *W.G. Sebald: A Critical Companion* (Edinburgh: Edinburgh University Press, 2004), pp. 77–88.

J Catling, W.G. Sebald: ein 'England-Deutscher'? Identität – Topographie – Intertextualität, in: I Heidelberger-Leonard, M Tabah (eds.), *W.G. Sebald: Intertextualität und Topographie* (Berlin: LIT, 2008), pp. 25–53.

J Catling, Gratwanderungen bis an den Rand der Natur: W.G. Sebald's Landscapes of Memory, in: R Görner (ed.), *The Anatomist of Melancholy: Essays in Memory of W.G. Sebald* (Munich: Iudicium, 2003), pp. 19–50.

JJ Long, W.G. Sebald: The Anti-Tourist, in M Zisselsberger (ed.), *The Undiscover'd Country: W.G. Sebald and the Poetics of Travel* (Rochester: Camden House, 2010), pp. 63–91.

J Ryan, Lines of Flight: History and Territory in ›The Rings of Saturn‹, in: G Fischer (ed.), *W.G. Sebald: Schreiben ex patria / Expatriate Writing* (Amsterdam: Rodopi, 2009), pp. 45–60.

5 Academia

D Lambert, R McGill, The Collected 'Maxims', in: *Five Dials* 5 (2014), pp. 8–9.

F Radvan, The Crystal Mountain of Memory: W.G. Sebald as a University Teacher, in: SM 154–160.

U Schütte, *Interventionen: Literaturkritik als Widerspruch bei W.G. Sebald* (Munich: Ed. Text +Kritik, 2014), pp. 9–63.

U Schütte, Out of the Shadows, in: *Times Higher Education*, 22 September 2011, pp. 44–47.

U Schütte, Wissenschaftliche Biographie, in: M Niehaus, C Öhlschläger (ed.), *W.G. Sebald-Handbuch* (Stuttgart: Metzler, 2017), pp. 2–5.
U Schütte, *W.G. Sebald* (Liverpool: Liverpool University Press, 2018), pp. 9–17.
G Turner, At the University: W.G. Sebald in the Classroom, in: SM 109–142.
L Williams, A Watch on each Wrist: Twelve Seminars with W.G. Sebald, in: SM 143–153.

6   The British Centre for Literary Translation

J Catling et al., Among Translators: W.G. Sebald and Translation, in: *In Other Words* 38 (2011), pp. 111–120.
D Large, A Goode, JE Hanson (eds.), *My BCLT: Celebrating 30 Years of the British Centre for Literary Translation* (Norwich: BCLT, 2019).
St. Jerome Lecture 2001: W.G. Sebald in conversation with Maya Jaggi and Anthea Bell, in: *In Other Words* 21 (2003), pp. 5–18.
U Schütte, *W.G. Sebald* (Liverpool: Liverpool University Press, 2018), pp. 26–27.

7   Between Germany and Britain

J Catling, W.G. Sebald: ein 'England-Deutscher'? Identität – Topographie – Intertextualität, in: I Heidelberger-Leonard, M Tabah (eds.), *W.G. Sebald: Intertextualität und Topographie* (Berlin: LIT, 2008), pp. 25–53.
R Görner, Im Allgäu, Grafschaft Norfolk: Über W.G. Sebald in England, in: *Text+Kritik 158* (2003), pp. 23–29.
P Schlesinger, W.G. Sebald and the Condition of Exile, in: *Theory, Culture & Society* 21:2 (2004), pp. 43–67.
U Schütte, *W.G. Sebald: Leben und literarisches Werk* (Berlin/Boston: De Gruyter, 2020), pp. 7–66.

8   Unpublished Juvenilia

U Bülow, H Gfrereis, Nachlass in: M Niehaus, C Öhlschläger (eds.), *W.G. Sebald-Handbuch: Leben – Werk – Wirkung* (Stuttgart: Metzler, 2017) pp. 73–77.
M Etzler, ›So ein langes Leben‹: Rebellious Writing and Philosophical Meanderings in W.G. Sebald's Juvenilia, in: U Schütte (ed.), *Über W.G. Sebald: Beiträge zu einem anderen Bild des Autors* (Berlin/Boston: De Gruyter, 2017), pp. 29–50.
M Hutchins, ›Der Gedanke kommt ihm wie eine Erlösung‹: Restitution and False Redemption in Dramatic Texts by W.G. Sebald, in: U Schütte (ed.), *Über W.G. Sebald. Beiträge zu einem anderen Bild des Autors* (Berlin/Boston: De Gruyter, 2017), pp. 51–64.
U Schütte, *W.G. Sebald: Leben und literarisches Werk* (Berlin/Boston: De Gruyter, 2020), pp. 7–66.

R Sheppard, The Sternheim Years: W.G. Sebald's ›Lehrjahre and Theatralische Sendung‹, 1963–75, in: SM 42–108.

9   Film Scripts

M Gotterbarm, *Die Gewalt des Moralisten: Zum Verhältnis von Ethik und Ästhetik bei W.G. Sebald* (Paderborn: Fink, 2016), pp. 487–492.

R Gray, *Ghostwriting: W.G. Sebald's Poetics of History* (London: Bloomsbury, 2017), pp. 27–57.

M Hutchins, *Tikkun: W.G. Sebald's Melancholy Messianism* (PhD thesis: Cincinnati, 2011) pp. 134–161.

M Hutchins, ›Der Gedanke kommt ihm wie eine Erlösung‹: Restitution and False Redemption in Dramatic Texts by W.G. Sebald, in: U Schütte (ed.), *Über W. G. Sebald: Beiträge zu einem anderen Bild des Autors* (Berlin/Boston: De Gruyter, 2017), pp. 51–64.

U Schütte, Durch die Hintertür: Zu W.G. Sebalds unveröffentlichter Szenenreihe über das Leben und Sterben des Immanuel Kant, in: U Schütte (ed.), *Über W. G. Sebald: Beiträge zu einem anderen Bild des Autors* (Berlin/Boston: De Gruyter, 2017), pp. 63–98.

R Weihe, Wittgensteins Augen: W.G. Sebalds 'Leben Ws', in: *Fair: Zeitung für Kunst und Ästhetik* 7:4 (2009), pp. 11–12.

10   The Prose Project

S Bartsch, 'W.G. Sebald's ›Prose Project‹: A Glimpse into the Potting Shed', in: U Schütte (ed.), *Über W.G. Sebald: Beiträge zu einem anderen Bild des Autors* (Berlin/Boston: De Gruyter, 2017), pp. 99–134.

R Gray, *Ghostwriting: W.G. Sebald's Poetics of History* (London: Bloomsbury, 2017), pp. 59–74.

U Schütte, *W.G. Sebald: Leben und literarisches Werk* (Berlin/Boston: De Gruyter, 2020), pp. 113–223.

11   Auto-/Biography

C Bigsby, *Remembering and Imagining the Holocaust: The Chain of Memory* (Cambridge: Cambridge University Press, 2006).

D Osborne, Memoirs of the Blind: W.G. Sebald's ›Die Ausgewanderten‹, in: J Baxter et al (eds.), *A Literature of Restitution: Critical Essays on W.G. Sebald* (Manchester: Manchester University Press, 2013), pp. 94–110.

R Gray, *Ghostwriting: W.G. Sebald's Poetics of History* (London: Bloomsbury, 2017).

U Schütte, *W.G. Sebald: Leben und literarisches Werk* (Berlin/Boston: De Gruyter, 2020).

F Schwamborn, *W.G. Sebald: Moralismus und Prosodie* (Munich: Iudicium Verlag, 2017).

L Ward, A Simultaneous Gesture of Proximity and Distance: W.G. Sebald's Empathic Narrative Persona, in: *Journal of Modern Literature* 36:1 (2012), pp. 1–16.

L Wolff, *W.G. Sebald's Hybrid Poetics. Literature as Historiography* (Berlin: De Gruyter, 2014).

12   Natural History and the Anthropocene

P Baumgärtel, *Mythos und Utopie: Zum Begriff der 'Naturgeschichte der Zerstörung' im Werk W.G. Sebalds* (Frankfurt: Lang, 2010).

R Gray, *Ghostwriting: W.G. Sebald's Poetics of History* (London: Bloomsbury, 2017).

C Hein, *Traumatologie des Daseins: Zur panoptischen Darstellung der Desintegration des Lebens im Werk W.G. Sebald* (Würzburg: Königshausen & Neumann, 2014).

T Hoorn, *Naturgeschichte in der ästhetischen Moderne: Max Ernst, Ernst Jünger, Ror Wolf, W.G. Sebald* (Göttingen: Wallstein, 2016).

A Maier, 'Der panische Halsknick': Organisches und Anorganisches in W.G. Sebalds Prosa, in: M Niehaus, C Öhlschläger (eds.), *W.G. Sebald: Politische Melancholie und archäologische Bastelei* (Berlin: Schmidt, 2006), pp. 111–126.

B Malkmus, The Anthroposcene of Literature: Diffuse Dwelling in Graham Swift and W.G. Sebald, in: S Wilke, J Johnstone (eds.), *Readings in the Anthropocene: The Environmental Humanities, German Studies, and Beyond* (London: Bloomsbury, 2017), pp. 263–295.

13   The Corsica Project

C Albes, Nature Writing: Zur Brauchbarkeit eines neuen Gattungsbegriffs für das Verständnis von Sebalds Prosa am Beispiel des Essays ›Die Alpen im Meer‹, in: G Dürbeck, C Kanz (eds.), *Deutschsprachiges Nature Writing von Goethe bis zur Gegenwart: Kontroversen, Positionen, Perspektiven* (Berlin: Metzler, 2020), pp. 265–280.

U Bülow, Sebalds Korsika-Projekt, in: U Bülow et al. (eds.), *Wandernde Schatten: W.G. Sebalds Unterwelt* (Marbach: Deutsche Schillergesellschaft, 2008), pp. 211–224.

G Gilloch, The 'Arca Project': W.G. Sebald's Corsica, in: J Baxter et al. (eds.), *A Literature of Restitution: Critical Essays on W.G. Sebald* (Manchester: Manchester University Press, 2013), pp. 126–148.

R Gray, *Ghostwriting: W.G. Sebald's Poetics of History* (London: Bloomsbury, 2017), pp. 361–411.

S Meyer, ›Campo Santo‹ und weitere Prosa, in: M Niehaus, C Öhlschläger (eds.), *W.G. Sebald-Handbuch: Leben – Werk – Wirkung* (Stuttgart: Metzler, 2017), pp. 58–65.

U Schütte, *W.G. Sebald: Leben und literarisches Werk* (Berlin/Boston: De Gruyter 2020), pp. 336–384.

14 Poetry

J Catling, Gratwanderungen bis an den Rand der Natur: W.G. Sebald's Landscapes of Memory, in: R Görner (ed.), *The Anatomist of Melancholy: Essays in Memory of W.G. Sebald* (Munich: Iudicum, 2003), pp. 19–50.

C Riordan, Ecocentrism in Sebald's ›After Nature‹, in: JJ Long, A Whitehead (eds.), *W. G. Sebald: A Critical Companion* (Edinburgh: University of Edinburgh Press, 2004), pp. 45–57.

U Schütte, *Figurationen: Zum lyrischen Werk von W.G. Sebald* (Eggingen: Ed. Isele, 2014).

L Wolff, *W.G. Sebald's Hybrid Poetics. Literature as Historiography* (Berlin/Boston: De Gruyter, 2014).

Volker Hage im Gespräch mit W.G. Sebald, in: *Akzente* 50:1 (2003), pp. 35–50.

15 The World War Project

U Bülow, The Disappearance of the Author in the Work: Some Reflections on W.G. Sebald's Nachlass in the Deutsches Literaturarchiv Marbach, in: SM 247–263.

T Honickel, *Curriculum Vitae: Die W.G. Sebald-Interviews*, ed. U Schütte, K Wolfinger (Würzburg: Königshausen & Neumann, 2021).

Arthur Lubow Crossing Boundaries [interview], in: EM 159–173.

J Wood, W.G. Sebald's Uncertainty, in: *The Broken Estate: Essays on Literature and Belief* (London: Cape, 1999), pp. 273–284.

16 Interviews

T Hoffmann, Das Interview als Kunstwerk: Plädoyer für die Analyse von Schriftstellerinterviews am Beispiel W.G. Sebalds, in: *Weimarer Beiträge* 55 (2009), pp. 276–292

T Hoffmann, Das Gewicht des Lebens: Nachwort, in: *W.G. Sebald, ›Auf ungeheuer dünnem Eis‹: Gespräche 1971–2001*, ed. T Hoffmann (Frankfurt: Fischer, 2011), pp. 264–280.

T Hoffmann, Sebald als Interviewter, in: M Niehaus, C Öhlschläger (eds.), *W.G. Sebald-Handbuch: Leben – Werk – Wirkung* (Stuttgart: Metzler, 2017), pp. 109–112.

R Sheppard, An Index to Interviews with W.G. Sebald, in: SM 592–618.

17 Critical Writings

L Banki, *Post-Katastrophische Poetik. Zu W.G. Sebald und Walter Benjamin* (Paderborn: Wilhelm Fink, 2016), pp. 189–217.

R Robertson, W.G. Sebald as Critic of Austrian Literature, in: *Journal of European Studies* 41:3–4 (2011), pp. 305–322.

E Santner, *On Creaturely Life: Rilke, Benjamin, Sebald* (Chicago: University of Chicago Press, 2006), pp. 97–141.

P Schmucker, *Grenzübertretungen: Intertextualität im Werk von W.G. Sebald* (Berlin/Boston: De Gruyter, 2012), pp. 240–354, 448–503.

U Schütte, *Interventionen: Literaturkritik als Widerspruch bei W.G. Sebald* (Munich: Ed. Text + Kritik, 2014).

U Simon, Der Provokateur als Literaturhistoriker, in: M Atze, F Loquai (eds.), *Sebald. Lektüren.* (Eggingen: Ed. Isele 2005), pp. 78–104.

18 Minor Writing

M Etzler, *Writing from the Periphery: W.G. Sebald and Outsider Art* (PhD thesis, Berkeley 2014)

U Schütte, *Interventionen: Literaturkritik als Widerspruch bei W.G. Sebald* (Munich: Ed. Text+Kritik, 2014), pp. 288–311.

U Schütte, Robert Walser, in: M Niehaus, C Öhlschläger (eds.), *W.G. Sebald–Handbuch: Leben – Werk – Wirkung* (Stuttgart: Metzler, 2017), pp. 591–601.

P Whitehead, *Im Abseits: W.G. Sebalds Ästhetik des Marginalen* (Bielefeld: Aisthesis, 2019).

19 Franz Kafka

R Gray, *Ghostwriting: W.G. Sebald's Poetics of History* (London: Bloomsbury, 2017), pp. 94–132.

M Klebes, Infinite Journey: From Kafka to Sebald', in: JJ Long, A Whitehead (eds.), *W.G. Sebald: A Critical Companion* (Edinburgh: Edinburgh University Press, 2004), pp. 123–139.

D Medin, *Three Sons: Franz Kafka and the Fiction of J.M. Coetzee, Philip Roth and W.G. Sebald* (Evanston: Northwestern University Press, 2010), pp. 80–145.

B Prager, Sebald's Kafka, in S Denham, M McCulloh (eds.), *W.G. Sebald: History, Memory, Trauma* (Berlin/Boston: De Gruyter, 2006), pp. 105–125.

P Schmucker, *Grenzübertretungen. Intertextualität im Werk von W.G. Sebald* (Berlin/Boston: De Gruyter, 2012).

U Schütte, *Interventionen. Literaturkritik als Widerspruch bei W.G. Sebald* (Munich: Ed. Text+Kritik, 2014), pp. 204–233.

20 Literary Predecessors

B Hutchinson, *W.G. Sebald: Die dialektische Imagination* (Berlin: De Gruyter, 2009).
K Jacobs, Sebald's Apparitional Nabokov, in: *Twentieth Century Literature* 60:2 (2014), pp. 137–168.
D Medin, *Three Sons: Franz Kafka and the Fiction of J. M. Coetzee, Philip Roth, and W.G. Sebald* (Evanston: Northwestern University Press, 2010).
U Schütte, Ein Lehrer: Über W.G. Sebald und Thomas Bernhard, in: J Lughofer (ed.), *Thomas Bernhard: Gesellschaftliche und politische Bedeutung der Literatur* (Vienna: Böhlau, 2012), pp. 303–319.
S Weller, Unquiet Prose: W.G. Sebald and the Writing of the Negative, in J Baxter et al. (eds.), *A Literature of Restitution: Critical Essays on W.G. Sebald* (Manchester: Manchester University Press, 2013), pp. 56–73.

21 Walter Benjamin

L Banki, *Post-Katastrophische Poetik. Zu W.G. Sebald und Walter Benjamin* (Paderborn: Fink, 2016).
J Dubow, Case Interrupted: Benjamin, Sebald, and the Dialectical Image, in: *Critical Inquiry* 33:4 (2007), pp. 820–836.
A Lemke, Figurationen der Melancholie: Spuren Walter Benjamins in W.G. Sebalds ›Die Ringe des Saturn‹, in: *Zeitschrift für deutsche Philologie* 2 (2008), pp. 239–267.
N Preuschoff, *Mit Walter Benjamin. Melancholie, Geschichte und Erzählen bei W.G. Sebald* (Heidelberg: Winter, 2015).
E Santner, *On Creaturely Life: Rilke, Benjamin, Sebald* (Chicago: Chicago University Press, 2006).
S Ward, Ruins and poetics in the works of W.G. Sebald, in: JJ Long, A Whitehead (eds.), *W.G. Sebald: A Critical Companion* (Edinburgh: Edinburgh University Press, 2004), pp. 58–74.
I Wohlfahrt, Anachronie. Interferenzen zwischen Walter Benjamin und W.G. Sebald, in: *Internationales Archiv für Sozialgeschichte der deutschen Literatur* 33:2 (2008), pp. 184–242.

22 Philosophical Models

M Häckel, *Zur Rezeption Ludwig Wittgensteins im literarischen Werk W.G. Sebalds* (Berlin: Lang, 2021)
M Klebes, *Wittgenstein's Novels* (Abingdon: Routledge, 2006), pp. 87–131.
L Kunze, *Der Schamane mit der Feder: Ökologie und Mitleidenschaft in W.G. Sebalds ›Nach der Natur‹* (Göttingen: Wallstein, 2022).

S Meyer, Keine Kausallogik: Zum Zusammenhang in W.G. Sebalds Schreiben, in: U Schütte (ed.), *Über W.G. Sebald: Beiträge zu einem anderen Bild des Autors* (Berlin/Boston: De Gruyter, 2017), pp. 19–28.

U Schütte, Negative Evolution. Zur Rezeption von Stanisław Lem bei W.G. Sebald, in: *Prace Literaturoznawcze* 10 (2022), pp. 23–48.

P Thompson, ›A walker's approach [. . .] is a phenomenological one‹: W.G. Sebald and the Instant, in: *Monatshefte* 112:3 (2020), pp. 411–428.

23 History

J Baxter et al. (eds.), *A Literature of Restitution. Critical Essays on W.G. Sebald* (Manchester: Manchester University Press, 2013).

C Bigsby, *Writers in Conversation with Christopher Bigsby*, vol. 2 (Norwich: EAS, 2001).

J Cowan, Sebald's ›Austerlitz‹ and the Great Library. History, Fiction, Memory. Parts I and II, in: *Monatshefte* 102:1 (2010), pp. 51–81 & 102:2 (2010), pp. 192–207.

H Finch, L Wolff (eds.), *Witnessing, Memory, Poetics: H.G. Adler and W.G. Sebald* (Rochester: Camden House, 2014).

A Fuchs, JJ Long (eds.), *W.G. Sebald and the Writing of History* (Würzburg: Königshausen & Neumann, 2007).

R Gray, *Ghostwriting: W.G. Sebald's Poetics of History* (London: Bloomsbury, 2017).

B Hutchinson, *W.G. Sebald: Die dialektische Imagination* (Berlin/New York: De Gruyter, 2009).

JJ Long, *W.G. Sebald: Image, Archive, Modernity* (Edinburgh: Edinburgh University Press, 2007).

L Wolff, *W.G. Sebald's Hybrid Poetics: Literature as Historiography* (Berlin/Boston: De Gruyter, 2014).

24 Polemics

R Burns, W Will, The Calamitous Perspective of Modernity: Sebald's negative Ontology, in: *Journal of European Studies* 41:3–4 (2011), pp. 341–358.

T Hoffmann, Polemik, in: M Niehaus, C Öhlschläger (eds.), *W.G. Sebald-Handbuch: Leben – Werk – Wirkung* (Stuttgart: Metzler, 2017), pp. 155–158.

M Joch, 4:2 für den Literaturpfaffen: W.G. Sebalds Angriffe auf Alfred Andersch und Jurek Becker, in: Schütte (ed.), *Über W.G. Sebald: Beiträge zu einem anderen Bild des Autors* (Berlin/Boston: De Gruyter, 2017), pp. 227–250.

U Schütte, Against ›Germanistik‹: W.G. Sebald Critical Essays, in: SM 161–182.

U Simon, Der Provokateur als Literaturhistoriker: Anmerkungen zu Literaturbegriff und Argumentationsverfahren in W.G. Sebalds essayistischen Schriften, in: M Atze, F Loquai (eds.), *Sebald. Lektüren.* (Eggingen: Isele, 2005), pp. 78–104.

25   Holocaust

J Hessing, V Lenzen, *Sebalds Blick* (Göttingen: Wallstein, 2015).
R Klüger, Wanderer zwischen falschen Leben: Über W.G. Sebald, in: *Text+Kritik* 158 (2003), pp. 95–102.
JJ Long, History, Narrative, and Photography in W.G. Sebald's ›Die Ausgewanderten‹, in: *Modern Language Review* 98:1 (2003), pp. 117–137.
B Prager, The Good German as Narrator: On W.G. Sebald and the Risks of Holocaust Writing, in: *New German Critique* 96 (2005), pp. 75–102.
S Taberner, German Nostalgia? Remembering German-Jewish Life in W.G. Sebald's ›Die Ausgewanderten‹ and ›Austerlitz‹, in: *Germanic Review* 79:3 (2004), pp. 181–203.
D Weidner, Holocaust, in: M Niehaus, C Öhlschläger (eds.), *W.G. Sebald–Handbuch: Leben – Werk – Wirkung* (Stuttgart: Metzler, 2017), pp. 232–239.
D Weidner, Judentum, in: ibid., pp. 239–245.

26   Photography

M Anderson, Documents, Photography, Postmemory: Alexander Kluge, W.G. Sebald, and the German Family, in: *Poetics Today* 29:1 (2008), pp. 129–153.
A Daubin, Donner à voir: The Logics of the Caption in W.G. Sebald's ›Rings of Saturn‹ and Alexander Kluge's ›Devil's Blind Spot‹, in: L Patt, C Dillbohner (eds.), *Searching for Sebald: Photography after W.G. Sebald* (Los Angeles: ICI Press, 2007), pp. 306–329.
C Eggers, *Das Dunkel durchdringen, das uns umgibt: Die Fotografie im Werk von W.G. Sebald* (Frankfurt: Lang, 2011).
JJ Long, *W.G. Sebald: Image, Archive, Modernity* (Edinburgh: Edinburgh University Press, 2007), pp. 46–70.
C Scott, Sebald's Photographic Annotations, in: SM 217–245.
C Scott, Still Life, Portrait, Photograph, Narrative in the Work of W.G. Sebald, in: J Baxter et al. (eds.), *A Literature of Restitution: Critical Essays on W.G. Sebald* (Manchester: Manchester University Press, 2016), pp. 203–230.
T Steinaecker. *Literarische Foto-Texte: Zur Funktion der Fotografien in den Texten Rolf Dieter Brinkmanns, Alexander Kluges und W.G. Sebalds* (Bielefeld: Transcript, 2015), pp. 247–314.

27   Paintings and Ekphrasis

L Patt, C Dillbohner (eds.), *Searching for Sebald: Photography After W.G. Sebald* (Los Angeles: Institute of Cultural Inquiry, 2007).
E Santner, *On Creaturely Life: Rilke, Benjamin, Sebald* (Chicago: Chicago University Press, 2006).

C Hünsche, *Textereignisse und Schlachtenbilder: Eine sebaldsche Poetik des Ereignisses* (Bielefeld: Aisthesis, 2012).

28 Media Theory

K Bonn, W.G. Sebalds laufende Bilder. Der Film und die Worte, in: *Arcadia* 42:1 (2007), pp. 166–184.

J Draney, W.G. Sebald's Paper Universe: ›Austerlitz‹ and the Poetics of Media Obsolescence, in: *Journal of Modern Literature* 45:3 (2022), pp. 155–172.

C Duttlinger, Traumatic Photographs: Remembrance and the Technical Media in W.G. Sebald's Austerlitz, in: JJ Long, A Whitehead (eds.), *W.G. Sebald: A Critical Companion* (Edinburgh: Edinburgh University Press, 2004), pp. 190–202.

F Kittler, *The Truth of the Technological World: Essays on the Genealogy of Presence* (Stanford: Stanford University Press, 2014).

S Pane, Trauma Obscura: Photographic Media in W.G. Sebald's ›Austerlitz‹ in: *Mosaic: A Journal for the Interdisciplinary Study of Literature* 38:1 (2005), pp. 37–54

C Pias, What's German About German Media Theory?, in: N Friesen (ed.), *Media Transatlantic: Developments in Media and Communication Studies between North America and German-speaking Europe*(Berne: Springer, 2016), pp. 15–27.

29 Travel Writing

D Anderson, *Landscape and Subjectivity in the Work of Patrick Keiller, W.G. Sebald and Iain Sinclair* (Oxford: Oxford University Press, 2020).

S Cooke, *Travellers' Tales of Wonder: Chatwin, Naipaul, Sebald* (Edinburgh: Edinburgh University Press, 2013).

P Farley, M Symmons Roberts, *Edgelands: Journeys into England's True Wilderness* (London: Vintage, 2012).

J Skinner (ed.), *Writing the Dark Side of Travel* (New York: Berghahn, 2012).

M Zisselsberger (ed.), *The Undiscover'd Country: W.G. Sebald and the Poetics of Travel* (Rochester: Camden House, 2010).

30 Eco-Criticism and Animal Studies

E Jones, Verschachtelte Räume: Writing and Reading Environments in W.G. Sebald, https://dash.harvard.edu/bitstream/1/9406020/3/Jones_gsas.harvard_0084L_10296.pdf.

K Kończal, Auf den Spuren eines 'verkehrten Miniaturuniversums': Tiere im Werk von W.G. Sebald, in: *Comparatio* 8:1 (2016), pp. 143–170.

B Mosbach, Schauer der ungewohnten Berührung: Zur Tieranalogie bei W.G. Sebald, in: N Eke, E Geulen (eds.), *Texte, Tiere, Spuren* (Berlin: Schmidt, 2007), pp. 82–97.

E Santner, *On Creaturely Life: Rilke, Benjamin, Sebald* (Chicago: Chicago University Press, 2006).

M Schmitz-Emans, Der Garten als Schwellenraum: Literarische Reflexionen über Kultivierung und Kultur, in: C Schmitt, C Solte-Gresser (eds.), *Literatur und Ökologie: Neue literatur- und kulturwissenschaftliche Perspektiven* (Bielefeld: Aisthesis, 2017), pp. 144–156.

31 Sebald Scholarship

JJ Long, W.G. Sebald: A Bibliographical Essay on Current Research, in: A Fuchs, JJ Long (eds.), *W.G. Sebald and the Writing of History* (Würzburg: Königshausen & Neumann, 2007), pp. 11–29.

R Sheppard, Dexter – Sinister: Some Observations on Decrypting the Mors Code in the Works of W.G. Sebald, in: *Journal of European Studies* 35:4 (2005), pp. 419–463.

R Sheppard, Woods, Trees, and the Spaces In-Between: A Report on Work Published on W.G. Sebald 2005–2008, in: *Journal of European Studies* 39:1 (2009), pp. 79–128.

R Sheppard (ed.), Special Issue: W.G. Sebald, in:*Journal of European Studies* 41:3–4 (2011).

L Wolff, Das metaphysische Unterfutter der Realität: Recent Publications and Trends in W.G. Sebald Research, in: *Monatshefte* 99:1 (2007), pp. 78–101.

L Wolff, Zur Sebald-Forschung, in: C Öhlschläger, M Niehaus (eds.), *W.G. Sebald-Handbuch: Leben – Werk – Wirkung* (Stuttgart: Metzler, 2017), pp. 312–317.

M Zisselsberger, A Persistent Fascination: Recent Publications on the Works of W.G. Sebald, in: *Monatshefte* 101:1 (2009), pp. 88–105.

32 Sebald in Translation

A Bell, Foreword: Translating W.G. Sebald, With and Without the Author, in: J Baxter et al. (eds.), *A Literature of Restitution: Critical Essays on W.G. Sebald* (Manchester: Manchester University Press, 2013), pp. 13–24.

J Catling, 'Doubly taxing': W.G. Sebald and Translation, www.uea.ac.uk/docu ments/96135/5136906/Catling+-+WG+Sebald+and+Translation.pdf/266912a9-a509-599e-5f84-4db705915be9?t=1639479221398.

J Catling et al., Among Translators: W.G. Sebald and Translation, in: *Other Words: The Journal for Literary Translators* 38 (2011), pp. 111–120.

P Charbonneau, Correspondence(s): Le traducteur et son auteur, in: R Vogel-Klein (ed.), *Mémoir, Transferts, Images / Erinnerung, Übertragungen, Bilder. Recherches germaniques*. Hors série 2 (2005), pp. 193–210.

M McCulloh, Two Languages, Two Audiences: The Tandem Literary Œuvres of W.G. Sebald, in: S Denham, M McCulloh (eds.), *W.G. Sebald: History – Memory – Trauma* (Berlin/New York: De Gruyter, 2006), pp. 7–20.

R Vogel-Klein, ›Stendhal nach Auschwitz‹? Zur Rezeption W.G. Sebalds in Frankreich, in: M Atze, F Loquai (eds.), *Sebald. Lektüren.* (Eggingen: Ed. Isele, 2005), pp. 133–142.

L Wolff, The ›solitary mallard‹: On Sebald and Translation, in: *Journal of European Studies* 41:3–4 (2011), pp. 323–340.

L Wolff, *W.G. Sebald's Hybrid Poetics: Literature as Historiography* (Berlin/Boston: De Gruyter, 2014), pp. 216–245.

33   The Sebaldian

C Martindale, *The Clockwork Muse: The Predictability of Artistic Change* (New York: Basic Books, 1990).

J Moran, *Star Authors: Literary Celebrity in America* (London: Pluto, 2000).

F Moretti, *Graphs, Maps, Trees: Abstract Models for a Literary History* (London: Verso, 2005).

T Pitts, Vertigo, https://sebald.wordpress.com/

AN West, Nostalgia for Probity in the Era of the Selfie: W.G. Sebald's American Imitators, in: U Schütte (ed.), *Über W.G. Sebald: Beiträge zu einem anderen Bild des Autors* (Berlin/Boston: De Gruyter, 2017), pp. 285–295.

34   Film

K Bonn, Sebalds laufende Bilder: Der Film und die Worte, in: *Arcadia* 42:1 (2007), pp. 166–184.

A Gnam, Fotografie und Film in W.G. Sebalds Erzählung *Ambros Adelwarth* und seinem Roman *Austerlitz*, in:S Martin, I Wintermeyer (eds.), *Verschiebebahnhöfe der Erinnerung: Zum Werk W.G. Sebalds* (Stuttgart: Königshausen & Neumann, 2007), pp. 27–47.

R Kilbourn, Architecture and Cinema: The Representation of Memory in W.G. Sebald's *Austerlitz*, in: JJ Long, A Whitehead (eds.), *W.G. Sebald: A Critical Companion* (Edinburgh: Edinburgh University Press, 2004), pp. 140–154.

E Rositzka, A Saturn State of Mind: ›Patience (After Sebald)‹, in: E Carter, B Malcomess, E Rositzka, *Mapping the Sensible: Distribution, Inscription, Cinematic Thinking* (Berlin/Boston: De Gruyter, 2023), pp. 125–155.

35 Pop Music

R Calzoni, Moments musicaux: W.G. Sebald und die Musik, in: R Calzoni et al. (eds.), *Intermedialität – Multimedialität: Literatur und Musik in Deutschland von 1900 bis heute* (Göttingen: V&R unipress, 2015), pp. 167–184.

U Schütte, *Annäherungen. Sieben Essays zu W.G. Sebald* (Cologne: Böhlau, 2019), pp. 248–256.

F Schwabel, Intermediale Formen der Sebald-Rezeption in der populären Musik, in: P Ferstl (ed.), *Dialogues Between Media* (Berlin/Boston: De Gruyter, 2021), pp. 251–261.

36 Literary Prizes

C Hein, Deutschsprachiger Raum, in: M. Niehaus, C Öhlschläger (eds.), *W. G. Sebald-Handbuch: Leben – Werk – Wirkung* (Stuttgart: Metzler, 2017), pp. 300–305.

U Schütte, Anglo-amerikanischer Raum, in: M. Niehaus, C Öhlschläger (eds.), *W.G. Sebald-Handbuch: Leben – Werk – Wirkung* (Stuttgart: Metzler, 2017), pp. 305–309.

U Schütte, Gratulationen: Sebalds Preise, in: C Jürgensen, A Weixler (eds.), *Literaturpreise: Geschichte und Kontexte* (Stuttgart: Metzler, 2021), pp. 367–390.

W Self, Absent Jews and Invisible Executioners, in: J Cook (ed.), *After Sebald: Essays and Illuminations* (Woodbridge: Full Circle, 2014), pp. 95–114.

37 Visual Arts and Exhibitions

S Bode (ed.), *Waterlog: Journeys Around an Exhibition* (London: Film and Video Umbrella, 2007).

R Krauss, *A Voyage on the North Sea: Art in the Age of the Post-Medium Condition* (New York: Thames & Hudson, 2000).

L Patt (ed.), *Searching for Sebald: Photography After W.G. Sebald* (Los Angeles: Institute for Cultural Inquiry, 2007).

38 The Cult of Sebald

S Denham, Foreword: The Sebald Phenomenon, in: S Denham, M McCulloh (eds.), *W.G. Sebald: History – Memory – Trauma* (Berlin/New York: De Gruyter, 2006), pp. 1–6.

U Schütte, *W.G. Sebald* (Liverpool: Liverpool University Press, 2018), pp. 107–115.

U Schütte, *Annäherungen: Sieben Essays zu W.G. Sebald* (Cologne: Böhlau, 2019), pp. 219–268.

AN West, Nostalgia for Probity in the Era of the Selfie: W. G. Sebald's American Imitators, in U Schütte (ed.), *Über W.G. Sebald: Beiträge zu einem anderen Bild des Autors* (Berlin/Boston: De Gruyter, 2017), pp. 283–295.

Index